Organizational
Communication

FOURTH EDITION

Organizational Communication

Balancing Creativity and Constraint

ERIC M. EISENBERG
University of South Florida

H. L. GOODALL JR.
University of North Carolina at Greensboro

Bedford / St. Martin's
Boston ◆ New York

For Bedford/St. Martin's

Developmental Editor: Terence Fitzgerald
Associate Editor, Publishing Services: Maria Burwell
Senior Production Supervisor: Joe Ford
Production Associate: Christie Gross
Marketing Manager: Richard Cadman
Project Management: Books By Design, Inc.
Cover Design: Lucy Krikorian
Cover Art: © Getty Images/Todd Davidson
Composition: Books By Design, Inc.
Printing and Binding: RR Donnelley & Sons Company

President: Joan E. Feinberg
Editorial Director: Denise B. Wydra
Publisher for History and Communication: Patricia A. Rossi
Director of Marketing: Karen R. Melton
Director of Editing, Design, and Production: Marcia Cohen
Manager, Publishing Services: Emily Berleth

Library of Congress Control Number: 2003101670

Manufactured in the United States of America.

9 8 7 6 5 4
f   e   d   c

For information, write:
Bedford/St. Martin's, 75 Arlington Street, Boston, MA 02116   (617-399-4000)

ISBN: 0-312-40859-5

Acknowledgments

¿Estan listos por lo siguiente?

Preface

As we set out to write this latest version of our textbook, the mood of the day had changed dramatically from that surrounding past editions. We found ourselves struggling more than ever to make sense of a world increasingly characterized by hazard and uncertainty both in business and in society at large. The burst of the "dot-com" bubble in industry caught many unaware and dealt a sobering financial blow to millions of people. The bankruptcy of massive energy conglomerate Enron further eroded the public trust in business auditors and regulators. And the willful destruction of one of the planet's leading business centers — New York's formidable World Trade Center — served as a horrific reminder that the institutions we take for granted in the West are seen as symbols of evil by others. Democracy remains a daily and fragile accomplishment, and real freedom is yet out of reach for most of the world's people.

Understanding this social context is important for a number of reasons. First and foremost, this book is as much a product of organizational communication as it is a treatise on the subject. A host of complex technologies and social structures make these ideas available to you. Even the most solitary aspects of the text — our writing of it, and your careful reading — are accomplished with *organizations in mind*, inasmuch as we are each born into a world of social norms and institutions. Like a set of nested Russian dolls, our identities sit inside of relationships, families, communities, businesses, societies, and nations, each of which shape how we think of ourselves and live in the world.

A chief purpose of a university education is to help us better understand how these social institutions developed and how we came to occupy our particular roles within them. Put differently, the purpose of this text is to make the familiar strange, to expose the assumptions we take for granted to thoughtful analysis. In our view, what distinguishes an educated person is the ability to reflect on the world in this way, to consider the numerous factors that motivate how we think, talk, and act.

As teachers, we put great faith in the power of this sort of reflection and in the profound conversations it can generate. In this edition, we do so with greater urgency. The present historical moment is characterized both by highly sophisticated technology and by primitive, inarticulate brutality. Rather than backing down from threats of violence and anarchy, however — or allowing for the steady abridgment of human rights and freedoms — *we choose to respond passionately as advocates of the power and promise of communication*. Effective communication is the key requirement for creating and sustaining a truly democratic way of life. As students of communication we are obligated to learn all that we can about this process, and to share what we know in the service of a more enlightened and peaceful future.

This book, therefore, distills what we have learned about the role and importance of organizational communication within today's rapidly evolving social context, and we proudly share it with you. From its inception to this fourth edition, our text has evolved to meet the demands of the field and the market. But it has remained unchanged in two important ways: its model and its goal. We emphasize balancing creativity and constraint, the ability to simultaneously consider the enabling and constraining aspects of communication. Striking this balance helps people to achieve their professional and personal goals. As humans we struggle to be individualistic and heroic (assert our creativity) yet still belong to a group (respond to social and institutional constraints). Our model examines this struggle through the lens of everyday communication practices as they play out in the workplace.

Likewise, our aim for this text has always been to help students bridge the gap between what they learn in school and what they experience at work. Toward this end, we have devised numerous case studies — the cornerstone of the classroom *and* the consultant's craft — with thought-provoking assignments to conclude each chapter. Our *What Would You Do?* ethics boxes, included in almost every chapter, challenge students to resolve various ethical dilemmas they might face in today's business world. (See the list of case studies with descriptions on the inside front cover.) Based in fact and relevant to the ideas discussed in each chapter, the scenarios posed in the case studies and ethics boxes truly place the concepts of organizational communication in the context of the workplace.

New to This Edition

Organizational Communication has been revised and updated in response to reviewers' and users' suggestions. Because concrete examples are paramount to a student's understanding of this field, we have expanded the number of real-life examples throughout the text and have included two new ethics boxes and ten new case studies. Of special note are the four "caselets" that conclude Chapter 12. Taken from our own consulting work, these thorny workplace scenarios end with the challenge, "It's Monday morning. What do you do?" Our revision was guided, as always, by research, providing our readers with as current and comprehensive a snapshot of the discipline as possible. We have:

- **Expanded coverage of the debate over globalization,** including the rise of resistance groups challenging global trade treaties and organizations such as the World Bank and the International Monetary Fund (IMF). In Chapter 6, for instance, we discuss how relaxed trade barriers have allowed employers to use lower-wage workers overseas, which has reshaped U.S. industries and drastically changed the social fabric of countries worldwide.

- **Increased coverage of ethics and personal responsibility within organizational contexts,** with special attention given to recent corporate scandals involving such companies as Enron, WorldCom, and Arthur Andersen. Look to our first chapter for one examination of how corporate misconduct has brought animosity from domestic and foreign populations. These events have influenced the ways in which the public views organizations and organizations view themselves, and they remind us that we are responsible as individuals, even when we act as part of a team.
- **Updated coverage of the latest information and communication technologies.** Digital networks, which allow us to transfer information and currency efficiently, are changing the ways in which we congregate and communicate — so much that the words *office, store,* and *bank* no longer refer only to physical places. In Chapter 6 we cover how new information technologies have helped flat, flexible organizational structures replace traditional communication hierarchies in many companies. This new model is so effective, in fact, that terrorist cells and drug traffickers have adopted it.
- **Added a new Chapter 7.** "Alternatives to Hierarchy" explores recent trends in organizational and communication scholarship that pose difficult questions about the viability of traditional structures in today's world and that advance various alternative models for working together.
- **Added a new Chapter 12.** "Working with Integrity: Organizational Communication as Disciplined Practice" makes explicit connections between the text's concepts and organizational life outside of school. Beyond talking about how and why conflicts arise in organizations, for example, this chapter lays out a series of useful questions (based on mindful communicative practices) that helps readers get to the heart of an actual dispute and resolve it.

In response to numerous requests from instructors, a new *Instructor's Manual* has been prepared by Raina Massand to supplement the fourth edition of the text. This new manual contains clear and concise lecture notes, lists of key terms, test questions, and engaging assignments, including Net Detective exercises aimed at providing students increased exposure to electronic research and communication technology using the concepts, ideas, and terminology in each chapter.

Overview of the Book

Part I of the text, "Approaching Organizational Communication," includes two chapters that provide readers with an overview of the discipline and the concepts they'll need to master the ideas and methods presented throughout the rest of the text. Chapter 1, "Communication and the Changing World of Work," introduces the idea of organizational communication, provides reasons for its study, and describes in detail the nature of work today. Chapter 2, "Defining Organizational Communication," examines four definitions of the concept and offers the notion of organizational dialogues as a productive way to think about communication at work.

Part II of the text, "Theories of Organizational Communication," covers five distinct theoretical perspectives on organizational communication that motivate research and practice. Chapter 3, "Three Early Perspectives on Organizations and Communication," reviews classical organizational theory and explores its implications for communication. Chapters 4 and 5 address what are perhaps the two leading perspectives on organizations today: systems and cultures. More specifically, Chapter 4, "The Systems Perspective on Organizations and Communication," applies various forms of systems theories and demonstrates how they are useful for thinking about communicating and organizing. Chapter 5, "Cultural Studies of Organizations and Communication," uses a metaphor borrowed from anthropology and adopted by many organizations to examine the role of communication in the creation, maintenance, and transformation of organizational reality. Chapter 6, "Critical Approaches to Organizations and Communication," takes a different approach altogether, starting with the premise that research should be directed at illuminating and correcting inequalities at work. Particular attention is paid to how privilege is distributed unevenly across race, gender, and class differences. Finally, Chapter 7, "Alternatives to Hierarchy," wraps up our examination of various theories of organization by examining how some organizations are addressing the failures of traditional hierarchical models.

Part III of the text, "Levels of Analysis," explores communication at work across a variety of different levels of understanding, from the individual's experience of work (Chapter 8), to the nature and functioning of communication in dyadic (two-person) relationships (Chapter 9), to interaction in teams, networks, and groups (Chapter 10). Chapter 11 takes the big-picture perspective by considering the role of communication in the strategic positioning of the total organization, as well as in the facilitation of strategic organizational change.

Finally, Part IV, "Applications," comprises one chapter. Chapter 12, "Working with Integrity: Organizational Communication as Disciplined Practice," is the capstone of the text, bringing a semester's worth of experiences and learning to bear on the realities of organizational life in the workplace. The book concludes with an appendix, "A Field Guide to Studying Organizational Communication," which provides students and instructors with a helpful step-by-step process for planning, researching, participating in, and writing a qualitative account of an organization's communication practices.

Acknowledgments

Textbooks are published with the authors' names listed on the cover, but in every way publishing a textbook is a team effort. We are especially grateful for the strong support this edition of *Organizational Communication: Balancing Creativity and Constraint* has received from Bedford/St. Martin's. In particular, we want to thank our publisher, Patricia Rossi; Terence Fitzgerald, our developmental editor; Emily Berleth, the manager of publishing services; and Nancy Benjamin at Books By Design. All of these fine professionals contributed to this project in ways that have made the fourth edition of this text the best book it could have been.

We also want to thank our colleagues and friends at other universities and colleges who reviewed the fourth edition and offered insightful suggestions for improvement: Mark J. Braun, Gustavus Adolphus College; Irwin Mallin, Indiana University–Purdue University, Fort Wayne; Steven K. May, University of North Carolina at Chapel Hill; Patricia S. Parker, University of North Carolina at Chapel Hill; Craig R. Scott, University of Texas at Austin; Paaige K. Turner, Saint Louis University.

In addition, we are personally and professionally indebted to a number of colleagues, students, and staff members for their support in this project: Pete Kellett, David Carlone, Dan DeGooyer, Spoma Jovanovic, Chris Poulos, Raina Massand, and Janice Smith of the University of North Carolina at Greensboro; Patricia Riley of the University of Southern California; Jay Baglia of the University of South Florida; Patricia Geist of San Diego State University; Alexandra Murphy of DePaul University; Carl Lovitt of Penn State Berks–Lehigh Valley; and Bruce Hyde of St. Cloud State University.

Finally, we could not have written this edition without the enthusiastic and loving support of members of our immediate families — Lori Roscoe, Evan and Joel Eisenberg, and Sandra and Nic Goodall — as well as of grandparents (especially Clarence and Martha Bray), siblings, and close friends. As always, we are grateful to those individuals who, despite the intellectual, social, political, economic, and spiritual turmoil of our time, remain committed to continuing the dialogue.

Eric M. Eisenberg
University of South Florida

H. L. Goodall Jr.
University of North Carolina at Greensboro

Contents

PART I Approaching Organizational Communication

CHAPTER 1 Communication and the Changing World of Work   *3*

CHAPTER **6** **Critical Approaches to Organizations and Communication** *147*

CHAPTER **9**   **Interpersonal Relationships and Organizational Communication**   *233*

CHAPTER **11** **Managing the Total Enterprise:**
Communication and Strategic Change   *310*

About the Authors

Eric M. Eisenberg first learned about the field of Communication from his father, Abne M. Eisenberg, a Communication Professor at Queens College in New York City. Abne enlisted Eric's help in grading exams and papers, and over the next fifteen years, despite numerous detours (e.g., microbiology, poetry, and pre-med), Eric kept returning to his first love. He graduated Phi Beta Kappa with a bachelor's degree in Communication from Rutgers University, having survived and at times even enjoyed a year-long simulation of a media marketplace called INTERACT.

When selecting graduate schools, Eisenberg went in search of quality training in communication research methods to complement his fine education in communication theory at Rutgers. Michigan State University was purported to be a methodological Mecca, so Eisenberg packed up his old yellow Ford Fairlane 500 (with no heater!) and headed west. It was at MSU that he discovered that the research that interested him most had a decidedly practical bent. He received his master's degree in Communication working with Dr. Cassandra Book on an experiment evaluating the most effective uses of simulations and games in the classroom. Dr. Book was a superb mentor and master teacher who encouraged Eisenberg to complete a second master's degree in Education in 1980. Book also gave him his first taste of organizational research — they conducted a needs assessment and communication network analysis of the American Dietetic Association. He got rid of the Ford the first winter in Michigan.

Having been raised in a household with no links to corporate America, Eisenberg was intrigued by the possibility of learning about the "real world" of organizational communication. Determined to become fluent in both management and communication, and under the expert guidance of Dr. Peter Monge, he immersed himself in management theory and practice, publishing work on organizational communication networks and superior-subordinate communication. Eisenberg received his doctorate in Communication from Michigan State University in 1982. He now owned two suits.

The city boy had learned to love the Midwest, but it was time to head east again. Intrigued by the original and expansive writings of Dr. Art Bochner (who had spent a fortuitous semester at MSU), Eisenberg took his first academic position in the Department of Speech at Temple University in Philadelphia. It was there that he wrote his award-winning paper on the strategic uses of ambiguity in organizations, and with the support of his colleagues at Temple, turned his attention more closely to the uses of language and symbols in organizational life. He stayed connected to business practice by launching and directing the Applied Communication master's program at Temple and teaching at the downtown campus. During this period, he married Lori Roscoe (whom he had met at Michigan State) and they started building a life together.

In 1984, Eisenberg left Philadelphia to join the Communication faculty at the University of Southern California. Over the next decade, he was promoted to Associate Professor with tenure, published numerous studies of organizational communication and culture, and received recognition as University Scholar and Outstanding Teacher. His paper "Jamming: Transcendence through Organizing" received the NCA research award for the best publication in organizational communication in 1990. At the same time, Eisenberg worked closely with Dr. Patricia Riley on numerous grants and contracts aimed at applying cutting-edge knowledge about communication to organizational practice across a variety of industries (e.g., aerospace, health care, electronics, manufacturing). Meanwhile, Evan and Joel were born at Good Samaritan Hospital in downtown L.A. Eisenberg published his bittersweet poems from this period in a collection called *Fire and Ice: Fiction as Social Research* (A. and S. Banks, ed.).

USC was a world-class institution, but Los Angeles was a hard place to raise a family. Eisenberg took a position as Full Professor at the University of South Florida in 1994, staying true to his lifelong pledge to remain within driving distance of a Disney amusement park. He was attracted to USF for its extraordinary faculty, the energy of a young school with a new doctoral program in Communication, and his old friend Art Bochner. Immediately he knew he had found his home — an eccentric but winning department where experience and philosophy were privileged over theory and method. More publications followed, including his first textbook (this one!) and other strange forays into the world of communication and organizational change.

Once in Florida, Eisenberg's consulting work shifted toward the hospitality and health care industries. He recently published an article for the *Journal of Communication* about the role of communication in the development of identity, which will be expanded into a book next year. In 1996, Eisenberg was elected Chair of the Department of Communication at USF, a position he continues to hold today. In 2000, his wife earned a doctorate in Aging Studies and is currently a Professor in the USF College of Medicine. Eisenberg and his family love the Tampa Bay area and he is grateful for the opportunities to teach and learn from exceptional people whenever and wherever he finds them.

Harold Lloyd (Bud) Goodall Jr. has been both a subject and a student of organizations since his birth, in King's Daughters Hospital, in Martinsburg, West Virginia, in 1952. Reared in a traditional family; educated in public and private schools and universities; employed by large and small businesses; participant and volunteer in community activities and church-sponsored events; and the owner of a publishing house and partner in a consulting firm — all of these organizational experiences have shaped his approach to studying, writing about, and living his many and varied organizational lives.

He first became interested in researching and writing about organizational communication while a new faculty member at the University of Alabama in Huntsville. As a resident "communication specialist," he was asked to develop training sessions in "effective communication" for scientific and engineering firms that supported NASA's Space Shuttle and the federal government's Star Wars project. Later, as his interest in organizations grew from training to consulting, and his scholarly interests shifted from traditional social science to interpretive forms of inquiry, he applied detective methods to various high-technology firms and government agencies. These interpretive methods included his going undercover in the organizations to experience firsthand the lives that were lived there. The result of those years of study and writing were captured in his first two organizational ethnographies, *Casing a Promised Land: The Autobiography of an Organizational Detective as Cultural Ethnographer* (1989), and *Living in the Rock 'n' Roll Mystery: Reading Context, Self, and Others as Clues* (1991).

Goodall received his B.A. from Shepherd College in 1973, his M.A. from the University of North Carolina at Chapel Hill in 1974, and his doctorate in Speech Communication from Pennsylvania State University in 1980. He has taught at the University of Alabama in Huntsville, the University of Utah, Clemson University, and the University of North Carolina at Greensboro. In three of his academic positions — UAH, Clemson, and UNCG — he applied his understanding of organizational and learning theories to create new communication departments and curricula in which vision, mission, values, and course work are strategically aligned and students are better served. Additionally, he is a partner in a consulting firm that specializes in transforming schools and organizations to better serve their communities. His work in the academic community was honored with the Gerald M. Phillips award for mentoring by the American Communication Association.

Goodall's primary scholarly mission has been to change the way texts about organizations and communication are written in an effort to make them more accessible, more representative of everyday life, and more creatively engaging. His ethnographies have received laudatory reviews and awards from both academic and nonacademic sources, and over two hundred colleges and universities worldwide have adopted his textbooks. He has been consistently featured in the popular press and media from coast to coast for his trade books. Overall, he is the author or co-author of eighteen textbooks, tradebooks, and scholarly volumes and over one hundred journal articles, book chapters, and scholarly presentations. He is listed in *Contemporary Authors, Dictionary of American Scholars,* and *Who's Who International.*

"Dr. Bud" is married to Sandra Goodall, who received her advanced training in communication at the University of Utah. She is a private organizational consultant and Feng Shui master with a passion for organizing workplaces and home spaces as sources of balance and harmony in people's lives. Together they have a son, Nicolas Saylor Goodall, who, although not yet a teenager, already aspires to a life full of rock 'n' roll, fencing, computers, and good friends. They make their home in the Greensboro area, where they have been blessed with many good friends, colleagues, and neighbors. All of these good people share with them stories of lives lived in organizations and families, and serve as constant reminders that finding the necessary balance is both a life goal and a daily challenge.

Approaching Organizational Communication

CHAPTER 1

Communication and the Changing World of Work

Globalization itself is neither good nor bad. It has the power to do
enormous good, and for the countries of East Asia, who have embraced
globalization under their own terms, at their own pace, it has been an
enormous benefit. . . . But in much of the world it has not brought
comparable benefits. For many, it seems closer to an unmitigated disaster.
— JOSEPH E. STIGLITZ, *Globalization and Its Discontents* (2002, p. 20)

Perspective

From the moment we are born, we are surrounded by people. With few in-
stincts, human beings need one another for survival. As we seek to understand
the people on whom we rely, we learn many related things at once — a language, a culture, and, most important, a sense of self. We discover who we are
through our communication with others.

Although each of us goes through this process, no two individuals come out
the same. Even small differences in genetics or upbringing result in marked
variations in character and perception. Over time, we each develop habitual
ways of seeing the world — called *worldviews* or *perceptual sets* — that reflect our
inclinations and experiences. Tall or short, male or female, manager or employee, African or Eastern European, what we know for sure is that people perceive the world differently in accord with their worldview, and no two are
exactly alike.

Where do these worldviews come from? Which life experiences are most influential in shaping who we become? We spend our lives as members of numerous social groups: family, church, school, business, country. Our membership in these groups shapes our sense of self. At the same time, participation in these groups requires ongoing interaction with others who are often different from us. To have a self, and to be a functioning member of a society, we must learn how to communicate with diverse others. In primitive times, humans banded together to hunt, gather, and grow food, as well as to propagate the species. Human survival has always hinged on our ability to work together. For this reason, the history of human civilization is fundamentally a history of organizing.

Although collaborating with diverse others may be unavoidable, it is by no means easy. What makes organizing so challenging? Let's start by acknowledging that some tasks are easier than others. In sports, where there are clearly defined rules, roles, and goals, coordination is mostly unproblematic. Simple bank transactions, mail delivery, and traffic patterns on an interstate are other examples of continuous coordination around clearly defined rules that are not open to interpretation. In each of these instances, people know what they want and have a well-defined notion of what it will take to get it.

Unfortunately, many organizing challenges are far more complex and ambiguous. For example, how does one build a successful business? What is the best structure for local government? What kind of communication characterizes a successful marriage? We are on very different ground here: Goals, rules, and roles are negotiable and open to interpretation. Particularly in modern societies (as opposed to traditional ones), there are few givens in social life — almost everything is negotiable.

In school, a mundane but emotionally charged example of the challenges inherent in organizing is the dreaded group project. On the surface, the assignment seems straightforward, and we tend to assume that our fellow group members have ideas similar to ours. In time, however, it becomes clear to us that people have different goals, values, motivations, and worldviews. Hence, for each group member who seeks perfection, there is someone who sees no problem settling for a C; for every person who likes to get work done in advance, there is someone who prefers to wait to finish the project the night before it is due.

So organizing takes work. In business, pulling a bunch of people together who are accustomed to working in isolation and calling them a "team" does more damage than good. The special challenge of organizing — which we have shown here also to be a central challenge of social life — is to collaborate in ways that both acknowledge and bridge differing worldviews.

The interaction required to direct a group toward a set of common goals is called *organizational communication*. Nothing about this process is automatic or easy; certain knowledge and skills are required to succeed. Moreover, as we go about our lives we enter into one interaction after another, always in the shadow of multiple large organizations, whether at a school, a hospital, or a local fast-food restaurant. In each of these interactions, we are occasionally satisfied but more often frustrated by incompetence, insensitivity, lack of coordination, and red tape, all of which result from ineffective organizational communication. A deeper understanding of communication permits us to better comprehend the factors that contribute to successful organizing, from both the customer's and the employee's standpoint. We designed this book to help you develop this deeper understanding.

The Changing World of Work

What kinds of communication are needed for survival today in the world of work? To answer this, we must first understand how this world has evolved and the conditions to which we must adapt and respond in order to be successful. These conditions have changed markedly in recent years, so it is especially important that we reexamine our assumptions about what is most likely to be effective as we strive to create a successful work life.

Questions, Not Answers

Students embarking on careers often harbor misconceptions about the world of work. Many expect their first "real" job to be more serious and orderly than it turns out to be. Likewise, they expect competent and fair managers. They are often disappointed. Once on the job, they may expect a stable career with a company, only to be continually surprised by the steady stream of mergers, acquisitions, and joint ventures that change their job duties and add to their workload. The near universal feeling of continuous change is disturbing to many people, and each of us, regardless of industry, is challenged to find ways to deal with it.

How can we deal with constant change in the business world? There are no easy answers. Even seemingly straightforward questions like "What is the best way to supervise employees?" or "How does one attract and keep customers?" don't permit a simple response. As a result, the definition of effective communication does not remain constant; rather, it varies by company or industry, the people involved, and the culture.

Put another way, answers to questions about organizational communication are highly situated and perishable. By "situated," we mean that the type of communication that works well for a small start-up clothing manufacturer may be inappropriate for a mature film-production company. By "perishable," we mean that patterns of interaction that were effective last year may be outdated today due to changes in customer tastes, technology, or the nature of the industry. Companies that fail to recognize the need for change may perish. One example from our experience involves a machine shop in California. The general manager, a

Marine Corps veteran, modeled the shop's management systems and structures on the military. Although this approach may have been effective for selected industries in the past, it did not work for the machine shop. Neither the managers nor the employees were comfortable with the rigid hierarchy and the intimidating management style. Eventually, employee resistance turned into open hostility, and the general manager was ousted by the board of directors and replaced by an outsider with a more participative approach.

The rapid changes taking place in today's social, economic, and political climate demand speedy, flexible responses. Flexibility is not a strength of the military model. In an historic company-wide restructuring in the 1980s, IBM escaped obsolescence by creating numerous independent business units to meet the demand for greater flexibility. Similarly, in the 1990s, General Electric reconsidered the wisdom of an autocratic management style, moving from a top-down approach to the current structure, in which employees are regularly given opportunities ("Workouts") to talk back to managers and to question the status quo.

When we first taught classes in organizational communication nearly twenty years ago, the banking, air transportation, and fast-food industries were considered to be relatively placid. Competition was weak, and there was room for many players in each industry. Today, these are among the most highly competitive industries in the world. Rapid change also means that the nature of organizational communication in the business world of even five years ago no longer applies. Moreover, what we might believe to be true today may have limited relevance in the future. For this reason, our focus here is on enabling you to ask good questions about organizations, the answers to which may change over time. Successful executives, consultants, researchers, managers, and employees have in common a talent for asking good questions about organizational communication situations. Over time, their actions are guided by how they see and make sense of such situations, by keeping an open mind to the various ways of interpreting those situations, and by remaining committed to a lifetime of learning. Flexibility will enable you to manage diversity more effectively and to adapt more readily to a turbulent business environment. You will be able to reinvent yourself and your organization both in response to and in anticipation of changing times.

New Developments in the World of Work

In the space of just a few years, tragic world events have transformed how Americans think and feel about organizations. The terrorist attacks on New York's World Trade Center and the Pentagon revealed the depth of animosity harbored by at least some of the world's citizens against capitalism and its most visible associations. At the same time, we were faced with less dramatic but similarly shocking news concerning massive financial misconduct by trusted executive officers and their accountants (e.g., Enron, WorldCom, Tyco, Arthur Andersen).

The ensuing dramatic decline of the stock market was only one symptom of the pain caused by these events; many thousands of layoffs provide further bleak testimony. Americans were left to wonder both "how could these things happen?" and "what next?" The current attitude toward organizations in the United States could well be characterized as one of deep skepticism, if not anger.

But alongside these hopeless feelings there is also some slim sense of a possible rebirth, of a desire to rediscover and recommit to the things that matter most, our core values and beliefs. At a superficial level, most corporate and government leaders have rewritten their public addresses to emphasize the importance of ethics and integrity. But regaining public confidence will not be easy, nor will these leaders reestablish credibility any time soon. For this to happen, these new claims to integrity will be tested repeatedly on a global economic stage that continues to reward ruthlessness, exploitation, and expediency.

The massive changes in the realities of organizing in the twenty-first century can be characterized using three critical dimensions: space, time, and loyalty. In the remainder of this chapter, we discuss each dimension and provide examples of how it has changed the nature and meaning of organizational communication.

Beyond Space: The Global Economy

Toward the end of the twentieth century, remarkable changes in global politics — the end of the Cold War, the breakup of the Soviet Union, the destruction of the Berlin Wall in Germany, and the forging of a unified European Community — altered or dissolved divisions that once seemed insurmountable. Many saw in the collapse of old ideas and structures the promise of new alliances striving to end poverty and suffering worldwide, and the potential to adopt a universal code of human rights. This is the dream of globalization, defined as:

> the closer integration of the countries and peoples of the world which has been brought about by the enormous reduction of costs of transportation and communication, and the breaking down of artificial barriers to the flows of goods, services, capital, knowledge and (to a lesser extent) people across borders. (Stiglitz, 2002, p. 9)

Many aspects of globalization, such as artistic exchange and easier access to medical care, are almost universally welcome. Much more controversial have been the economic issues, specifically the policies, agenda, and effectiveness of the international institutions that have emerged to regulate the global economy: the World Bank, the International Monetary Fund (IMF), and the World Trade Organization (WTO). Both the World Bank and the IMF were formed in 1944 to rebuild a war-torn Europe and to prevent future international economic depressions. (Note the focus on Europe: Many of today's so-called third world countries were colonies of European nations at the time, and their development was clearly a secondary concern.) The same 1944 agreement called for the formation of a facilitating body that would encourage the free flow of goods through such measures as lowering tariffs. More than fifty years later, the World Trade Organization finally came into being, and its conferences have become a lightning rod for those protesting the negative economic effects of globalization on the environment and the world's poor. Violent protests accompanying WTO meetings (in Washington, D.C.; Seattle; and Genoa, Italy, during 2001 and 2002) highlighted for the first time the widespread opposition to economic globalization.

There is growing recognition among social commentators that the institutions promoting a global economy have made a number of serious errors. Most critical have been those involving the pace at which it is possible or desirable for a country to make the transition to a market economy where prices and wages are determined mainly by the laws of supply and demand, rather than being regulated by the government. An unreasonably optimistic belief in the self-regulating power of a market economy has led the IMF in particular to force nations needing its help to privatize their industries and open their markets before adequate regulatory frameworks are in place. Disastrous results can be seen, for example, in Russia, where the poor are worse off under market capitalism than they were under their prior socialist regime. A second problem with the current approach has been the failure to recognize that there are multiple models for a market economy, and that, for example, the Japanese, German, and Swedish versions have advantages that may be more useful (and a better fit than the American model) for developing countries. On a more hopeful note, those countries that have not relied on the magic of self-regulation but have recognized the role government could play in the transition to markets (e.g., Thailand, Indonesia) have been more successful (Stiglitz, 2002).

Amidst this struggle, the number of organizations that operate globally has grown exponentially. As of 2002, more than one hundred thousand U.S. companies conduct business internationally, which includes having foreign customers, suppliers, and employees. More than one-third of the profits of U.S. companies and one-sixth of the nation's jobs come from international business. While half of Xerox's 110,000 employees work overseas, half of Sony's employees are not Japanese. The United States enjoys imported music, and American music, films, and television command large markets abroad.

Three regions will dominate the global marketplace during the next few decades: North America, the Pacific Rim, and the European Union (EU). Although globalization gives the United States an expanded market for its products and services, it also threatens to erode U.S. business because of increased foreign competition. At one time, U.S. consumers could respond meaningfully to these challenges by "buying American," but the globalization of business has made this slogan almost meaningless. For example, in October 2002 VF Corporation — the largest apparel firm in the world — shut down its only remaining American plant. Many new automobile buyers who want to remain loyal to

American brands have discovered that their supposedly "American cars" are manufactured or assembled in foreign countries. Similarly, it is harder to define precisely what is "foreign." Consider that Jaguar, once a British manufacturer, is now a Ford subsidiary, as is Volvo, which was once a Swedish company.

But globalization has provided far more challenges to our way of thinking and working than simply complicating how we define the origin of a particular product or service. It has also brought new issues concerning questionable labor practices, multicultural management, and communication technology.

Questionable Labor Practices

The emergence of a new world labor pool has encouraged businesses to search the globe for the lowest possible labor costs, moving jobs wherever cheap labor can be found. Although such practices have long been commonplace in textiles and other kinds of manufacturing, they were confined almost exclusively to blue-collar jobs. Today, white-collar jobs in most industries are affected by this trend. For example, most U.S. software designers employ engineering staffs in India and the Philippines.

Not all prospecting for cheap labor leads to the loss of U.S. jobs, however. In many cases, European and Japanese companies have set up operations in the United States, particularly in the Southeast: "The highest concentration of foreign investment [in the United States] is in South Carolina, which is now home to 185 non-U.S. companies. BMW is likely to pay around $12 an hour in South Carolina rather than the $28 it has to pay in Germany" (Barnet & Cavanagh, 1994, p. 321).

The potential consequences of U.S. jobs being moved overseas were at the center of the debate over the North American Free Trade Agreement (NAFTA), an attempt to reduce restrictions on trade between the United States, Canada, and Mexico. On the one hand, an expanded labor pool makes U.S. companies more competitive by allowing them to hold down costs. In addition, by hiring people from less developed countries (thereby putting money in their pockets), U.S. companies gain new consumers for their products and services. On the other hand, sending work elsewhere may lead to the destruction of U.S. communities that are unable to withstand plant closings or massive job losses. Furthermore, the low wages paid to workers in less developed countries — as little as 10 to 15 percent of comparable U.S. wages — raise questions about exploitation.

But exploitation is not limited to offshore ventures. One domestic statistic neatly reflects the distinct nature of management-labor relations in the United States today. Between 1980 and 2000, the average pay of regular working people increased just 66 percent, while CEO pay grew a whopping 1,996 percent. According to *Business Week*, the average CEO of a major corporation made 42 times the average hourly worker's pay in 1980, 85 times in 1990, and a staggering 531 times in 2000 (to compare working people's salaries with those of CEOs, visit <www.aflcio.org/paywatch/ceou_compare>). In 2000, the United States became the Western industrial nation with the largest percentage of the world's rich and the biggest gap between rich and poor (Phillips, 2002).

Multicultural Management

Another challenge associated with globalization involves the multicultural management of customers, suppliers, and employees. Globalization does not eliminate differences in language and culture. The challenge is to introduce a product or service that is an identifiable example of the brand but still reflects local tastes and tolerances. McDonald's, for example, has many locations in India, where cows are sacred. In a great example of flexibility, the company's "Maharaja Macs" are made with mutton.

Success across national boundaries requires highly sophisticated, global communication skills (Dalton, Ernst, Deal, & Leslie, 2002). At a minimum, this means that employees must speak the language of their customers and suppliers and, preferably, understand the subtleties of the other cultures. Finland has relied on export markets throughout much of its history, and consequently many Finns speak four or more languages. Similarly, Western countries doing business with Japan have learned much about the Asian tendency to spend what westerners perceive as an inordinately long time planning and developing relationships.

An infamous example of an error in multicultural management is Disneyland Paris (formerly Euro Disney). After achieving outstanding success with Disneyland in Japan, where the meticulously designed theme park was consistent with the local culture, Disney opened a park in France. In this case, however, the park ignored important aspects of French culture and climate. For instance, the American-style hotels built around Disneyland Paris costing $300 a night were not practical for the typical French family, which takes a three- to six-week vacation. In addition, when the park first opened, it did not serve alcohol, which conflicted with the French custom of drinking wine at lunchtime (this policy was soon changed). More recently, it appears that Disney has learned its lesson; the appointment of a French citizen to run Disneyland Paris and the serving of alcoholic beverages on the property have eased tensions somewhat.

Starbucks' experience expanding into Asia further illustrates the complexity of multicultural management. When seeking to open his first store in Japan, Starbucks founder Howard Schulz was strongly cautioned by market researchers that the Japanese would not accept European-style coffee, that they preferred their coffee light and sweet. Schulz refused to budge, insisting that once they had experienced his product, the Japanese would enjoy it. After initial success in marketing the Starbucks product to the Japanese, customer acceptance of the new product declined significantly. At this writing, Starbucks Japan has 398 shops open nationwide, and while sales for 2002 were up 22 percent, profits were down 55 percent due to rising import and expansion costs combined with less apparent enthusiasm for its once-popular coffee.

With the acquisition of global markets, businesses have no choice but to acquire a more culturally diverse workforce. At Sheraton's Vistana Resort, an award-winning resort hotel in Orlando, Florida, the Environmental Services Department meets regularly to address communication issues pertinent to the multiethnic staff, which is mainly Latino, Anglo, and Haitian. At computer hardware supplier Kyocera America in San Diego, California, a Japanese management team struggles to communicate effectively with the mostly male African American supervisors and female Filipino employees on the line. As these examples show, effective organizational communication today must address a host of multicultural and multinational concerns.

Being able to manage across cultures can be useful even within the same country. In one case, software managers at Lucent Technologies (the high-technology company that spun off from AT&T in 1996) were challenged to create the most complex product in their company's history, using five hundred engineers scattered over three continents and thirteen time zones. The product was a fiber-optic phone switch called the Bandwidth Manager. The work process was called "distributed development," and the managers found that the technology was the easy part. The hard part was agreeing on the meanings of basic words, like *test*, and reaching consensus on procedures and protocols, since each location had its own culture and traditions. Personality tests revealed that New Jersey employees, who were mostly former professors, exhibited a highly rational style of thinking. In contrast, Massachusetts employees (who were mostly manufacturing engineers) were more in tune with values and the human impact of decisions. In the end, the managers' ability to work with these differences and across these vast distances paid off handsomely, with the switch shipping on schedule, within budget, and technically better than expected. The project is now described as a success story showing the potential of distributed development.

The Center for Creative Leadership, a research and development firm in North Carolina, has studied the factors that lead "global managers" to succeed, and have identified four pivotal skills: (1) international business knowledge; (2) cultural adaptability; (3) perspective-taking; and (4) ability to play the role of innovator (Dalton et al., 2002). The thread connecting these capabilities is effective communication, the ability to forge relationships with others in an open, informed way.

Communication Technology

Although we will detail the role of communication technology in contemporary organizations in Chapter 11, it is important to know up front that the global business community — and the global markets, economy, and joint ventures implied therein — is in large part made possible by recent advances in communication technology.

Globalization requires companies to communicate in ways that transcend space and time. Computerized communication networks — ranging from those that operate over short distances (called *intranets*) to those that span the globe (such as the *Internet* and the *World Wide Web*) — allow companies to coordinate production, take and service orders, schedule work, recruit employees, and market their services. Microsoft executive Bill Gates (1999) called this emerging configuration of point-to-point (or place-to-place) connectivity a company's "digital nervous system." Indeed, some of the most ingenious applications of new communication technology have been in software manufacturing. Software and hardware manufacturer Texas Instruments has operations in Texas, Ireland, and Indonesia that allow it to conduct business continuously. Before the workday ends in Indonesia, employees forward their work electronically to employees in Ireland, who are just starting the workday. The employees in Ireland, in turn, transmit their work to those in Texas before they sign off.

Communication technology enables businesses to structure themselves in novel ways. Some observers credit the development of the telephone with the creation of the modern skyscraper, which would have been impractical and unsafe without the ability to communicate quickly between floors. Advances in communication technology both promote global business and create new sites for work, such as offices in cyberspace. As a billboard for telecommunications giant AT&T proclaims, "The office of the future has no office."

Perhaps the most profound impact of new communication technology on organizations within the last decade has been the emergence of electronic commerce as a viable way of doing business. Today, an enormous number of consumer products and services are available for purchase over the World Wide Web, and even those that cannot be purchased that way offer product education and some kind of preview. A study by DaimlerChrysler showed that over half of the car maker's customers visiting their dealerships had already visited the company Web site for information about models and available options. Consumer hesitations associated with security and privacy have proved no match for the convenience of on-line shopping. One consequence of this shift is that *store* (along with *bank*, and, soon, *library*) no longer refers to a physical place. Reverberations of this are also being felt in colleges and universities; nearly one hundred educational institutions now offer virtual degree programs that can be completed anywhere. The relationships and interactions that constitute organizing can now occur without regard to physical distance or geography.

Beyond Time: Competition and the Urgent Organization

Were these changes not dramatic enough, similar ones have taken place with regard to time. In fact, these changes are so profound that we see most businesses today as "urgent organizations," companies whose main challenge is to shorten the time in which they develop new products and respond to customer demands.

A trend that began with fast food, fax, and overnight mail continues today with the proliferation of automated teller machines, virtual libraries, and customer service call centers that are open twenty-four hours a day, seven days a week. The main motivation for all this emphasis on speed is increased competitiveness. Customers increasingly expect to get exactly what they want, exactly when they want it (Gleick, 1999). The volume of calls to 911 has prompted some communities to create 912 numbers for serious conditions, reserving 911 for real emergencies. If quality was the watchword of the last decade, velocity is ruling the early years of this one (Gates, 1999).

Speed conveys a number of advantages to one company over another (Stalk, 1988). Consider three examples. First, companies vie to see how quickly they can bring a new product or service to market. Often, the first company to release a new product has an edge and, in computers and electronics, can sometimes set the standard by which future products are measured. Second, businesses today compete over who can provide the quickest response time to customer inquiries and concerns. In the personal computer industry, Dell has made an enormous investment in one-year, next-day, on-site service if needed — but most problems can be resolved over the phone through a customer service representative. Finally, companies today strive to shorten delivery times so that the product or service is available to you as close to the moment of purchase as possible. In the past, it was common to hear that delivery would take six to eight weeks for a simple order; today people are demanding that customized products be both assembled and shipped within a few days at most.

Turbulent Organizational Environments

One useful way of thinking about how organizations are changing their relationship with time and space is to introduce the concept of an organization's "environment." The environments in which organizations exist vary in terms of character and complexity. They include their customers, competitors, suppliers, and relevant governments, along with the sometimes very real natural environment. From a biological perspective, we typically think of successful organisms as effectively adapting to changes in their environment. The same can be said for organizations; only in this case these changes could be happening at any time, anywhere in the world. Who could have predicted the struggles of Levi-Strauss, an otherwise superb organization, when millions of young people abandoned classic "501" jeans for radically oversized brands and styles (e.g., JNCO)? Often, companies don't know the extent of their environment until a crisis reveals it to them.

The classic analysis of organizational environments employed a weather metaphor to describe variations in speed and complexity (Emery & Trist, 1965). At one extreme is the so-called turbulent environment — dense, complicated, and hard to predict. An organization in such an environment is in constant fear of environmental jolts (unexpected events that can negatively affect its business) and has difficulty forecasting the consequences of its actions (such as a new marketing strategy, distribution policy, or product feature). At the other extreme is the placid environment — uncomplicated, calm, and predictable. A company in a placid environment need not fear unexpected events and is better able to predict the consequences of its actions. Unfortunately, placid environments no longer exist outside of our grandparents' memories. It's turbulence from here on out.

The unpredictable nature of a turbulent organizational environment has led some companies to focus on rapid retrieval of information about environmental conditions. This can involve such traditional methods as market research and customer focus groups or more innovative scanning approaches using the Internet. Recently, many companies have increased their environmental scanning efforts, but most firms still have not taken full advantage of the available wealth of information.

Perhaps the simplest, although often overlooked, way to keep in touch with environmental conditions is through *boundary spanners*, company employees who have direct contact with the public (Adams, 1980). Bank tellers, telephone receptionists, repair technicians, market researchers, salespeople, and customer service representatives can provide important information about the outside world. Boundary spanners serve at least three functions: (1) They can access the opinions of people outside of the organization and use that information to guide organizational decision making; (2) their awareness of subtle trends in the environment can serve as a warning system for environmental jolts; and (3) they serve as important representatives of the organization to its environment (Adams, 1980).

An interesting tension emerges from the twin pressures to provide responsive service, on the one hand, and to remain speedy and flexible as a company, on the other. The ability to provide instantaneous, customized responses — or what one observer calls "just-in-time, just-for-me" service — requires an enormous investment in people, training, and technology. As a result, only very large companies with sufficient financial resources have the ability to compete. Since size is itself an obstacle to flexibility and innovation, these large firms are seeking to provide more responsive service through consolidation — by purchasing smaller companies with proven technologies and a loyal customer base. One consequence of this pattern is that it is nearly impossible to compete in any industry today as a midsize company. Midsize companies have neither the entrepreneurial swiftness of the small companies nor the megacapital and reputation of the big firms to sustain them. Although we do not necessarily welcome this change, it seems inevitable that in most industries we will soon have three or four major players that control the vast majority of the market.

Beyond Loyalty: The New Social Contract

Over the past hundred years, people have left their homes, farms, and communities to work for large companies in exchange for wages. Many worked all their lives for a single company and were rewarded with job security and a decent pension. The old social contract stipulated that acceptable performance and good behavior would be rewarded with lifetime employment. At the close of the twentieth century, this relationship between organizations and employees became obsolete, both in the United States and abroad. With global competition came plant closings, downsizing, and cutbacks. As the economies picked up, people were rehired, but under different terms, either as temporary or limited-contract employees. This change is having a dramatic impact in Japan, where individual identity is closely tied to corporate membership; layoffs there have caused skyrocketing stress levels and an increase in the suicide rate.

Today, few employees believe that their employer will remain loyal to them, and, indeed, the feeling is mutual. Owners jump at the possibility of selling out for a fortune, and employees are always on the lookout for a better opportunity. Many business schools teach their students to think of themselves as a small business, and to see their careers as a series of finite contracts with corporations. In this new environment, employees must engage in continual learning to remain in demand; at the same time, businesses must strive to attract and retain the best talent. In this spirit, one of Warner-Lambert Company's (now a part of Pfizer) senior human resources managers is now director of "talent management," with the job of continually "re-recruiting" the best employees, making sure that they are challenged, satisfied, and likely to stay with the firm.

Perhaps the greatest challenge to employee loyalty in recent years has been the extraordinary number of corporate officers (e.g., CEOs, CFOs), corporate directors, and corporate accountants who are either being investigated for or have been indicted for criminal behavior. Fueled by an arrogance and sense of invulnerability not seen since the robber barons of the 1920s, these individuals are accused of a range of self-serving behaviors aimed at adding to their fortunes at the expense of average employees. A partial list of recent indictments includes:

- CEO, WorldCom, for hiding $3.9 billion in expenses as a way of boosting profit numbers
- CEO, Tyco International, for tax evasion and evidence tampering
- CEO, ImClone Systems, for insider trading, that is, tipping off friends and family to sell stock
- CEO, Enron Corporation, for creating a maze of off-the-book partnerships to hide losses
- CEO, Arthur Andersen LLP, for obstruction of justice by shredding documents providing evidence of willful wrongdoing

Perhaps the most storied of these cases is Enron, now synonymous with grievous ethics violations. As the company was clearly moving toward bankruptcy, it paid out $681 million in cash and stock to its 140 most senior managers in 2001 (nearly $5 million per manager), while most of Enron's former employees received a maximum of only $13,500 in severance pay ("Managing to make money," 2002).

Shifting Power Bases

In nineteenth-century America, power was measured by a person's tangible assets: land, equipment, oil, and even slaves. Not surprisingly, those in control of these resources wielded the greatest power. By the second half of the twentieth century, information resources replaced tangible resources as a measure of power. By the year 2000, more than half of the U.S. labor force was involved in the transfer, reprocessing, or transmittal of information, a figure that is predicted to increase significantly by 2010 (U.S. Department of Labor, 2002). A growing number of people can be classified as "knowledge workers," and those with the best access to information are the most likely to succeed. Indeed, such companies as TRW and American Airlines cite the information aspects of their business (credit verification and computerized reservations, respectively) as their greatest financial successes (Davis & Davidson, 1991).

However, some observers argue that having the right information is not sufficient for achieving and maintaining power. According to Rosabeth Moss Kanter (1989), informal communication networks are the most dynamic source of power in contemporary organizations because of the role they play in responding to a turbulent business environment. In this challenging environment, the formal reporting relationships specified by the organizational chart (for those companies that still have organizational charts!) are far too limiting to be effective. Increasingly, employees rely on quick, verbal communication with trusted co-workers. These informal relationships allow employees to get things done across functions within organizations, across organizations, and among business, government, and other stakeholders. Under the new social contract, loyalty is limited to those trusted colleagues who can be relied on in a pinch.

Finally, under the new social contract, the career ladder (an expectation that one's career will follow an orderly progression of increasingly responsible jobs in the hierarchy) has been replaced by the opportunity to work on an expanding set of challenges to hone one's own skills and the strategic application of those skills through an expanding web of work opportunities and projects. Since careers no longer follow predictable paths, personal connections and interpersonal relationships have become essential for success.

New Values and Priorities

At the same time that competition has increased and managers demand more from employees, new values and priorities about home and family have emerged. The desire for balance between work and family is increasing among many workers (Hall, 1986); at the same time, people seek more meaningful, involving work experiences. In short, many American workers are changing their definition of success to include not only a career, but also family and community (Bellah, Madsen, Sullivan, Swidler, & Tipton, 1985).

Two primary factors have contributed to this shifting of priorities. First, with fewer high-paying, unionized manufacturing jobs available in the United

States, two-career families are prevalent. More than 40 percent of the workforce consists of dual-earner couples (Zedeck & Mosier, 1990). Second, because grandparents and other members of extended families rarely live nearby, child care is in high demand. As a result, family issues have become a big part of the national political agenda.

It was not that long ago that the model American employee came to work early, stayed late, and was willing to travel anywhere at a moment's notice. Being a success meant putting one's job ahead of almost everything else, leading many to become "workaholics" (see *What Would You Do?* 1.1). Today's men and women are redefining the work ethic of the past. Although some are willing to work as hard as needed to get ahead, others seek more balanced lives. Businesses are moving to accommodate these needs by providing child care, flexible hours, and parental leave (Moskowitz & Townsend, 1991; Zedeck & Mosier, 1990).

In sum, there is an overriding trend to consider overall quality of life as an important concern of organizations today. Nevertheless, this value is easier to espouse than to enact, given varying definitions and priorities among employees. For example, an unmarried colleague of ours recently confided that he resents "family-friendly" company policies because they favor the personal lives of families over those of singles. On-site day care is seen as a boon by many but is resisted by some who see it as further encroachment by business into employees' personal lives. In the end, probably the best any organization can do is attempt to treat employees as whole people while maintaining a great deal of latitude in how particular individuals seek to establish balance in their own lives.

The Meaning of Work

Some of the values being espoused today about work signal not a retreat from it but a transformation of its meaning — from drudgery to a source of personal significance and fulfillment. Employees want to feel that the work they do is worthwhile, not just a way to draw a paycheck. This trend is increasingly pervasive. For example, while white-collar workers and college students tend to view blue-collar workers as being motivated primarily by money, job security, and benefits, the most important incentives for workers at all levels include positive relationships with co-workers and managers. Also important are opportunities to participate in organizational decision making. Without these major determinants of job satisfaction, worker stress and burnout may occur. Work has considerable social significance for Americans, who, despite increased concerns for balance, as a rule spend more time on the job than they do with their families.

Who Can Afford to Prioritize?

For many people, prioritizing work, family, and other needs is a luxury. "Sure," they say, "I want all those things — more meaningful work, more time for myself, more time with family and friends. But most of all I really need this job to survive!"

What Would You Do? 1.1

ORGANIZATIONAL STRUCTURE AND EMPLOYEE WELL-BEING

Workaholic is a term used to describe a person who is unnaturally preoccupied with work. Typically, a workaholic spends long hours at work, including nights and weekends. Family relationships and friendships are often abandoned in favor of relationships with co-workers or other workaholics. Some workaholics truly enjoy their work, but most worry obsessively about getting unfinished work done. Workaholics are often viewed as people who choose to dedicate themselves to their work at the expense of their health, family, and friends. Some organizations consider the behavior of workaholics desirable — a sign of the employee's dedication to the job and the company and a source of increased productivity.

Several organizational theorists propose a new interpretation of workaholism as a disease, a condition brought about by the profound influences that organizations have over how people define themselves through their work (Alvesson, 1993; Deetz, 1991; Karasek, 1979). In this view, organizational power structures may destabilize the employee's personality and produce an unhealthy level of dependency.

The causes and symptoms of workaholism are in a sense ethical problems. As organizational theorist Stan Deetz argues, "It is wrong to knowingly do physical or psychological harm to others" (1991, p. 38). This raises several ethical questions:

Discussion Questions

1. To what extent do organizations intentionally reward unhealthy but productive behavior as a way of maximizing employee output?
2. As a manager in a company that rewards workaholic behavior, how would you counteract the problem? What questions would you ask? Who in the company would you consult?
3. As an employee of a company that rewards workaholic behavior, how would you address the problem? Who would you discuss it with?
4. As an employee or manager, would you have an ethical obligation to help a co-worker who is a workaholic? Explain why or why not.

Any discussion of the quality of work life must take into account the millions of U.S. workers who are either unemployed or underemployed and live below the poverty line. As we struggle to make work more meaningful, we must also seek to improve the education, living standards, and working conditions of those at the bottom of the economic ladder by setting priorities that include everyone. More specifically, we must recognize that traditionally disadvantaged groups — for example, people of color and women — are disproportionately represented among the working poor. This awareness must lead us to redouble our efforts to fight both racism and sexism on the way to establishing economic parity.

SUMMARY

Defining organizational communication for the twenty-first century requires the identification of important social trends and the repositioning of communication practices in this changing landscape. In the present turbulent environment, traditional ways of doing business — and of communicating — are no longer effective. Instead, new principles of effective organizational communication must be developed to reflect the new environment — principles that transcend time and space and that acknowledge the formation of a new social contract between owners and employees. Dissatisfaction with current forms of economic globalization and corporate corruption on an unprecedented scale have created conditions for a new activism around the nature of work.

As we stated at the outset, the history of humanity is the history of organizing, which is in turn accomplished through communication. In the next chapters we will consider more specifically the theories and definitions that will guide us toward a better understanding of organizational communication today.

QUESTIONS FOR REVIEW AND DISCUSSION

1. Explain what is meant by the idea that organizing in business always entails bridging diverse perspectives. How is this idea directly related to the study and practice of communication at work?

2. What do we mean by the statement, "Answers to questions about organizational communication are highly situated and perishable"? How is the answer to this question directly related to the idea that there are no hard-and-fast rules for effective communication?

3. Why is it more important to learn how to ask good questions than it is to have pat answers about communication in organizations?

4. Describe how the global economy, changing management practices, and information technologies have reshaped the world of work. Then explain how each of these changes has affected the study and practice of communication in organizations.

5. Describe the concept of the urgent organization. Explain how this concept relates to the idea of today's business being done in a "turbulent environment."

6. What is meant by the "new social contract"? What social changes have helped create it?

7. How can studying organizational communication prepare you for the world of work?

CASE STUDY

The Case of the Corporate Peacemakers

Darshan Rao is an assistant professor of management who specializes in management communication, corporate ethics, and global economics. Born in New Delhi, India, he came to the United States for college and never left. He became a U.S. citizen in 1995 and three years later took a faculty position at Rutgers University in New Jersey.

In 2001, Professor Rao was visiting family in New Delhi when India and Pakistan's long-standing conflict over the Kashmir region flared up. He was never physically in danger, but war rhetoric from both sides brought back terrible memories; his father had fought in two wars with Pakistan over the same issue, and he was angry that peace seemed so elusive. The fact that both countries had nuclear weapons only added to his anxiety, and, for a time, they seemed on the brink of using them. Darshan thought about changing his plane ticket so that he could be with his parents in case things got any worse. Then, in June 2001, the sabre-rattling suddenly stopped. Parties on both sides were surprised and confused about what had led to the sudden de-escalation. Further investigation by Darshan turned up some amazing information.

He knew, of course, that Indian companies provided critical support to some of the world's biggest companies, including Dell, Reebok, VF, Avis, Sony, and American Express. He also discovered that General Electric's largest research center is in Bangalore, a city with over 1,700 engineers and scientists. When the U.S. State Department had advised Americans to leave India because war prospects with Pakistan had risen to serious levels, information technology ministers from every Indian state approached the government and warned them about the economic chaos that would be caused by a disruption of this magnitude. One American journalist even concluded: "The cease-fire is brought to you by GE — and all its friends here in Bangalore" (Friedman, 2002, p. 8A).

Professor Rao has mixed feelings about this situation. As one of his best students, you hope to understand his thoughts and feelings and perhaps even provide some counsel.

ASSIGNMENT

1. What are the social, political, and economic conditions that made this scenario possible?
2. Why is Professor Rao feeling conflicted over corporate influence in government matters?
3. What aspects of globalization are highlighted by this case, and how might they be applied to other situations?
4. What should be the relationship, if any, between multinational corporations and nation-states? Explain your answer.

CHAPTER 2

Defining Organizational Communication

The mere fact that communication can be theorized in various ways . . . does not give us any good reason to do so. . . . In a practical discipline of communication, theory is designed to provide conceptual resources for reflection on communication problems.

— ROBERT CRAIG, "Communication Theory as a Field" (1999)

As we stated in the last chapter, as long as there have been humans there has been organizing, and with organizing comes an enduring concern about how to do better, whether the task is hunting, coaching a sports team, or running a multinational corporation. Unfortunately, those with practical interest in organizational communication have not as a rule ascribed to the same definitions and assumptions. For example, when engineers speak of the importance of communication, they often (but not always) refer to its role in promoting clarity and consensus. In contrast, a group of clergy calling for improved communication would likely focus on the evocative and emotional power of discourse. In this chapter, we describe some prevalent approaches to organizational communication, beginning with the evolving models of communication as information transfer, transactional process, strategic control, and a balance of creativity and constraint, and concluding with a model of communication as dialogue.

Approaches to Organizational Communication

Of the various conceptions of organizational communication, four stand out as exemplars that have attracted the greatest number of adherents. These are communication as (1) information transfer, (2) transactional process, (3) strategic control, and (4) a balance of creativity and constraint.

Communication as Information Transfer

The information-transfer approach views communication as a metaphoric pipeline through which information "flows" from one person to another. Managers thus communicate well when they transfer their knowledge to subordinates and others with minimal "spillage." According to Steven Axley (1984), this version of communication theory rests on the following assumptions:

1. Language is capable of transferring thoughts and feelings from one person to another person.
2. Speakers and writers insert thoughts and feelings into words.
3. Words contain those thoughts and feelings.
4. Listeners or readers extract those thoughts and feelings from the words.

The information-transfer approach sees communication as a tool that people use to accomplish their objectives. This view, popularized in the early to mid-1900s, compared human communication to the flow of information over a telegraph or telephone wire. During this period, clear, one-way communication was emphasized as a means of impressing and influencing others. In this view, communication is typically defined as "the exchange of information and the transmission of meaning" (Dessler, 1982, p. 94). It is further characterized as "information engineering," wherein information functions as a tool for accomplishing goals, but the process of transmission is not seen as problematic; that is, "If I say it and you can hear it, you ought to understand it" (Feldman & March, 1981).

According to this perspective, miscommunication occurs only when no message is received or when the message that is received is not what the sender intended. Typical communication problems include information overload, distortion, and ambiguity.

Information overload occurs when the receiver becomes overwhelmed by the information that must be processed. Three factors can contribute to information overload: (1) amount, or the absolute quantity of information to be processed; (2) rate, or the speed at which the information presents itself; and (3) complexity, or the amount of work it takes to interpret and process the information (Farace, Monge, & Russell, 1977). Information overload situations can vary in intensity and type. A government worker in a severely understaffed bureaucracy, for example, may have to deal with mountains of simple, steady work. In contrast, a police officer on patrol is faced with varying amounts of complex information that often presents itself at a fast rate.

Distortion refers to the effects of noise on the receiver's ability to process the message. Noise can be semantic (the message has different meanings for the sender and the receiver), physical (the sound of static on a telephone line or of a jet plane passing overhead), or contextual (the sender and the receiver have different perspectives that contribute to the miscommunication). A typical example would be trying to communicate with a co-worker who is experiencing a personal crisis; although you may be saying important things, the co-worker's emotional "noise" may prevent him or her from getting the message you intend to send.

Finally, ambiguity occurs when multiple interpretations of a message cloud the sender's intended meaning. Abstract language and differing connotations are common sources of ambiguity. When a manager asks two employees to work "a little bit harder," for instance, one might put in an extra half-hour a day, and the other might work all night.

David Berlo (1960) offered a communication model that reflects the information-engineering approach. According to his SMCR model, communication occurs when a sender (S) transmits a message (M) through a channel (C) to a receiver (R). The sender "encodes" an intended meaning into words, and the receiver "decodes" the message when it is received. Keith Davis (1972) offers a similar definition: "Two-way communication has a back-and-forth pattern similar to the exchange of play between tennis players. The speaker sends a message, and the receiver's responses come back to the speaker."

The information-transfer model, while dated, remains a useful way to explain certain communication situations in organizations, such as the giving and receiving of technical instructions. To illustrate a more complex application of the information-transfer approach, let's assume that an advertising agency has just received a new account. The senior account representative calls a team meeting and gives assignments to the junior people. One of the team members, however, has difficulty with the assignment. He found the senior representative's presentation confusing, and was distracted by people coming in and out of the room during the team meeting. The deadline arrives, and his assignment is not complete. In this situation, communication is said to have broken down because the intended meaning of the sender (the senior representative) did not reach the receiver (the junior member).

Critics of the information-transfer approach argue that it is simplistic and incomplete, painting a picture of communication as a sequential process (i.e., "I throw you a message, then you throw one back"). In addition, the model assumes that the receiver remains passive and is uninvolved in constructing the meaning of the message. Finally, this theory is incomplete due to its inability to take into account important — and often ambiguous — nonverbal signals.

Communication as Transactional Process

Dissatisfaction with the information-transfer approach to communication led to the development of the transactional-process model. It asserts that in actual communication, clear distinctions are not made between senders and receivers. Rather, people play both roles simultaneously. "All persons are engaged in sending (encoding) and receiving (decoding) messages simultaneously. Each person is constantly sharing in the encoding and decoding processes, and each person is affecting the other" (Wenberg & Wilmot, 1973, p. 5). The transactional-process approach highlights the importance of feedback, or information about how a message is received, and particularly *nonverbal* feedback, which may accompany or substitute for verbal feedback. Consider, for example, the nonverbal messages that students send to instructors during a lecture to indicate their degree of attention and comprehension. While the members of one class may be on the edge of their seats and making consistent eye contact with the teacher, the members of another class may be slouching, fidgeting, and avoiding the instructor's gaze. Rightly or wrongly, most teachers will imbue these nonverbal behaviors with meaning and interpret the first class as more engaged and intelligent. The importance of nonverbal communication is captured by the famous axiom, "You cannot not communicate" (Watzlawick, Beavin, & Jackson, 1967). In other words, a person need not speak to communicate; nonverbal messages are conveyed through a person's silence, facial expressions, body posture, and gestures. As a result, then, any type of behavior is a potential message (Redding, 1972).

The transactional-process model differs from the information-transfer approach in terms of the presumed location of the meaning of the message. In the information-transfer model, the meaning of a message resides with the sender, and the challenge of communication is to transmit that meaning to others. The transactional-process model rejects this idea in favor of one in which meanings are in people, not words (Richards, 1936). It focuses on the person receiving the message and on how the receiver constructs the meaning of that message. As a result, says Steven Axley (1984), "Miscommunication is the normal state of affairs in human communication. . . . Miscommunication and unintentional communication are to be expected, for they are the norm" (p. 432).

One area to which the transactional-process model may be applied is leadership. Ideas about leadership have evolved from the simple belief that certain people are born with leadership skills to the acknowledgment that leadership involves a transaction between leaders and followers. Thus, successful leaders can shape the meanings that followers assign to what leaders say or do. In this sense, then, leadership is the transactional management of meaning between leaders and followers. Compare this to the information-transfer model, which would gauge a leader's effectiveness solely on his or her ability to "put across" an inspirational message. In contrast, the transactional-process model predicts that a common understanding will emerge between a leader and his or her followers over time through communication.

Many experts criticize the transactional-process view for its emphasis on the creation of *shared* meaning through communication. This bias toward shared meaning may be based more on ideology than on empirical research. The degree of shared meaning between people can never be truly verified; all one ever has as proof is people's reports about what they mean, which can be manipulated and may be unreliable. Shared meaning implies consensus, and it is commonly observed that organizational communication is more typically characterized by ambiguity, conflict, and diverse viewpoints.

Communication as Strategic Control

Unlike the transactional-process model, which assumes that effective communicators are clear and open in their efforts to promote understanding and shared meaning, the strategic-control perspective regards communication as a tool for controlling the environment (Parks, 1982). It recognizes that, due to personal, relational, and political factors, greater clarity is not always the main goal in interaction. The strategic-control perspective sees communicators as having multiple goals. For example, in a performance review, a supervisor might have two primary goals: to be understood and to preserve a positive working relationship. In this view, a competent communicator is one who chooses strategies that are appropriate for accomplishing multiple goals.

In addition, the strategic-control approach to communication recognizes that while people may have reasons for their behavior, they cannot be expected to communicate in an objective or a rational way. Communicative choices are socially, politically, and ethically motivated. We recognize that others break the communicative expectations of clarity and honesty when it is in their interest to do so.

The limits of general statements about what constitutes "effective" communication led to a focus on communication as *goal attainment*, or as a means to accomplish one's ends through adaptation and saying what is appropriate for the situation. Communicators must be "rhetorically sensitive" (Hart & Burks, 1972); they must also be able to recognize the constraints of the situation and to adapt to multiple goals simultaneously, such as being clear, assertive, *and* respectful of the other person (Tracy & Eisenberg, 1991).

In organizational communication, strategic ambiguity is an important concept that describes the ways in which people may communicate unclearly but still accomplish their goals (Eisenberg, 1984). Specifically, strategic ambiguity

- Promotes unified diversity
- Preserves privileged positions
- Is deniable
- Facilitates organizational change

First, strategic ambiguity takes advantage of the diverse meanings that different people can give to the same message. For example, the mission statement "Quality is job one" is sufficiently ambiguous to allow all Ford employees to read their own meanings into it. In contrast, the more specific statement "Quality through cutting-edge engineering" is less inclusive and less likely to inspire unity, particularly in the manufacturing and administrative ranks of the company.

Second, strategic ambiguity preserves privileged positions by shielding those with power from close scrutiny by others. A seasoned diplomat or a professor emeritus giving a speech, for example, is traditionally given the benefit of the doubt by supporters who may have to fill in some gaps in their understanding. Fans of seasoned performers often come to shows rooting for their heroes, willing to overlook what may seem to others as signs of weakness. Similarly, by being less than precise, employees can protect confidentiality, avoid conflict, and conceal key information that may afford them a competitive advantage. In this sense, strategic ambiguity is said to be deniable; that is, the words seem to mean one thing, but under pressure they can seem to mean something else.

Finally, strategic ambiguity facilitates organizational change by allowing people the interpretive room to change their activities while appearing to keep those activities consistent. For example, with the advent of air travel, transatlantic ocean liner companies that provided overseas passage by ship were faced with a major challenge to their service. The firms that defined themselves as transportation companies did not survive, whereas those that interpreted their business more broadly (and ambiguously) as entertainment went on to develop vacation or leisure cruise businesses. An example of the pros and cons of strategic ambiguity appears in *What Would You Do?* 2.1.

Unlike other models of communication, the strategic-control approach opposes the idea of shared meaning as the primary basis or motivation for communication. Rather, it holds that shared meaning is an empirically unverifiable concept (Krippendorff, 1985) and that the primary goal of communication should be organized action (Donnellon, Gray, & Bougon, 1986). If we accept that the meaning one person creates may not correspond to the meaning that another person gives to the same communication, it is less important that the two people fully understand each other than it is that they act in mutually satisfying ways (Weick, 1995).

Although the strategic-control perspective advances our appreciation of the subtleties of communication, it is not without significant problems. First, it minimizes the importance of ethics. While strategic ambiguity is commonplace in organizations, it is often used to escape blame. Consider one executive's now classic definition of effective communication: "All you have to remember is . . . let the language be ambiguous enough [so] that if the job is successfully carried out, all credit can be claimed, and if not, a technical alibi [can] be found" (in Whyte, 1948).

Another limitation of the strategic-control approach is its strong emphasis on the behavior of individuals (or on individuals controlling their environment through communication), often at the expense of the community. As such, it clouds issues related to cooperation, coordination, power and inequality, and the interdependent relationships of individuals and groups. The strategic-control model suggests that the world is composed of independent communicators, each

---

What Would You Do? 2.1

ORGANIZATIONAL AMBIGUITY IN ACTION

The strategic uses of ambiguity can have positive or negative influences on the quality of organizational life. Viewed positively, strategic ambiguity can encourage employees to define corporate vision statements, objectives, and goals in personal and productive ways. When DaimlerChrysler says that its vehicles are "engineered to be great cars," everyone from assembly-line workers to top management is encouraged to take the initiative to ensure a quality product. However, ambiguous statements used to define performance objectives can have negative or prejudicial applications. *Quality* is an ambiguous term. When it is left solely to the discretion of managers and employees to define, misunderstandings often result. Similarly, because rewards based on quality attainments are subject to organizational power relationships (see Chapter 6), there is a potential for abuse in the form of favoritism or inequitable application of quality standards.

Strategic ambiguity thus raises important ethical questions. Consider the following scenarios:

1. You are a manager charged with the responsibility of implementing a Total Quality Commitment program in your company. At a preparatory training seminar, you learn that successful quality commitment programs leave determinations of quality standards to employees. You are concerned about the potential differences of opinion among employees regarding quality and how it should be measured. What steps can you take to make strategic use of the ambiguity while also preserving equity among employees? Should the process begin with your definition of quality? Why or why not?

2. You work for a company that has just adopted a Total Quality Commitment program. Your supervisor, unhappy about the program, tells you (off the record) of his intentions to sabotage the program by rewarding only employees who work overtime and on weekends. You are shocked by his behavior. You also believe that the program will improve the workplace. Do you have an ethical obligation to confront your supervisor? To inform co-workers of his intentions? To report him to his superiors? What would you do?

---

working to control his or her own environment, and that meaning exists only within people's minds. It thus overemphasizes the role and power of individuals in creating meaning through communication.

Communication as a Balance of Creativity and Constraint

Since the late 1960s, the central focus of social theorists has been the relationship between individuals and society, which in our case translates to the relationship between employees and organizations. Two competing perspectives examine this relationship. The *macro* perspective sees individuals as being molded, controlled, ordered, and constrained by society and by social institutions. In contrast, the *micro* perspective sees individuals as creating society and its social systems. This dichotomy has obvious implications for organizational communication, depending on whether the emphasis is on how employees communicate to create and shape organizations or on the constraints organizations place on that communication. In other words, while we no doubt conform to social pressures, rules, laws, and standards for behavior, "we are rule and system users and rule and system breakers as well" (Wentworth, 1980, p. 40).

In their foundational text on the individual and society, *The Social Construction of Reality* (1967), Peter Berger and Thomas Luckmann argue that societies and organizations are constructed as people act in patterned ways; over time, people take those behavior patterns for granted as "reality." In other words, most of what we take for granted in organizations is created or constructed through people's choices and behavior. Over time, routines develop and members amass a general knowledge of "how things are done." What results is a tension between the need to maintain order and the need to promote change.

Although many writers have contributed significantly to this line of thought, Anthony Giddens's (1984) theory of structuration is especially relevant to students of organizational communication. In discussing the relationships between individual communication and social systems and structures, Giddens focuses on the creative and constraining aspects of structure, or what he calls the duality of structure. In this view, the designer of a new product advertisement is both bound by the rules, norms, and expectations of the industry and open to the possibility of transcending those structures by designing a creative ad. In this sense, creativity is the design and modification of social systems through communication. The communication process is not viewed as what goes on inside organizations but as how people organize (Barnard, 1968; Farace, Monge, & Russell, 1977; Johnson, 1977). This does not mean that the process is always deliberate or rational; to the contrary, much of what is taken for granted as organizational reality is either unintentional or based on people's perceptions and assumptions (which may or may not be valid). Moreover, people create social reality through communication in an ironic sense: They rarely get the reality they set out to create (Ortner, 1980). The process of designing a new retail store, for example, is necessarily a series of compromises among differing dreams and worldviews; rarely does one individual get to call all the shots. Both the physical design and the interpretations of that design are the result of overt and covert negotiation.

The theory of structuration thus sees human behavior as an unresolvable tension between creativity and constraint. William Wentworth (1980) acknowledges as much when he describes the conflict between under- and oversocialized images of people. For Wentworth, the idea that people are either inherently constrained or inherently creative does not offer a complete characterization of the relationships between individuals and society. Instead, he argues, social life is a balance of creativity and constraint — of constructing social reality and of being constrained by those constructions — and it is through communication that the balance is achieved.

Our definition of organizational communication in this text is derived from the perspectives of Wentworth and others. We believe that communication is the moment-to-moment working out of the tension between individual creativity and organizational constraint. The phrase "moment-to-moment working out of the tension" refers specifically to the balance of creativity (as a strategic response to organizational constraints) and constraints (as the constructions of reality that limit the individual's choice of strategic response).

As an example of how the tension between creativity and constraint is constructed through communication, we can cite the meetings we attended at a company that manufactures hydraulic lifts. These staff meetings were controlled by the company president according to an agenda that he prepared. Most discussions were marked by short briefings on various topics (such as new sales, personnel changes, and capital equipment expenditures) and little actual decision making. Although the executives in attendance were experienced decision makers, they knew that the president viewed any opposing viewpoint as a sign of disloyalty. Nicknamed "Little General," the president routinely embarrassed employees who disagreed with him or who attempted independent action. Over time, employee nonconfrontation was taken for granted, and what had started out as a human construction came to be accepted as an organizational reality (Berger & Luckmann, 1967). Despite the strong constraints on communication and the norm of nonconfrontation at the company, however, occasionally the urge to be creative emerged during meetings. An employee might, for instance, introduce a topic that was not on the president's agenda or present new data that conflicted with data given by the president. By observing communication in these ways, we saw both creativity and constraint in action, as the company's norms were applied or challenged.

Notice that this balancing act activates creativity as a strategic response to organizational constraints. In our example, the staff members acted on information they already had to guide their choices of when to speak and what to say. Unfortunately, however, the organizational reality of nonconfrontation limited their strategic choices and their ability to respond. Because the president seemed unable to respond to their initiatives positively and because they were unable to alter his construction of reality, the balance was tipped toward constraint and away from creativity. It was this lack of balance that made the staff meetings relatively unproductive, one-sided affairs.

The main advantage of this approach appears to be the ability to simultaneously consider the enabling and constraining aspects of communication. Occasionally, researchers and theorists lose this important point and harken back to the information-transfer approach, suggesting that individuals create society, which then in turn constrains the individual. This is a serious misunderstanding of the theory. Finally, there are some who object to the use of the balance metaphor to characterize what happens between people and institutions, claiming that there is an implied norm of "good balance" that might not be in anyone's best interest. Further study and discussion of these ideas is needed.

Having now reviewed the high points of organizational communication theory — communication as information transfer, transactional process, strategic control, and a balance of creativity and constraint — we can use the best concepts from each perspective to develop our own model of organizations as dialogues. A summary of the perspectives appears in Table 2.1. A specific representation of the "balance" metaphor for understanding organizational communication is shown in Figure 2.1 (p. 34).

Organizations as Dialogues

We are both social and private beings. As such, we establish a sense of self that is apart from the outside world (an identity) that engages in a lifelong conversation with another sense of self that is a part of the outside world (a member of a community). If we could somehow construct reality all on our own — as a monologue — we would then be totally alone. Conversely, if our contexts for interpretation came entirely from others, we would lose our identity. The critical issues, then, revolve around these concepts of identity and community, or self, other, and context.

Foundations of Dialogue: Self, Other, and Context

Our self-concept is formed in part from the social relationships we have with others and from others' responses to what we say and do (Bakhtin, 1981; Blumer, 1969; Jackson, 1989). According to George Herbert Mead (1934), the self consists of two interrelated "stories": (1) the story of "I," or the creative, relatively unpredictable part of a person that is usually kept private, and (2) the story of "me," or the socially constrained, relatively consistent part of a person that is more openly shared with others. The "I" is impulsive, whereas the "me" strives to fit into society's rules and norms. The creative aspect of the self (the "I") desires meaningful action with others. The constraining aspect of the self (the "me") guides this action by anticipating responses and applying social rules of behavior.

TABLE 2.1

Organizational Communication: Preliminary Perspectives

COMMUNICATION AS INFORMATION TRANSFER	COMMUNICATION AS TRANSACTIONAL PROCESS	COMMUNICATION AS STRATEGIC CONTROL	COMMUNICATION AS A BALANCE OF CREATIVITY AND CONSTRAINT
Metaphor: Pipeline or conduit — sender transmits a message to receiver.	*Metaphor:* Process — communication is a process that creates relationships; "You cannot not communicate."	*Metaphor:* Control — individuals attempt to control their environments.	*Metaphor:* Balance — individuals attempt to develop distinct identities while participating in an organized community.
Assumptions: (1) Language transfers thoughts and feelings from person to person; (2) speakers and writers insert thoughts and feelings into words; (3) words contain the thoughts and feelings; (4) listeners or readers extract the thoughts and feelings from the words.	*Assumptions:* (1) There are rarely clear distinctions between senders and receivers; (2) nonverbal feedback accompanies or substitutes for verbal messages; (3) meanings are in people, not words.	*Assumptions:* Strategic ambiguity gains control because it (1) promotes unified diversity, (2) preserves privileged positions, (3) is deniable, and (4) facilitates organizational change.	*Assumptions:* All communication accomplishes two things at once: It reflects historical constraints of prior contexts, and it represents individuals' attempts to do something new and creative. This is the duality of social or organizational structure.
Description: Source transmits a message through a channel (air or light) to a receiver; communication is a tool people use to accomplish objectives.	*Description:* Person receiving the message constructs its meaning; the idea is for senders to adapt their messages to the needs and expectations of their listeners.	*Description:* Strategic ambiguity takes advantage of the diversity of meanings people often give to the same message; choices of what to say are socially, politically, and ethically motivated; strategies can be selected to accomplish multiple goals.	*Description:* Communication is the moment-to-moment working out of the tension between individual creativity and organizational constraint. Approaching organizations as constructed through communication requires simultaneous attention to the ways in which groups of people both main-

TABLE 2.1

Organizational Communication: Preliminary Perspectives *(continued)*

COMMUNICATION AS INFORMATION TRANSFER	COMMUNICATION AS TRANSACTIONAL PROCESS	COMMUNICATION AS STRATEGIC CONTROL	COMMUNICATION AS A BALANCE OF CREATIVITY AND CONSTRAINT
			tain order through their interactions, and allow individual actors the freedom to accomplish their goals.
Measure of effectiveness: Receiver of communication understands (or does) precisely what the speaker intended.	*Measure of effectiveness:* Shared meaning.	*Measure of effectiveness:* Coordinated actions accomplished through diverse interpretations of meanings.	*Measure of effectiveness:* A balance between satisfied individuals and a coherent community.
Limitations: (1) Overly simplifies communication: Treats transmission of the message as linear and unproblematic; (2) sees the receiver as a passive receptor uninvolved with the construction of the meaning of the message; (3) does not account for differences in interpretation between speaker and listener.	*Limitations:* (1) Emphasis on shared meaning is problematic and ultimately unverifiable; (2) bias toward clarity and openness denies political realities; (3) does not account for ambiguity, deception, or diversity in points of view.	*Limitations:* (1) Can minimize the importance of ethics; (2) places strong emphasis on individuals over communities; (3) overemphasizes the role and power of individuals to create meaning through communication.	*Limitations:* Can sometimes be difficult to identify what counts as a constraint; also tends to draw attention away from material economic realities that may threaten the system independent of member behaviors.

This definition of the self has important implications for interpreting organizational communication. Because the self is constructed out of our need to balance our own needs with those of others, the self is necessarily dialogic, or made in concert with others (Bakhtin, 1981). At work, we engage in conversations that affect our perceptions of ourselves. We retell stories that were told to us by others, and we use and comment on others' opinions of who we are

FIGURE 2.1

Communication as a Balance of Creativity and Constraint

Metaphor: Balance

Assumptions

1. The duality of structure: Individuals are molded, controlled, ordered, and shaped by society and social institutions; individuals also create society and social institutions.

2. Communication is the moment-to-moment working out of the tensions between the need to maintain order (constraint) and the need to promote change (creativity). As such, communication is the material manifestation of

    a. institutional constraints
    b. creative potential
    c. contexts of interpretation

Representative Model

Creativity ▬▬▬▬▬▬▬▬▬▬▬▬ Constraint

Communication

Description

Creativity	Communication	Constraints
Interpretations of meanings; all forms of initiative; new ways of organizing tasks and understanding relationships; resistance to institutional forms of dominance; uses of storytelling and dialogue to alter perceptions; uses of social constructions of reality to forge new agreements and to shape coordinated actions at work	Reveals interpretations of contexts; asks questions about resources for creativity and the presence of constraints; suggests the possibility of dialogue	Social and institutional forms, laws, rules, procedures, slogans, and management styles designed to gain compliance and limit dialogue at all costs; top-down decision making and problem solving

(Blumer, 1969; Laing, 1965). We make use of both real and imagined characters and relationships (Goodall, 1996). The voice of our experience, therefore, carries with it the perceptions, memories, stories, fantasies, and actions of the many people who shape our lives — co-workers, family members, friends, teachers, students, enemies, celebrities, heroes, and villains (Conquergood, 1991). In other words, our identity only makes sense in relation to others.

At the same time, we construct the *other* in relation to our conception of self. It is said that people who consistently speak badly about others often reveal their own negative self-concept. Conversely, people who generally speak well of others may have a positive self-concept. Our construction of others is not entirely of our own making. It is constrained by the self's culture, race, gender, and subconscious. How we learn to see and respond to the presence, actions, and meanings of others is shaped by many influences. In this sense, then, the self's symbolic construction of the other is also always complex and dialogic.

Especially interesting is the role of others in our understanding of organizations. As noted earlier in the chapter, the information-transfer, transactional-process, and strategic-control models of communication focus on how the sender (self) acts toward the receivers (others). The sender is usually viewed as a manager and the receiver as a subordinate, reflecting the managerial bias of these theories (Putnam, 1982). Employees are too often viewed as "others" to be acted upon, communicated to, ordered, and controlled, rather than as participants in an organizational dialogue. This concept of others as partners to the dialogue contains the important idea of plurality, which refers to the fact that the self and others mutually construct the meanings they have for each other. It also encompasses the idea that multiple interpretations of a relationship are possible and that neither the self nor the others alone can control those interpretations.

Context refers to where communication occurs (i.e., the physical setting) and the interpretive frameworks used to make sense of the communicative exchange. Context is vital to our understanding of organizational communication. For one thing, it shapes our interpretations. In addition, multiple contexts are always available for sense making, and the concept of context tells us much about organizational dialogue.

There can be no meaning without context (Bateson, 1972). If we think of a message as a text, the context is information that goes with and helps make sense of the text. For example, if you overhear a friend call someone you don't know a "loser," how would you make sense of the comment? You would need to know more about the relationship between your friend and the other person and about what happened just before your friend made the comment. You might even need to know where the comment was made. Relationship and situation, two basic aspects of context, would affect your interpretation. If your friend and the other person had been teasing each other all day, the comment might be interpreted as a sign of friendship.

The role of context is always complex. We cannot fully understand the meaning of a message without first examining the relationship, its history, and the immediate situation for clues. This is especially true in organizations, where lines of authority, personal relationships, politics, the business situation, and other factors affect the interpretation of communicative exchanges. Because it is impossible to communicate in isolation, people necessarily communicate in contexts. However, contexts are not stable. According to the *Oxford English Dictionary*, the word *context* originated as a verb meaning "to weave together, interweave, join together, compose." We favor this older definition because it highlights context as "a verbal process aimed at the manufacture of something . . . the seaming together of otherwise disparate elements, perceptions, fabrics or words, the piecing together of a whole out of the sum of its parts" (Goodall, 1991a, p. 64).

When we say that individuals communicate in contexts, we use that term to refer to both (1) how a person defines a situation at any given moment and (2) the process of altering that definition over time. Our definition of context reflects the duality of structure: People both create contexts through communication and are constrained by those contexts once they are created (e.g., one's creative decision to tell off one's boss will constrain future interactions with him or her). As Linda Putnam (1985) puts it, "People establish the context, use the context to interpret messages, and use the messages to change the context" (p. 152). Over time, what we define as context becomes the constructed reality that we take for granted. Therefore, when we say that individuals communicate in context, we mean that they communicate in accord with their constructions of reality, or with their interpretations of the evolving situation.

Please notice that we are, in a way, redefining what it means to work in an organization. Rather than viewing employees as the product of a corporate culture, we believe that a large part of working is the interpretation of contexts. Although most obvious in white-collar jobs, this applies to blue-collar work as well. How people think and talk about their work and how they feel about the relationships they maintain at work and about the company itself all have a significant impact on their behavior choices and, ultimately, on the performance of the organization.

Suppose you are a supervisor in a large bank and during lunchtime you discover one of your employees sobbing in the rest room. What would you do or say? Your first challenge would be to interpret the situation and the context because human communication makes sense only in context. What do you know about this employee that could help you make sense of his behavior? Might personal problems, layoffs at work, or stress play a role? Recalling that the employee's mother had been ill, you inquire about the situation and discover that his mother's illness has become life threatening. This is the relevant context; it makes sense of the employee's behavior and allows you to offer an appropriate response. Furthermore, your interaction with the employee will affect your future interactions in ways that depend on how you and the employee interpret the situation. Thus, your relationship might become more aloof — or more friendly — as a result. Not only is context necessary to make sense of the initial communication, but that communication will, in turn, shape the context for making sense of future interactions.

Dialogue and the Situated Individual

Multiple contexts exist for interpreting communication. What are multiple contexts? Consider this definition provided by Goran Ahrne (1990):

> From birth every human being is affiliated to a family and a nation-state. Children's first experiences of the exercise of power occur within the family. After some years all children will have to yield to the power of the nation-state in the form of school. Growing up, children will slowly get to know the world outside the family and the school. Gradually the everyday world will be larger, adolescence being the typical time for activities in groups or gangs of various kinds. . . . Having married and settled down and started to work, people fill their everyday lives with organizational affiliations. In the course of their lives individuals orient themselves within the existing organizations in the social landscape. Every individual attempts to establish a domain within this landscape, balancing between different organizational influences and leaving some unorganized space. (p. 72)

In other words, we grow up and learn about life in multiple contexts, each of which has its own constraints — or rules, norms, and expected understandings — that make it unique. These constraints play two roles: (1) They limit creativity and individual freedom, and (2) they suggest particular constructions of reality that assist in interpretation. For example, if a co-worker leans over and kisses you (against your wishes), it would be clear from the business context that such behavior is inappropriate and that a strong negative reaction on your part is warranted. If a family member does the same thing, the meaning would be entirely different, as would your likely response.

Consider also how interpretation is complicated by multiple contexts in the typical family business or when husband and wife work together in the same company. You can imagine the conversations: "Dad, you can talk to me that way at home, but not here in front of the other employees!" or "How could you, my own wife, vote against me at the faculty meeting!" Different contexts suggest different rules for action and interpretation. Even within a small organization, multiple contexts are always available for interpretation.

In conducting performance appraisals, how tough should supervisors be on marginal performers? Seen in the context of the business as a financial entity accountable primarily to shareholders, the supervisor should be direct and tough. In a context that emphasizes the supervisor-employee relationship, however, the supervisor could justify being more understanding. Interpreting and communicating in multiple contexts is the tough stuff of organizational life.

This brings us to our key point: All individuals are situated in multiple contexts. In a broad sense, this means that behavior is both guided and constrained by the types of organizations with which we affiliate, whether they be capitalist enterprises, voluntary associations, nation-states, or families. More specifically, all behavior is situated in smaller, or more local, contexts:

> The situated individual is a person who is constructing the everyday business of the maintenance and construction of the social realities in which we live. The situated individual is connected to others through a network of shared, mutually negotiated, and maintained meanings. These meanings provide location, identity, action, and purpose to the individual. They tell me where I am, who I am, what I am doing, how to do it, and why. . . . The network of meanings is not independent of the situated individual. It is the product of the interaction among situated individuals. (Anderson, 1987, p. 268)

Difficulty is encountered when the multiple contexts impinging on an individual suggest inconsistent or conflicting communication or behavior. A study of Disneyland's corporate culture provides a detailed example of multiple conflicting contexts for interpretation (Smith & Eisenberg, 1987). In the early days of the theme park, employees used two metaphors, "the show" and the Disney "family," which were keyed to larger contexts. The first metaphor — of Disneyland as a show — suggested that employees were actors who played important roles. They could thus be told by the "director" to act in particular ways because of "box office concerns" (e.g., to smile more or to style their hair). The other metaphor — Disneyland as a family — however, suggested a different and sometimes opposing context in which management, like a concerned parent, took care of its employees and provided a nurturing environment. These conflicting contexts for interpretation had very different consequences for Disney policy, and in the mid-1980s, company employees actually called a strike in response to a pay cut that was being sold by management as a "sacrifice families are sometimes called upon to make." In fact, recent case studies suggest that the drama metaphor — so compatible with business — has in fact won out.

The situated-individual model of organizational communication may be summarized as follows:

1. The individual is an actor whose thoughts and actions are based on the interpretation of contexts.
2. More than one context always exists to guide the individual's actions and interpretations.
3. Communication is a practice that includes both interpretation and action; as such, it can reveal sources of creativity, constraint, meaning, interpretation, and context.

A final example can help clarify this notion of the situated individual. One of the authors of this textbook became involved with a problem facing a customer service manager at a large travel agency. The manager (we'll call her Laura) sought to convince management of her need for a full-time accountant to manage the record keeping of customer service billings. Laura's initial request was met with assurances from her boss that an accountant would be hired, but then management decided suddenly to deny her request. The problem, then, was how to interpret the denial and what, if anything, to do about it. There were various possible ways to make sense of (or contextualize) the situation. From Laura's point of view, the problem centered on a lack of expertise in her department and the need to address it by hiring the accountant. The finance department saw the situation differently. Because it had sought for several years to hire its own accountant, it strongly resisted the idea that one might now be hired in customer service. As a result, rumors surfaced among the finance department staff about Laura's competency as a manager, suggesting that she would not need the new position if she were doing her job properly. Still another view of the situation came from the general manager of the travel agency. He resisted the new hiring simply because none of the companies he had worked for in the past had had an accountant in customer service. The board of directors based its disapproval on economic concerns. Any new hires in a recession would not please shareholders. Finally, Laura's peers perceived her as aloof and a loner, rather than as a team player. Consequently, no informal group within the company was inclined to support Laura's agenda to hire an accountant. Laura might not have faced this problem if she had been more involved in informal communication networks or if the company had ways of considering multiple interpretations side by side in conversation — that is, in some form of dialogue.

Keep in mind that this is a simple example of how multiple contexts can inform the interpretation of selves, others, and action. Although the facts remain the same — whether to hire an accountant in customer service — the meanings of those facts are constructed differently depending on which context is applied. Because no one individual has access to all potential contexts, each individual's interpretation is based on a limited understanding of the reality being constructed. The information drawn on to build a context for interpretation is varied, multiple, and always limited. All interpretations, therefore, are partial, partisan, and problematic (see Chapter 3). Fortunately, however, the limitations of one person's interpretations are usually offset by others' perspectives. Because sense making is a social activity, more than one person is always involved in the construction of reality. When individuals work to coordinate their contexts, interpretations, communication, and actions, they are said to be organizing. One way of viewing this organizing process is as dialogue.

Definitions of Dialogue

In our working definition of communication as a balance of creativity and constraint, we maintain that dialogue is balanced communication, or communication in which each individual has a chance to both speak and be heard. Dialogue has three levels representing an increasing degree of collaboration and respect for the other: dialogue as (1) equitable transaction, (2) empathic conversation, and (3) real meeting.

Dialogue as Equitable Transaction

An equitable transaction from a communication perspective is one in which all participants have the ability to voice their opinions and perspectives. In defining dialogue this way, we call attention to the fact that not everyone in an organization has an equal say in making decisions or in interpreting events. In the traditional organization of the early twentieth century, people in low-level jobs were discouraged from "interact[ing] with anybody in the organization unless [they] got permission from the supervisor, and then he wanted to know what [they] were going to talk about. So there's this notion in an organization that talking to people is not what your job is, that talking to people [means] interfering with . . . productivity" (Evered & Tannenbaum, 1992, p. 48). Even in some of the most progressive companies today, certain people's voices are valued more highly than others'. These people are said to have power because they can back up what they say with rewards or sanctions. The extent to which one person's remarks carry more weight than another's is not always obvious to the casual observer because a deeper exercise of power is applied to the shaping or defining of context. That is, determinations of whose voice counts most are either well established before the observer arrives on the scene or are created by those who define what is addressed. Numerous contextual factors — the structure of rooms, the arrangement of furniture, differences in dress and appearance, the length of time scheduled for meetings, who is invited (or not invited) to attend meetings, and norms derived from prior communication situations — affect how much weight is given to the points of view of certain people. Once we are in a situation we can try to speak as if from a position of power, but this is difficult given the numerous contextual factors involved.

One way to learn about how individuals participate in organizational dialogues is to ask questions about voice (who does and does not get to speak on organizational issues) and to pay close attention to when, where, and for how long individuals speak. *Voice* manifests itself in the ability of an individual or group to participate in the ongoing organizational dialogue. In most organizations, a few voices are loud and clear (e.g., those of the owners or senior managers), while others are muted or suppressed (e.g., those of the janitorial and clerical staffs). In the literature on organizations, voice has a more specific meaning: It refers to an employee's decision to speak up against the status quo rather than keep quiet and stay or give up and leave (Hirschman, 1970). In an ideal world, voice is the preferred option because it raises important issues and encourages creativity and commitment. In most companies, however, many barriers to voice exist. The suppression of employee voice within organizations can lead to whistle-blowing, wherein frustrated employees take their concerns to the media, the courts, or others outside of the organization (Redding, 1985). In extreme cases of suppressed employee voice, the results may include sabotage and violence in the workplace (Goodall, 1995).

At a minimum, then, dialogue requires that communicators be afforded equitable opportunities to speak. While the notion of dialogue as equitable transaction is a good starting point for thinking about organizational communication, it does not address the quality of that communication.

Dialogue as Empathic Conversation

In defining *dialogue* as empathic conversation, we refer to the ability to understand or imagine the world as another person understands or imagines it. Achieving empathy is difficult for people who believe that their view of reality is the only correct view and that others' perceptions are misinformed or misguided. Indeed, Western communication is largely based on assumptions of what is "right." As a result, it becomes much more difficult to accept the validity of a different perspective, especially a radically different one. However, empathy is crucial in organizations. It promotes understanding among different departments, makes managing diversity possible, and acknowledges that although individuals and groups have different perspectives on the organization, no single perspective is inherently better than others. In this way, we can focus on common problems without immediately turning those who have a different view of these problems into enemies. The challenge, of course, is in learning to appreciate differences in interpretation without feeling pressured to either demonize the other or to strive for complete agreement. Put differently: "Can I recognize the value of your [perspective] . . . without us having to somehow merge into something that's less rich than the community of differences?" (Evered & Tannenbaum, 1992, p. 52).

Researchers at the Massachusetts Institute of Technology (MIT) take a similar view of organizational dialogue in their efforts to create learning communities (Isaacs, 1999; Senge, 1991; Senge, Roberts, Ross, Smith, & Kleiner, 1994). Building on the work of physicist David Bohm, the researchers define *dialogue* as a kind of "collective mindfulness" in which the interactants are more concerned about group process than about individual ego or position. From this perspective, dialogue affords new opportunities for people in organizations to work together. Not merely a set of techniques, dialogue requires that people "learn how to think together — not just in the sense of analyzing a shared problem or creating new pieces of shared knowledge, but [also] in the sense of occupying a collective sensibility, in which the thoughts, emotions, and resulting actions belong not to one individual, but to all of them together" (Isaacs, 1999, p. 358). The MIT dialogue project has attracted the attention of business because it links the fate of whole systems of individuals (e.g., organizations, societies, species) with dialogue, flirting with the idea that our relationships with others can possess a spiritual quality.

We know that treating people like objects is inappropriate, but are understanding and empathy enough? These questions recall the work of contemporary philosophers Martin Buber and Mikhail Bakhtin, whose critique of empathy as the goal of dialogue leads us to yet another definition.

Dialogue as Real Meeting

In defining *dialogue* as real meeting, we mean that through communication, a genuine communion can take place between people that transcends differences in role or perspective and that recognizes all parties' common humanity. John Stewart (2000) refers to this state as "letting others happen to you while holding your ground." The notion of dialogue as empathic conversation is insufficient because it assumes that one individual experiences the other as a kind of object, rather than as a fellow interpreter. In other words, even empathic communicators, once the conversation has ended, may continue to view the dialogue as mainly instrumental in accomplishing their personal and professional goals. Therefore, one's performance of empathy may be false or even a means to a personal strategic end.

Certain types of dialogues are valuable in and of themselves. Buber distinguishes between interhuman dialogue, which has inherent value, and social dialogue, which has value as a route to self-realization and fulfillment. According to Buber, "We are answerable neither to ourselves alone nor to society apart from ourselves but to that very bond between ourselves and others through which we again and again discover the direction in which we can authenticate our existence" (quoted in Friedman, 1992, p. 6). Consider also this quote from Bakhtin:

> A single consciousness is a contradiction in terms. Consciousness is essentially multiple. . . . I am conscious of myself and become myself only when revealing myself for another, through another and with the help of another. . . . The very being of man [*sic*] is the deepest communion. (quoted in Emerson, 1983)

From this perspective, since life exists only in communion with other humans, dialogue is a fundamental human activity. How do meetings in organizations resemble Buber's ideal? Buber sees it as a relationship between "I and Thou," wherein two individuals acknowledge that each is an interpreter and that neither reduces the other to an object of interpretation within a context that has already been constructed. For example, we have seen senior managers who have struggled to understand each other deeply move to an even higher level of trust and coordination in which their respect and regard for the others appear as the foundation of each of their conversations. This respect for another's subjectivity and worldview is the key ingredient in real meeting.

Seeking dialogue because it has value for itself can often result in positive consequences for the organization:

> [Dialogue] is one of the richest activities that human beings can engage in. It is the thing that gives meaning to life, it's the sharing of humanity, it's creating something. And there is this magical thing in an organization, or in a team, or a group, where you get unrestricted interaction, unrestricted dialogue, and this synergy happening that results in more productivity, and satisfaction, and seemingly magical levels of output from a team. (Evered & Tannenbaum, 1992, p. 48)

This definition of *dialogue* combines the abstract or spiritual with the more practical aspects of how we communicate. Are we open to the voices of others? Do we recognize that all views are partial and that each of us has the right to speak? Are we open to the possibility of maintaining mutual respect and openness of spirit through organizational communication? Such questions are not easily answered by people in organizations today. Although people may desire to maintain an open dialogue, they may be constrained by learned behaviors that guard against intimate disclosure, by the social, professional, and political consequences of those disclosures, and by the habit of separating emotions from work.

To establish dialogue as real meeting, we must learn to interpret communication as a dialogic process that occurs between and among individuals, rather than as something we do to one another. All parties are responsible for the dialogue as well as for the risks taken; only together can they make progress. We engage in dialogue to learn more about the self in context with others. Dialogue helps us attain new appreciations for the multilayered dimensions of every context: "The crucial point is to go into a dialogue with the stance that there is something that I don't already know, with a mutual openness to learn. Through dialogue we can learn, not merely receive information, but revise the way we see something. Something about the dialogue honors inquiry and learning from the inquiry" (Evered & Tannenbaum, 1992, p. 45).

Authentic dialogue also provides a practical communication skill that is invaluable: We learn to speak from experience and to listen for experience. By sharing and risking the truth of our experience, we discover important questions that can guide our interpretations of contexts, of others, and of ourselves. We gain access to the shaping forces of our own and others' experiences. These forces guide our individual and collective constructions of reality, teach us about what counts as knowledge as well as how to value it, and influence how we generate our evaluations of people and things.

Dialogue as real meeting is difficult to achieve, which is why it does not characterize most relationships inside or outside of organizations. Most organizations readily acknowledge the importance of equitable transactions and are pleased to create increased empathy across hierarchical levels and professional groups. Still, dialogue as real meeting is an important communicative goal because it can transform organizations into energetic and dynamic workplaces. Such organizations are both effective and enjoyable because they encourage the kinds of communication required for real human connection.

There are advantages and limitations associated with promoting dialogue in organizations. It can increase employee satisfaction and commitment, reduce turnover rates, and lead to greater innovation and flexibility within the organization. However, it is also time-consuming, requiring that issues be screened in terms of the amount of dialogue they warrant. Although certain people will possess the power to decide which issues are most important, this is necessary in a turbulent business environment. In addition, promoting dialogue may lead communicators to assume that their ideas and opinions will be implemented. Although there may be an equitable distribution of power and voice in the group, within a capitalist system the owners and their agents make the final decisions. Recent moves to develop employee-owned companies are beginning to address this concern. Finally, dialogue may lead to a lack of closure or to the feeling that "no right answer" can be found. This problem is related in part to the nature of Western society, in which people expect definitive answers about science, medicine, politics, and technology. In organizational communication, it may be more appropriate to focus on practical guidelines for action.

We conclude this section with two important questions. First: Is dialogue possible in organizations? Our experiences lead us to believe that while dialogue is possible in organizations, it is exceedingly rare. More common is communication that creates barriers to real meeting by attempting to convince others that their perceptions are faulty: "Management shouldn't think that way," "That idea will never fly," and "I know my people aren't dissatisfied." Much may be gained by expanding the current interest in coordinating the diverse voices in business.

Our second and more difficult question is: What role can the situated individual play in constructing organizational reality through communication? Some observers take exception with the concept of the situated individual. They argue that it simply restates the idea that a person has a political ideology in favor of free will and capitalism (Grossberg, 1991). In their view, most choices are so constrained that decisions are made for us, and what we believe to be free or motivated action is actually the force of the world acting through us. Other observers, however, are less willing to underestimate the experiences of the situated individual (Jackson, 1989). In this view, we are born into a society that expects us to act out a balance of individual and social responsibilities. We are expected to make decisions about ourselves and about how our actions may in-fluence and be influenced by others. Ultimately, however, the responsibility for those actions is our own. If someone commits a serious crime, for example, so-ciety may be implicated, but it is the criminal who goes to jail.

SUMMARY

This chapter begins by introducing four definitions of organizational commu-nication that are commonly encountered in the research literature: communica-tion as information transfer, transactional process, strategic control, and a balance of creativity and constraint. This list is roughly chronological and re-veals an increased interest in feedback and two-way interaction as key to orga-nizational sense making. We next extend this trend by offering our own view of organizations as dialogues.

Recasting organizations as dialogues (in contrast, say, with economic or po-litical models) focuses us on the interplay between self and other in multiple, changing contexts and situations. We next explain how each of these founda-tional elements arises in relationship with the others, culminating in the idea that every individual is "situated" in flows of communication.

Finally, we explain that when situated individuals come together to orga-nize, they may vary considerably in the sort of communication in which they engage. On one end of the spectrum is discussion, wherein people seek to dom-inate others. At the other end is dialogue. Writers on dialogue (and there has been an explosion of recent interest in the subject) have outlined what we cate-gorize as three levels that increasingly reveal people with a fundamental respect for the subjectivity and differing worldview of the other. The three levels are di-alogue as equitable transaction, dialogue as empathic conversation, and dia-logue as real meeting. We close the chapter on an optimistic note, suggesting from our experience that some level of dialogue is indeed possible in contempo-rary organizations.

QUESTIONS FOR REVIEW AND DISCUSSION

1. What are the major approaches to communication discussed in this chapter? What insights does each approach provide?

2. Explain what we mean by our definition of organizational communication. What are the sources of individual creativity? Of organizational constraints?

3. How do the concepts of self, other, and context contribute to our under-standing of organizational communication? How do these concepts help us understand the differences among the major approaches?

4. Strategic ambiguity is discussed as a way to encourage empowerment by allowing employees at different levels within the company to interpret the meaning of statements in relation to their own jobs. However, it doesn't always work out that way. What potential problems are associated with using strategic ambiguity?

5. What is dialogue? Of the types of dialogue described in this chapter, which ones do you believe are most likely to be available to organizational employees? Why?

C A S E   S T U D Y

The Many Robert Smiths

JASON, THE JANITOR

"Smith is a tidy man. I pass by his desk at night when I'm cleaning up, and his area is the only one that's perfect. Nothing is ever out of place. I've made a kind of study out of it. You know, paid lots of attention to it on account of it being so unusual. So I've noticed things.

"I'd say Smith must be a single man. There are no pictures of family on his desk or on the walls. Most people leave keys to their personal life in the office — photographs, items they picked up during vacations, stickers with funny sayings on them. But not Smith. In Smith's area, there is no trace of anything personal. Just some books and the computer. The books never change positions, which tells me he never has to look things up. So I think Smith must be a smart man, too.

"I've never met him. Or if I did, I never knew it. But I see him in my mind as a tall, thin guy with glasses who doesn't smile too often. He may be shy, too. Fastidious people are often shy. Maybe he's an accountant or a computer programmer. It's hard to say. But Smith makes my job interesting. I look at his desk every night to see if anything has changed."

CATHERINE, THE RECEPTIONIST

"Smith is okay, a little shy maybe. He says 'hello' to me every morning. Just a 'hello,' though — nothing more, not even my name. I didn't know his name for months. But then, I didn't say much to him either.

"Then one afternoon he had a visitor. It was a woman — a beautiful woman in her late twenties or early thirties. She asked to speak to Bobby. 'Bobby who?' I asked. She looked confused; then she smiled and said, 'Bobby Smith, I thought everyone knew.' Well, this was interesting. I mean, I suddenly realized Smith had a first name — Robert. I had never thought of him as anyone's 'Bobby' before.

"I paged Smith, and he came downstairs. When he saw the woman, his face turned white like he'd seen a ghost. She called his name, and he stood still. I thought he was about to cry or something, but instead he just shook his head, as if to say, 'No.' He didn't say anything. Just shook his head. Then he turned and walked back upstairs, slowly. The woman just

(continued)

watched him. Then she turned around and walked out. I never saw her again. I don't know if she was a girlfriend, sister, or friend. Smith never said anything about her.

"In this job, I meet all kinds of people. I've learned a lot about people while working here as a receptionist. But Smith is still a mystery to me. I don't know much about him. All I know is that his first name is Robert but that some people call him Bobby, that he says 'hello' to me every morning like clockwork, and that there was once a beautiful woman in his life. Oh yeah, and he's about 5 feet, 7 inches tall, has short hair and a big mustache, wears an earring, and obviously works out a lot."

WILSON, THE BOSS

"Smith is a strange guy, but a good worker. He never misses a day and is even willing to work nights or weekends to get the job done. His work is always neat and well organized. Personally, I wish he would get rid of his earring and mustache, but that's just him, I guess.

"I hired him five years ago as an entry-level accountant. His work in that position was good. He was promoted to a senior accountant position very quickly, as if someone up there in the company ranks were watching out for him. Usually it takes the best accountant five to seven years to make it to senior status; Smith made it in three. Last fall I asked him to take charge of a major audit, and he's been diligently working on that project ever since.

"Smith never talks about his life outside of work. And I never ask him. He seems to like it that way. But from the way he is built, I'd say he spends a lot of time working out at a gym. He drives a vintage black sports car, a Speedster, and it is always clean. He leaves it open during the day with a pair of Ray-Bans on the dash, always in the same position.

"I figure he comes from a wealthy family. He graduated from Stanford. But he doesn't act like a Californian. I'd say he's from Pittsburgh. I don't know why I say that.

"Actually, to be honest, Smith scares me a little bit. I don't know anyone who's as calm and collected and perfect as Smith is. In movies it's always the mass murderer who's like that. Not that I think Smith is that way. But I wouldn't be surprised, either. I wish his starched shirts would just one time come back with a rip in them or something. I know that sounds small. I can't help it. Smith does that to me."

FELICIA, A CO-WORKER

"Robert is my good friend. He's a warm, sensitive person with a heart of gold. He and I have talked a lot over the past couple of years. Mostly about our dreams. We both want to work hard, save a lot of money, and be able to do something else with our lives while we are still young enough to enjoy it.

"Robert came from a poor family. He grew up moving around from town to town while his mother looked for work in construction. He had two brothers and a sister, all older. He was the baby. His father was killed in the Vietnam War. His older brothers are both in the military and don't have much in common with Robert, and his sister is a successful lawyer in Washington. Robert showed me a picture of her once; she's a beautiful woman. They had a big argument a while back. He wouldn't say much about it, except that he hasn't seen her since. His mother died of lung cancer two years ago.

"Robert worked hard in school but won an athletic scholarship to Stanford. He was a gymnast. Or still is, because he spends two or three nights a week working with underprivileged kids downtown, teaching them gymnastics. And he is big in Adult Children of Alcoholics, which I took him to. That's a whole story in itself. He has a lot of hobbies, which, when he does them, aren't exactly hobbies anymore. He is such a perfectionist! Like that car of his, for instance. He built it himself, out of a kit. And you should see his apartment."

JENKINS, THE RETIRED CEO

"Robert Smith is one of the company's finest employees. And he is an exceptional young man. I recruited him at Stanford when I was teaching there right after I retired. Since then, I've followed his career. I asked him not to say much about our relationship because a lot of people might get the wrong idea. I want him to make it on his own, which he has. I put in a good word for him here and there, but never anything too pushy.

"I knew his father in Vietnam. He served in my command and was a good soldier. He was due to be shipped home later in the week when he was killed. It was sad. I wrote the letter to his family myself. When I got out of the Army, I moved into the private sector. You can imagine how odd it was for me to walk into that accounting class at Stanford and see

(continued)

Robert Smith, who looks just like his dad except for the mustache and earring, sitting in the front row. I couldn't believe it. Still can't.

"In a way, I feel related to Robert. He still comes to visit us on the holidays. I like that."

ASSIGNMENT

1. You are the executive recruiter (or headhunter) who compiled the preceding information about Smith from interviews with his colleagues. You also have Smith's résumé and performance appraisal reports to supplement the interviews. Your job is to prepare a personality profile of Smith for a firm that may be interested in hiring him. What would you write? How would you explain the different perspectives on Smith? If you were Robert Smith, what would you say about the interview statements?

2. We live complex (and often contradictory) lives as situated individuals in organizations. This should make us sensitive to the various ways in which meanings are constructed through communication. Construct an investigation of yourself, using interview statements by others describing who you are. Supplement these statements with your own résumé. What do the statements tell you about yourself? About your construction of others? About yourself as a situated individual in an organization? About the complexities of interpreting meaning?

3. As a student of communication, you are interested in finding ways to improve your own and others' interpretations of meanings. Review the case study as if you were the communication consultant working with the executive recruiter. Your job is to help the headhunter construct better follow-up questions and produce a complete report on Smith. What questions would help explain the different views of Smith?

PART II

Theories of Organizational Communication

Three Early Perspectives on Organizations and Communication

No one ever walks into a McDonald's and asks, "So, what's good today?" except satirically. The heart of McDonald's success is its uniformity and predictability. Not only is the food supposed to taste the same every day everywhere in the world, but McDonald's promises that every meal will be served quickly, courteously, and with a smile. Delivering on that promise over 20 million times a day in 54 countries is the company's colossal challenge. Its strategy for meeting that challenge draws on scientific management's most basic tenets: find the One Best Way to do every task and see that the work is conducted accordingly.

— ROBIN LEIDNER, *Fast Food, Fast Talk* (1993)

We have thus far discussed the pervasiveness of organizational communication in society and have given you some definitions for thinking about the nature and process of communication in general. In this chapter, we hone in on the organizational context and discuss in some detail three early *theories* of organizations that were not written with a communication focus, although they do have implications for communication. Instead, they had more of a business focus, but we must begin here since the ways they defined (or failed to define) communication have had enormous impact on organizational practice both historically and even today. The three organizational perspectives are classical management, human relations, and human resources. Before we start, however, we want to make sure that you have a thorough understanding of what is meant by "theory."

Why Theory?

Theories of human behavior run the gamut from simple ideas to formal systems of hypotheses that aim to explain, predict, and control. All theories share two features: They are historical and metaphorical. Any theory of organizational communication is historical in that it is a product of the time in which it emerged, reflecting the concerns and interests of the culture that produced it. A theory is metaphorical in that it uses language to suggest enlightening comparisons between organizational communication and other processes. For example, scientific management theory, which we will discuss in this chapter, compares organizations to machines.

Our approach to the role of theories in understanding organizations is a practical one that recognizes both their uses and limitations. As students of organizational communication, we choose to participate in a particular discourse community, which in this case is made up of individuals who share an interest in organizations and communication. Communication and literary theorist Kenneth Burke (1989) likened participation in a discourse community to entering a room in which conversation is already in progress. We wander around for a while, listen, and occasionally join in the talk. Sooner or later, we find ourselves engaged in conversation that seems important. As time passes, we have many such conversations. Eventually, we notice that the hour is late and that it is time to leave, but the conversation continues without us. Here we recognize that participation in the discourse community requires detailed attention to the talk that preceded our entry into the room.

Theories function as resources in that they enhance our ability to explain and to act on a wide variety of practical issues, such as what motivates people to work. The way we talk about an issue or problem influences the solutions we can propose. But theories are also historical narratives, or goal-oriented stories told for the purpose of explanation. Theories may offer a creative integration of disparate issues (such as how organizations can be both pro-profit and pro-people or why communication and efficiency are linked), or they may provide a complete explication of a narrow topic (such as how to lead an effective decision-making group or how to relieve employee stress). In either case, theories reflect unique historical circumstances and diverse cultural and political interests.

Because organizational communication theories are evolving episodes in an ongoing historical narrative, it is important that we not strive to choose one theory over another. Instead, we should learn to see each theory as a participant in a larger, ongoing dialogue. Consequently, our interest in theories goes beyond what they help us to explain. We are also interested in the position of theories in the general stream of events, in their relationship to other theories, in their unique properties, in their strengths and limitations, in the interests they represent or exclude, and in the effects of retelling them on our conversation and the world.

Organizational Communication Theories as Historical Narratives: The Three *P*'s

The three *P*'s of historical writing — that such writing is partial, partisan, and problematic — provide an important perspective on communication and reveal the limitations of any account. All talk is partial, partisan, and problematic, and theories are no exception. The kinds of questions we raise about our reading of theory add to our understanding of organizational communication.

Theories Are Partial

An argument could be made that any attempt to trace the history of organizational communication is necessarily incomplete and therefore misleading. Obviously, we have chosen to write this chapter anyway. Our primary condition is partiality: Our account tells only part of the story. However, the inability to articulate a complete account of the history of organizational communication is not unique to our field, nor is it disabling. As French philosopher Jacques Derrida (1972) notes, all thought is inscribed in language, and language is rooted in an inescapable paradox: There is no point of absolute meaning outside of language from which to view — or to prescribe — the truth of the world. Furthermore, it is logically impossible to say everything about anything; new perspectives are always possible, now and into the future. Because all language is partial (regardless of length!), there can be no absolute history, no full account, no complete story of organizational communication. Therefore, from this perspective, our account is necessarily partial.

Theories Are Partisan

We write this chapter, and indeed this book, under the limitation of partisanship: The story we tell is one that we favor. The history of organizational communication typically emphasizes the interpretations of dominant white males in Western culture, with little attention given to how members of oppressed, marginalized, or subjugated groups like women and minorities would tell the story. Compare, for example, how a Native American might interpret the nineteenth-century expansion of railroads, mining, and manufacturing interests across the Great Plains with the account given in many U.S. history textbooks. Depending on one's interests, or partisanship, this story can be seen as one of tragedy or opportunity. Notice that although there may be disagreement about how the story gets told and who should tell it, there is likely to be agreement on at least some of the story's events and characters. Everyone agrees that Native Americans considered the Great Plains their natural hunting grounds and that westward expansion by white settlers took place. Partisanship, then, is not so much about identifying facts as it is about interpreting their meanings.

All thought is partisan. Knowledge is shaped by the theories and interpretations we use to make sense of the world, or to create what we call a worldview. If we think of each theory as a kind of mini-worldview, then we see clearly that one theory cannot explain everything. No one partisan view can comprehend all the interests of all people over all time. When we read about theories, then, it is useful to think of each theory as telling a particular story. Because each story represents the interests of the storyteller, it is a partisan perspective on broader, more complex stories about the world. In this sense, many theories contribute to the complex story of organizational communication.

This principle can be directly applied to routine episodes of communication at work. For example, let's assume that Deon makes this announcement at a team meeting: "I just talked to Beth about our project, and she thinks we ought to go with the approach I suggested last week." His comment may be viewed as partisan on several accounts. The other team members might consider whether Deon's interpretation of his conversation with Beth was influenced by what he wants to happen. Alternatively, perhaps Deon influenced Beth's opinion. The key point here is not that Deon has intentionally misrepresented Beth's opinion at the team meeting, but that all talk is partisan. When we speak, we tend to represent our views of situations in ways that favor our interests and goals.

Theories Are Problematic

Finally, we write this chapter knowing that the story itself will be problematic: Our account asks more questions than it can answer, and the answers it does provide are based on what is currently known rather than on all that could be known. In admitting the problematic nature of our narrative, we also invite dialogue, asking our readers to bring to our account their experiences and understandings. Consider how this concept can inform our understanding of everyday organizational communication. Rather than making ultimate statements, it encourages us to ask more questions and thereby to invite others into the dialogue. Rather than assuming that we know the whole truth about any issue, it encourages us to ask for the input of others who may hold different perspectives. This is very much in line with our philosophy and conception of this text — not as a book of answers, but rather as a way of thinking that produces good questions across multiple contexts and situations.

Now that you have a clearer understanding of our perspective on theories, it is time to examine some specific theoretical perspectives on organizations with implications for communication.

Classical Management Approaches

Classical management approaches are represented by a collection of theories that share the underlying metaphor of organizations modeled after efficient machines. This section shows the evolution of this idea from the eighteenth century to more recent times, beginning with the nature of preindustrial organizations and concluding with the apex of the classical approaches, the Industrial Revolution.

From Empire to Hierarchy

From the eighteenth to the early twentieth centuries, organizations functioned much like empires. Corporations were viewed as extensions of governments; they expanded trade, provided employment for the masses, and contributed to economic and social development (Rose, 1989). Cities in the New World (North America) were even mapped according to the appropriation of territories by organizations. Today, we can still see the close relationship between homes and factories in some regions, and we can also see how wealth and status allow a family to move farther away from the site of production. The closer a house is to a factory, the less material power and social status the family living in that dwelling tends to have. Thus, social control is effectively produced in part by the relationship between the location of industry and neighborhoods.

In the mid-eighteenth century, Benjamin Franklin (1706–90) popularized some early notions of empire and pragmatism in his *Poor Richard's Almanac*. It is primarily a collection of parables and quotations that elevate hard work (called "industry"), independence (the accumulation of wealth on individual, corporate, and national levels), and the virtues of planning, organizing, and controlling one's life through work. Here are some sample axioms from Franklin's almanac (1970):

- Industry need not wish — There are no Gains without Pains.
- God gives all things to industry.
- God helps them that help themselves.
- Sloth makes all things difficult, but industry all easy.
- Early to Bed, early to rise, makes a Man healthy, wealthy, and wise.

Although Franklin was not the only writer to express these ideas (similar sentiments are found in Japanese and Chinese proverbs, the Old Testament, and the Talmud), he was the first to popularize them as the foundation for an American work culture. Moreover, the proverbs were influential precisely because they fit neatly into the wisdom of older narratives used in churches, schools, and business.

During this same period, Frederick the Great (1712–86), king of Prussia, organized his armies on the principles of mechanics: ranks, uniforms, regulations, task specialization, standardized equipment, command language, and drill in-struction (Morgan, 1986). His success served as a model for organizational ac-tion, one based on the division of labor and machinelike efficiency. Given this historical background, it is perhaps no surprise that inventor Eli Whitney's (1765–1825) groundbreaking demonstration of mass production in 1801 was based on the production of guns, whose purpose was to maintain order and ex-tend the power of empires.

Adam Smith (1723–90), a philosopher of economics and politics, published *Wealth of Nations* in 1776, which praised the divisions of labor evident in factory production. As Karl Marx (1818–83) would demonstrate in the mid-nineteenth century, division of labor was essential to organizing corporations and societies along class lines. By 1832, a blueprint for such an organizational form had emerged. Characterized by strict divisions of labor and hierarchy, it would later be called the "classical theory of management." Notice in Figure 3.1 that the classic bureaucratic organization privileges a top-down or management-oriented approach. Two assumptions of this perspective are worth noting. First, the em-phasis on developing scientific methods for production is politically and socially linked to providing that information only to managers and supervisors, who in turn use it to organize and control workers. Second, the model endorses the need to foster a passive audience in the workplace. In other words, workers are viewed as silent receptors of management information, incapable of responding, interpreting, arguing, or counteracting this subtle but persuasive form of con-trol. Thus, effective communication in the nineteenth century meant giving or-ders and emphasized the downward transmission of information. Managerial authority and the presumption that there was "one best way" of doing things (which, of course, only managers knew) effectively stifled any upward commu-nication. Despite its considerable drawbacks, we continue to see significant rem-nants of this sort of chart (and of this management philosophy!) in some organizations today.

The top-down flow of information in hierarchies also led to the emergence of domination narratives, which ascribed particular readings of how truth, power, and control were constituted in everyday conversation. These are dis-cussed next.

From Resistance to Domination

The rapid expansion of industrialization in nineteenth-century northern Eu-rope and North America created the need to organize and manage labor in ways that mirrored dominant social and political values. In the United States, slavery both supplied the laborers for agricultural work in the South and mirrored a view of hierarchy that was based on the racial divisions sanctioned by white slaveholders. One result of the deep divisions between ways of organizing labor and the social values that supported them was the Civil War (1861–65). The outcome of that war is an interesting, but often overlooked, part of the history

FIGURE 3.1

Organization Chart Illustrating the Principles of Classical Management Theory and Bureaucratic Organization

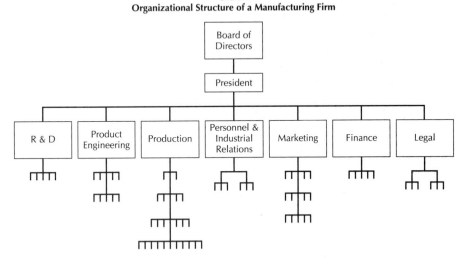

Chart A
Organizational Structure of a Manufacturing Firm

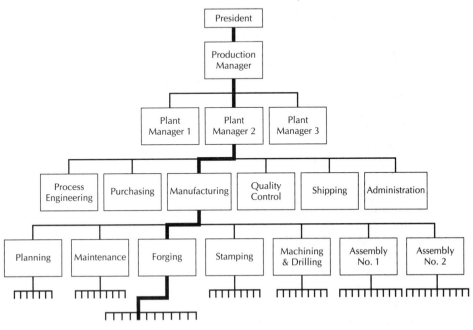

Chart B
Detailed Structure of the Production Department

Source: Gareth Morgan, *Images of Organization* (Newbury Park, Calif.: Sage, 1986). Reprinted by permission of Sage Publications, Inc.

of organizations and communication in this country. It can be viewed as a struggle between social values that coincided with the hierarchical division of organized labor and the different interpretations of how hierarchies should be determined. Whereas the South supported a racial hierarchy, the increasingly industrial North favored one governed by social class. This accounts for the observation on the part of some freed slaves that the hidden "slavery" of the northern factories was in many ways just as bad as the overt slavery practiced by plantation owners in the South.

Where differences exist in the type of work that people do, there will also be differences in how that work is done, evaluated, valued, and compensated. Those in power control the interpretation of such differences; the story they tell favors their interests. For white slaveholders in the South, slavery was justified on economic and moral grounds. They believed they had a right to a cheap source of labor to farm their lands and that their accumulation of wealth was at the heart of Calvinist moral advancement (Raban, 1991). From their perspective, then, slavery was necessary for the productive accomplishment of work that would grant them entry to a Protestant heaven. This partisan view of racial division and moral order gave slaveholders the power to control both the daily lives of slaves and the means of resolving conflict. Thus, any slave attempt to challenge white authority was viewed as a challenge to the moral order. As a result, communication between slaveholder and slave was one-sided, favoring the slaveholder's interests.

One feature of societal dialogue helps us understand organizational dialogue: resistance to domination. In addition to the domination narratives discussed earlier in the chapter, all societies have narratives of resistance. These are the narratives of the less powerful and the powerless, of those who ordinarily have little or no voice in organizational and societal dialogue. They provide different accounts of events and the meanings those events had for the participants (Freire, 1968). Unless the domination is eventually overturned, these stories only rarely make it into textbooks. Slave narratives are an example.

James Scott (1990) points out how the accounts of the powerless can function as "hidden transcripts" of the other side of the story. Narratives of resistance gave slaves a way to express their outrage among others in the same situation. Their stories reversed the order of things, placing slaveholders in inferior intellectual, moral, and performance positions. In this "world turned upside down" (Scott, 1990; Stallybrass & White, 1986), those without power could take control of the story and use it as a "performative space for the full-throated acting out of everything that must be choked back in public" (Conquergood, 1992, p. 91). By looking at the dominant narrative alongside the slave narrative, we get a sense of the potential dialogue that might have occurred between the two groups. Unfortunately, however, that dialogue remained mostly implicit because the dominant group's narrative was told in public and the slave's narrative in private.

In addition to slave narratives, other forms of resistance to domination came with the slave songs, ditties, and dirges that would later become known as "the blues." This, in turn, would lead to two other musical forms of resistance to domination: rock and roll and rap music (Goodall, 1991a). Similarly, there are accounts of resistance to domination from those who were once among the dominant and powerful. Perhaps the best known of these accounts is the gospel hymn "Amazing Grace," which combines the rhythms and sensibilities of a slave song with words penned by a former slave trader turned English minister, John Newton (1798):

> Amazing Grace, how sweet the sound,
> That saved a wretch like me.
> I once was lost, but now I'm found,
> Was blind, but now I see.

Newton's diaries also contain evidence of the values of hierarchy, empire, and scientific management in the operation of slave ships (Moyers, 1989). Dramatic testimony is found in Newton's drawings of how chained slaves were "scientifically organized" for the long voyage between Africa and the New World (Figure 3.2). Like cattle or dry goods, slaves were kept in tight, straight lines to minimize wasted space in the ship's hull. Meager food and water were dispensed according to a rigid schedule. Management took the form of absolute tyranny and utilized scientific principles of cost efficiency and production.

Although in later decades many economic and technical advances would attest to the benefits of rational approaches to organization, the scientific management that was applied to slave ships shows how it can be abused in cases of absolute power. In the twentieth century, the Holocaust provides yet another example of the abuse of classical principles of organization. Unfortunately, abuses of power based on hierarchically ordered systems of domination continue to persist in areas under severe political and military occupation as well as in illegal sweatshops employing immigrant laborers the world over. One study suggests that as recently as 1999 up to 27 million people were made to endure some form of forced servitude, including such activities as brickmaking, logging, sewing, and prostitution (Bales, 1999).

The Industrial Revolution

Although organizations and communication existed before the steamboat, railroad, and cotton gin, it was not until the Industrial Revolution that modern machinery and methods of production emerged, with the accompanying rise of the factory bureaucracy (Perrow, 1986).

The rise of the modern factory during the industrial period was an extension of a social (and racial) class structure that sought to stabilize power relations among people by controlling the means of production and consumption

FIGURE 3.2

Diagram Showing How Slaves Were Stowed on Ships

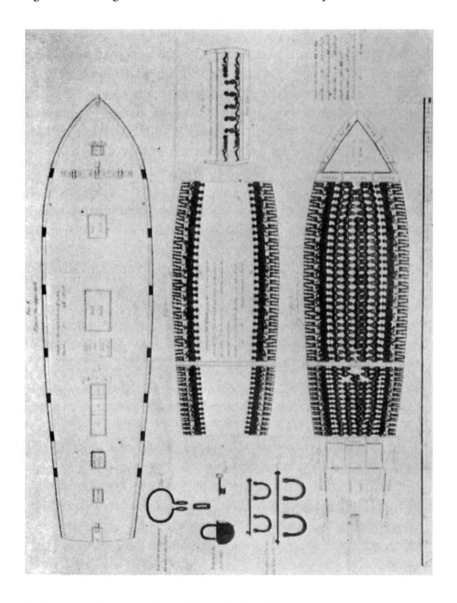

Source: Reproduced from *Slave Ships and Slaving* (1969), p. 159.

in society (Foucault, 1972, 1979). This period also marked an important shift. Before the Industrial Revolution, only rarely did anyone work for someone else in exchange for wages. In the mid-1980s, in contrast, only about 15 percent of our working population was able to get by without working for someone else (Perrow, 1986). (Interestingly, as we discuss in Chapter 8, this trend may now be reversing, as businesses downsize, restructure, or move operations overseas and more people are becoming self-employed providers of goods and services.)

The organization of work and communication in the early factories was highly influenced by the then-emerging concepts of division of labor and hierarchy. *Division of labor* refers to the separation of tasks into discrete units; *hierarchy* refers to the vertical arrangement of power and authority that distinguishes managers from employees. These concepts, which form the foundation of the modern organization, originated in an affluent, class-conscious view of social control in which the rise of the middle class was seen as a threat to the upper class. The rationale was that the work institution should mirror the organization of the ideal society. (This may help explain why prisons and factories were modeled on the same architectural principles and why the behavior of inmates and workers was monitored and controlled in similar ways.) Another clue about why organization and order were linked to hierarchy may be found in Kenneth Burke's work on purposive (i.e., rhetorical) language. Burke (1989, p. 69) states that people are symbol users moved to a sense of order. From his perspective, language is a hierarchical and symbolic construction of order that we use to attempt to "perfect" nature. In our construction of language-based realities, we create rules for organizing sentences (grammar) and arguments (logic) and for cooperating with audiences through symbols (rhetoric). It can be argued, then, that hierarchical forms of organization mirror the hierarchical nature of language.

The relationships among class consciousness, purposive language, and social control developed simultaneously with the rise of science. With science came much more than a highly ordered method of explaining phenomena: From explanation emerged the ability to predict, and from the ability to predict came the potential to control. Thus, the underlying theme of the classical management approach to organization is the *scientific rationalization of control*. Organizations are viewed as the primary vehicle through which our lives are rationalized — "planned, articulated, scientized, made more efficient and orderly, and managed by experts" (Scott, 1981, p. 5).

Scientific Management

The years 1880 to 1920 were characterized by both significant racial and class prejudice and unprecedented economic expansion in the United States. With massive industrialization came ruthless treatment of workers by owners who subscribed to a "survival of the fittest" mentality. Those employees who succeeded were deemed to be morally strong; those who failed were deemed to be unworthy of success (Bendix, 1956).

Born in this era was the middle-class engineer Frederick Taylor (1856–1915), a pioneer in the development of scientific management. His classic book, *The Principles of Scientific Management* (1913), is based on the assumption that management is a true science resting on clearly defined laws, rules, and principles. Taylor's time and motion studies led to improved organizational efficiency through the mechanization of labor and the authority of the clock. Work was divided into discrete units that were measured by how long it took a competent worker to accomplish them. This principle was then used to plan factory outcomes, to evaluate worker efficiency, and to train less skilled workers. The production system thus required divisions of labor, carefully developed chains of command, and communication limited to orders and instructions.

Taylor's goal was to transform the nature of both work and management. He hoped that cooperation between managers and employees would bring a new era of industrial peace: "Under scientific management, arbitrary power, arbitrary dictation, ceases; and every single subject, large and small, becomes the question for scientific investigation, for reduction to law" (Taylor, 1947, p. 211). However, things didn't work out that way. Instead of industrial peace, scientific management led to increased conflict because it reinforced hierarchical distinctions and further objectified the already downtrodden worker. Although Taylor claimed that he was developing his ideas to help the working person, by the end of his life he was cursed by labor unions as "the enemy of the working man" (Morgan, 1986). Even so, Taylor's work ushered in a new focus on the relationship between managers and employees as a key to organizational productivity.

Scientific management, then, is a management-oriented, production-centered view of organizations and communication. Its ideal, the efficient machine, holds that humans function as components or parts. It also assumes a fundamental distinction between managers and employees: Managers think, workers work (Morgan, 1986). The ideal of scientific management can be realized only in straightforward task situations that require no flexibility in responding to contingencies and that offer no opportunities for initiative. This description of an organization does not take into account human motivations for working, personal work relationships, and the flexibility required by the turbulent nature of organizational environments. Moreover, efforts to improve efficiency by raising production levels often alienate workers, as in Henry Ford's automobile plant, which experienced a turnover rate of 280 percent annually under scientific management (Morgan, 1986).

Fayol's Classical Management

At roughly the same time Taylor was working on scientific management in the United States, the French industrialist Henri Fayol (1949) was developing his influential theory of "administrative science," or classical management. Fayol was a highly successful director of a French mining company, and his management principles became popular in the United States and elsewhere in the late 1940s. He is perhaps best known for articulating the five elements of classical management: planning, organizing, commanding (goal setting), coordinating, and controlling (evaluating). He was even more specific in detailing how this work ought to be done.

Katherine Miller (1995) groups Fayol's principles into four categories: structure, power, reward, and attitude. Regarding structure, Fayol prescribed a strict hierarchy with a clear vertical chain of command; he called this the "scalar principle." He believed that each employee should have only one boss and should be accountable to only one plan. Like Taylor, Fayol advocated division of labor through departmentalization (the grouping of similar activities together). The resulting organizational structure is the classic hierarchical pyramid.

In terms of power, Fayol advocated the centralization of decision making and respect for authority. He held that authority accrues from a person's position and character and that discipline and obedience could only be expected if both were present. Moreover, he viewed discipline as a respect for agreed-upon rules, and not solely a respect for position.

Mirroring Taylor's view of rewards, Fayol advocated fair remuneration for well-directed efforts, foreshadowing the potential of profit sharing as a compensation system (Tompkins, 1984). Most concerned about the employee's perception of equity in pay and other issues, Fayol believed in the value of a stable workforce. He was thus a proponent of stable tenure for employees as a means of avoiding high turnover rates and recruitment costs.

Finally, regarding organizational attitude, Fayol held that employees should subordinate their personal interests to those of the organization. He also saw rational enforcement of agreements through fair supervision as the method for ensuring this organizational attitude. At the same time, Fayol encouraged employee initiative, or the capacity to see a plan through to completion, and believed that supervisors should work hard to foster positive employee morale.

Fayol intended to develop a set of guidelines for organizational administration that would be useful across a variety of situations. Some of his principles, most notably those related to unity of command and centralization, are especially relevant for students of communication (Tompkins, 1984). However, as Fayol cautioned, "There is nothing rigid or absolute in management affairs, it is all a question of proportion. Seldom do we have to apply the same principle twice in identical conditions; allowances must be made for different changing circumstances" (1949, p. 19).

Bureaucracy

A final piece of the classical approach fell into place with the development of the idea of bureaucracy. In the harsh working conditions of the early 1900s, job security did not exist, young children worked long hours for meager wages, and workers were hired and fired for reasons that had to do with their race, religion, sex, attitude, or relationship to the boss. This method of dealing with employees, called *particularism*, was expedient for owners and managers but had dire consequences for employees. Particularism also presented an ideological conflict in the United States: "On the one hand, democracy stressed liberty and equality for all. On the other hand, large masses of workers and nonsalaried personnel had to submit to apparently arbitrary authority, backed up by local and national police forces and legal powers, for ten to twelve hours a day, six days a week" (Perrow, 1986, p. 53).

It was this conflict between ideology and practice that gave rise to a system that protected employees better than particularism. That system we now call *bureaucracy*. According to W. Richard Scott (1981), organizational bureaucracy has the following characteristics:

1. A fixed division of labor among participants
2. A hierarchy of offices
3. A set of general rules that govern performances
4. A rigid separation of personal life from work life
5. The selection of personnel on the basis of technical qualifications and equal treatment of all employees
6. Participants' view of employment as a career; tenure protecting against unfair arbitrary dismissal

Although the well-known German scholar Max Weber (1864–1920) was not a blind advocate of bureaucracy (he feared that its sole focus on instrumental rationality would drive out mystery and enchantment from the world), he saw it as technically superior to all other forms of organization. Furthermore, he was a strong advocate for *universalism*, or equal treatment according to ability. Most people today associate bureaucracy with the red tape and inflexibility of public agencies. However, these may not be necessary results of a bureaucratic approach. In his famous defense of bureaucracy, Charles Perrow (1986) argues that the machine itself ought not be blamed, but rather the people who misuse it to further their own interests.

It is useful to examine bureaucracy in terms of both what came before it — particularism — and Weber's goal of universalism, which sought to introduce standards of fair treatment in the workplace. Even today, managers struggle to hold on to the powers to hire, fire, promote, and discipline employees at will. In addition, prebureaucratic decision making is viewed by managers as easier and more expedient than decision making in a bureaucracy. The latter makes decisions harder to implement, at the same time that it protects employees from abuse.

The ideal bureaucracy cannot be fully realized for several reasons: (1) It is not possible to rid organizations of all extraorganizational influences on member behavior; (2) bureaucracy does not deal well with nonroutine tasks; and (3) people vary in terms of rationality (Perrow, 1986). These inadequacies of bureaucracy became the basis for other theories. Alternative forms of organizing were proposed that loosened the rigid assumptions of classical management theory, thus paving the way for new insights into human organization.

Implications for Organizational Communication

Classical management approaches view communication as unproblematic. They posit that in organizations, communication is simply a tool for issuing orders, coordinating work efforts, and gaining employee compliance. Moreover, in a hierarchical world, the primary function of communication is the transfer of information through the proper channels. In the classical management approach, any attempt at achieving a balance between individual creativity and organizational constraint through dialogue will tilt in favor of constraint. This approach raises several ethical questions, some of which are addressed in *What Would You Do?* 3.1.

It is important to recognize, however, that many of the tenets of the classical approach to management are alive and well in organizations today. The military still maintains strict divisions of labor and a scalar, chain-of-command hierarchy, and Taylor's ideas about designing jobs scientifically, making work routine, and hiring people fit to accomplish a specific task can be found in contemporary corporate concerns with organizational efficiency. In applications ranging from software design to fast food sales to the creation of computerized accounting systems, the goal of reducing the number of steps involved to reliably produce a quality result is still paramount (Miller, 2003). Additionally, the classical management objective of fitting the right person to the right job is now called "individualizing the organization" (Lawler & Finegold, 2000), wherein physical criteria have been replaced by psychological profiles that focus on individual differences in abilities, needs, and career aspirations. In the next section we will explore the origins of many of these challenges to, and modifications of, the classical approach.

The Human Relations Approach

Noted communication theorist Kenneth Burke was once asked how he became interested in the study of human communication. Burke replied, "People weren't treating each other very well. I wanted to help find a way to make relationships better" (quoted in Goodall, 1984, p. 134). Burke's comment was made during the 1930s, a time of unparalleled economic depression when models of bureaucracy were questioned and theories of human relations emerged.

Historical and Cultural Background

Three major events — the Great Depression, World War II, and a new way of understanding human behavior — came at a time when the perceived limitations of scientific management were at their peak. The Great Depression

What Would You Do? 3.1

RANK HAS ITS PRIVILEGES: INFLUENCES OF THE BUREAUCRATIC ORGANIZATION ON HOME AND FAMILY LIFE

Among the world's largest bureaucracies is the U.S. military. Characterized by principles of scientific rationality, the military is organized according to hierarchies or ranks and relies on standardized procedures for behavioral control. It seeks to operate as an efficient machine.

Often neglected in studies of bureaucracy is its influence on employees' home and family life. How do those who work for bureaucracies make the daily transition from a highly controlled work life to a more loosely organized home life? Does the bureaucracy have an effect on home and family management?

In the following excerpt from Mary Truscott's *Brats: Children of the American Military Speak Out* (1989), the narrator explains how growing up in the military deeply affected her childhood and family life.

> I learned to snap off a salute before I learned to ride a bike. There were plenty of role models for me to imitate; people who were always saluting my father. It didn't seem unusual. Some men saluted, and others were saluted.
>
> The military jargon that was so pervasive on the post and in our household included many rank-related qualifiers. The size and location of our houses were based on rank. We lived on "Colonel's Row" in stately three-story duplexes with full maid's quarters in the basement, but we had done our time in apartments before my father made colonel. . . . My mother came home from the Officers' Wives Club functions and frequently told my father about the "little captain's wife" or "little major's wife" she had met. Too young to remember when my father had been a lowly major, I developed a mental image of a community of Lilliputian people, captains and majors and their families, inhabiting the smaller and, I knew, inferior housing on the other side of the post.
>
> The ascending rank was always part of a family name. I answered the telephone with "Colonel Truscott's quarters, Mary speaking." I addressed all adults with their surname and current rank. I never knew many men who were "mister," with the exception of school principals.
>
> We lived on the post for the most part, only minutes away from my father's office, but I had no idea of what my father did at work. . . . In his study at home he had a framed poster from a lecture he had given that had his picture on it and the caption "the nation's foremost expert on radioactive fallout." Whatever it was that my dad did at work, I felt certain that if we were bombed and fallout came raining out of the sky, my father would lead us to the designated fallout shelters on the post and we would survive, no matter how awful the blast, because he was "The Nation's Foremost Expert."

We visited my father's office a few times, and it was remarkably devoid of any sign or indication of his work. The walls in his office were pale green, with perhaps a flag and a strictly functional map or two to break the monotony. . . .

Rank truly had its privileges. The written and unwritten rules that established the chain of command for the men in uniform also applied to their families. Rank created a virtual caste system, and life on a military post had no uncertainties. There were stripes and insignia on uniforms, stickers on cars, and name-plates on houses. Families were segregated, by rank, in separate and not necessarily equal enclaves, and there were separate club facilities for officers and enlisted men. Post housing was the most obvious indicator of rank. . . .

Regardless of who the father was and what he did, rank was either a source of pride and status or an embarrassing label that put the military brat on the wrong side of the tracks. And all military brats, no matter where their father had fit in the hierarchy of rank, emphasized, over and over, that rank was pervasive and clearly defined.

Ethical questions can be thought of as sources of creativity or constraint. On the basis of the preceding narrative, how would you respond to the following questions?

1. What ethical issues surround the notion that rank has its privileges? Is it ever appropriate for those privileges to extend beyond the duties and responsibilities of work? Why or why not?
2. How does hierarchical thinking influence the narrator's view of the world? How does this type of thinking contribute to your own understanding of social divisions in class, race, age, and gender?
3. Is the integration of home and work as described by the narrator necessary to the survival of all bureaucracies or only the military? Explain.

(1929–40) created economic and social hardships for millions of people and led to major changes in government policies regarding Social Security, public assistance, and the funding of public improvement projects. The Depression also contributed to major migrations of workers — from the drought-ridden central farming states to the West Coast, and from the impoverished rural South to northern cities — as people went in search of jobs to support themselves and their families. A surplus of available workers and a lack of employment opportunities meant keen competition for jobs and widespread abuse of workers by employers. It is not surprising, then, that this period was also marked by the expansion of powerful labor unions. These organizations advocated human rights, fair wages, and improved working conditions for the labor force.

Although divisions between managers and workers had existed since the Industrial Revolution, they became more intense during the Depression. Demands for improved working conditions were accommodated only when the improvements increased productivity and profits. Wages were determined by factory output, but increased output tended to increase the number of incidences of work-related injury, illness, or death. In addition, the typical twelve-hour workday, six days a week, with one half-hour break for a meal contributed to the strained relationship between workers and managers.

With World War II, however, came an enormous expansion of new jobs in both the military and the private sector. The war also placed academic researchers, managers, and military personnel in direct communication with one another. W. Charles Redding (1985), a pioneer of organizational communication and one of its leading historians, refers to this threesome as the "Triple Alliance." He argues that through the alliance, managers and military officers benefited from new ideas about organizing work and developing trust among workers, while academic researchers benefited from their access to industrial plants and their involvement in training workers, military personnel, and managers. The effects of this war-formed alliance would have a lasting impact, particularly on the subdiscipline that was created out of that alliance: organizational communication (Redding, 1985).

Finally, the period was marked by a new approach to understanding human relationships and behavior, which Herbert Blumer (1905–89) would later call "symbolic interactionism." Symbolic interactionism draws on the pragmatism of social philosophers Charles Pierce, William James, and John Dewey; the writings of George Herbert Mead; and the Freudian interpretation of the symbolic realms of experience. According to Blumer (1969), symbolic interactionism is a simple but revolutionary alternative to behaviorism: *Humans respond to the meanings they have for things* (Figure 3.3). A meaning-centered, rather than behavior-centered, approach to understanding human action was thus born.

FIGURE 3.3

Behaviorism versus Symbolic Interactionism

BEHAVIORISM

Stimulus ⟶ Response

SYMBOLIC INTERACTIONISM

Stimulus ⟶ INTERPRETATION ⟶ Response

What Is Human Relations?

Although Frederick Taylor had hoped to emphasize the importance of cooperative relationships between managers and employees, his methods did little to contribute to the quality of those interactions in the early twentieth century. It was not until the 1920s–1930s that Mary Parker Follett, Elton Mayo, and Chester Barnard would examine the employee-manager relationship in an entirely new way. Their work would provide the foundation for the human relations approach and would become a precursor of contemporary thinking about management and leadership. Their perspective marked a clean break from earlier points of view. They believed that "people are tractable, docile, gullible, uncritical — and want to be led. But far more than this is deeply true of them. They want to feel united, tied, bound to something, some cause, bigger than they, commanding them yet worthy of them, summoning them to significance in living" (Bendix, 1956, p. 296).

Mary Parker Follett (1868–1933), whom Peter Drucker calls "the brightest star in the management firmament of her time" (1997, p. 24), was a Boston social worker who used her experience running vocational guidance centers to develop new ideas about leadership, communication, social processes, and community, which she expressed in a controversial series of articles, books, and lectures on management that were far ahead of their time. In contrast to the dominant scientific management preoccupation with efficiency and strict divisions of labor and decision making, Follett was a democratic pragmatist who believed that only cooperation among people working together in groups under visionary leadership produced excellence in the workplace, in the neighborhood, and in the community (Dixon, 1996; McLarney & Rhyno, 1999). She advocated what we would consider today a feminist view of management that focused on empowering workers by sharing information with them, emphasizing cooperation to solve problems, and by organizing teams to accomplish tasks. She believed that "genuine power can only be grown . . . for genuine power is not coercive control but coactive control" (cited in Hurst, 1992, p. 57), and that workers at all levels in any organization were sources of creativity whose loyalty "is awakened . . . by the very process that creates the group" (cited in Hurst, 1992, p. 58). The democratic ideal, she believed, was achieved by integrating organizations, neighborhoods, and communities through teamwork and by encouraging individuals to live their lives fully. These ideas, considered radical in their time, marked the start of a new way of thinking about leadership, groups, communication, and relationships between managers and workers that still holds sway today (Graham, 1997).

Elton Mayo, a Harvard professor, also set out to critique and extend scientific management. Like Follett, Mayo did not share Taylor's view of organizations as comprising wage-maximizing individuals. Instead, Mayo stressed the limits of individual rationality and the importance of interpersonal relations. In contrast to scientific management, Mayo (1945) held that

1. Society comprises groups, not isolated individuals.
2. Individuals are swayed by group norms and do not act alone in accord with self-interests.
3. Individual decisions are not entirely rational; they are also influenced by emotions.

Chester Barnard, a chief executive at Bell Telephone in New Jersey, the author of the influential book *The Functions of the Executive* (1938), and a man very much influenced by Mary Parker Follett, asserted the importance of cooperation in organizations: "Organizations by their very nature are cooperative systems and cannot fail to be so" (Perrow, 1986, p. 63). The key to cooperation, he argued, lay in persuading individuals to accept a common purpose, from which all else would follow. Unlike Taylor's emphasis on economic inducements, for Barnard the role of management was largely communicative and persuasive. Effective managers thus strived to communicate in ways that encouraged workers to identify with the organization. Barnard also valued the contributions of informal contacts to overall organizational effectiveness. For the first time, then, the purpose of management was seen as more interpersonal than economic.

The Hawthorne Studies

While Barnard was running New Jersey Bell, a landmark event was taking place at another subsidiary of AT&T: the Hawthorne plant of Western Electric in Cicero, Illinois. Mayo and F. J. Roethlisberger (also a Harvard professor) were called into the Hawthorne plant by W. J. Dickson, a manager and industrial engineer concerned about widespread employee dissatisfaction, high turnover rates, and reduced plant efficiency. Previous efforts to correct these problems by using principles of scientific management had failed. Perrow (1986) picks up the story:

> The researchers at Western Electric took two groups of workers doing the same kinds of jobs, put them in separate rooms, and kept careful records of their productivity. One group (the test group) had the intensity of its lighting increased. Its productivity went up. For the other group (the control group), there was no change in lighting. But, to the amazement of the researchers, its productivity went up also. Even more puzzling, when the degree of illumination in the test group was gradually lowered back to the original level, it was found that output still continued to go up. Output also continued to increase in the control group. The researchers continued to drop the illumination of the test group, but it was not until the workers were working under conditions of bright moonlight that productivity stopped rising and fell off sharply. (pp. 79–80)

Over time, Mayo and his colleagues realized that the productivity improvements they had measured had little to do with the degree of illumination or other physical conditions in the plant. Instead, they found that the increased attention given to the workers by management and researchers was the key to increased productivity. This finding — that increased attention raises productivity — has come to be known as the Hawthorne effect.

Further research supported Mayo's critique of scientific management. A prominent finding of the Hawthorne studies was drawn from an experiment in the bank-wiring observation room, where it was found that even under poor working conditions, supportive informal group norms could have a positive effect on productivity. For the first time, then, it was shown that individual workers were complex beings, sensitive to group norms and possessing multiple motives, values, and emotions. Studies after Hawthorne have been greatly influenced both by its sociopsychological model of human motivation (it's not always about money) and its description of the informal organization.

Reflections on Human Relations

It is difficult to criticize the primary goal of the human relations approach — to restore whole human beings and quality interpersonal relationships to their rightful place in what had become an overly rational view of organizations. In this spirit, the work of Chris Argyris has been influential. According to Argyris (1957), the principles of formal organization, such as hierarchy and task specialization, are incongruent with the developmental needs of healthy adults. But do real alternatives exist? Critics have labeled Argyris and others who share his views "romantics," arguing that alienation is an inherent part of organizational life (Drucker, 1974; Tompkins, 1984).

Indeed, there is little empirical evidence to support the effectiveness of the human relations approach, particularly the claim that positive employee morale fosters productivity (Miller & Form, 1951). Nevertheless, the approach, reflecting the romantic ideals of the time, has played an important role in further research on organizational behavior. (Table 3.1 summarizes the move from classical management to human relations in the study of organizations and communication.) Generally, however, research that applies human relations thinking to the relationship between management and organizational effectiveness has been inconclusive and disappointing. Its underlying ideology has been interpreted as an unacceptable willingness to trade profitability for employee well-being. William Whyte (1969), in his classic critique, criticizes the human relations approach for attempting to replace the Protestant work ethic and entrepreneurialism with a social ethic of complacency that emphasizes dressing well, acting nice, and "fitting in." Another critic has referred to human relations as "cow sociology": "Just as contented cows [are] alleged to produce more milk, satisfied workers [are] expected to produce more output" (Scott, 1981, p. 90).

A similar critique of a simplistic connection between good feeling and organizational effectiveness has been offered by communication scholars (Eisenberg & Witten, 1987). Although we would all like to believe that openness,

TABLE 3.1

Summary of Historical and Cultural Influences on the Classical Management and Human Relations Approaches to Organizations and Communication

CLASSICAL MANAGEMENT	HUMAN RELATIONS
Theme: Scientific rationality leads to improved efficiency and productivity	*Theme:* Improved human relations leads to improved efficiency and productivity
Enlightenment ideals	Romantic ideals
Industrial Revolution	Development of psychology
Scientific methods	Social scientific methods
Dominant metaphor: Organization as an efficient machine	*Dominant metaphor:* Organization as the sum of relationships
Supporting principles: *Ideal form of society* is authoritarian and values hierarchical organization	*Supporting principles:* *Ideal form of society* is democratic and values open and honest relationships
Divisions of labor/social classes/races/ sexes/nations; if "the rules" were applied equally to everyone, individuals who worked hard and obeyed instructions could better themselves	*Divisions* of labor/management honored; negotiation of differences through open communication valued
Conflict based on divisions; dialectical relationships between management and labor based on power and money	*Conflict* based on lack of shared understanding; dialogic model of relationships between management and labor based on trust, openness, honesty, and power
Application of the principles of mechanics to organizations and communication led to operationalizing the machine metaphor (e.g., "This business runs like clockwork.")	*Application* of humanistic and behavioral psychology to organizations and communication led to operationalizing "relational metaphors" (e.g., "This business is like family.")
Communication — top-down and procedurally oriented; following "the rules" is valued, and opposing them calls into question the whole moral order	*Communication* — relational and needs-oriented; self-actualization is valued if it occurs through work

TABLE 3.1

Summary of Historical and Cultural Influences on the
Classical Management and Human Relations Approaches
to Organizations and Communication *(continued)*

CLASSICAL MANAGEMENT	HUMAN RELATIONS
Dominant form of organizing: Bureaucracy	*Dominant form of organizing:* Teams or groups within bureaucracies
Stability best obtained through adherence to procedural forms of order	Stability best obtained through relational and personal happiness
Limitations: Too constraining; encourages mindless adherence to details and procedures and discourages creativity	*Limitations:* False openness, abuse of trust and/or honesty; equation of employee happiness with efficiency or productivity

self-disclosure, and supportive relationships have positive effects on organizational productivity, research does not support that contention. Instead, models of employee motivation have become increasingly complex, refining what is meant by good leadership and the conditions under which a focus on interpersonal relations may be desirable. However, the applicability of these contingency models is limited to specific situations, resulting in a body of research with no clear implications for practice.

Beyond Human Relations

The foundational work in human relations led to three very different lines of research that merit our consideration. The first sought to investigate the effects of leadership style on worker productivity. The second line of research, typically associated with Herbert Simon and built on Mayo's critique of Taylor's wage-maximizing model of individuals, sought to identify the limitations of decision making in organizations. Finally, the institutional school extends Barnard's ideas about executives by focusing on the communication between senior managers and the organizational environment.

Leadership Style

From World War II through the 1960s, a fundamental shift in thinking about worker motivation and performance led to numerous studies of the relationship between leadership style and worker productivity. No longer ascribed to the unmotivated worker, poor performance was now seen as a result of poor management. Thus, increasing worker productivity became the job of management, and the search for ways to lead, manage, and supervise people began. No other problem in the history of organizations would prove as challenging.

A ten-year study of leadership characteristics at Ohio State University began in 1945. It attempted to identify leadership traits associated with work group productivity. The research team isolated two factors — *initiating structure* and *consideration* — to describe leaders. A person "high" in initiating structure was active in planning, communicating, scheduling, and organizing, while a person high in consideration showed concern for the feelings of subordinates, promoted mutual trust, and fostered two-way communication. A leader could score high on one or both factors (Perrow, 1986). The study's major finding was that the traditional management skills associated with initiating structure were as important as the interpersonal skills in promoting worker productivity.

In a similar research effort conducted at the University of Michigan at about the same time, leaders were classified along a continuum ranging from employee-oriented to production-oriented, but the study provided no definitive conclusions about effective management skills. Later research offered more complex models of managerial behaviors that could be applied to certain situations. Frederick Herzberg's (1966) two-factor theory of job satisfaction, for instance, assumes that people have two independent sets of needs — to avoid pain and to grow psychologically — and that management strategies need to be tailored to address each set of needs. According to Herzberg, reducing "pain" does not increase job satisfaction but does decrease dissatisfaction (making one more neutral). Conversely, promoting psychological growth increases satisfaction but may have no effect on dissatisfaction. For example, improving working conditions and increasing salaries (what Herzberg calls "hygiene factors") would be expected to reduce dissatisfaction, but they would not necessarily promote satisfaction. On the other hand, changing the design of the work to make it more rewarding would most likely increase satisfaction. To motivate worker performance, according to Herzberg, managers need to maintain a clear distinction between the two sets of needs because changes in hygiene factors are not likely to affect productivity or morale.

Similarly, Fred Fiedler's (1967) contingency theory of leadership maintains that different leadership styles are appropriate for different situations. For example, when a group is either extremely favorable or unfavorable toward a leader, a task-oriented style of management is considered most effective, whereas in less extreme cases an interpersonal style may be effectively applied. Contingency theories of management continue to enjoy popularity today.

Simon's Decision-Making Model

In Herbert Simon's (1957) decision-making model of individuals in organizations, people attempt to make rational decisions, but their ability to do so is hindered by both the situation and their limited processing ability. Specifically, people lack knowledge not only of the consequences of their actions, but also of the alternative courses of action and of the criteria on which to judge the choices available. Rather than attempting to maximize all factors in decision making, the best we can do, according to Simon, is to "satisfice." "Satisficing" means that people tend to "settle for acceptable as opposed to optimal solutions, to attend to problems sequentially rather than simultaneously, and to utilize existing repertoires of action programs rather than develop novel responses for each situation" (Scott, 1981, p. 75). Communication is thus critical in Simon's model; it establishes the definition or interpretation of the situation, which, in turn, guides individual decision making:

> This definition of the situation . . . is built out of past experience (it includes prejudices and stereotypes) and highly particularized, selective views of present stimuli. Most of the individual's responses are "routine"; they invoke solutions . . . used before. Sometimes [individuals] must engage in problem-solving. When they do, they conduct a limited search for alternatives along familiar and well-worn paths, selecting the first satisfactory one that comes along. They do not consider all possible alternatives, nor do they keep searching for the optimum one. Rather, they "satisfice" or select the first satisfactory solution. Their very standards for satisfactory solutions are a part of the definition of the situation. . . . The organization can control these standards . . . only to a limited extent are they up to individuals. (Perrow, 1986, p. 122)

Simon's decision-making model is further refined in his collaborative work with James March, *Organizations* (March & Simon, 1958). The writers detail the ways in which organizations control individuals by influencing their definition of the situation or by actively shaping their assumptions and decision premises. The more isolated an individual is in an organization, the more the leader's communication resembles monologue and the more constrained the individual member's decision premises become. In contrast, the more sources of information in an organization, the greater the likelihood of divergent opinions, interpretations, definitions of the situation, and dialogue.

According to March and Simon (1958), then, organizations can exert unobtrusive (or hidden) control over members by limiting alternatives and shaping decision premises. From one perspective, such controls as division of labor, job titles, a formal hierarchy, and key rules and regulations are necessary to the ideal of cooperation popularized by Chester Barnard at Bell Telephone. From another perspective, however, such controls represent the triumph of owners and managers over workers, whose freedoms are increasingly restricted by limited definitions of the situation. We will discuss this latter point of view in the context of critical theory in Chapter 6.

Institutional Theory

Like Simon's decision-making model, Philip Selznick's (1948, 1957) institutional view of organizations is counterrational, meaning that people do not always behave in ways that make the most sense. Unlike Simon's focus on the individual, the institutional approach is more interested in the total organization, which is viewed as having a life of its own. Specifically, the institutional perspective is based on the following major assumptions:

1. The differences among organizations are important: A case study method is used to expose the ways organizations differ from one another and to identify their unique characteristics (foreshadowing the organizational culture approach discussed in Chapter 5).
2. Organizations are not the sum of individual actions; rather, they take on lives of their own that no single individual can control: This assumption reinforces the idea from Chapter 2 that meanings are coconstructed in dialogue (and foreshadows key aspects of systems theory discussed in Chapter 4).
3. The relationship between an organization and its environment is a key to its survival: Earlier theories focused almost exclusively on the inner workings of an organization, primarily because environments were relatively stable. As environmental turbulence has increased, its impact on organizations has become more important.

However, the institutional approach does not apply to all organizations. Only some organizations become institutions in the sense that society prizes them more for the values they embody than for a particular service or level of performance. Examples include libraries, universities, and medical centers. People identify with institutions, associating them with what it means to live well in a good society. Institutions thus become invested with community values, and the managers of institutions must be skilled in communicating with the public (Perrow, 1986). In theory, the institution's survival depends on the public's image of it, not on performance, productivity, or effectiveness.

John Meyer and Brian Rowan (1977) describe how the institutionalization process works in hospitals and schools. To protect their legitimacy, the leaders of these organizations must communicate effectively with the community while also shielding data about technical performance from outside scrutiny. Thus a college or university has numerous and complex requirements for awarding a degree or for majoring in a particular field of study. However, similar quantification is rarely, if ever, applied to the supposed technical output of the university: student learning. Professors are not routinely evaluated on the basis of how much their students have learned in their courses. And until just recently, hospitals were not scrutinized in terms of the quality of their patient care.

Today, however, the legitimacy of institutions is being questioned. Schools and hospitals are being pressured to account for the effectiveness of their technical work. The results will likely be dramatic. In a study of the California state mental health system, J. Rounds (1984) notes that after the traditional decision premises of the institution were questioned (in this case, rules about who could be categorized as mentally ill), pandemonium ensued as different groups with various degrees of technical expertise scrambled to participate in an increasingly frustrating dialogue. The collapse of an institution's legitimacy both opens the possibility for positive change and complicates further action by the institution.

The institutional model emphasizes the relationship between the organizational environment and communication and redefines the role of at least some senior managers to that of political statesperson. It also provides further evidence for the importance of communication, not only in the area of information transfer, but also in defining situations and creating organizational reality. Finally, it illustrates that limiting communication about certain issues (e.g., technical performance) can help preserve legitimacy and support the status quo.

The Human Resources Approach

In retrospect, the human relations approach identified many important issues (e.g., that informal communication is important and that human decision making is emotional as well as rational), but it fell short of truly valuing employee perceptions, worldview, and voice. Whereas human relations encouraged employee communication mainly to "blow off steam," it took another set of thinkers — collectively characterized as the human resources approach — to fully assert the crucial role all employees can play in promoting organizational effectiveness. While incorporating most of the assumptions of human relations, the human resources approach is concerned with the total organizational climate as well as with how an organization can encourage employee participation and dialogue. Three theorists best capture the spirit of the original human resources movement: Abraham Maslow, Douglas McGregor, and Rensis Likert.

Maslow's Hierarchy of Needs

According to Abraham Maslow's hierarchy of needs, people's basic needs for food, shelter, and belonging must be satisfied before they can move toward achieving their full human potential, or what Maslow calls "self-actualization" (Figure 3.4).

FIGURE 3.4

Maslow's Hierarchy of Needs

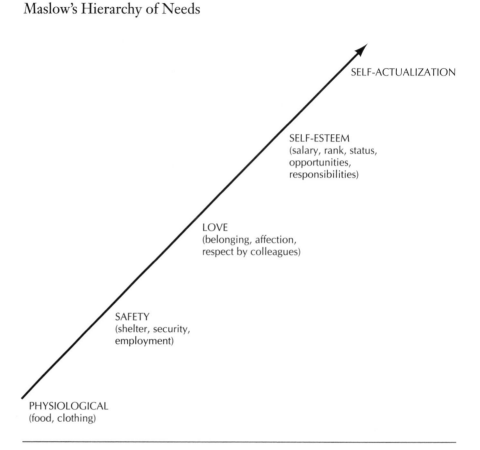

In *Eupsychian Management* (1965), Maslow poses the question, "What kinds of management and what kinds of reward or pay will help human nature to grow healthily into its fuller and fullest stature?" He concludes that the conditions that foster individual health are often surprisingly good for the prosperity of the organization as well. He thus defines the problem of management as that of setting up social conditions in the organization so that the goals of the individual merge with those of the organization. In many ways, Maslow's work paved the way for more recent theories of performance, including Mihalyi Csikszentmihalyi's (1990) theory of flow.

McGregor's Theory Y Management

Sharing Maslow's view that classical management theory fails to address important individual needs, Douglas McGregor (1960) argued that classical approaches are based in part on an assumption that the average employee dislikes work and avoids responsibility in the absence of external control. He calls the control-oriented, bureaucratic style of management "Theory X," which he summarizes as follows:

1. The average human being has an inherent dislike of work and will avoid it if he [or she] can.
2. Because of [their] . . . dislike of work, most people must be coerced, controlled, directed, [or] threatened with punishment to get them to put forth adequate effort toward the achievement of organizational objectives.
3. The average human being prefers to be directed, wishes to avoid responsibility, has relatively little ambition, and wants security above all. (pp. 33–34)

Although Theory X may seem quite limited, it helps identify some of the implicit and explicit assumptions of the traditional organization.

McGregor (1960) advances an alternative set of assumptions or principles in his Theory Y:

1. The expenditure of physical and mental effort in work is as natural as play or rest.
2. External control and threat of punishment are not the only means for bringing about effort toward organizational objectives. [People] will exercise self-direction and self-control in the service of objectives to which [they are] committed.
3. Commitment to objectives is a function of the rewards associated with their achievement (including the reward of self-actualization).
4. The average human being learns, under proper conditions, not only to accept but [also] to seek responsibility.
5. The capacity to exercise . . . relatively high degree[s] of imagination, ingenuity, and creativity in the solution of organizational problems is widely, not narrowly, distributed in the population.
6. Under the conditions of modern industrial life, the intellectual potential . . . of the average [person is] only partially utilized. (pp. 47–48)

In Theory Y, McGregor builds on the best of the human relations approach to offer fundamentally different views of employees and of their relationship with management. Employees are viewed as possessing a high capacity for autonomy, responsibility, and innovation. Unlike the Theory X manager, the Theory Y manager has a more participative and facilitative management style that treats employees as valued human resources. Optimistic about incorporating the individual's desires in an organizational framework, McGregor argues that "the essential task of management is to arrange things so people achieve their own goals by accomplishing those of the organization" (Perrow, 1986, p. 99). In contrast to the scalar principle of classical management, in which decision-making ability is centralized within management, McGregor offers the principle of integration, wherein employees are self-directed as a result of their commitment to organizational goals.

Likert's Principle of Supportive Relationships

Continuing the trend toward employee participation in decision making, the work of University of Michigan professor Rensis Likert has contributed to our understanding of high-involvement organizations. Likert's (1961) principle of supportive relationships holds that all interactions within an organization should support individual self-worth and importance, with emphasis on the supportive relationships within work groups and open communication among them.

Likert divides organizations into four types, or "systems," based upon degree of participation: System I — exploitative/authoritative, System II — benevolent/authoritative, System III — consultative, and System IV — participative. The principle of supportive relationships considers open communication to be among the most important aspects of management. It also favors general oversight to close supervision and emphasizes the role of the supportive peer group in fostering productivity. Therefore, Likert's principle supports System IV, participative management.

Research on Likert's systems has been inconclusive (Perrow, 1986). Many studies have shown that good classical changes in organizations (e.g., improved work procedures and plans) are as important as participation in increasing organizational effectiveness. The human resources approach continues the human relations tendency to treat all organizations as similar, which opponents in the institutional school and the cultural approach (see Chapter 5) view as inappropriate. Moreover, while human resources emphasizes employee participation in organizational decision making, it does not explain the pragmatics or politics involved in establishing such a voice for employees. (See *What Would You Do?* 3.2 for an example of these complexities.) As a result, its prescriptions for participation tend to have limited practical use. Nevertheless, the quest for effective forms of participative decision making continues (Miller & Monge, 1986).

SUMMARY

This chapter discusses the communication theories associated with three general approaches: classical management, human relations, and human resources.

What Would You Do? 3.2

THE POLITICS OF MIDDLE MANAGEMENT

A key assumption of the human resources approach is that happy employees are also productive employees. However, in the act of defining happiness, there is the potential for tyranny. Consider the following perspectives on happiness (Shorris, 1984, pp. 17–34):

1. The most insidious power is the power to define happiness. Happiness cannot be described, and what cannot be described cannot be attained. So it is that we create imagined happiness as the opposite of what we can describe — dissatisfaction.

2. All leaders must have the ability to define happiness. In the absence of absolute happiness, we content ourselves with relative happiness.

3. There are three ways in which capitalism and the bureaucratic society conspire to use happiness as a source of fear and reward:

   a. The merchant offers happiness in the immediate future. Commodity purchases offer material rewards; failure to consume commodities suggests material poverty and, therefore, a lack of relative happiness.

   b. The manager offers happiness in the future. According to human relations theory, his or her power is largely symbolic (kind words, generous deeds, a pat on the back). Because being in management is a source of symbolic attainment in our society, the manager represents what the rest of us aspire to. As such, the manager is the enforcer of our moral code.

   c. The despot offers happiness in the historical future. By making prophetic claims about the historical future, he or she is like a secular god and only lacks immortality to be a god. The despot combines displays of material and symbolic happiness and suggests that others may attain them only if they do as they are commanded.

4. When work becomes rationalized and bureaucratized, the resulting order symbolizes levels of happiness. The manager has the power to define happiness as the next step up the career ladder. The manager's definition of happiness creates the moral system in which white-collar workers and some managers live, but the despot's definition, with its ultimate promises and religious demands, has a greater effect on the middle manager's life. In return for happiness, middle managers agree to the abolition of their

(continued)

freedom, thereby becoming a part of the organization and accepting the notion that any sin against the organization may cast them out of heaven and into the limbo of the unemployed.

Given these thoughts, consider how you would handle the following situations:

1. Your supervisor explains that you will be promoted if you can find ways to cut costs by one-third in your department. You know this will mean cuts in personnel, even though your boss never says so directly. However, you are already working with a limited staff, and stress is high among employees as a result of the heavy workload. In addition, you fear that any further reduction in staff may affect employee morale and perhaps lower productivity in your department. At the same time, you are heavily in debt and in need of the promotion to make ends meet. How will you handle the situation? Should you gain some happiness at the expense of others? Is the short-term gain of a promotion worth the long-term risks of negative morale and reduced productivity?

2. You are a midlevel manager privy to information about your company's intent to restructure and downsize its operations. You know this will put you in intense competition with other midlevel managers to keep your job. The vice president of personnel, whom you have long considered an ally, has asked you to keep this information to yourself. She has also asked you to prepare a speech on "Working Your Way Up the Ladder" to be delivered to members of the supervisory training group, most of whom will lose their jobs in the downsizing of the company. You are faced with an ethical dilemma. How will you handle the situation? What will you say in the speech? Will you use the opportunity to help protect your own job or to address broader issues?

It is important to remember that all historical narratives and all human communication exhibit the three *P*'s: They are partial, partisan, and problematic.

The classical management approach emerged during the Industrial Revolution, a period characterized by a quest to adapt the lessons of science and technology to make perfect machines. These early organizations were built on the model of the efficient machine, and management was characterized by a machinelike dependence on hierarchy, divisions of labor, strict rules for communication between management and workers, and formal routines. The term *bureaucracy* is often used to describe the structure of these early organizations. In some industries, similar attempts to rationalize organizations continue today.

In the image of the ideal machine, communication happens before the machine is turned on, such as when a manager explains how to operate the machine to the workers responsible for the labor. Communication that occurs *during* work tends to slow down production; therefore, informal talk is considered unnecessary and costly. Morgan (1986) suggests that the machine metaphor is useful for organizing work that is straightforward and repetitive in nature and performed in a stable environment by compliant workers. He attributes the limitations of this approach to its narrow focus on efficiency: It does not adapt well to changing circumstances, and it can have a dehumanizing effect on employees. When opportunities for dialogue do not exist, employees' resentment may be expressed as resistance, leading to work slowdowns or sabotage.

In the classical management approach, any attempt at achieving a balance between individual creativity and organizational constraint through dialogue will tilt in favor of constraint. The individual needs of workers are largely ignored, communication is limited to the giving of orders, and the strict imposition of rules and routines seeks to maintain order above all else. When such strict adherence to hierarchical power remains in place for too long, underground opposition or resistance is likely to emerge. During the latter stages of the Industrial Revolution, for example, slavery was abolished and labor unions became more prevalent.

The human relations approach to organizations and communication emerged against the cultural and economic background of the Great Depression. Studies demonstrating a positive correlation between managers who paid attention to workers and improved productivity led to new theories about the role of communication at work. The balance in the organizational dialogue thus tipped back toward a concern for individual creativity and the satisfaction of needs. However, critics argued that the balance had tipped back too far and that making workers happy did not necessarily make them more productive. They saw the new social ethic as a threat to the Protestant work ethic with its emphasis on achievement and entrepreneurship.

Refinements in human relations theory led to the human resources approach. Through this approach, advances were made in our understanding of the relationship between individual needs for creativity and organizational structures. In the period following World War II, studies of leadership style, decision making, and organizations as institutions served to redefine the individual in organizations as socially situated and rational only within limits.

This highly contingent and dynamic view of the individual suggests a new role for communication: the construction of definitions of the situation, of decision premises, that shape individual behavior. It also suggests a new view of employee motivation and performance: The employee's motivation is derived from his or her interests, which constitute the individual's definition of the situation. Hence, situations are symbolic constructions of reality that are individualized according to personal needs, desires, and interests. This suggests that many employees are motivated as much by symbolic rewards (e.g., identification with the organization, quality of information, praise, satisfying relationships with co-workers) as they are by their paychecks.

The human resources movement is a precursor of many of today's most common management practices. Most firms have given the personnel department a new name — the human resources department — and an increasing number of companies emphasize respect in their relationships with employees. As a result, employees are given more freedom to construct organizational reality through opportunities for dialogue. Their increased involvement, however, has also meant greater responsibility and accountability for their actions and decisions. Of all the approaches to management that we have observed in action, participative management is the most difficult to understand and to implement. However, when applied successfully, it most certainly fosters more satisfied, committed employees and more productive organizations.

Two extremes of thought on organization and management — tightly controlled formal bureaucracies versus a looser, more empathic view of employees as valuable human resources — are at the opposite ends of our theoretical continuum for understanding organizational communication. At the far right is bureaucracy, which holds that formal structure and communication that respect the chain of command ensure productivity and stability. At the far left is the human resources approach, which holds that open communication between managers and employees ensures creativity, adaptability to change, and satisfaction of the individual's needs and motivations. In this chapter, we have seen the problems associated with an organizational dialogue that is tipped too far in favor of either approach. In the following chapters, we will examine new theories that propose solutions to these problems.

QUESTIONS FOR REVIEW AND DISCUSSION

1. Why do we need theory to study organizational communication? What do we mean by the idea that all theories are metaphors?

2. Why is all communication partial, partisan, and problematic?

3. What is the classical management approach? What does the machine metaphor imply about communication in organizations based on classical management? What is "scientific" about Henri Fayol's approach to decision making?

4. What is useful about the idea of resistance to domination when it is applied to classical management theories? Do you think this idea has relevance in today's organizations? If so, why and how?

5. Why do you think Mary Parker Follett's ideas about management were considered "radical" in her day? What specific influences of her work can you see in human relations and human resources theories?

6. What are the principles of the human relations and human resources approaches to organizational communication? What was the influence of the "Triple Alliance" on the historical development of organizational communication? Why do you think Elton Mayo's work had so much impact?

7. Why do you think Abraham Maslow's hierarchy of needs has had such far-ranging implications for the development of human resources approaches to management and communication? What are the fundamental differences between McGregor's Theory X and Theory Y when applied to human communication at work?

8. What is a leadership style? What are the relationships between concepts of leadership style and theories within the classical approach?

CASE STUDY

Riverside State Hospital

BACKGROUND

Riverside State Hospital is a five-hundred-bed, state-supported psychiatric facility located along the scenic banks of the Tennessee River. Admission to the facility requires a physician's order or court referral. The hospital staff consists of physicians, psychologists, psychiatrists, nurses, dietitians, pharmacists, therapists, technicians, and general housekeeping and groundskeeping personnel, all of whom are state employees. The hospital is run primarily as a bureaucracy, with levels of authority and salary based on seniority and rank.

All employees hold a government service (GS) rank, the lowest being GS-1 (groundskeeping trainee) and the highest GS-15 (administrator or CEO). In addition, within each rank are seven to ten steps, which are determined by seniority and achievement. Performance reviews are conducted annually, at which time promotions in steps or in GS rank may occur. Employees are given annual salary adjustments for inflation or cost-of-living increases. Full state benefits are provided to all workers.

Riverside employees work an eight-hour shift. Employees below rank GS-12 (head or chief) take a thirty-minute lunch break and two fifteen-minute breaks during their shift. Members of the professional staff (physicians, nurses, pharmacists, and the like) work on a three-shift schedule: 7 A.M. to 3 P.M., 3 P.M. to 11 P.M., and 11 P.M. to 7 A.M. The hospital operates year-round.

THE PROBLEM

A few days ago, a resident patient at Riverside State Hospital was killed when part of the wall next to his bed collapsed. Horris James Wilcox Jr. was fifty-six years old when he died. He had no family and had been a resident at the hospital for three years. He suffered from traumatic amnesia and scored in the borderline range on intelligence tests. He was otherwise in good health. He was also well liked and seemed to be responding to treatment.

In statements made to state investigators and the news media, hospital administrators called the accident a "tragedy." They explained, "There had been no indication that the wall was weak or that Wilcox was in any danger."

You are the government investigator assigned to the Wilcox case. Your job is to determine whether any evidence exists that would make Riverside State Hospital liable for Wilcox's death.

THE INVESTIGATION

You learn from your investigation that Wilcox was a quiet man who tended to keep to himself, although he did join the other patients on the ward for scheduled games and activities. During these times, he talked a lot about current news events. Watching the cable news channel was his favorite source of entertainment. He was known among the staff as the most informed patient on the ward.

Your investigation also reveals that Wilcox's amnesia was complicated by his belief that he was directly affected by whatever he saw on television. News events — particularly family tragedies — affected him deeply. The hospital staff had tried reducing his television viewing time to prevent further complications, but he became depressed. His television privileges were restored as a result, and the staff tried instead to use the emotions he displayed about news shows in his therapy. Perhaps, they reasoned, some family tragedy had produced the traumatic amnesia.

In addition, for the past month Wilcox had repeatedly exclaimed, "The sky is falling," especially when he was confined to his bed at night and in the mornings upon awakening. He would also point at the ceiling and walls of his room and cry out, "There is trouble here, trouble from the sky." On several such occasions he had to be physically restrained and calmed with drugs. During this same month, an air force fighter plane had exploded in the sky during an air show, and videotaped replays of that event had appeared frequently on the television news. Given Wilcox's past history of responding emotionally to tragedies reported in the news, the staff linked his most recent behavior to the air show disaster. However, you think there may be more to it. Considering Wilcox's unwillingness to go to bed at night, his complaints about an impending tragedy may have had an altogether different meaning: Perhaps "the sky" was a reference to perceived structural defects in the walls and ceiling of his room. You wonder whether Wilcox was trying to direct attention to the actual physical deterioration of his room. Moreover, his psychiatric history may have led those in charge of his care to dismiss his allegations.

Upon further investigation, you learn that the walls and ceiling in Wilcox's room had been repainted three times during the past twelve months due to stains from a leaking water pipe. You think the leak may

(continued)

have seriously weakened the wall, and you feel that hospital personnel should have followed up on this warning. You also discover that state funding for maintenance had been cut back severely during the previous summer and that although there was structural damage to the wall, there was no indication that it was unsafe. From the hospital administrators' perspective, then, the culprits were an aging building and insufficient state funding to repair it. Even so, they maintain that the collapse of the wall was "an unforeseeable accident."

You obtain copies of the building inspection reports for the past three years. You note that in the past year, state inspectors recorded the deteriorating condition of the wall and ceiling that eventually collapsed. These forms are signed by Hillary Hanks, the head of resident life.

In an interview with Hanks, you discover that although her name appears on the state inspection forms, she did not actually sign them. She explains that her secretary, Nancy Ellis, regularly signs her name on state forms to save time. She adds, "There are so many forms to sign that if I signed them all, I wouldn't get any real work done." When you speak to Ellis, she confirms Hanks's story. Furthermore, Ellis is annoyed because the man who delivered the forms to her was supposed to point out any problems that required attention. The problem with the walls and ceiling in Wilcox's room had not been reported verbally to Ellis, and therefore she didn't notify Hanks. Now Hanks is in trouble with her superior, and that means Ellis will lose her chance at a promotion. Any trouble for Hanks generally means trouble for Ellis, too. Ellis admits that she regularly avoids telling her boss any bad news for exactly that reason, but this time, Ellis claims, she was unaware of the bad news. You ask Ellis what she did with the inspection report. She points to the overstuffed filing cabinet behind her. "That's where I put it," she says, "along with all the other paperwork that never gets read around here."

You find out that the report was prepared by state inspector Blake Barrymore, who gave it to a groundskeeper for delivery to the appropriate hospital administrator because "it was raining that day, and I was late for another inspection." He adds that it is not his official responsibility to deliver the report himself or to follow up on it. You discover that the inspection report was delivered by Jack Handy, a reliable and well-liked groundskeeper, but you also discover that Handy is illiterate. He did not know what the forms contained because he could not read them. He did not report any problems with the walls or ceiling because Barrymore didn't tell him there were any problems. Besides, Handy added, "Nobody listens to a groundskeeper anyway. I could tell the administrators that there was a bomb in the hospital and because I'm just a groundskeeper, they'd let it pass. So I just do what I'm told to do."

You file your report. The insurance company claims that gross negligence on the part of Riverside State Hospital indirectly caused the death of Horris James Wilcox Jr. At a press conference, the hospital spokesperson places the blame for Wilcox's death on Nancy Ellis, claiming that it was her responsibility to report the problem to her superior, Hillary Hanks. He adds that Hanks has been "reassigned" to other duties and is unavailable for comment. In a final statement, the spokesman says, "The hospital deeply regrets this tragic accident, and reminds the state legislature that until the requested funds for structural repairs are made available, the hospital administration cannot be held accountable for structural defects that are beyond its control."

ASSIGNMENT

1. What management approach does Riverside State Hospital most resemble?
2. How does the management approach influence communication at the hospital?
3. Should Ellis be held responsible for Wilcox's death? Why or why not? In what ways did the hospital's organizational structure contribute to Wilcox's accidental death?
4. What recommendations would you propose to help Riverside State Hospital avoid similar occurrences in the future? How can organizational communication be improved?

CHAPTER 4

The Systems Perspective on Organizations and Communication

The human being experiences himself . . . as something separated from the rest — a kind of optical delusion of [the] consciousness. This delusion is a kind of prison for us, restricting us to our personal desires and to affection for a few persons nearest to us. Our task must be to free ourselves from this prison by widening our circle of compassion to embrace all living creatures and the whole of nature in its beauty.

— ALBERT EINSTEIN, *Relativity: The Special and General Theory* (1921)

In life, the issue is not control, but dynamic connectedness.

— ERICH JANTSCH, *The Self-Organizing Universe* (1980)

Try the following exercise. Close your eyes, and imagine growing yourself (a feat that you in fact once achieved . . .). Imagine all the branchings, the self-differentiations, that necessarily take place in the process, and imaginatively identify with this process. If you take this exercise seriously, you may discover it is somehow illuminating to get in touch with this "you." Why? And what does this experience tell us about what it means to say "I"? Now entertain the notion that the "you" that grew yourself has analogues in all living things, in ecologies of living things, and in the whole of biological evolution, as well as in the evolution of ideas.

— RODNEY DONALDSON, introduction to Gregory Bateson's
   Sacred Unity: Further Steps toward an Ecology of Mind (1991)

In this and the following chapter, we continue our story of organizations and communication by considering two prominent metaphors — systems and cultures — that seek to describe the contemporary world. According to one well-known observer of business, "The unhealthiness of our world today is in direct proportion to our inability to see it as a whole" (Senge, 1990, p. 168). By thinking in terms of systems and cultures, however, we find ways of thinking about wholes, and in so doing we may learn how to survive in an era of economic and environmental limits. Unlike the machine metaphor of classical management theory, the focus of the systems and cultural approaches is not on individual parts or people but instead on relationships, or on "the pattern that connects" (Bateson, 1972). As such, these approaches give supreme emphasis to communication — that is, to the development of meaning through human interaction.

We begin, then, with the systems approach. It broadens our way of looking at organizations by borrowing concepts from other, seemingly unrelated, areas of study, including engineering, biology, chemistry, physics, and sociology. Associated with the nature of a system are such components as environment, interdependence, goals, feedback, and order. In addition, the systems approach has important implications for the situated individual striving to balance creativity and constraint.

The Systems Perspective

An advertisement for BMW poses this question: "What makes the BMW the ultimate driving machine?" Is it the car's superb handling and braking? Aerodynamic design? Powerful engine? According to the advertisement, no single feature makes the BMW special; rather, the car is unique in the way that all of its qualities work together as a whole to create "the ultimate driving machine."

This advertisement nicely illustrates the systems approach, which emphasizes the important difference between a collection of parts versus a collection of parts that work together to create a functional whole. That functional whole is called a "system," and in a system *the whole is more than the sum of its parts.* Sociologist Walter Buckley (1967) translates this expression as follows: "The 'more than' points to the fact of organization, which imparts to the aggregate characteristics that are not only different from, but [also] often not found in the components alone; and the 'sum of the parts' must be taken to mean, not their numerical addition, but their unorganized aggregation" (p. 42). In other words, organization makes a social system more than just its components. In a marriage, family, team, or business, the relationships that exist among people are what make the group a system.

Historical and Cultural Background

Although it has come to be applied broadly to social systems, the systems approach has its roots in the sciences, notably physics, information theory, and biology. The impact of each is discussed below.

The Origins of Systems Theory in the Sciences

Before the work of Albert Einstein, Isaac Newton's concepts of the universe prevailed. Space and time were viewed as distinct entities operating "in a fixed arena in which events took place, but which was not affected by what happened in it. . . . Bodies moved, forces attracted and repelled, but time and space simply continued, unaffected" (Hawking, 1988, p. 33). There is a clear parallel between this view of the physical world and classical approaches to organization. Scientific management, for example, relied heavily on time and motion studies (whose principles were drawn from Newtonian physics) to provide data to managers about worker productivity.

Einstein's theory of relativity radically transformed how we saw our world. This new way of seeing brought new questions: What if time and space are not fixed but relative? If, as Einstein's general theory of relativity suggests, time runs slower nearer the earth due to the influence of its gravitational pull, does this imply that observations of what appears to be a fixed reality are skewed by the observer's position? For example, when seeing a commercial jetliner pass overhead it often appears to be floating, almost standing still, when in fact it is traveling at hundreds of miles an hour. Relativity theory explains what is wrong:

> Space and time are . . . dynamic quantities: when a body moves, or a force acts, it affects the curvature of space and time — and in turn the structure of space-time affects the way in which bodies move and forces act. Space and time not only affect but also are affected by everything that happens in the universe. (Hawking, 1988, p. 33)

In other words, rather than conceptualizing time and motion studies within the limited framework of a specific task, the interpretation of the task is expanded to include how it functions as part of a dynamic interdependent system. For example, a company can work hard to lower the cost of its product through more efficient production, but if it fails to closely monitor consumer tastes, it may end up failing in any case. Systems theory encourages us to explore how organizational effectiveness depends on the coordination of the total enterprise. Appropriate questions might include: What are the intended and unintended consequences of increased or decreased efficiency? How do pressures to reduce time and eliminate unnecessary motion affect employee morale, absenteeism, commitment, and turnover? How, in turn, do these factors affect productivity in important but potentially unexpected ways?

This major shift in our understanding of the laws of the universe does more than simply call into question the rationality of time and motion studies. It also brings to our attention the idea of dynamic systems of interacting components, whose relationships and interactions point to a new kind of order based on pattern of interaction. The ideas of dynamic systems have been applied to atomic physics, navigational science, aerospace, and electronics, but it was not until World War II that a general systems paradigm emerged with applications to organizations. Indeed, today we don't have to look far to see the impact of systems theory on the field of communication. Consider some of the terms we routinely use to describe communication: sender, message, channel, receiver, and feedback. Before 1948, the vocabulary of communication developed by the ancient Greeks was still in use (e.g., speech, speaker, audience, ethos, pathos, and logos). Since then, our language about communication processes has been transformed by the information revolution. As Stuart Clegg (1990) puts it, "Systems ideas are now so much a part of the modernist consciousness that they barely require elaborate iteration" (p. 51).

In addition to the theoretical advances in physics, new technologies have been spawned by industries capitalizing on scientific advances. Primarily an outgrowth of transistors and, later, the microchip, communication technologies like television, satellites, and computers have contributed to the emergence of what Marshall McLuhan called the "global information society" (1964). McLuhan's idea is simple but profound. The instantaneous transfer of information across cultural boundaries means that our perceptions of reality, of cultural differences, of political and social events, and of what constitutes the news cease to be mediated by fixed notions of space or time. Because information now connects us in ways not possible before, the world has become — in McLuhan's famous phrase — a "global village."

Biology and General Systems Theory

Within the broad context of the information revolution there emerged a more specific contributor to systems theory — the life sciences, especially biology. It is easy to see why. A system is alive not because of any particular component or component process (e.g., a respiratory or digestive system), but because of the relationships and interchanges among processes. Within any system there are subsystems, and it is the *connections* between subsystems (e.g., how oxygen gets from the lungs into the blood, then into the muscles and synapses) that define the characteristics of biological or living organisms. To take a holistic approach means to consider the properties of systems that come out of the relationships among their parts.

Biologists Ludwig von Bertalanffy (1968) and J. G. Miller (1978) are credited with advancing the study of living systems, and von Bertalanffy with pioneering the development of general systems theory in particular. General systems theory applies the properties of living systems, such as input, output, boundaries, homeostasis, and equifinality (that there is more than one right way to accomplish the same goal), to a dazzling array of social phenomena. (Table 4.1 provides an overview of the hierarchy of general systems theory.) As biologist Lewis Thomas explains in his landmark work, *The Lives of a Cell* (1975),

> Although we are by all odds the most social of all social animals — more interdependent, more attached to each other, more inseparable in our behavior than bees — we do not often feel our conjoined intelligence. Perhaps it is in this respect that language differs most sharply from biological systems for communication. Ambiguity seems to be an essential, indispensable element for the transfer of information from one place to another by words, where matters of real importance are concerned. It is often necessary, for meaning to come through, that there be an almost vague sense of strangeness and askewness. Speechless animals and cells cannot do this. . . . Only the human mind is designed to work this way, programmed to drift away in the presence of locked-on information, straying from each point in the hunt for a better, different point. (pp. 89–94)

In other words, the ambiguity of language makes the interdependencies between members of a social system (i.e., among people) looser than those found in biology or those that connect the parts of a car. Put another way: "social organizations, in contrast to physical or mechanical structures, are loosely coupled systems" (Scott, 1981, p. 103).

Thus, with the advent of relativity and the initiation of analogies between organic systems and human societies, the concept of *dynamic systems* was born, offering innovative ways of understanding the relationships among functioning components in space and time. However, applying systems theory to human language would prove to be challenging. The work of chemist Ilya Prigogine (1980) has helped to expand the potential application of systems thinking to social organization. By studying chemical reactions, Prigogine found that in open systems (i.e., those that *must* interact with their environments to survive), a movement toward disorder often precedes the emergence of a new order. In contrast to the Newtonian vision of a universe constantly falling apart, Prigogine's findings suggest that both living and nonliving systems have the potential for *self-organization or self-renewal* in the face of environmental change, and that disorder is a natural part of the renewal process.

More recently, biological concepts and processes have gained greater prominence in organizational theory and practice. Most notably, manufacturing and information (computer) system designs are now being fashioned after robust biological systems. Abandoning the top-down, "central-processing" model implicit in classical approaches, all manner of new organizational structures and processes are being modeled after living systems, which tend to exhibit distributed intelligence. By "distributed intelligence" we mean that all members of the system — whether they be people or cells — play an important role in the system's ongoing self-organization. Imagine for a moment what life would be like under a central-processing model! What would happen if your brain had to "turn

TABLE 4.1

The Hierarchy of General Systems Theory

LEVEL	DESCRIPTION AND EXAMPLES	THEORY AND MODELS
Static structures	Atoms, molecules, crystals, biological structures from the electron microscope to the macroscope level	Structural formulas of chemistry; crystallography; anatomical descriptions
Clockworks	Clocks, conventional machines in general, solar systems	Conventional physics, such as the laws of mechanics (Newton and Einstein)
Control mechanisms	Thermostat, servomechanisms, homeostatic mechanism in organisms	Cybernetics; feedback and information theory
Open systems	Flame, cells, and organisms in general	Expansion of physical theory to systems maintaining themselves in flow of matter (metabolism); information storage in genetic code (DNA)
Lower organisms	Plantlike organisms: increasing differentiation of system (so-called division of labor in the organism); distinction of reproduction and functional individual ("germ track and soma")	Theory and models mostly lacking
Animals	Increasing importance of traffic in information (evolution of receptors, nervous systems); learning; beginnings of consciousness	Beginnings in automata theory (stimulus-response relations), feedback (regulatory phenomena), autonomous behavior (relaxation oscillations)
Humans	Symbolism; past and future, self and world, self-awareness as consequences; communication by language	Incipient theory of symbolism
Sociocultural systems	Populations of organisms (humans included); symbol-determined communities (cultures) in humans only	Statistical and possibly dynamic laws in population dynamics, sociology, economics, possibly history; beginnings of a cultural systems theory
Symbolic systems	Language, logic, mathematics, sciences, arts, morals	Algorithms of symbols (e.g., mathematics, grammar); "rules of the game," such as in visual arts and music

Source: Ludwig von Bertalanffy, *General Systems Theory* (New York: George Braziller, 1968), pp. 28–29.

on" the rest of the body's systems each morning? Our tendency to equate rationality with intelligence has caused us to miss the very real (but non-linguistic) forms of intelligence that are distributed throughout our bodies.

The advantage of modeling organizations after living systems is that living systems — which exhibit distributed intelligence and seek to organize — are far more adaptive to a changing environment than are closed systems such as most machines. Even theories of artificial intelligence have moved from centralized models to linked computers that share information in a weblike fashion. The tentative conclusion appears to be that people learn best in a complex environment when they are only loosely connected and are free to initiate action from any place in the organization.

From Biology to Organizational Communication

Academic disciplines whose traditional focus had been on complex processes of information exchange embraced systems theory. Sociologist Albion Small (1905) used concepts of systems theory in his field-defining work at the University of Chicago, and other prominent social theorists, such as Talcott Parsons (1951) and George Homans (1961), followed suit. Similarly, the initial popularity of the systems approach to organizational communication studies was enormous. Daniel Katz and Robert Kahn's *The Social Psychology of Organizations* (1966), a landmark application of systems theory to organizations, argues that organizations are fundamentally open systems that require a constant flow of information to and from their environment. In the field of organizational communication, then, systems theory provided a new connection between communicating and organizing.

Enthusiastic about the potential of this approach, Richard Farace, Peter Monge, and Hamish Russell devoted an organizational communication textbook to the systems approach — *Communicating and Organizing* (1977) — thereby endorsing the now commonly heard statement, "Communication is the process of organizing." This means that only through communication can organizations come into being and continue to exist. In addition, communication is not inside, outside, or tangential to the organization; rather, it *is* the organization.

What Is a System?

As you can tell from the preceding discussions, a system may be defined as a complex set of relationships among interdependent parts or components. In the study of organizational communication, we are concerned both with the nature of those components in organizations and the relationships among them.

Environment and Open Systems

According to systems theory, organizations do not exist as entities isolated from the rest of the world. Rather, organizations exist in increasingly turbulent environments which both provide inputs to the organization and receive outputs in the form of products and services. For a company to succeed today, some of its members must spend a significant amount of time engaged in environmental scanning, the careful monitoring of competitors, suppliers, government legislation, global economics, and consumer preferences. Failure to do so leaves an organization open to unexpected environmental jolts, which can have disastrous consequences. In most successful companies, environmental scanning is done by boundary spanners, those employees who have the greatest opportunity for interaction with people outside of the company.

An organization's relationship with its environment, however, is not limited to scanning. As open systems, organizations must also work with their environments to be successful (e.g., by establishing joint ventures and strategic partnerships). This is a significant change from traditional "us-against-them" theories of competition. In today's world, it is difficult for companies to know who is a potential enemy or friend, so the best strategy is usually something called "co-opetition," a blend of cooperation and competition that tries to reap the best of both worlds (Brandenburger & Nalebuff, 1996). A landmark example of co-opetition is SEMATECH, a semiconductor consortium formed by the U.S. federal government to improve the global competitiveness of the entire semiconductor industry (Browning & Shetler, 2000). At first, participating companies (e.g., Intel, HP, Motorola) were very uncomfortable sharing information with their "enemies"; they later came to the important realization that their individual competitiveness was enhanced, not hindered, by a certain level of cooperation.

This critical insight can be useful in the development of cross-functional collaboration within organizations. Open systems theory encourages individual members (whether they be people, departments, or organizations) to be mindful of the importance of the overall health of their industry "ecosystem" (Lewin, 1997). The analogy between organizations and living organisms helps to further explain the concept of open systems. Organisms are open systems in that they rely on exchanges with their environment to survive (human beings, for example, need food, air, and sunlight to live). Similarly, organizations rely on communication with their environments. As Walter Buckley (1967) explains, "That a system is open means, not simply that it engages in interchanges with the environment, but that this interchange is an *essential factor underlying the system's viability*, its reproductive ability or continuity, and its ability to change" (p. 50). Therefore, an open system that interacts productively with its environment tends to create structure or, more simply, to organize, whereas in a closed system there is little or no interaction with the environment and the organization may approach entropy or disorder. (See *What Would You Do?* 4.1 for an example.)

What Would You Do? 4.1

THE ADDICTIVE ORGANIZATIONAL SYSTEM

Organizational systems are not always open, nor do they always foster openness. An addictive system is one that encourages individuals to become dependent on the system and to shut out external influences. As a result, employees may become addicted to their work, overworking, covering up, and striving to please the boss. As Anne Wilson Schaef and Diane Fassel (1988) explain,

> The addictive system operates from the same characteristics that individual addicts have routinely exhibited. The major defense mechanism of the addictive system is denial, which supports a closed system. If something does not exist, it simply does not have to be considered. Corporations frequently say, "We have a minor problem, but certainly not a major one." "We are having a sales slump, but it is only temporary." The alcoholic says, "I am not an alcoholic. I may have a small drinking problem, and I may overdo it a bit on weekends or under stress, but I do not have a severe problem." (p. 62)

In addition, an addictive (or closed) organizational system has the following characteristics:

1. *Confusion.* Confusion prevents an organization and its employees from taking responsibility, and therefore they remain powerless over the addiction.
2. *Self-centeredness.* This characteristic allows the organization and its members to interpret all actions of others as either "for" or "against"; it also reduces the complexities of living to whatever is necessary to get a "fix."
3. *Dishonesty.* Like addicts who are master liars and have perfected the "con," members of addictive organizations lie to themselves, to the people around them, and to the world at large.
4. *Perfectionism.* Like addicts who are obsessed with not being good enough, addictive organizations and the individuals in them compensate by trying to never make mistakes. This gives them the illusion of control (Schaef & Fassel, 1988).

Addictive organizational systems raise ethical concerns. Consider how you would deal with the following situations:

1. You work for an organization that is proud of its strong culture and work ethic. You and your co-workers enjoy the benefits of working for a highly successful company and feel very much a part of the dominant culture. However, you routinely give up your evenings

and weekends to participate in work-related activities for no additional pay or recognition, and your family life has suffered as a result. For the past two years, your family vacationed without you while you stayed home and worked. You love your job and the people you work with, but you feel estranged from the world outside of the organization, and you want to improve your family life. What can you do to address the situation? Quit your job? Redefine your relationship with the company? Speak to co-workers about your dilemma? In particular, think about the ethical issues raised by your participation in an addictive organization.

2. Your supervisor is a perfectionist, though she denies it. You think you do your job well, but your supervisor is not satisfied with your output. She often points out "small areas that need improvement" and has suggested that you give up some of your spare time to improve the quality of your work. You believe your supervisor is addicted to the organization, but she is viewed as a highly valued member of the company, and her work habits are the standard for all employees. You respect your supervisor, but you resent her implication that you do not contribute enough to the company. You are concerned about an ethical issue: How much personal sacrifice should a company expect from its employees? What might systems theory suggest as a remedy to your situation?

Interdependence

Another essential quality of a system, interdependence, refers both to the wholeness of the system and its environment and to the interrelationships of individuals within the system. These relationships can vary in terms of their degree of interdependence. For example, a student's refusal to acknowledge the legitimacy of a particular instructor would have a negative effect on the student's performance in the course but only a minimal effect on the instructor because of the lopsided nature of the student-teacher relationship: The student is dependent on the instructor, but the instructor is only minimally interdependent. In contrast, because most marriages are characterized by a high degree of interdependence, the decision of one partner to withdraw emotionally from the relationship puts the whole system at risk. In systems theory, then, the interdependent relationships between people not only give an organization its character, but are established and maintained through communication.

The failure to recognize interdependence in dynamic systems leads to what ecologist Garrett Hardin (1968) called the "Tragedy of the Commons." The tragedy occurs when a group of people (or organizations, or departments within organizations) with access to a common resource use it in ways that focus on personal needs rather than on the needs of the whole, leading to the destruction of rain forests, the exploitation of grazing land, and the pollution of major waterways. While each individual's actions may make sense from his or her perspective, the failure to recognize the interdependency and consequences of one's actions can be devastating to both the individual and the collectivity.

In organizations, division of labor can cloud peoples' perceptions of the interdependent nature of their work. For example, when we toured a company that manufactures high-technology radio transmitters, we asked employees to describe the various kinds of jobs available in the company and whether they had considered cross-training or moving to a different department. We found that most employees in the company were completely ignorant of the nature of their co-workers' jobs. Although familiar with the processes they controlled directly, they were not aware of the origin of their work materials or the destination of their finished products. Even employees within the same work group had little knowledge of each other's jobs, despite their daily contacts. One employee, who for fifteen years had been handing over his finished parts to a co-worker (through a small window in an interior wall), had no idea what the co-worker did with the parts. A worst-case scenario from a systems perspective, the company's employees did not see themselves as part of an interdependent system because of the strict division of labor. In an interdependent system, no part of the system can stand alone but relies on the other parts to do its job effectively. Breakdowns in communication anywhere in the system run the risk of negatively impacting the whole.

Goals

Organizational goals are defined in various ways in theories of organization and communication. From a scientific management perspective, goals are central: Both individuals and organizations direct their activities toward goal attainment. From an institutional perspective, organizations and their members may espouse goals, but rarely do their goals guide their behavior (Scott, 1981, p. 21). From the open-systems perspective, however, goals are negotiated among interdependent factions in the organization and are heavily influenced by its environment.

Michael Keeley (1980) makes an important distinction regarding organizational goals. Examining the traditional view of organizations as mobilized around common goals, he distinguishes between the goals *of* individuals, which are personal and highly variable, and the goals individuals have *for* their organization, which are more likely to be shared.

Goals can also differ across systems levels. For example, a unit at one level within a large corporation may seek the goal of profitability. At the next level, however, the corporation may be under pressure from stakeholders to raise cash; this corporate goal may cause it to try to sell the business unit (a decision that is unfavorable to the unit). At the same time, the other unit's goal of profitability may conflict with the individual goals of workers or managers within the unit, who may advocate such goals as improving product quality or focusing on strategic products at the expense of others. Thus, systems theory emphasizes that what is good for one level of the system may or may not be good for the other levels.

Processes and Feedback

A system is not simply an interdependent set of components; it is also an interdependent collection of processes that interact *over time*. For instance, to sell radio transmitters, we would not only have to submit the orders to engineering or manufacturing, but we would also have to do so in a timely fashion to avoid inefficiency and other work-flow-related problems. Engineering, in turn, would need to deliver accurate drawings to manufacturing on schedule, and manufacturing would be required to meet the customer's quality standards and delivery date. The reengineering approach is often directed at minimizing the time it takes to execute these processes.

Suppose, however, that the customer is dissatisfied with the radio transmitters and calls to cancel future orders, or that he or she is generally pleased with the product but requests changes in its design. These are examples of *feedback*, which can be defined as a system of "loops" that connect communication and action. Individuals provide messages to others, who then respond to those messages in some way. The response closes the loop, providing communicators with information about how their messages were received. In other words, feedback contains information about the influence of a particular message or action, and it is usually expressed as a deviation from what the sender intended.

Feedback thus controls systems of communication by regulating the flow and interpretation of messages. In systems theory, there are two main types of feedback: negative and positive. Negative, or deviation-counteracting, feedback is illustrated by the customer's complaint about the radio transmitters. The negative feedback seeks to reestablish the goals or quality levels that were initially established for the product. (This type of feedback is sometimes referred to as "cybernetic," after the Greek word for "steersman," or someone who used oars to stay on course.) The other type of feedback, positive, or deviation-amplifying, feedback, is illustrated by the consultant who suggests changes in product design. It seeks to find new avenues of growth and development. Positive feedback is often referred to generally as "second cybernetics" (or "morphogenesis") (Maruyama, 1963). (Other, more complex forms of feedback, such as causal loops and cause maps, are discussed later in the chapter.)

In their work on learning organizations, Chris Argyris and Donald Schon (1978) assert that today's businesses need *both* deviation-counteracting and deviation-amplifying feedback to achieve success. While deviation-counteracting feedback encourages adherence to an established strategy or course of action, deviation-amplifying feedback ensures that alternative strategies or courses of action are considered. Argyris calls the latter practice "double-loop learning," or the ability to "learn how to learn" by reexamining established assumptions and decision premises.

Openness, Order, and Contingency

Systems theory evokes the image of a complex, interdependent organization that operates within a dynamic environment and is engaged in an ongoing struggle to create order in the face of unpredictability (Clegg, 1990; Thompson, 1967). In retrospect, it is indeed surprising that classical management theories paid so little attention to an organization's environment, focusing instead on treating organizations equally and directing management to conduct careful studies of the "one best way" to accomplish work within the boundaries of the organization. Ideas about environments or global economics were considered irrelevant or misplaced.

In contrast, today's open systems are less reassuring and more unpredictable. Environmental openness helps organizations see themselves as part of a dynamic system of intricate interdependencies and relationships. Openness in the organization-environment relationship also has implications for some of the more prescriptive aspects of organizational theory. The existence of diverse environments across industries, companies, and even geographic regions means that the same organizing principles and solutions cannot be applied in all situations; rather, they are contingent on various factors. In systems theory, the term *equifinality* means that the same goal may be reached in multiple ways. Jay Galbraith (1973) summarizes the two basic tenets of contingency theory as follows:

1. There is no one best way to organize.
2. All ways of organizing are not equally effective.

These principles imply not only that the forms of organizing that will work best depend on the environment, but also that the match between certain organizational approaches and specific environments should be explored because some approaches will work better than others. Organizations that exist in complex and highly turbulent environments require different forms of leadership, interpersonal communication, decision making, and organizational structure than those in relatively predictable environments (Lawrence & Lorsch, 1967).

The Appeal of Systems Theory for Organizational Communication

Systems theory appeals to those who are interested in organizational communication because it highlights the importance of communication processes in organizing. In addition, it is theoretically capable of capturing much of the complexity of these processes. While experience teaches us that communication is complex and takes place over time, earlier theories were based on the overly simplistic idea that communication involved the sending and receiving of messages.

Research on systems theory has also been disappointing. Researchers have had difficulty translating the concepts of systems theory into research designs. Scholars unable to create dynamic systems theories of communication often lack the methodological tools needed to analyze complex systems of communication and feedback. Systems theories are ideally tested using statistical methods that accommodate multiple factors interacting over time. Unfortunately, few people studying social systems are well trained in how to use these new statistics. As a result, studies of complex systems often apply the wrong analytic techniques or remain untested at the theoretical level. Because actual studies of complex social systems are rare, systems theory has been characterized as an appealing but abstract set of concepts with little applicability to actual theory or research (Poole, 1996). Recently, however, efforts have been made to reinvigorate systems theory in ways that are compatible with organizational communication. We are referring specifically to the innovative theories of Margaret Wheatley, Peter Senge, and Karl Weick, which we discuss next.

Margaret Wheatley's New Science of Leadership

Management professor Margaret Wheatley (1992) has received a great deal of acclaim for her efforts to bring to management the principles and aesthetics of what she calls "new science" — a combination of quantum physics, self-organizing systems theory, and chaos theory. "In new science, the underlying currents are a movement toward holism, toward understanding the system as a system and giving primacy to the relationships that exist among seemingly discrete parts" (p. 9). (In this regard, Wheatley's critique of the machine metaphor of organizations is consistent with our argument thus far.) Wheatley relies heavily on Prigogine's (1980) theory of "dissipative structures," which views disorder as "a full partner" in the search for order. Just as Frederick Taylor's (1947) first "scientific management" required what he called a "mental revolution," so too does Wheatley's new science depend on major changes in the way we think about the world. Wheatley argues the following six points:

1. There are no "things" in themselves; even particles of matter are "intermediate states in a network of interactions." This is true for people and organizations as well.
2. Information, not matter, is the creative energy of the universe.
3. All living things are naturally engaged in self-renewal, and organizations do this by making creative use of their environments.
4. The search for machinelike control by management is counterproductive. "The more freedom in self-organization, the more order" (Jantsch, 1980, p. 40).

5. What we would call "disorder" is part of the natural process of order making.
6. The desire to make meaning is the "strange attractor" that keeps human beings in a constant tendency toward self-organization.

The main implication of Wheatley's approach is that people in organizations — and especially leaders — must take a different attitude toward order and control. This is important because what appears as disorder may well be an important pattern that has not yet been recognized. Encouraging disorder is a way of remaining open to change and innovation. Wheatley further suggests that positive outcomes are more likely to occur in an atmosphere that fosters collaboration, experimentation, and self-renewal than in one characterized by regulation and top-down control. In addition, communication is critical to the organization's ability to organize. Wheatley has had a big impact on communication researchers, and more recent work on self-organizing systems inspired in part by her approach will be covered in Chapter 7.

Peter Senge's Learning Organization

Management theorist Peter Senge (1990) has succeeded at bringing systems thinking to those who actually manage corporations. Like Wheatley, he is both concerned with holism and inclined to use scientific terminology. However, Senge focuses on the distinction between what he calls "learning organizations" and organizations that have a learning disability or a lack of understanding about how they function as systems. Learning organizations exhibit five features:

1. *Systems thinking.* Combining holism and interdependence, systems thinking claims that for any one member to succeed, all members must succeed.
2. *Personal mastery.* All members share a personal commitment to learning and self-reflection.
3. *Flexible mental models.* Mental models are those patterns of belief that shape and limit an individual's interpretations and actions. In a learning organization, members engage in self-reflection, allowing them first to understand and then to change the mental models that tend to guide their thinking.
4. *A shared vision.* In learning organizations, tight hierarchical control is replaced by "concertive control" (Tompkins & Cheney, 1985), whereby members act in concert because they share a common organizational vision and understand how their own work helps to build on that shared vision.
5. *Team learning.* Team members in a learning organization communicate in ways that lead the team toward intelligent decisions, with an emphasis on dialogue as the key to team learning.

According to Senge (1990), developing a learning organization requires a major "shift of mind" toward a more participative and holistic notion of effective organizing. What one does with differences in mental models — and how one moves on to team learning — is critical to Senge's approach and our interest in it.

Senge and his colleagues (Senge et al., 1994) at the MIT Dialogue Project (designed to promote dialogue in businesses around the world; see Isaacs, 1999) build on the work of physicist David Bohm (1980) on the role of consciousness in communication problems. Bohm is critical of the human tendency to see ourselves as separate from the rest of the world. Bohm argues that the result of such thinking is discussion, or "participative openness," wherein we advocate our opinions, but because we are unwilling to suspend our certainty about our own worldview, no real learning takes place. In contrast, dialogue, or "reflective openness," "starts with the willingness to challenge our own thinking, to recognize that any certainty we have is, at best, a hypothesis about the world" (Senge, 1990, p. 277). From this point, dialogue progresses through a combination of advocacy and inquiry, wherein we collectively offer and expose our ideas to tough scrutiny by others. The primary distinction between dialogue and the typical problem-solving meeting in business is that the former places more value on the communication process, and group members are thereby more willing to distance themselves from their own opinions and ideas.

Karl Weick's Sense-Making Model

Karl Weick's exploration of sense making, developed in his books, *The Social Psychology of Organizing* (1979) and *Sensemaking in Organizations* (1995), has strongly influenced the fields of organizational behavior and communication. In particular his work has reinvigorated systems theory by connecting it with issues of sense making, meaning, and communication, while also providing a bridge for the development of cultural studies of organizations (see Chapter 5).

According to Weick (1979), organizations exist in highly complex and unpredictable environments. The job of organizing involves making sense of the uncertainties in environments through interaction, a process that Weick calls "equivocality reduction." In the process of identifying the meaning of a given situation or event, the same facts can be interpreted in various ways by different observers. How the members of an organization communicate to make sense of equivocal situations is central to Weick's approach.

As illustrated in Figure 4.1, Weick's (1979) model of organizing has three parts: enactment, selection, and retention. In enactment, organizational members create environments through their actions and patterns of attention, and these environments can vary in terms of their perceived degree of equivocality or uncertainty. For example, college presidents and their staffs are struggling these days to decide what to include in their enacted environment. The usual list of students currently registered in courses and alumni is now being augmented by local communities, governments, senior citizens, and technology companies running virtual universities. School administrations vary greatly in the degree to which they pay attention to any of these forces.

FIGURE 4.1

Weick's Model of Organizing

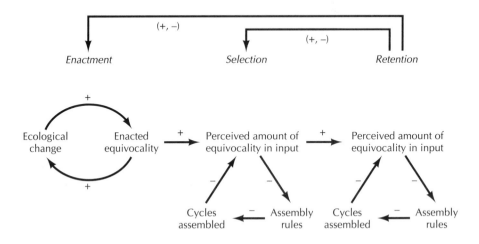

Source: Karl Weick, *The Social Psychology of Organizing* (Reading, Mass.: Addison-Wesley, 1979).
Reprinted by permission.

Once an environment is enacted, the organizing process requires the participants to select the best explanation of the environment's meaning from a number of possible interpretations. In selection, then, collective sense making is accomplished through communication. In the case of higher education, some universities (like Portland State University, the University of North Carolina at Greensboro, and the University of Alabama at Birmingham) have chosen to interpret their purpose and mission as in close partnership with the local community, and have even redesigned their reward systems to align with this interpretation. For example, the mission statement of one of these universities begins with the words "The University of North Carolina at Greensboro is a student-centered university, linking the Piedmont Triad to the world through learning, discovery, and service" (UNCG Undergraduate Bulletin, 2002–2003, p. 9). As a result of establishing "learning, discovery, and service" connections to the Piedmont Triad (e.g., the communities of Greensboro, Winston-Salem, and High Point) as first and foremost in its mission, the faculty and administration also revised promotion standards to include a track based primarily on service to the Triad area. Additionally, the university's Provost announced that one of UNCG's "Signature Programs" would be Service Learning, which means that each and every academic department is expected to develop core service learning opportunities for students within the Piedmont region and that academic departments will be evaluated, in part, based on the success of those community programs and initiatives.

Finally, in retention, successful interpretations are saved for future use. In the case of UNCG, time will tell what lessons are learned from their choice; success will not only reinforce their selection, but also allow others to see this as a legitimate option for their institutions. Retained interpretations also influence future selection processes, as indicated by the feedback arrow in Figure 4.1. Weick thus represents sense making as a set of interdependent processes that interact with and provide feedback to one another. In this sense, his model connects systems thinking with interpretation.

Perhaps Weick's (1979) most revolutionary concept is that of the enacted environment. Unlike theories of species evolution, in which degrees of environmental variation are determined objectively, in organizational environments people look for clues to threats or opportunities. Their perception is highly selective and dependent on their interests, motives, background, and behavior. Therefore, a company dominated by engineers would focus on changes in science and technology, whereas an organization made up mainly of accountants would focus on financial markets and global economic trends. This concept of the enacted environment is especially important in today's business world, wherein environmental scanning is crucial to an organization's survival. Among the most critical but often overlooked keys to organizational success involves keeping in touch with current issues through scanning relevant articles in newspapers and journals and maintaining contacts with others. Many times businesspeople overlook the importance of environmental scanning and miss articles that have a direct bearing on their company. Because the enacted environment is always limited by subjective perception, organizational success requires an ongoing examination of current issues.

Weick extends his model of organizing through three important concepts: retrospective sense making, loose coupling, and partial inclusion.

Retrospective Sense Making

An underlying assumption of Weick's model is that decision making is largely retrospective. In other words, although people in organizations think they plan first and then act according to a plan, Weick argues that people really act first and later examine their actions in an attempt to explain their meaning. He sums this up in what he calls a "recipe": "How can I know what I think until I see what I say?" (1979). Weick (1995) goes on to identify seven "properties of sense making" as follows:

1. *Identity construction.* Who I am is indicated by how and what I think.
2. *Retrospection.* To learn what I think, I look back over what I said earlier.
3. *Enactment.* I create an object to be seen and inspected when I say or do something.

4. *Socialization.* What I say, single out, and conclude are determined by who socialized me and how I was socialized, as well as by the audience I anticipate will audit the conclusions I reach.
5. *Continuation.* My talking is spread across time, competes for attention with other ongoing projects, and is reflected on after it is finished (which means my interests may already have changed).
6. *Extracted cues.* The "what" that I single out and embellish as the content of the thought is only a small portion of the utterance that becomes salient because of the context and personal dispositions.
7. *Plausibility.* I need to know enough about what I think to get on with my projects, but no more, which means sufficiency and plausibility take precedence over accuracy. (pp. 61–62)

The seven properties also apply if we change the pronouns in the recipe to reflect a collective actor (e.g., "How can we know what we think until we see what we say?").

However, Weick's theory of retrospective sense making does not take into account that some people do act first and interpret later while others strive to act only in accordance with predetermined plans. Perhaps both processes are always at work. The important point in Weick's argument is that the balance between planned and unplanned behavior is often the reverse of what we assume it to be. Such challenges to commonsense beliefs have been called "counterrational" approaches to organizational theory. Weick pushes this position to the limit, even arguing that random decision-making processes may be superior to rational methods of decision making and planning. His work in this area further challenges the scientific approach to management, wherein communication serves only as a conduit for the one best way of doing things. In contrast, the manager in Weick's model is a manipulator of symbols who motivates employees to make sense of their work life. Interaction is thus emphasized over reflection, with an accompanying bias for action. According to Weick, employees do not need common goals to work well together, nor do they need to know precisely what decisions they will make before they make them. More important, according to Weick, is a willingness to engage in coordinated action aimed at reducing equivocality, which over time may lead employees to discover (in retrospect) the meaning of what they have done.

Loose Coupling

At the same time that Weick stresses the importance of communication at work, he points out that unlike the connections among biological systems, the communication connections among people in organizations vary in intensity and are often loose or weak. Weick's (1976) concept of loosely coupled systems has had a major impact on our understanding of organizations as communication systems.

Consider, for example, the typical college or university, in which a great deal of interaction occurs within departments but not across various fields of study. The activities of the history department have little effect on those of the engineering department. Similarly, loose or weak connections usually exist among the university's nonacademic units (staff, administration, and faculty). The university is a classic example of a loosely coupled system.

Whereas strictly rational approaches maintain that loose connections tend to deter people from working together to achieve a common goal, Weick (1979) argues that such connections can sometimes be advantageous. The multiple goals of an organization can be coordinated without extensive communication or consensus (Eisenberg, 1984, 1986, 1990, 1995). In addition, a loosely coupled system is better able to withstand environmental jolts. In a system of close or tight connections, environmental jolts can affect the entire system, whereas in a loosely coupled system, the whole is less affected because of the weak connections among units. Although it is subject to redundancy and inefficiency, a loosely coupled system may still be more effective in the long term.

Partial Inclusion

In analyzing the balance between work and other activities, Weick (1979) uses the theory of partial inclusion to explain why certain strategies for motivating employees are ineffective. He holds that employees are only partially included in the workplace; that is, at work we see some but not all of their behaviors. An unmotivated employee at work may be a church leader or a model parent, whereas the top performer at a company may engage in few outside activities. In either case, simple theories of organizational behavior are limited when they fail to consider the employee's activities, roles, and interests outside of the workplace.

Weick (1979) mainly differentiates himself from those who value profitability above all else. He sees organizations as communities or social settings in which we choose to spend most of our adult lives. As such, organizations provide opportunities for storytelling and socializing; according to Weick, "they haven't anything else to give" (p. 264). A closer analysis of organizations as communities is the primary goal of the cultural approach, our focus in Chapter 5.

SUMMARY

The broad term *systems approach* encompasses many theories with various assumptions and implications for action. In contrast to earlier organizational theories (many of which can be classified according to their underlying view of the goals of organizing and of workers), systems theory is more open-ended. Adopting a systems approach requires acknowledging the openness and complexity of social organizations as well as the importance of relationships among individuals over time. Table 4.2 provides an explicit comparison of scientific management and systems theories.

TABLE 4.2

Scientific Management and Systems Theories

SCIENTIFIC MANAGEMENT	SYSTEMS THEORIES
Metaphor: Machines.	*Metaphor:* Biological organisms.
Theme: Efficiency — a machine is the sum of its parts.	*Theme:* Complexity — a system is greater than the sum of its parts.
Influences: Industrial Revolution, modernity, capitalism, and empire; assembly-line production and management; division of labor, interchangeable parts, coordination of many small, skilled jobs.	*Influences:* Einstein's theory of relativity; McLuhan's global information society; Miller's biological systems; von Bertalanffy's general systems; information engineering model of communication.
Focus of management principles: "The only things that count are the finished product and the bottom line"; time and motion studies.	*Focus of management principles:* "Everything counts"; studies of interdependent processes, information flows and feedback, environments and contingencies.
Management of individuals as interchangeable parts	*Management of relationships* among components; focus on groups and networks
Planning the work, working the plan	*Planning* the work, using feedback to correct the plan
Motivation by fear and money	*Motivation* by needs and contingencies
Theory of communication:	*Theory of communication:*

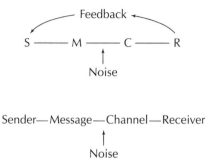

S ——— M ——— C ——— R
e   e   h   e
n   s   a   c
d   s   n   e
e   a   n   i
r   g   e   v
        e   l   e
                        r

Sender—Message—Channel—Receiver

Table 4.2

Scientific Management and Systems Theories *(continued)*

SCIENTIFIC MANAGEMENT	SYSTEMS THEORIES
Theory of leadership: Trait (tall, white males with blond hair and blue eyes, who come from strong moral backgrounds).	*Theory of leadership:* Adaptive (rhetorical contingency) — anyone can learn the skills of leading by attending to the requirements of behavioral flexibility.
Limitations: (1) Forgets that humans are more complex than machines; (2) encourages individual boredom and deep divisions between managers and employees; (3) discourages communication, individual needs, job initiative, task innovation, personal responsibility, and empowerment.	*Limitations:* (1) Forgets that humans are symbolic as well as biological; (2) encourages mathematical complexities that are difficult to put into everyday practices; (3) equates communication with information.

In practice, however, a systems approach can either help or hinder situated individuals. It can help individuals better understand overall workings of the organization. It can emphasize the importance of relationships and networks of contacts in allowing groups and organizations to achieve goals that are greater than those of the individual. A systems perspective can also reveal important interdependencies, particularly the connections with organizational environments that can affect an organization's survival. Despite its focus on communication and relationships, however, systems theory does not help to explain the meanings constructed by interactions. It can identify the potential participants in a productive organizational dialogue, but it cannot tell us about the content of that dialogue. It is in this area that Weick augments systems theory with issues related to sense making, arguably the central process of organizing.

Systems theory may also be applied in a way that elevates the whole and ignores or dehumanizes individuals. Any recognition of the role of whole systems must be accompanied by an understanding of how individuals create, refine, and destroy them. In the following passage, one of the founders of systems theory admits to its limited applicability to the individual in social organizations:

> [A human being] is not only a political animal, he [or she] is, . . . above all, an individual. The real values of humanity are not those it shares with biological entities, the function of an organism or a community of animals, but those which stem from the individual mind. Human society is not a community of ants or termites,

governed by inherited instinct and controlled by laws of the superordinate whole; it is based on the achievements of the individual and is doomed if the individual is made a cog in the social machine. This, I believe, is the ultimate precept a theory of organization can give: not a manual for dictators of any denomination to more efficiently subjugate human beings by the scientific application of iron laws, but a warning that the Leviathan of organization must not swallow the individual without sealing its own inevitable doom. (von Bertalanffy, 1968, pp. 52–53)

Systems theory is likely to continue to exert significant influence on the field of organizational communication. Particularly in organizations that produce complex products or provide complex services, systems theory is evident in discussions of work-flow analysis, internal customers, and cross-functional work groups, as well as in the use of control charts and process maps. Businesses are increasingly recognizing the critical role of markets and environments in their survival. In Chapters 7 and 10, we will return to the discussion of systems theory with specific application to the development of network forms of organizing.

QUESTIONS FOR REVIEW AND DISCUSSION

1. How has the information revolution influenced the development of systems theory?

2. How are biological systems and organizational communication systems similar? How are they different?

3. In what ways is organizational learning connected to the processes associated with systems thinking?

4. How has the sense-making model reinvigorated the application of systems theory to organizational communication?

5. Describe Margaret Wheatley's "new science of leadership." What characteristics of this "new science" can be directly connected to systems thinking? Why couldn't this theory of leadership have been a part of human relations or scientific management approaches?

6. Why do you think it has been difficult to operationalize systems thinking? In terms of doing systems research in an organization, what would you consider to be the major challenges?

CASE STUDY

Crisis in the Zion Emergency Room

A recent issue of *U.S. News & World Report* declared the nation's emergency rooms (ERs) to be in crisis. Part of the problem is a lack of qualified nurses. Nurses everywhere are in short supply, and those who can work effectively in the emergency environment are even rarer. But there are other reasons for the widespread overcrowding of ERs. A large and growing population of people without insurance continue to make use of them for primary care needs. Emergency rooms, staffed primarily to serve the victims of trauma or acute illness, are increasingly overburdened by mothers and infants without adequate prenatal and pediatric care; the chronically ill and disabled; persons with HIV/AIDS; individuals with mental illnesses, including drug and alcohol addiction; and the homeless. The end result is excessive wait time, angry patients, and substandard care. The ER at Zion Hospital is no different.

On any given night, Zion's ER looks like a war zone. The halls of the ER are lined with twenty to twenty-five patients on gurneys, lying in limbo until one of the forty-five regular ER beds opens up; just walking through the ER can be tricky. The overcrowding of the ER creates a distinct lack of privacy and, more important, the potential for serious errors resulting from the confusion about the location and status of patients. And more patients keep coming.

You have recently accepted the position of Director of Emergency Medicine at Zion. Expectations are high that you will be able to do something quickly about the dreadful patient satisfaction ratings that have appeared in recent months. Your initial assessment of the situation, however, is discouraging. For the reasons described above, there appears to be an endless and growing stream of new patients into the ER, and the hospital financial committee looks unfavorably at turning people away. Meanwhile, all of your beds are taken, half of them by people who have already been admitted to Zion but have yet to be assigned a bed upstairs in one of the hospital wards/units. Your staff has to find a way of serving these bored and hungry patients, while handling the more critical patients lined up in the hall.

Further investigation reveals that your patients are waiting for beds for a number of reasons: (1) Other units in the hospital, such as the heart

(continued)

center and the pediatric unit, have priority over the ER in getting beds; (2) all of the beds in the hospital are full, and those that are physically empty are locked in units that have been temporarily closed due to the lack of qualified nurses to staff them; and (3) there are long delays from the time a viable bed actually becomes empty, to when housekeeping gets around to cleaning the room for the next patient, to when floor nurses make themselves available to accept the new patient to their unit.

The situation is miserable and deteriorating. The nursing shortage is not going to end anytime soon, your current nurses are all threatening to quit, patients are furious, and hospital administration is urging you to "think outside the box" to find some relief.

ASSIGNMENT

Using what you know about systems theories of organization, answer the following questions:

1. How would you define the problem systemically in this case? How does your choice of definition affect your likely course of action?
2. Using the language of systems theories, what are the "realities" in this case that would be most difficult to change, and which are more malleable?
3. What role does communication play in perpetuating the current situation? How does your understanding of the systems approach help you identify specific communication issues?
4. Using your knowledge of systems, what kinds of communication might you use to address the situation? What obstacles would you expect to encounter, and how would you deal with them? Wouldn't dealing with those obstacles — in whatever way you choose to deal with them — also necessarily create new systemic issues? Given your choice of how to deal with the obstacles, what might these new issues be?
5. What role might communication technology play in developing a systems approach to your solution or solutions?

CHAPTER 5

Cultural Studies of Organizations and Communication

Man is an animal suspended in webs of significance which he himself has spun. I take culture to be those webs.

— CLIFFORD GEERTZ, *The Interpretation of Cultures* (1973)

This chapter introduces the idea of organizations as cultures. The cultural approach departs from the more rational and formal approaches that preceded it, bringing a new focus on the language of the workplace, the routine versus dramatic performance of managers and employees, and the formal and informal practices that mark an organization's character, such as rites and rituals and the display of meaningful artifacts like architecture, interior design, posters, and furniture. Moreover, the cultural approach foregrounds the human desire to see organizational life as an opportunity to do something meaningful (Gendron, 1999). In this chapter, we trace the history of the cultural approach, explore the social, methodological, and practical reasons for its popularity, and look at some of the ways it has been applied by researchers and managers. Finally, we outline a communication view of organizational culture to show how an organization's unique patterns of interaction and sense making work together over time to create its culture.

The Cultural Approach

Culture is undoubtedly a term with which you are familiar. When you hear the term, you most likely think about it in a broad sense, such as the differences between American culture and French culture. A closer view, however, reveals that within every national culture there are thousands of smaller cultures based on religion, ethnicity, and geography — among other things. Taking this one step farther, some have argued that individual organizations also develop cultures. In this chapter, we will talk at length about organizational culture, for whenever people organize in any fashion, a culture inevitably develops. But this still seems vague. What precisely do we mean by "culture"? How can one word serve to describe so many different kinds of social groups?

Anthropologist Marshall Sahlins (1976) defines culture as "meaningful orders of persons and things." By "meaningful orders," he means complex processes and relationships in a social grouping that are revealed through symbols. Thus, we learn about a culture not only by what its members say, but also by the tools they use to create the culture, by the values they display in cultural artifacts, and by their development and possession of things. More concretely, Clifford Geertz (1973) expands on his brief statement at the start of this chapter by defining culture as "an historically transmitted pattern of meanings embodied in symbols, a system of inherited conceptions expressed in symbolic form by means of which men [*sic*] communicate, perpetuate, and develop their knowledge about and attitudes toward life" (p. 89). And Edgar Schein (1994) offers this variation: "An organizational culture is a pattern of shared basic assumptions that have been invented, discovered, and/or developed by a group as it learns to cope with problems of external adaptation and internal integration" (p. 247).

A culture is also something like a religion. According to T. S. Eliot (1949), "No culture has appeared or developed except together with a religion . . . [and] the culture will appear to be the product of the religion, or the religion the product of the culture" (p. 13). Put another way, a culture is like a religion in that both locate a set of common beliefs and values that prescribes a general view of order (the way things are) and explanation (why things are that way). The tie between religion and culture is important to organizational studies because it indicates how the search for order and explanation compels beliefs.

However, not all members of a culture accept or practice those beliefs in the same way. Culture is never so much about agreement as it is about a common recognition or intelligibility. Like religions, most cultures include various sects or subcultures that share the common order but whose ways of understanding or carrying out their beliefs differ. This point underscores the importance of understanding an organization's culture or cultures as a dialogue with many different voices.

Cultures as Symbolic Constructions

The term *culture* is itself a symbol. For our purposes, it stands for the actions, practices, stories, and artifacts that characterize a particular organization. Similarly, we study the culture of an organization through its symbolic environment (e.g., the arrangement of parking lots, office cubicles, and conference rooms) as well as through its uses of symbols (e.g., topics of conversation, key vocabulary and jargon, treasured accomplishments and awards). The study of organizational cultures thereby involves interpreting the meanings of these symbolic constructions.

Viewing organizations as symbols requires several assumptions. First, all cultural studies begin with a fundamental appreciation of how human conceptions are formed in language. In this sense, then, language is the tool that both creates organizations and permits our understandings of them. Our search for meaningful orders of persons and things begins with what people say to one another about the meanings of things.

In addition, viewing organizations as symbolic constructions involves defining human beings as symbol-using animals, as Kenneth Burke does in his classic essay, "Definition of Man" (1966). (Table 5.1 provides a more detailed look at the terms of his definition.) Burke's view helps us understand why symbols both

TABLE 5.1

Burke's Definition of Man

Humans are:

1. *Symbol-using (and -abusing) animals:* Symbols are shorthand terms for situations (how we talk about an event reveals how we understand it). Symbols contain motives for actions (the words we use induce us to behave in particular ways).

2. *Inventors of the negative:* "Thou shalt not . . ." (we know what to do, in part, because of what we cannot or should not do). Action involves choice (choice assumes alternatives; alternatives imply opposites).

3. *Separated from our natural conditions by instruments of our own making:* Language separates us from other animals. Culture is made out of the technologies of language (e.g., alphabets), and culture further separates us from nature. Progress is a symbol that motivates technologies.

4. *Goaded by the spirit of hierarchy (or moved by a sense of order):* Just as language separates us from other animals, it also induces us to separate members of our culture from each other. Divisions among social classes, divisions of labor, and divisions of race, age, or gender start as divisions in language and end up as divisions in how we act toward each other. Guilt rooted in these divisions produces conflict and cooperation, both of which are necessary to maintain hierarchy.

5. *Rotten with perfection:* We strive toward absolutes (e.g., what we name as "right," "progress," "good," "beautiful," or "true").

Source: Kenneth Burke, *Language as Symbolic Action* (Berkeley: University of California Press, 1966).

represent, or stand for, other things and evoke other symbolic possibilities. For example, an organizational chart simultaneously provides information about hierarchy and relationships (e.g., formal lines of communication; formal status relations) and suggests possibilities for future action (e.g., getting promoted). That is, symbols do not only stand for other things; they also shape our understandings of those things and help us to identify their meanings and uses. As such, symbols are instruments of human understanding and action. A company that anticipates being sold, for example, begins to "talk" differently to itself, and these new ways of communicating in turn affect action, as a culture of apathy or cynicism may develop. The culture of an organization induces its members to think, act, and behave in particular ways. For instance, the homogeneous organizational cultures of PepsiCo and Disney are symbolically constructed by their individual members and serve as constraints on their members' actions and views.

Moreover, symbol using (or, depending upon one's perspective, symbol abusing) is an inherently human activity. As Kenneth Burke (1982) points out, "All animals eat, but we are the only [animals] who gossip about restaurants or exchange recipes." Similarly, cultures are human constructions of reality. Only human beings both make languages out of symbols and make cultures out of languages. Therefore, studying how and why we make cultures out of symbols and languages can tell us much about ourselves.

Historical and Cultural Background

The first known reference to organizational culture appeared in a 1979 article by Andrew Pettigrew published in *Administrative Science Quarterly*. The concept became immediately popular for a variety of reasons.

Factors Contributing to the Rise of Organizational Culture

Social Trends

The economic framework of the United States following World War II contributed to the popularity of the cultural approach to organizations in the Western nations. As sociologist Todd Gitlin (1987) explains,

> By 1945, the United States found itself an economic lord set far above the destroyed powers, its once and future competitors among both Allies and Axis powers. Inflation was negligible, so the increase in available dollars was actually buying more goods. Natural resources seemed plentiful, their supplies stable. . . . The Depression was over. And so were the deprivations of World War II, which also brought relative blessings: While European and Japanese factories were being pulverized,

new American factories were being built and old ones were back at work, shrinking unemployment to relatively negligible proportions. Once the war was over, consumer demand was a dynamo. Science was mobilized by industry, and capital was channeled by government as never before. The boom was on, and the cornucopia seemed all the more impressive because the miseries of the Depression and war were near enough to suffuse the present with a sense of relief. (p. 13)

As Gitlin goes on to point out, these sources of renewal and promise were balanced by powerful threats of nuclear holocaust in an atomic age. The tension created by these opposing influences helped shape the values of the new generation. Social, ethnic, racial, political, sexual, and economic tensions contributed to the complexity of the post–World War II climate, as did the new role of science in society, industry, and ideology. Since the Enlightenment, science had delivered on its promise of creating a more progressive and rational society. In the twentieth century, however, science demonstrated a new ability to create weapons that could destroy humanity. In industry, which since the Industrial Revolution had delivered the products and services that made life easier and more humane, inequalities between women and men and among ethnic and racial groups were sanctioned, and fierce competition for scarce natural resources and commodity markets contributed to worldwide tension. Similarly, new information technologies like radios, stereos, televisions, and satellites made information more accessible as well as more open to commentary. Ideological battles among capitalism, socialism, and communism threatened world peace and led to the Cold War.

The political landscape changed as well in the decades that followed World War II. The mid-1960s are commonly referred to by anthropologists, historians, and literary critics as the end of Western colonialism; European countries like England were forced to give up their colonies in Africa and elsewhere (Greenblatt, 1990; Said, 1978, 1984). With the end of colonialism came a redefinition of the role of Western interests in the political and economic subordination of Third World countries (Bhabha, 1990; Clifford & Marcus, 1985; Marcus & Fischer, 1986; Minh-Ha, 1991).

New global economic and political concerns also increased critical scrutiny of organizations. The emergence of multinational firms and a world economy dominated by capitalism and dependent on cheap labor in Third World countries exposed global problems and inequities, and the management of cultural differences in the workplace became important to firms doing business in other countries. Finding ways to improve cross-cultural understandings and communication skills was an integral component of the cultural approach to organizational communication.

In this turbulent social environment, new questions about organizations addressed such topics as power, participation, domination, and resistance in the workplace. For example, men exerted power over women by defining "real work" as that which was done outside of the home (by men) and "housework" as less worthy of compensation or respect. Housework was not valued for its major contributions to the ideals of family and society. As a result, housework brought women less status than men received for performing "real work." Furthermore, when women began to assert their right to work outside of the home and to assume positions of responsibility in the workforce (in secretarial, food preparation, elementary school teaching, and custodial jobs), they encountered widespread opposition by men.

Similarly, in the 1950s to 1970s, members of minority groups posed serious challenges to the Anglo elite that had long controlled their access to equality (the civil rights movement in the United States being a well-known example). These groups included people whose racial, ethnic, or religious heritage distinguished them from the dominant white majority, people with physical and mental disabilities, people who had served in the armed forces, and the elderly. They protested against unfair social and professional practices, discrimination, and oppression.

The social climate in which cultural studies of organizations emerged, then, was characterized by increased participation, globalization, diversity, and resistance to domination on the part of minority groups. The popularity of the cultural approach was thus tied to its focus on cultural differences within an organization or a society.

Methodology

The new focus on organizational cultures required a new vocabulary and new approaches for analyzing organizations and communication. Previously, the dominant vocabulary, derived from the fields of psychology, sociology, communication, and management, covered such topics as performance, motivation, and rewards, as well as work units, hierarchies, and the outcomes of group problem solving, decision making, and leadership. Our knowledge about organizations and communication was thus symbolically structured out of the theories, methods, and findings of the social sciences.

The anthropological vocabulary of the cultural approach gave organizational researchers, managers, and members new ways of viewing organizations, applying long-standing cultural concepts like values, rituals, and socialization (Table 5.2). Today, this language is commonly used by members of large corporations. It has both broadened the scope of what is considered important about organizations and communication and complicated our thinking about organizational communication processes. For example, the study of an organization's values is no longer limited to the domain of verbal messages; those values may also be found in artifacts and cartoons, in the layout of work space, even in the arrangement of cars in the employee parking lot (Goodall, 1989, 1990b).

How does one analyze organizational culture in a systematic way? The most common methodology has its roots in anthropology and is called "ethnography."

TABLE 5.2

Cultural Terms Applied to Organizational Communication Studies

SYMBOLS	LANGUAGE	METAPHORS

Words/actions	In-group speech
	    Technical terms
	    Jargon
	    Jokes
	    Gossip
	    Rumors
	    Gendered usage
		Determined by use within
		the culture

Artifacts
    Objects
    Cartoons
	Arrangement of the physical
	work space
	Personal meanings
	Humor in the workplace
	Social/political commentary
		Power/status
		Irony/contrast
		Resistance to domination

ROUTINES	RITUALS/RITES	COMMUNITIES
Repetitive behaviors	Individual performances Group performances New employee orientation Acceptance into group Promotions Annual celebrations Shunning/exclusion Retirement/layoffs	Continuity Acculturation Difference

USE OF OBJECTS	EMPLOYEE HANDBOOKS	REPRESENTATION
  Logos Awards	Company brochures Annual reports Identification Reward	 Symbolic unity Enhancement

Because anthropologists have long studied cultures, researchers sought to integrate anthropological research methods into cultural studies of organizations and communication (Geertz, 1973; Goodall, 1989, 1991a; Van Maanen, 1979, 1988). Successful organizations (e.g., Xerox) hire ethnographers to review and evaluate their company cultures. Ethnography, or the "writing of culture"

(Clifford & Marcus, 1985), recounts the researcher's reflections on the experiences of members of the culture. In writing an ethnographic account of Disneyland, John Van Maanen (1991), a management professor at the Massachusetts Institute of Technology with ties to anthropology and communication, relies on his recollections of working there while he was a student as well as his more recent observations of and interactions with employees and guests. Unlike traditional research methods in the social sciences, in which the researcher maintains distance from the group under study, ethnography requires the researcher to experience the culture firsthand. Van Maanen (1988) identifies three general types of ethnography: the *realist* tale, which conveys the basic elements of the culture in an objective way; the *impressionist* tale, which presents the research experience along with the findings, often in creative ways; and the *confessional* tale, which focuses on the emotional experience of the ethnographer in the cultural setting.

Organizational ethnography provides rich (or "thick") descriptions of organizational life, often capturing subtle points that are overlooked by traditional research methods. For example, consider the difference between a traditional written survey of patient satisfaction in a hospital and an ethnography of a hospital unit. Whereas the findings of the survey would likely be cut and dried and limited to the questions the researchers posed in advance, the ethnography would reveal more about the communication and sense-making processes of all parties involved, including many findings that might surprise the researcher. Ethnography is a stimulus for cultural dialogue as it exposes sources of power and resistance and reveals values and beliefs that might otherwise be taken for granted. Moreover, organizational ethnography encourages us to look beyond the managerial and profitability aspects of organizations and toward a definition of the workplace as a community. Office parties, softball games, provocative e-mail, rumors, and jokes can reveal much about the nature of an organization as a business and as a community.

The cultural approach attempts to bring communication research in line with developments in the philosophy of science. As physicists were altering their narratives about the universe based on Albert Einstein's relativity theories and, later, Werner Heisenberg's uncertainty principle, the social sciences were struggling for legitimacy. Measurements of human behavior continued to be modeled on the Newtonian notion of physics and mathematics, as social scientists remained loyal to the same model of theoretical physics that science had demonstrated as flawed (Smith, 1972). Relativity and uncertainty had yet to be incorporated into the new interpretive approach to the social sciences (Rabinow & Sullivan, 1986).

One way to understand the distinction between scientific and interpretive approaches to organizational communication is to think of relevant research questions as either problems or mysteries (Figure 5.1). Traditional social science research is based on the problem-solution method: Name a problem, and then work to solve it. This assumes that a known order already exists, or that the

FIGURE 5.1

Seeing an Issue as a Problem or Mystery

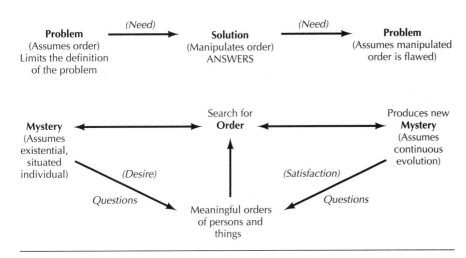

framework for understanding and making sense of an issue is already in place. The perception of a problem produces the need for a solution to the problem, and achieving a solution requires manipulating people or things within the existing order. These manipulations produce findings (the effects of the manipulations) and, it is hoped, solutions to the problem. In turn, the solutions to existing problems tend to produce new problems that call for new solutions. Thus, while the solutions tend to solve part of the puzzle, they also create new puzzles. But some researchers find fault with the problem-solution framework, arguing that the order being manipulated may not be representative of the actual order.

In contrast, cultural studies of organizations, and particularly ethnographies, tend to assume that the puzzle *is* the search for order. Researchers accept ambiguity, rather than try to resolve it. Furthermore, symbolic constructions of reality are mysteries containing clues for reading the culture. Mystery produces the desire for order — that is, for ways to question meaningful orders, for ways to make stories out of questions, and for ways to appreciate the critical terms of the ongoing dialogue. What can be known about organizations always exists in tension with what is unknown, and given the partiality of theory, nothing can ever be known completely. Thus, at the same time that they serve to explain some things, cultural studies of organizations also produce new mysteries about the meanings of orders, the functions of stories about the orders, and the relationship of these orders to a greater order beyond the organization.

While there are many ways to conduct interpretive research, the best studies capture the spirit and diversity of an organization's values and practices through evocative vocabulary or metaphor. For example, Van Maanen (1991) uses the metaphor of a "smile factory" in his cultural study of Disneyland. The image of smiles (friendly, fun, courteous) being manufactured (e.g., the products of a rigid assembly-line factory) establishes the tensions of a cultural dialogue between Disney management and Disney employees. By using this language, Van Maanen delineates the interplays of a staged performance: Employees are "members of a cast" who wear "costumes," not uniforms, and who exhibit onstage, offstage, and backstage behaviors. He also uses the image of the factory to discuss the production of smiles: formal rules about informal behaviors, and the prevalence of supervisory spies who note every infraction. The result is an account of a strong culture whose everyday use of language constructs a metaphor that, in turn, becomes its unique sense of place.

Organizational culture is the result of the cumulative learning of a group of people, and that learning manifests itself as culture at a number of levels. According to Edgar Schein (1991), culture is defined by six formal properties: (1) shared basic assumptions that are (2) invented, discovered, or developed by a given group as it (3) learns to cope with its problems of external adaptation and internal integration in ways that (4) have worked well enough to be considered valid and, therefore, (5) can be taught to new members of the group as the (6) correct way to perceive, think, and feel in relation to those problems.

Practicality

As we alluded to above, the study of organizational culture developed in response to global changes in society and new developments in science and social research. The business climate of the 1970s further contributed to the widespread popularity of such studies. This period was characterized by a significant increase in global competition that highlighted productivity problems in the United States. Although for many years the United States had been the world leader in many industries, it suddenly found itself eclipsed by other nations, most notably Japan. In many industries, Japanese manufacturing techniques threatened to prevail, and many wondered what made them so successful.

William Ouchi (1981) developed what he called "Theory Z" to describe Japanese management. As noted in Chapter 3, Douglas McGregor's (1960) Theories X and Y distinguish between the assumptions of classical management and human resources concerning individuals in organizations (i.e., people work because they *have to* versus people work because they *want to*). Ouchi's Theory Z holds that the survival and prosperity of organizations depend heavily on their ability to adapt to their surrounding cultures. He uses the term *culture* to refer to national standards of organizational performance, and in comparing those standards in the United States and Japan, he found some major differences at the time. For example, he contrasted the American emphasis on individual achievement with the Japanese emphasis on the performance and well-being of the collective. Ouchi thus proposed a Theory Z type of organization that would integrate individual achievement and advancement while also developing a sense of community in the workplace. A Theory Z organization would be capable of reducing negative influences and segmented decision making by incorporating new cultural values into the work environment.

The economic troubles of Asia at the closing of the twentieth century came as a surprise to most people and has caused many theorists to question the seemingly "magical" Japanese formulas. With hindsight, it appears that much of Japan's success was gained the old-fashioned way — through close informal contacts and partnerships, research and development of new products and services, and clever competitive tactics and strategy. As we write this, the Japanese are regrouping by revisiting what has worked for them in the past. Specifically, they are seeking to extend the Internet revolution to the majority of people in Japan.

By the mid-1980s, many traditional organizations were failing financially or soon in danger of doing so. The old prescriptions — more hierarchy, bureaucracy, division of labor, and standardization — were no longer effective, and it became clear that radical changes were required for companies to remain competitive. As business leaders began speaking of organizational change — in attitudes, values, and practices — they also began thinking about a holistic transformation in terms of organizational culture. One of the authors of this textbook (Eisenberg) received a phone call in 1983 from a CEO in search of someone who could "install a new culture" at his company. Managers were attracted to the idea even without much knowledge of how culture develops, much less how it could be altered. Many questions remained: What types of cultures are most productive? What aspects of culture are most closely associated with business success? Some tentative answers were provided in two successful books, both sponsored by the McKinsey Corporation, a management consulting firm. The first, Terrence Deal and Allen Kennedy's *Corporate Cultures: The Rites and Rituals of Corporate Life* (1982), defined the elements of strong cultures as (1) a supportive business environment; (2) dedication to a shared vision and values; (3) well-known corporate heroes; (4) effective rites and rituals; and (5) formal and informal communication networks. The other book, *In Search of Excellence* (1982) by Tom Peters and Robert Waterman, made the *New York Times* bestseller list for nonfiction. Its authors studied sixty-two financially successful companies and found eight common characteristics of their cultures:

1. *A bias for action.* Top-performing companies are characterized by active decision making; they are not characterized by thinking about decisions for long periods of time or relying on a lot of information to make decisions. If a change occurs in the business environment, they act.
2. *Close relations to the customer.* Top-performing companies never forget who makes them successful: their customers. One of the basics of excellence is to remember that service, reliability, innovation, and a constant concern for the customer are vital to any organization.

3. *Autonomy and entrepreneurship.* Top-performing companies empower their employees by encouraging risk taking, responsibility for the decisions they make and the actions they perform, and innovation. If an organization is too tightly controlled and the worker's performance is too tightly monitored, initiative, creativity, and willingness to take responsibility all tend to decay.

4. *Productivity through people.* A quality product depends on quality workers throughout the organization. Good customer relations depend on valuing service throughout the organization. Top-performing companies recognize these factors and rally against we-them or management-labor divisions.

5. *Hands-on, value-driven.* Top-performing companies are characterized by strong core values that are widely shared among employees and by an overall vision — a management philosophy — that guides everyday practices. Achievement is dependent on performance, and performance is dependent on values.

6. *Stick to the knitting.* Top-performing companies tend to be strictly focused on their source of product and service excellence. They tend not to diversify by going into other product or service fields. They expand their organization and profits by sticking to what they do best.

7. *Simple form, lean staff.* Top-performing companies are characterized by a lack of complicated hierarchies and divisions of labor. None of the companies surveyed maintained a typical bureaucratic form of organizing. Many of them employed fewer than one hundred people.

8. *Simultaneous loose-tight properties.* Top-performing companies are difficult to categorize. They encourage individual action and responsibility and yet retain strong core values; they encourage individual and group decision making. They are neither centralized nor decentralized in management style because they adapt to new situations with whatever is needed to get the job done.

Over two decades later, this list of qualities remains a good reference point for the design and analysis of organizational cultures. Since the publication of *In Search of Excellence*, Peters has gone on to refine his thinking in a series of books, placing even more emphasis on customers and the need to manage amidst chaos. An interesting aside is that some of the companies that made Peters and Waterman's initial list have had great difficulty sustaining their success, partly because they misread market trends and partly because a value-based system is difficult to sustain over a long period of time. A related critique is that "strong corporate cultures" naturally spawn employee resistance and may eventually lead to serious internal conflicts. All of this is further proof of our contention that no single approach to organizing will work everywhere and for all time.

Academic ethnographers have a lot to say about the failures of strong corporate cultures. In 1993, Gideon Kunda published an ethnographic study on the power relationships affecting workers' lives in a high-tech engineering firm that challenges many of the assumptions of Deal and Kennedy (1982) and Peters and Waterman (1982). From interviews, observations, and a close reading of the culture's everyday activities, Kunda concludes that the control and commitment features of strong cultures are the most problematic. Specifically, attempts to "engineer culture" to look a certain way are flawed. Over time, workers may come to question the authenticity of any emotions and beliefs associated with the company. Moreover, workers may learn the lessons of strong cultural performances so well that they seem driven to make irony "the dominant mode of their everyday existence" (Kunda, 1993, p. 216). In such an organization, employee talk is uniformly cynical and sarcastic, reflecting a deep discomfort with commitment to the "party line" endorsed by the organization. This has happened to a degree in the way some Disney employees talk about their "loyalty" to "the mouse."

Kunda's study is valuable because it offers balance to what can at times seem to be a one-sided conversation about the benefits of a strong culture. In our role as organizational communication consultants, we are more often confronted by just the opposite: companies who claim dysfunctional cultures and seek our assistance in determining how they got that way and how they might change. A worst-case scenario is a company culture that supports unethical behavior. The following kinds of cultures are most likely to encourage questionable ethical practices:

1. A culture of broken promises
2. A culture where no one takes responsibility
3. A culture that denies participation and dissent

In 2002 the dramatic implications of questionable ethical practices within one well-known corporate culture — Enron — provided many people with new doubts about the benefits of working in a strong culture. In what was widely reported as a business culture of "cockiness and arrogance" (Sloan, 2002) that thrived on acute competitiveness among employees and intense aggressiveness in the marketplace, meteoric success quickly turned into dramatic failure. Enron, a Houston-based natural gas and electricity company, whose stock in December 2000 had been valued at $84.87/share, and whose sign greeting visitors at corporate headquarters proclaimed it to be "the world's leading company," found itself bankrupt with shares trading for less than $1/share less than one year later. The question quickly became: How did this happen? Soon, news reports of questionable or illegal accounting practices, dishonest communication with stockholders and customers, and insider loans to employees holding the highest positions in the company provided striking evidence of what can go wrong when the shared cultural values that help make a company strong cross moral, ethical, and legal boundaries.

Enron's collapse was not suffered in isolation, however, as corporate cultures around the globe came under scrutiny. New ethical questions — about the need for corporations to keep their promises to employees, customers, and stockholders; the moral climate informing accounting practices, including personal and fiscal responsibility for decision making; and the role of employee voice and dissent — have contributed to criminal indictments for executive officers of other large, publicly traded companies as well as major revisions to the codes of conduct guiding corporations and their boards. A new federal law now requires the signature of the CEO on all annual financial reports, which, for those who study organizational cultures, is a potent legal symbol that must be read as an important cultural sign.

Not all strong cultures behave badly. By contrast, one need only look to the heroic efforts of firefighters and police — notoriously strong cultures — in the events immediately following the collapse of the World Trade Center towers on 9/11 — to locate the other side of this story. This is because not all strong cultures are formed out of the same values and practices, nor are they guided by the same vision of leadership. Unlike the individualized corporate greed, aggressiveness, and "winner take all" attitude of the Enron executives, the women and men of the police and fire departments responding to 9/11 shared the values of teamwork, cooperation, and personal sacrifice, and were guided by a responsible vision of leadership, which translated into doing their jobs, to the best of their abilities, for the greater good of the public (Langewiesche, 2002).

These examples teach us that the story of organizational cultures is both important and multifaceted. In the next section we explain five ways to help make sense of it.

Five Views of Organizational Culture

As we have seen, various social, methodological, and practical concerns contributed to the rise of the cultural approach. Research on organizational culture has focused on five major areas of study: comparative management, corporate culture, organizational cognition, organizational symbolism, and critical and postmodern perspectives.

Comparative Management

The comparative management view of organizational culture treats culture as some "thing" imported into organizations through the national, regional, and ethnic affiliations of employees. It looks at companies operating in various parts of the world to show how differences in national and local culture are revealed in the workplace. Among the best-known researchers in this area of study, Grete Hofstede (1983, 1991) found that at IBM offices, which are located all over the world, there is no uniform culture; instead, versions of the company's culture are adapted to local ways of life. In a more recent study of comparative management, Miriam Erez and Christopher Earley (1993) define organizational culture as a set of mental programs that control behavior. They determine that these programs vary among countries due to differences in national cultures. A familiar contrast exists between geographical regions that emphasize rules and procedures (e.g., North America) versus those that rely more on personal relationships and politics (e.g., Latin America).

A fascinating example of the comparative management approach is Hedrick Smith's (1995) work on global capitalism. According to Smith, the vast differences among organizations in the United States, Japan, and Germany are largely tied to aspects of their national cultures. Organizations in the United States tend to develop cultures that value individual achievement rather than team recognition and reward. In contrast, Japanese organizational cultures place a high value on teamwork and community and tend not to tolerate creative individuals who are isolated from the community. In Germany, workers are both individually and communally oriented, define creativity as precision, and expect to be led by a strong national government. The limitation of the German view is that it is more rigid and less open to change in response to a changing economic and social environment.

The comparative management view of culture is not limited to the comparison of whole countries; regional differences can also influence organizational cultures. For example, a brokerage house with offices in Mississippi and New York can expect differences in how employees at the two offices relate to deadlines and schedules. Southern culture tends to be more laid-back, whereas New Yorkers by and large pride themselves on moving at a frenetic pace.

Despite these interesting contrasts, the comparative-management view of culture may become less useful as global economics turns many organizations and their employees into travelers and differences among national cultures dissolve (Clifford, 1992). In the past, employees traveled less, and the differences between countries were marked. Today, many big cities look alike. The homogenization of global culture bears directly on the tension between creativity and constraint. As large multinational organizations pursue global markets, corporate colonization threatens to minimize local differences. This means that people everywhere, as both employees and consumers, feel more constrained by dominant multinational companies (e.g., we are forced to organize our lives around Microsoft, GE, McDonald's, and Disney) and are increasingly less able to create and sustain anything that is genuinely different or out of line with dominant trends.

Corporate Culture

Whereas comparative management sees culture as a "thing" imported into an organization, the corporate-culture view sees culture as something that an organization possesses, manages, and exploits to enhance productivity. Culture is "a rational instrument designed by top management to shape the behavior of the employees in purposive ways" (Ouchi & Wilkins, 1985, p. 462). PepsiCo, Hyatt, McDonald's, Microsoft, and Disney, for example, are noted for their strong corporate cultures. Each invests tens of millions of dollars annually in the selection and indoctrination of employees into their company's way of doing things. Companies with strong corporate cultures can be highly profitable. They also tend to encourage a strong sense of commitment among their employees. However, such companies may require employees to give up significant freedoms (even in the area of personal appearance) in exchange for membership.

Moreover, managers seeking to manipulate corporate culture for business results may do an inadequate job of considering the investments in people and processes that are required to reach these goals. Bausch & Lomb is a famous example of a company aggressively pursuing a "culture of accountability" that stumbled due to its neglect of the reward systems and company values needed to support improved performance.

Not all companies with strong corporate cultures are this unbalanced, however. Many successful companies today are in the process of replacing top-down management processes with management that is driven by a vision of the future and a set of corporate values. Under this scenario, leadership's main role is to help employees understand and work according to the organization's vision and values. When this approach succeeds, the result is an organizational culture characterized by attention to process improvement as well as employees' supervision of their own behavior. (More on the pros and cons of this development in the next chapter.)

In a multisite study relating corporate culture to performance, John Kotter and James Heskett (1992) found that value consensus can enhance organizational performance, but only under the following circumstances:

1. When people agree on the importance of adapting to a changing environment (i.e., continuous learning or improvement);
2. When a strong entrepreneur is present who also adapts well to change; and
3. When an effective business strategy is in place to supplement the organization's vision and values.

Despite sustained criticism of the corporate-culture view as too controlling and reminiscent of Theory X (Alvesson, 1993; Smircich & Calas, 1987), it continues to have currency in contemporary organizations. Despite its misalignment with the anthropological view (which sees cultures as organic, emergent, and impossible to control), the approach — much like early human relations — has brought certain benefits. It has introduced a useful vocabulary for directing managers' attention toward communication practices and the human side of business, for example.

Organizational Cognition

The organizational-cognition perspective defines culture not as something imported or imposed, but as a way of thinking that is shared by members of an organization. As such, it is implicit in discussions of shared meaning, shared values, and shared rules. Robert LeVine (1984) points out the value of cognition with respect to human communities in general:

> Every human community functions with a group consensus about the meanings of symbols used in the communications that constitute their social life, however variable their behavior and attitudes in other respects, because such a consensus is as necessary for encoding and decoding messages in social communication in general as agreement about speech rules is to encoding and decoding in linguistic mode. (p. 69)

Many other observers have applied organizational cognition to the study of organizations. For example, Mary Mohan (1993) examines cultural "penetration," or the degree to which an organization's members share similar meanings for things. Similarly, Sonja Sackmann (1991) asserts that "a collection of people [is] a cultural grouping [because] the people hold the same cognitions in common" (p. 40). Pamela Shockley-Zalabak and Donald Morley's (1994) analysis of shared values in a computer company demonstrates a strong relationship between the values of the company's founders and of new employees that persists over time.

The organizational-cognition view of culture is appealing in part because it reflects how most people think about communication and relationships: that people have ideas and through communication they can share meaning with one another. However, no precise method exists for verifying whether two or more people actually share meanings of values or rules. These determinations are made only on the basis of what people say and do. For this reason, critics of organizational cognition argue that culture is more closely tied to coordinated practices than to cognitive alignment. Although the sense-making process contributes to the development of culture, that process is viewed as occurring between people rather than within people (such that social reality is coconstructed in communication). Therefore, while culture is still related to "the meaningful orders of persons and things," meaning is viewed as public or social, not private, and the importance of cognition is dependent upon its relationship to ongoing actions and behaviors.

Organizational Symbolism

According to organizational symbolism, culture is not what is imported, imposed, or shared directly. Instead, culture is indirectly revealed through language, stories, nonverbal messages, and communicative exchanges. Although management scholars have long limited their use of the term *symbolism* to the meanings of such things as corporate logos and value statements, more recent scholars focus on a broader view of symbolism in organizations. This broader view focuses on the subtle ways in which communication works to build, reproduce, and transform the taken-for-granted reality of organizational culture. Studies of this kind adopt the more general label *interpretive*, suggesting a move from focusing on specialized symbols to the interpretation of all organizational action as potentially having meaning. This research can be traced to a group of management and communication scholars who first met in Alta, Utah, in 1983. Organized by Linda Putnam and Michael Pacanowsky, this conference and a resulting book (Putnam & Pacanowsky, 1983) helped legitimize interpretive and cultural studies of organizational communication. Around the same time, an influential article by Pacanowsky and Nick O'Donnell-Trujillo (1983) helped establish organizational communication as a form of cultural performance.

David Boje (1991, 1995), an organizational researcher, has suggested that organizations are mainly storytelling systems. The stories or narratives about the organization's culture convey information about its current state of affairs, and as such the stories serve as resources for everyday sense making (Wilkins, 1984). As noted in Chapter 4, when an organization is viewed as a system — in this case, a storytelling system — modifications represent feedback. Paying attention to stories and how they change can be important for employees and managers alike (Mitroff & Kilmann, 1975).

Organizational stories may be found in speeches and casual conversations, as well as in employee newsletters, company brochures, strategic planning statements, corporate advertisements, fund-raising campaigns, and training videos (Goodall, 1989; Pacanowsky, 1988). These forums provide opportunities for the organization to talk about its values and aspirations. However, different stories about the organization are told by different narrators. The corporate or official story about the organization may be told by advertising agents working in conjunction with high-level managers and stockholders. The inside stories are told by employees of the organization, who may offer different accounts. In two recent investigations into the working conditions of fruit pickers and employees of manufacturing plants in the Carolinas, the accounts given by the business owners and managers differed greatly from the accounts given by the employees. The story told by the owners and managers focused on the number of people employed by the companies, product quality, and reasonable cost to consumers. In contrast, the story told by employees focused on low wages (sometimes paid in the form of crack cocaine or alcohol) and unsafe workplaces. Federal investigations and congressional hearings followed.

Clearly, organizational stories represent the interests and values of the storytellers. In the preceding example, neither side's narrative captured the whole story. Usually, multiple stories or interpretations are needed to describe an organization's culture. These stories represent different voices as well as potential dialogues among individuals and groups within the organization. Therefore, we can think of an organization's culture as a potential dialogue of subcultures or as a many-sided story (Boje, 1995).

In an attempt to advance the study of organizational symbolism, Charles Bantz (1993) describes a technique for analyzing messages and their interpretations. Using his method, one can analyze important aspects of vocabulary, identify key themes, and infer norms, motives, and interpretations that characterize a particular organization's culture. However, there is a risk associated with making inferences about an organization's culture from its members' use of symbols in that the use and meaning of symbols change over time. Another study attempts to deal with this issue by extending Edgar Schein's (1988) six-part definition of culture to include how, over time, people's assumptions develop into values, how those values become realized as artifacts, and how the artifacts take on meaning through symbols (Hatch, 1993).

Despite the lack of agreement on how to define symbolism, this approach to understanding culture has shifted our focus toward how people communicate and create meaning in dialogue. However, symbolic displays must be considered in practical contexts, not as isolated events. Just as a joke, a story, choice of words, or a ritual can be misleading out of context, symbols should be studied in ways that link them to the realities of work (Alvesson, 1993). In so doing, this view of culture gives us access to the social construction of meaning as well as its consequences.

Critical and Postmodern Views

Research on organizational culture has moved significantly in the direction of the critical and postmodern views (which is why Chapters 6 and 7 are devoted to more detailed discussions of these topics). Three researchers who have made significant contributions to this line of work are Stanley Deetz, Dwight Conquergood, and Joanne Martin.

Deetz and others (Atkouf, 1992; Smircich & Calas, 1987) argue that the managerial bias in culture research reinforces the "corporate colonization of the life-world" through which the interests of corporations frame all aspects of daily living (Deetz, 1991). These critics call for organizational ethnographers to examine issues of power and domination associated with the development, maintenance, or transformation of a particular culture. They believe the transcripts chronicling the lives of those with less power in organizations should be exposed and read, so that alternatives to the dominant culture can be considered.

According to Conquergood (1991), cultures are composed of ongoing dialogues that are variously "complicit" or "engaged." A dialogue is complicit when the participants accept or go along with the dominant interpretation of meaning. In contrast, a dialogue is engaged when the participants challenge the dominant interpretation with an alternative explanation. Both types of dialogue exist in most organizations. As a result, an organization's culture is characterized by multiple conflicting meanings and a constant struggle for interpretive control.

Conquergood's ethnographic work, which focuses on Chicago street gangs, Hmong refugees, and Palestinians, prompts a radical rethinking of cultural study. His critique moves us toward a critical perspective on issues of power and a postmodern perspective on the research process. He outlines four themes in the critical rethinking of cultural study: (1) the return of the body; (2) boundaries and borderlands; (3) the rise of performance; and (4) rhetorical reflexivity.

By the first, the return of the body, Conquergood calls for the physical immersion of the researcher in the organization. Although participant observation has always been an integral part of ethnographic study, Conquergood's version of it is more radical and based on the idea that closeness brings the ethnographer in touch with more than just the visual aspects of a culture (Stoller, 1989):

> This rethinking of ethnography is primarily about speaking and listening, instead of observing. . . . Sight and surveillance depend on detachment and distance. . . . Metaphors of sound, on the other hand, privilege temporal processes, proximity, and incorporation. Listening is an interiorizing experience . . . whereas observation sizes up exteriors. . . . The return of the body . . . shifts the emphasis from space to time, from sight and vision to sound and voice, from text to performance, from authority to vulnerability. (Conquergood, 1991, p. 183)

In discussing boundaries and borderlands, Conquergood advances the idea that "pure" cultures are an endangered species, as formerly isolated organizations dissolve their boundaries through strategic alliances, joint ventures, and global marketing. As employees increasingly see themselves as self-employed providers of skills under the new social contract (see Chapter 1), cultures may come to exist between organizations as well as within them.

By the rise of performance, Conquergood focuses our attention on behaviors, practices, and other nonverbal modes of communication within cultures. "Issues and attitudes are expressed and contexted in dance, music, gesture, food, ritual, artifact, symbolic action, as well as words" (p. 189).

Finally, rhetorical reflexivity refers to the realization that there is no single authoritative account of a culture. Instead, organizational ethnographies reflect as much the writer's biases and worldview as they do the place and people under study. Therefore, multiple studies of an organization's culture need not agree to be useful; each ethnography adds dimensions and voices that the others may have missed. It is this attitude toward knowledge and truth as never final and best found in speaking and listening that characterizes the postmodern approach to organizational culture.

The final writer we will consider is Joanne Martin, who has contributed significantly to the development of a taxonomy of perspectives on organizational culture that takes into account the movement toward a postmodern view. According to Martin (1992), perspectives on culture can be characterized as highlighting integration, differentiation, or fragmentation. Although studies of organizations typically take one perspective, most organizations contain all three. Each perspective reveals a different orientation to three key features of cultural study: orientation to consensus, relation among divergent manifestations, and orientation to ambiguity. Let us consider each perspective in detail.

Integration

The integration perspective portrays culture in terms of consistency and clarity. From this perspective, it appears that cultural members agree about what they are to do and why they do it. There appears to be no room for ambiguity. In addition, an organization's culture is portrayed as a monologue, not a dialogue (May, 1988). This tradition in the cultural study of organizations is evident in Tom Peters and Robert Waterman's (1982) descriptions of excellent companies with strong cultures that adhere to a narrow set of shared values, meanings, and interpretations. Similarly, studies that analyze the influence of the organization's founder tend to trace those influences throughout the organization (Barley, 1983; Pacanowsky, 1988; Schein, 1991), sometimes to the neglect of competing values within the company (McDonald, 1988). Indeed, the integration perspective typically favors the story of those in power over other competing stories.

Differentiation

Whereas an integration perspective focuses on agreement, a differentiation perspective highlights differences. The differentiation perspective portrays cultural manifestations as predominantly inconsistent with one another (such as when a formal policy is undermined by informal norms). Furthermore, when consensus does emerge, the differentiation view is quick to point out its limitations (e.g., that agreement may only exist among a group or subculture of members). From the standpoint of the total organization, differentiated subcultures can coexist in harmony, conflict, or indifference to one another. These subcultures are viewed as islands of clarity, and ambiguity is channeled outside of their boundaries (Frost, Moore, Louis, Lundberg, & Martin, 1991).

In addition, the differentiation perspective sees organizational cultures as contested political domains in which the potential for genuine dialogue is often impaired. The various subcultures may seldom speak to one another, instead reinforcing their own accounts of organizational meanings without seeking external validation. As a result, they do not actively participate in the broader interests of the organization.

For example, one study revealed that a computer software firm had created barriers to its subcultures' communication when it moved to a new location (Goodall, 1990a). Work groups were physically separated from one another, promoting competition for resources among them. In another study, a conflict between managers and employees over a pay freeze was masked at an annual breakfast by a group of speakers hired to create a story that favored management's position (Rosen, 1985). The ploy was unsuccessful and deepened the division between the two groups. Divisions among classes of employees often occupy the interests of subcultures, and the differentiation perspective can show how conflict among subcultures may be avoided, masked, or neglected.

Fragmentation

From a fragmentation perspective, ambiguity is an inevitable and pervasive aspect of contemporary life. Studies in this area focus on the experience and expression of ambiguity within organizational cultures, wherein consensus and dissensus coexist in a constantly fluctuating pattern of change. Any cultural manifestation can be interpreted in a myriad of ways because clear consensus among organizational subcultures cannot be attained.

Consistent with newer theories of organizations and society (see Chapter 7), the fragmentation perspective replaces certainty with ambiguity as a model for interpretation. Furthermore, ambiguity can be manipulated by management to support management's interests and by disempowered employees to cope with their interests (Eisenberg, 1984; Myerson, 1991). Ambiguity's application to organizational communication has been varied. For example, it has been used to explain the divergent accounts of an airline disaster given by eyewitnesses (Weick, 1990), the writing of noninfluential policy statements by analysts with vested interests in writing influential statements (Feldman, 1991), and the ways in which urban dwellers interpret the meanings of living space in cities and parks (De Certeau, 1984).

The meaning of ambiguity for our concept of organizational cultures as dialogue depends on how we define dialogue. If dialogue is viewed as a means of generating consensus, then ambiguity makes dialogue unlikely. Conversely, if dialogue is thought of as embodying a respect for diversity — and perhaps a form of consensus based on acknowledgment of differences — then ambiguity is a necessary component of dialogue. Furthermore, unlike ambiguity about shared meanings or interpretations of culture, multiple meanings are inevitably found in ambiguities about shared practices. Recall that in the interpretive perspective, shared practices and multiple interpretations of meaning for those practices are highly valued. For us, then, ambiguity is a necessary component of dialogue. Indeed, genuine dialogue probably would not exist without ambiguity, for if everything were clearly understood, there would not be much left to talk about (Boje, 1995).

A recent ethnography focusing on how one university selected its chief academic officer shows the usefulness of Joanne Martin's taxonomy (Eisenberg, Murphy, & Andrews, 1998). In this year-long study, various interpretations of the university's search process were offered by both participants and the researchers, and these accounts are shown to reflect all three of Martin's perspectives. Some saw the search process as highly rational, with the choice of the leading candidate an inevitable result. Others described the process as highly political; still others saw it as rife with ambiguity and confusion from the outset. A traditional researcher might ask, Who is right? We chose instead to describe the ways in which participants selected their interpretation with their audience in mind and felt free to offer differing interpretations at different occasions. We concluded that using all three perspectives provided a richer view of the search process than any one taken alone.

A Communication Perspective on Organizational Culture

Reviewing the body of research on organizational culture is a tantalizing and confusing task. Just about anything is regarded as culture, and studies purporting to study culture do so in dramatically different ways. As a result, no consistent treatment of communication has emerged in the culture literature.

For this reason, we propose the following view of communication and organizational culture. From this perspective, theories of organizational culture have the following characteristics:

1. They view communication as the core process by which culture is formed and transformed and see culture as patterns of behavior and their interpretation.
2. They acknowledge the importance of everyday communication as well as more notable symbolic expressions.
3. They encompass not only words and actions, but also all types of nonverbal communication (such as machinery, artifacts, and work processes).
4. They include broad patterns of interaction in society at large and examine how they are played out in the workplace. Therefore, they view each organization's culture as a cultural nexus of national, local, familial, and other forces outside of the organization (Martin, 1992).
5. They acknowledge the legitimacy of multiple motives for researching culture, from improving corporate performance to overthrowing existing power structures.

SUMMARY

Cultural studies of organizations and communication emerged in response to a variety of social, historical, and political issues. These studies focus on the meaningful orders of people and things and are usually written as ethnographies. The ethnographic format has been the focus of much controversy, such as whether the ethnographer's perspectives can be generalized and translated into practical managerial strategies. Studies of organizational cultures also tend to use the research methods and vocabulary of cultural anthropology. References to rituals, rites, cultural performances, symbols, languages, values, and artifacts are made to discuss the meanings of individuals and groups in organizational cultures. Researchers tend to classify cultures as integrated, differentiated, or fragmented and tend to use these distinctions in discussions of consensus, values, and conflict. Some researchers look beyond these categories toward a postmodern account of culture that is based on immersion in the organization. *What Would You Do?* 5.1 encourages you to think more deeply about the decisions behind conducting an organizational ethnography.

Although the cultural approach to organizations and communication yields interesting and informative accounts of everyday work life, questions have emerged about how much trust we can place in these accounts and what we can productively do with them. However, these limitations are not unique to the cultural approach; the systems, human relations, human resources, scientific management, and critical approaches share the potential for misunderstanding, misapplication, and abuse. Unlike these other approaches, however, the cultural approach relies on literary narratives about personal experiences and meanings. It is this characteristic of the cultural approach that has been criticized by researchers, managers, and employees who favor the more traditional social science methods aimed at explanation, prediction, and control.

Changes in the world of work will inevitably affect the usefulness of the cultural approach to organizations. As the relationships between employers and employees change from long-term to shorter-term commitments, organizational cultures may become more homogeneous or less well defined. In addition, communication technology is likely to affect organizational cultures as interaction via computers continues to augment face-to-face communication. The smaller cultural networks created by electronic communication may eventually provide alternatives to a corporate culture.

What role does the cultural approach play in achieving a balance between individual creativity and institutional constraint? While scientific management had tipped the scale toward institutional constraints, and human relations and human resources had tipped it back toward individual creativity, the same equation does not apply to systems and cultures. These perspectives complicate our thinking about organizational communication as well as issues of creativity and constraint. Gone is the straightforward view of creativity versus constraint; we are now faced with such complex issues as the ambiguities of symbols used to construct and interpret potential meanings for creativity or constraint. Apparently "simple" messages serve multiple, even conflicting, purposes, depending on where you stand. Studying organizations today is — much like actually participating in one — an activity rife with possibility. It is our relationship with such possibilities (whether it makes us anxious or excited) that in part determines our success in working with these ideas.

What Would You Do? 5.1

THE POLITICS OF INTERPRETING CULTURE

Ethnographers (Conquergood, 1991; Thomas, 1993) often ask the question, Who gets to speak for whom? In studies of organizations, this question targets fundamental communication problems: Who owns the right to speak for a company's culture? Do employees own that right, and if so, at what level is the correct interpretation of meaning found? At the senior executive level? Middle manager? Staff? Customer and supplier? Some combination of these levels? Or does the right to speak for the culture reside with academic researchers and other outsiders?

Within these issues lie many challenges to researchers. Every act of communication is partial, partisan, and problematic; this is true of interpretation as well. The issues also speak to an ethical challenge: What are the consequences of making statements about an organization's culture? This challenge often divides researchers into two ideological camps. On the left are those who assert that Marxist, feminist, and critical theories of the "production and consumption of culture" provide the appropriate frameworks for the interpretations of cultures (see Chapter 6). On the right are those who assert that what gets lost in leftist critiques about production and consumption is a literature that can be appreciated for its inspiration and poetry.

While this debate rages on campuses and in academic journals, organizations struggle to survive in the increasingly competitive global marketplace. Academic studies of organizational culture, particularly those derived from liberal sympathies, often seem unnecessarily tedious. Although we have learned that culture is important to the success of a business, seldom do these studies present clear findings that can be applied to all organizations. As a result, the gulf between academic and business interests has widened.

Let's assume that you are interested in conducting a cultural analysis of an organization. For the purposes of self-reflection, let's assume this organization is either a political party or a religious foundation.

Discussion Questions

1. What ethical issues would you address? How would your ideological commitments shape your study?
2. Why do a cultural analysis of an organization? Who would benefit? Who would you speak for?
3. How has culture itself affected your style of seeing, observing, talking about, writing about, and thinking about cultural issues? What directs your critical attention to particular interpretations of meanings?

The cultural approach values meaningful orders derived from symbolic constructions, but further research is needed to determine whether those meaningful orders are limited to what appears on the surface of a culture or whether clues to deeper structures of power, status, or personality exist. In conclusion, then, we offer the following thoughts on organizational culture and research:

> A culture — any culture — is like an ocean. There are many wonderful things and creatures in it that we may never understand; they change and so do we, regardless of the depth or perspective of our study. But the ocean is also made up of waves that are as regular as the cycles of the moon, and just as mysteriously musical, powerful, and enchanting. The top millimeter of the ocean is a world unto itself, and a vital one, in which the broader secrets of biological and evolutionary life . . . are contained. But even their meanings must be read in a vocabulary that is separate and distant. . . . So it is that within that millimeter, among those waves, we find clear and recurring themes. Like the great questions about culture that we pursue, those themes are always with us and not yet fully understood. (Goodall, 1990a, p. 97)

QUESTIONS FOR REVIEW AND DISCUSSION

1. What is culture? What makes studying an organization's culture different from studying French or British culture?

2. Why are symbolic action and metaphor central to the study of organizational cultures?

3. What were the historical, political, and social trends that contributed to the development of cultural studies of organizations?

4. What major questions are posed by viewing organizations as cultures?

5. Compare and contrast the major characteristics of the five approaches to organizational culture.

6. What are the advantages and limitations of studying organizations as cultures?

7. What are the characteristics of a communication perspective on organizational culture?

CASE STUDY I

The New Dojo

The sport of Judo has been good to Hank Tagawa. A sixth-degree (dan) black belt in the sport, Hank was born in Osaka, Japan, in 1965. He competed for years at the highest international level and won both a world championship and a silver medal in the 1992 Olympics. Eventually he settled in Pensacola, Florida, where he met and married an Anglo woman and began to put down roots in the community.

A shy, focused, but highly likeable man, Hank had been encouraged for years to consider opening his own judo school (dojo). About a year ago, Hank got the money together and did so. At first, the new dojo, at which Hank was the head teacher (sensei), had few students, but he was not interested in advertising, which he felt would appear too pushy. After a few months, however, there was an explosion of interest, both from parents bringing their small children for lessons and from men and women from a nearby military base who had heard of Hank's history and sought out the new dojo as a solid place to train. He set up classes for both children and adults and enjoyed both the cashflow and the camaraderie. He recruited a number of his former Olympic teammates from Osaka to visit for extended periods and to help out as instructors in the new dojo.

Hank's foremost concern is his desire to teach judo the "right" way, the way he was taught at the Kodokan Judo Dojo in Japan. This includes enforcing strict rules for the cleanliness and appearance of mats and uniforms, as well as rules for the respectful address of people of more senior ranks. Students are taught to bow to their teachers and superiors, speak some Japanese, and carry themselves with a quiet dignity both in and outside of the dojo.

After a year in operation, however, the dojo's attendance is starting to drop off. Sensei Tagawa has not deviated in his commitment to "doing things the right way," but many students have been unwilling or unable to tolerate his discipline. Furthermore, students from the military base resent his characterization of them as too aggressive, and parents are concerned about the visiting instructors, who force their children to do push-ups for bad behavior or, worse yet, to exercise to the point of exhaustion as a way of building endurance.

(continued)

Sensei Tagawa has come to you for advice about saving his dojo. He's ready to conclude that he is just not cut out for teaching, but you suspect that there is more to the story.

ASSIGNMENT

Given what you know about organizational communication and culture, answer the following questions:

1. Describe the organizational culture of the dojo. What is the origin of these beliefs, assumptions, attitudes, and practices?
2. Would you characterize the dojo culture as strong or homogeneous? Why or why not? Are there subcultures? Kinds of resistance?
3. How would you describe the interaction among different cultural perspectives at the dojo?
4. How do you feel about the Sensei's desire to ensure that his school teaches the "right" way? What are the pros and cons of his taking this approach?
5. At this point in the story, what advice would you give Sensei Tagawa about future actions? Can the dojo be saved, and if so, how?
6. How is this case similar to challenges faced by other organizations? How might we apply lessons from the dojo to a start-up plan for another, similar organization?

CASE STUDY II

Studying the Culture of Meetings

Helen Schwartzman asserts in *Ethnography in Organizations* (1993) that "nothing could be more commonplace than meetings in organizations," yet most studies of organizational cultures fail to look closely at the exchanges of talk at those meetings (p. 38). She argues that close readings of those exchanges can tell us much about various aspects of a company's culture: power; domination; resistance to domination; gender, race, and class divisions; concepts of time and money; and regional differences, among others. Her argument is compelling.

ASSIGNMENT

As a student of organizational communication and a member of an organization (your class, college, sorority/fraternity, or place of employment), you are likely intrigued by the idea that meetings hold important clues to organizational cultures. For this case study, you will immerse yourself in a culture in order to understand, analyze, and write about it in the form of an ethnography. You will collect the data to be analyzed and then write about it using what you have learned in this and other chapters. Here are some guidelines for conducting your cultural study:

1. Record and transcribe the exchanges between members of the group, team, or organization at one or more of its meetings. Use the following questions and illustrations to guide your work:

    a. Who opens the meeting? Who takes notes? Answering these questions should tell you something about the leadership of the meeting, as well as the role of one or more of the group members.

    b. In general, who says what to whom with what effect? Answering this question may help you isolate particular relationships and power structures.

    c. Pay close attention to exchanges of conversation — both on-topic and off-topic — that occur during the meeting. What are the exchanges "about"? What do they say about the role and relative power of the group members? What is the role of silence in the group? Is anyone excluded from the talk?

    d. What is the function of humor in the group, if any?

(continued)

e. What clothing do the group members wear to the meeting? Is there a relationship between their clothing and the conduct of the meeting (e.g., formal, informal)?

f. Does the group use a particular style of language? For example, is it highly technical? Does it contain a lot of jargon or slang? Can you tell "who is in the know" just by listening? Can you tell who isn't? Is there any attempt to mentor newer group members? Are there any metaphors that recur in the group and seem to suggest a common understanding?

g. What other affiliations or associations can you assume characterize these group members' lives outside of this meeting? How much of those extra-meeting cultures are brought into the culture of the meeting?

h. How do the meetings end? Are assignments made? Are they equitably apportioned? How much does expertise play a role in the assignments? How about friendship?

2. Decide how you will analyze the data based on your reading in this and other chapters. For example,

a. What management or communication approach (e.g., scientific management, human relations, human resources, systems, cultures, etc.) best characterizes the meeting?

b. Does the group operate like a system? If so, how? If not, why not?

c. What is the role of leadership in the group?

d. How are power relations established and maintained? How are they challenged?

e. What is the role of gender, race, class, or sexual orientation in the group? How do you know?

3. Perform your analysis.

a. Write a narrative account (i.e., a story) about the group meeting. Be sure to include as much detail about the conversations and your impressions as you can. Make sure your story has an identifiable beginning, middle, and ending.

b. Where possible, apply material from the chapters you have read to the story. When you are finished with a draft, add an introduction that theoretically frames the story and a conclusion that attempts to "sum up" what you have learned about this culture from the study.

4. Share your ethnography with your class.

CHAPTER 6

Critical Approaches to Organizations and Communication

If you pick up one of the many books written about American business in the 1950's, you will find a typical corporate employee who is unrecognizable today. The Organization Man, the Man in the Gray Flannel Suit — whatever you call him, he seems as freakish today as a bearded lady or a six-toed foot. The worker who is willing to subordinate his identity to some giant corporation is so deeply unfashionable that, for cultural purposes, he might as well not exist. Where did he go? One answer is that he was set free.

— MICHAEL LEWIS, "The Artist in the Gray Flannel Pajamas" (2000)

The various approaches to organizations discussed in the preceding chapters pose questions from within the dominant frameworks of Western capitalism, behavioral science, and modern organizational studies, but they do not for the most part challenge those frameworks. Although more recent cultural approaches have been more critical, blurring the distinction between cultural and critical approaches (see the work of Conquergood and Martin discussed in the last chapter), even more subversive approaches exist.

The perspectives considered in this and the next chapter examine and oppose the assumptions of the dominant frameworks. Critical organizational theory, which we address in this chapter, reveals the often hidden but pervasive power that organizations have over individuals, and more generally, questions the assumed superiority of market capitalism. Critical approaches, as we will see, pose important questions about power.

Critical Theory

Historical and Cultural Background

When we think of people as "critical," we may imagine them challenging some action or decision that they consider inappropriate or unfair. And this is precisely what critical approaches to organizations do: They are concerned mainly with challenging the unfair exercise and abuse of power. Critical theory emerged in response to the growing power a small part of society held over the rest of the public during the Victorian period. This era was marked by an abusive system of low wages, squalid working conditions, and wealthy, isolated business owners (Mead, 1991). Child labor was common, particularism was the rule, and consequently employees had little protection from the whims of their employers. Women and minorities were paid substantially less than white men for performing the same work, and their opinions about how work should be done or how workplaces could be improved were largely ignored (Banta, 1993). Practically speaking, the implementation of scientific management was fragmented along economic, ethnic, and gender lines.

It was under these circumstances of exploitive capitalism that critical theory found its earliest expression in the work of Karl Marx (1818–83). He viewed the division between business owners and employees as misguided and unfair, and he believed it would eventually lead to a violent overthrow of the owners as workers seized the means of production. The world has since witnessed many practical adaptations of Marx's ideas (e.g., China, Cuba, and the former Soviet Union). However, one particular theoretical adaptation merits our attention: that of a group of professors from the University of Frankfurt, referred to collectively as the Frankfurt school, who used some of Marx's ideas to develop what is now known as "critical theory" (Adorno & Horkheimer, 1972).

The Rise of Critical Theory in the United States

Critical theory gained considerable popularity in the United States during the 1980s (Strine, 1991). Practical and intellectual reasons account for the current interest in critical theory.

At the turn of the twentieth century, U.S. industrialists broke from traditional capitalism, which funneled the lion's share of wealth and responsibility to the top. For the first time, a clear connection was made between the wages paid to employees and their ability to be active consumers. At Ford Motor Company in the 1920s, for example, workers were paid the then-high wage of $5 a day. Ford reasoned that to sell his cars to the masses, workers had to earn enough to buy them. This strategy, known as "progressive capitalism," dominated U.S. industry from the Industrial Revolution until the early 1970s, when the average, inflation-corrected weekly wage of Americans reached its peak. Throughout this period, both individuals and corporations experienced enormous increases in economic well-being (Mead, 1991). In addition, for the first time in human history, more individuals worked for someone else than for themselves.

Moreover, these decades of progressive capitalism gave way to revolutionary changes in the world of work. With globalization, "a phenomena that has remade the economy of virtually every nation, reshaped almost every industry, and touched billions of lives" (Rosenberg, 2002, p. 28), employers had the option of hiring lower-wage workers overseas. Although this practice was deeply reminiscent of the earlier abuses of capitalism, it occurred far enough away from home to be ignored by most people until fairly recently. For example, Tina Rosenberg (2002) investigated the impact of globalization in Latin America and found that although it has produced additional jobs, it has also led to dramatic increases in crime, to the rise of new dictatorships, to the economic collapse of Argentina, to the financial panic that haunts Brazil, and to the new economic woes of Uruguay and Venezuela. In India, Rosenberg discovered that the sudden influx of new money to support high technology investments by American firms in recent years has led to further economic and social division between the 30 percent literate and 70 percent illiterate populations, and has rekindled old cultural and religious tensions over the importation of Western capitalist values. The same story has generally been true throughout Southeast Asia, where the widespread use of child labor in sweatshops over the past two decades by large American firms (e.g., Nike) created a public outcry and has led to some reforms. Ironically, as most economic observers admit, the idea of international integration of economies to produce and consume products and services is essential for the poor of the world, but unfortunately, "no nation has ever developed over the long term under the rules being imposed today on third world countries by the institutions controlling globalization" (Rosenberg, 2002, p. 30), such as the World Trade Organization.

Beginning in the 1980s, elected leaders of both the United States and Britain have adopted an economic philosophy in direct opposition to decades of progressive capitalism. With this new approach, more resources were given to big business (e.g., tax exemptions and reduced regulatory fines and controls) in the hope that increased profits would "trickle down" to the average individual (this approach has also been labeled "supply side economics"). Instead of promoting a more equitable sharing of wealth, however, the result has been a steady decline in the average employee's real wages, benefits, and standard of living. Even more recently, as wages have improved and unemployment rates hit an all-time low in the United States, many people work at one or more low-paying service jobs and struggle to make ends meet. In one notable investigative study, Barbara Ehrenreich (2001) decided to live life as a minimum wage earner in Florida, Minnesota, and Maine by working as a waitress, hotel maid, nursing home aide, house cleaner, and Wal-Mart salesperson. She discovered, along with the estimated 12 million women who were moved off welfare roles into minimum wage jobs as a result of welfare reform legislation during the 1990s, that the work was physically, mentally, and emotionally exhausting and that "you need at least two [jobs] if you intend to live indoors." Clearly, the division between people who own things (homes, cars, stocks, and stock options) and those who do not is wide.

As the gap between rich and poor widened, new information technologies offered companies unprecedented opportunities to rethink the relationships between global communication and local organization. One major result of this rethinking has been the flat, flexible organization, in which traditional communication hierarchies have been replaced by a team-based organization that can respond more quickly to worldwide economic patterns. This ability enabled technology rich companies to rethink the relationship between organizational structures and their ability to compete for fewer dollars distributed among larger markets. By flattening their hierarchies and outsourcing work previously done in-house (increasingly to poorer or Third World nations), these firms learned to maximize profits for shareholders while, at the same time, contributing significantly to the widening income gap worldwide. Additionally, the ability of flexible, team-based organizations who make use of computers and the Internet to respond quickly to changing circumstances has become so pervasive as a business model that recent studies have shown this form of organizing has even been adopted by illegal groups to operate terrorist cells (Langeweische, 2002) and to distribute heroin internationally (Brzezinski, 2002).

Finally, as U.S. scholarship became more international, European and postcolonial studies in critical theory were discovered and imported back to the United States. Given the economic and political climate at the time, the European studies helped to generate interest in applying the questions and lessons of critical theory to organizations and communication in the United States, and postcolonial studies have implicated the politics of organizational colonization and strategies for communication within the broader "historical structures of knowledge production that are rooted in various histories and geographies of modernity" (Shome & Hegde, 2002, p. 250).

Together, these changes have had a revolutionary impact on our lives. When the world of work changes fundamentally, every institution in society is challenged. At the very core of this challenge are questions of power.

The Centrality of Power

Early attempts to define power were based on the assumption that it is something a person or group possesses and can exercise through actions. In a classic paper on the subject, Robert French and Bertram Raven (1968) proposed five types of social power, following the assumption that person A has power over person B when A has control over some outcome B wants:

1. *Reward power.* Person A has reward power over person B when A can give some formal or informal reward, such as a bonus or an award, in exchange for B's compliance.
2. *Coercive power.* Person A has coercive power over person B when B perceives that certain behaviors on his or her part will lead to punishments from A, such as poor work assignments, relocation, or demotion.
3. *Referent power.* Person A has referent power over person B when B is willing to do what A asks in order to be like A. Mentors and charismatic leaders, for example, often have referent power.
4. *Expert power.* Person A has expert power over person B when B is willing to do what A says because B respects A's expert knowledge.
5. *Legitimate power.* Person A has legitimate power over person B when B complies with A's wishes because A holds a high-level position, such as division head, in the hierarchy.

French and Raven's approach to power is reflected in much of the research on compliance-gaining (Kipnis, Schmidt, & Wilkinson, 1980) and on behavior-altering techniques (Richmond, Davis, Saylor, & McCroskey, 1984). Examples include research on how supervisors can persuade subordinates to do undesirable tasks, how employees can persuade supervisors and co-workers to give them desired resources, and even how teachers can encourage students to complete assignments.

However, this approach to understanding power is incomplete. By focusing on the overt or surface exercise of power by individuals, we learn little about the more covert structures of power (Conrad, 1983). Unlike overt power, which is easy to spot and can in principle be resisted (though often at great costs), covert or hidden power is more insidious. Critical theory focuses on the control of employers over employees (Clegg, 1989) wherein power "resembles a loose coalition of interests more than a unified front. Critical theory is committed to unveiling the political stakes that anchor cultural practices" (Conquergood, 1991, p. 179).

Consider, for example, just how much invisible power is exerted over your choice of major or, for that matter, of being in school. Since the Industrial Revolution, nations have created "public schools" to educate society's young as a way of preparing them for a lifetime of work in organizations. Pennsylvania State University's motto, for instance, says the purpose of the university is "to educate the sons and daughters of the working classes in the agricultural and mechanical arts and sciences." A closer look at that sentence reveals evidence of a nineteenth-century separation of the "managerial" and "working" classes (wherein the rich attend "private" schools) alongside the belief that education should serve practical, state-mandated needs (in this case, those related to agriculture and engineering). Despite fiery debates among ideologically opposed camps, today's educational reforms are largely evolutionary: The question everyone shares is how best to educate students for our high-tech, networked world of work. As we will see, one challenge posed by critical approaches is that our system of education — and our outmoded assumption of lifetime employment with a company — are overdue for reform.

Power and Ideology

An ideology is a system of ideas that are the basis of a political or economic theory (as in Marxist or capitalist or feminist ideology). In conversation, ideology often refers to our basic, often unexamined, assumptions about how things are or, in some cases, how they should be. During the era of classical management, for example, the dominant ideology about work was based on various assumptions: that men (especially white men) were better suited to assembly lines than were women; that white men could learn faster than women and minorities and, therefore, should hold supervisory positions; that the U.S. system of work was second to none in the world; that Americans had a right to use the world's natural resources to build their cities, roads, and systems of commerce and industry; and that the American form of government was superior to all other forms (Banta, 1993).

Ideology touches every aspect of life and is manifested in our words, actions, and practices. The existence of ideology encourages us to understand that power is not confined to government or politics, nor is it always overt or easy to spot. Because it structures our thoughts and controls our interpretations of reality, it is often beneath our awareness. It seems "natural," and it makes what we think and do seem "right." According to philosopher Michel Foucault (1979), ideological power is a widespread, intangible network of forces that weaves itself into subtle gestures and intimate utterances. As such, ideology does not reside in things but "in a network of relationships which are systematically connected" (Burrell, 1988, p. 227). Ideology exists in the practices of everyday life.

Moreover, ideology is never neutral. It is associated with the interests of dominant individuals and groups, and it is often exercised unconsciously. The pervasive powers of a group, at least from the perspective of people outside of the group, rest with its ideology. In this sense, ideology is always something the other person has. According to Jurgen Habermas (1972), a leading modern proponent of critical theory, most people think along these lines: "I view things as they really are, you squint at them through a tunnel vision imposed by some extraneous system or doctrine."

One notable effort to investigate the relationship between ideology and organizational practices is Patricia Geist and Jennifer Dreyer's (1993) critique of the dominant model of health care in the United States. They explore this model's ability to define and control what is considered appropriate, professional, or ordinary health-care communication through the routine doctor-patient interview. The result often gives less weight to the patient's perspective. Using dialogic theory (Bakhtin, 1986), Geist and Dreyer propose an alternative model for communication encounters between health-care providers and their patients. By refocusing the dialogic encounter on what is created in communication (as opposed to what is given through scientific authority), Geist and Dreyer aim to empower those who seek medical treatment through the deliberate inclusion of the patient's voice in the doctor-patient interaction. Hence, two major challenges to the power of received ideology are present in their research agenda: (1) the power of the traditional medical model of scientific information gathering and (2) the power of traditional models that distance researchers — and research practices — from the people they study.

Again, the powerful influences of ideology are linked to everyday organizational and research practices in ways that complicate our understanding of what happens in organizations and of the role researchers and their theories should play in those happenings. Before we extend the latter argument, however, we need to examine some of the sources of the hidden powers of ideological control.

The Hidden Power of Cultures: Native Assumptions

Ideology operates locally, regionally, nationally, and internationally. For example, ideology can operate internationally in our reactions to other cultures. Iris Varner and Linda Beamer (1995) identify three reactions that we typically have to people who do not share our native culture:

1. *Assumptions of superiority.* Many cultures assume that their own values and practices are superior to those of others in the world. Hence, when cultural differences in understanding or in ways of doing things exist, English-speaking people tend to ideologically code those differences as primitive or backward, reserving for their own practices a culturally superior position that they assume is "normal." One example is our Western view that the possession of advanced technologies — computers, fax machines, telephones, televisions — equates with being educated or knowledgeable. However, many of the so-called Third World or underdeveloped countries of the world have better systems for handling conflict and sustaining marriages and families.

2. *Ethnocentrism.* There is a tendency for people to view their own culture as the "right" one. This leads to frustration in our dealings with others who do not share our culture or its assumptions. American businesses, for example, have attempted to apply to their business dealings overseas the same assumptions they apply at home, often with disastrous results. The typical American tendency to jump to action, for example, conflicts with Asian tendencies to plan and deliberate for long periods of time. Adapting to another's culture requires an openness to different ways of doing things, but ideology often makes this difficult.

3. *Assumptions of universality.* People often mistakenly assume that beneath differences in dress and behavior, all people are basically alike. This assumption can lead to misunderstanding and conflict among people from different cultures who interpret and understand the world from different perspectives. The key is to find ways for people who think differently to work together.

Ideology exists at the surface of cultures. A German manufacturer, for example, recently told us that he had learned that "Americans are like peaches, while Germans are like coconuts." When asked to explain this statement, he added that "Americans like to present a soft, warm, and appealing surface to others, but at their very core is something very hard and impenetrable. Germans, on the other hand, present the world with a hard exterior, often perceived as cold, distant, difficult to crack, but inside they are the ones who are truly soft and warm." His statement is about ideology as much as it is about perception, and his delineation of cultural differences is much deeper than simple labels suggest. Abstract ideological terms like *conservative* and *liberal* often obscure important individual differences and similarities. Consider also the many differences among those of us who call ourselves "college-educated Americans" or "IBM (or Mac) users." Ideology is both pervasive and complex.

The Hidden Power of Ideology: Manufactured Consent

The hidden power of organizational systems and structures has been a central focus of critical theory. Habermas (1972) argues that social legitimation plays a major role in holding contemporary organizations together. According to Habermas, capitalist societies are characterized by the manufacture of consent, in which employees at all levels willingly adopt and enforce the legitimate power of the organization, society, or system of capitalism. Furthermore, only when this perceived legitimate power is challenged might the basic order face a crisis.

The fact that this kind of power is hard to see only increases its strength. Practically from birth, westerners are immersed in capitalism and are trained to be consumers first, citizens second, if at all. Most of our activities these days are structured around consumption, on either consuming or finding ways to "add value" to ourselves and our families (Carlone & Taylor, 1998). Moreover, employees have for some time now accepted the label of *human resources*, which suggests an objectification of people that in turn makes it easier to mold or get rid of them. The magic of consent is that the people themselves buy into the vocabulary and, despite how it casts them as disposable objects, have difficulty imagining an alternative reality (Communication Research, 1997).

Manufactured consent is evident when an employee says, "I'm just doing my job," to justify some decision or action. As Dennis Mumby (1987) points out, domination involves leading people to organize their behavior around a rule

system. The system, not individual managers or actors, can then be blamed —
but not held accountable — for actions taken in its name (p. 115). A recent law
aimed at correcting this situation makes the senior management of large corporations personally responsible for any criminal actions taken on behalf of the
company. Similarly, both Exxon and Union Carbide were held (somewhat) financially accountable for, respectively, a major oil spill in Prince William Sound,
Alaska, and the release of deadly gas in Bhopal, India. Even more recently in the
wake of the accounting scandals of 2002, the Securities and Exchange Commission (SEC) proposed holding corporate officers — CEOs and CFOs — personally responsible for the truthfulness, timeliness, and fairness of all public
disclosures, including their financial statements.

Not all consent has purely negative consequences for members. The
Grameen bank in Bangladesh is an interesting example of how the self-policing
quality of ideology can have its benefits. The Grameen bank "enables the poor,
landless, and mostly illiterate people of rural Bangladesh to assist themselves, by
extending them small loans, loan utilization training, and various social services" (Papa, Auwal, & Singhal, 1995). People use the loans to start small enterprises that pull them out of poverty. Incredibly, the payback rate on these loans
is 99 percent. This is because the members themselves maintain a structure of
guilt and peer pressure that stigmatizes those who would fail to repay their
debts. At the same time, this normative structure can be seen as a kind of support system, as the bank provides "required" motivational programs and strict
daily monitoring of performance as well as weekly review meetings. In this way,
members come to identify strongly with the bank and to feel a shared responsibility for the repayment of all loans. Defying simple analysis, it appears that
Grameen is both incredibly empowering and controlling at the same time (Papa,
Auwal, & Singhal, 1997).

The Hidden Power of Communication:
Myths, Metaphors, and Stories

Myths contribute to the strength of a culture's ideology and its sources of power.
These narratives often reveal the beliefs and values of a culture as they tell the
stories of legendary heroes, of good and evil, and of origins and exits. In myths,
we find evidence of basic metaphors that structure "our" view of things. For example, both H. L. Goodall (1995) and Janice Rushing (1993) suggest that in the
American West there is a dominant mythic narrative that describes the origins
of order and power and that features three main characters: (1) power, the expression of a sovereign, rational, unified, or modern self; (2) other, the force
that resists the domination of the self by glorifying its opposites; and (3) spirit, a
mysterious force that is capable (at least narratively) of resolving the differences
between, and therefore uniting, power and other. We are yet again in the midst
of *Star Wars* mania, the story behind which is utterly familiar and resonates with

us precisely because it reflects the dominant cultural narrative. On the one hand, there is Luke Skywalker and the forces of good; on the other there is the "Dark Side" led by Darth Vader (and others). At the same time, we learn from Yoda of a transcendent "force" that can somehow end the conflict forever. Nearly every American story — from movie to novel to television drama — reflects some version of this narrative.

More specific stories exist at the organizational level as well. Organizational narratives, metaphors, and stories are important sources of power and ideology. Indeed, critical theory seeks to understand why organizational practices that maintain strong controls over employees are considered legitimate and, hence, are not resisted (McPhee, 1985). This kind of legitimation is maintained through such symbolic forms as metaphors, myths, and stories. At Ben & Jerry's, for instance, a theme of "social consciousness" is employed to justify managerial decisions regarding hiring, firing, promotions, and raises. Employees generally accept these controls as part of the "story" that distinguishes the organization and its culture. Over time, such myths, metaphors, and stories can come to define appropriate behavior and to suspend employees' critical thinking. (See *What Would You Do?* 6.1.)

One of the most pervasive myths in American culture is the idea of what constitutes (and fails to constitute) a "real job" (Clair, 1996). Although the phrase has the effect of naturalizing the idea that some jobs are more "real" than others, it can also be seen as a way of privileging certain kinds of work. Specifically, most people think of a real job as one that involves collecting good wages from an organization. This relegates all kinds of important work — nonorganizational, unpaid, home-based, odd-hours, service-oriented — to the margins. Another pervasive myth in our culture is the idea of a "career" being tied to societal norms or a "social contract" (Buzzanell, 2000). As Buzzanell points out, when the old social contract (that idealized individual commitment, hard work, and loyalty to a company in exchange for lifetime employment and a good retirement program) was replaced with the new social contract (that promises only a series of work contracts over a lifetime to those able to keep abreast of technological change), the career aspirations of many "marginalized workforce members (people of color, white women, poor and lower class persons, and the less educated)" (2000, p. 211) were sacrificed. Once again, a critical perspective helps us see how our taken-for-granted ways of thinking and speaking can mask important power relationships (Clair, 1996; Mumby, 2000).

Cultural stories about power tend to acquire not only the status of legend, but also the influence of myth. A story circulating at a large consulting firm tells of a senior consultant rushing to meet a client, ignoring traffic laws, driving through fences and onto sidewalks, and speeding the wrong way down one-way streets, while the new junior consultant sits white-knuckled in the passenger seat. They make it to the meeting on time. Afterward, the junior consultant confronts her boss: "Why did you drive like that? If we had been a few minutes late, the client would have understood!" Later that day, the junior consultant is

What Would You Do? 6.1

METAPHORS CAN SUSPEND CRITICAL THINKING

Family is a common metaphor used by companies in the United States. For some companies, like entertainment giant Disney, the metaphor has been very useful. The ideal family includes a warm, wholesome, caring, mutually supportive set of interdependent relationships characterized by open and honest communication. Viewed in this way, family is a positive metaphor for any firm.

Not all families conform to this ideal, however. Do the terms for describing the ideal family sometimes obscure dysfunctional power relationships between parents and children, among siblings, and with relatives? Should all families strive to achieve the same ideals? Are all successful businesses alike? Consider these questions as you respond to the following situations:

1. You dislike your supervisor's frequent use of the family metaphor to explain his behavior (e.g., "Yes, I yelled at you about that report, but even in the best families that sometimes happens" and "We're all family here, so if you have personal problems, you can tell me about them"). You believe your supervisor uses the family metaphor as an excuse for his irrational behavior as well as to gain unwarranted access to employees' private lives. What is wrong with the supervisor's behavior? What should you do?

2. Your company has just announced that at its annual holiday party, skits will be performed by employee work teams. Your team has been asked to write, produce, and perform a skit that portrays the company as a family. You view this as an opportunity to reveal both the positive and negative aspects of the organization's use of power and informal relationships. However, two members of your team argue against your proposal; they agree with your ideas, but they fear management's response to the negative portrayals. How will you argue your case at the next team meeting?

3. What other metaphors can be used to describe and to organize work relationships? Describe at least one such metaphor and its ethical dimensions.

told to clean out her desk (she was fired). The moral of this story is twofold: (1) Do what you must to accommodate a client, and (2) do not challenge the judgment of superiors. The story — regardless of its actual truth or falsity — reinforces existing power relations in the consulting firm.

The Hidden Power of Organizational Communication: Politics

Dennis Mumby (1993) reminds us of a principal tenet of critical theory: "that organizations are not neutral sites of sense making; rather, they are created in the context of struggles between competing interest groups and systems of representation" (p. 21). Although researchers attempt to show how such struggles are carried out in organizations, they seem less attuned to the roles of internal politics and ideologies in their own explanatory systems.

Mumby goes on to suggest three ways to improve organizational communication research:

1. *Connect the political to the poetic.* Most research in organizations takes place behind the scenes; employees and managers are observed rather than engaged by the researcher, and their behaviors and practices are analyzed on the basis of critical, cultural, or other theories. Researchers should move to more actively engage their subjects and turn the critical lens back upon themselves and their methods of study (see Goodall, 1989, 1991b, 2000). In this way, the reader can more fairly judge the interpretations that are offered through a better understanding of the particular biases that led to their development.

2. *Conduct more participatory research.* "To break down the bifurcation between researchers and those being studied," academics should engage themselves in the types of work they investigate (Mumby, 1993, p. 20). This means that researchers should, where possible, physically engage in the type of work they are studying, to get a better bodily sense for the experience of that work. Participatory research would help researchers identify sources of authority beyond the usual realm of academic theory (or at least reexamine the privileged position of current theory), as well as bring to workplaces the insights of those theories. As a result, the research process would encompass not only a search for knowledge, but also mobilization.

3. *Conduct more critically oriented research.* Traditional studies of organizations often shy away from critical research because it eschews objectivity and carries with it an agenda (i.e., to reveal sources of domination). More dialogue between advocates of theories of organization that explicitly consider issues of power and those who do not would benefit both types of research. In particular, more attention should be paid to the relationships among specific communicative practices as well as to structures of power and domination (see Conrad, 1988; Rosen, 1985).

Mumby's (1993) suggestions target the general need to challenge the assumptions, definitions, and research methods of organizational communication.

The good news is that this challenge is being met by scholars using feminist, postcolonial, ethnographic, and cultural studies methods. For example,

Marline Fine and Patrice Buzzanell (2000) use personal diaries to reconceptualize leadership as a form of feminist service. Viewed this way, leadership is revisioned as a form of resistance to managerial control in which "multiple commitments to self, others, community, and principles" allow leaders to "serve themselves with and through their connections to others" (2000, p. 152). Similarly, a team of feminist researchers recently challenged the American Medical Association's prescriptions for how to reduce workplace stress-induced heart attacks (controlling weight, lowering cholesterol, exercising, quitting smoking) by pointing out that what studies have shown to cause the workplace health problem (the stress induced by bosses meeting critical deadlines or firing employees) was not being addressed by this prescription (Mattson, Clair, Sanger, & Kunkel, 2000). Instead, using evidence collected from employees' poems, diaries, and stories, these researchers isolated four "real" causes of workplace stress: undervalued jobs, the politics and social interaction of the workplace, the ways in which "reality" is constructed in managerial environments, and an unwillingness to connect the concerns and emotional needs of a public work life with the ongoing inner private lives of employees. Additionally, Brenda Allen (2000), using testimony drawn from her own experiences, points out that the politics of organizational socialization (see Chapter 8 for detailed discussion) is both a gendered and a racial issue, and that "learning the ropes" of any new job requires understanding the contextual influences that shape these social processes.

The Hidden Power of Society: Hegemony

Antonio Gramsci (1971) uses the term *hegemony* (pronounced "heh-jeh'-mohnee") to describe the hidden power of society. It encompasses the power of rules, standard operating procedures, and routines. At a public swimming pool, for example, we abide by the posted rules, such as "No running or jumping." Rarely do we question these rules or seek to find out who posted them (in this case, most likely the person holding the insurance policy for the pool).

Similarly, managers of organizations work hard to achieve routine. This occurs when employees come to believe that their behavior is controlled not by other people, but by the rules of the company. A subtle transformation takes place — from "This is how we've decided to do things" to "This is how things are done." Only rarely does the latter situation remain negotiable. In most cases, members are not given the opportunity to redefine the situation.

An instance of hegemony frequently cited by critical theorists is most Americans' steady diet of television news. Although each network strives to offer an authoritative portrayal of "Here's what happened in the world today," certain kinds of stories are always highlighted (e.g., fires, wrecks, crime, scandal, and disaster) and others are actively suppressed (e.g., stories about economic inequality, pollution, and social class). These omissions (which are predictable given that the three major television networks are owned by large multinational corporations) become hegemonic when the audience is unaware of the extent to which "reality" is being preselected for them. The merger in January 2001 between Time Warner and America Online threatens to make this situation even worse, as large-scale "content providers," such as AOL Time Warner, drive out alternative media voices.

Once you start trying to understand the interests behind taken-for-granted assumptions, many new possibilities appear. For example, some writers critique the entire human effort at organization as an attempt to devalue other species by privileging our unique characteristic, linguistic rationality. In a world in which everything revolves around human beings, order, rationality, and hierarchy are the order of the day, and any challenge to these core beliefs is summarily dismissed as "meaningless." It is interesting to speculate about what organizational theories might emerge in a world where humans were forced to share power with other animals and with intelligent machines. Some would argue that this world may soon be at hand (Haraway, 1991).

Critical Theories of Power

Feminist Theory

Feminist theory focuses on the oppression and exploitation of women in the workplace and on giving women more power and voice in organizations. Research on women in organizations has followed closely the view of power described thus far in this chapter. Early studies sought only to identify strategies and behaviors women needed to succeed at work. *Games Mother Never Taught You: Corporate Gamesmanship for Women* (Harrigan, 1977) and *The New Executive Woman: A Guide to Business Success* (Williams, 1977), for example, did not challenge the status quo in organizations. Instead, they adopted a deficiency model of women, claiming that women needed to learn certain behaviors to succeed in organizations. This approach generally corresponds to the examination of overt power strategies.

Rosabeth Moss Kanter's *Men and Women of the Corporation* (1977) marked a turning point in the history of thinking about women in organizations. In particular, her discussion of tokenism — the promotion of a few women into highly visible positions — argues that increased publicity and attention actually result in greater pressure to perform and an increased likelihood of failure. Kanter also argues that the responsibility for change should be at the system level because individuals working alone are likely to fail. Other researchers adopt a more radical critique of definitions of *organization*. Focusing on the underlying assumptions and ideologies of a male-dominated society, they identify hidden aspects of patriarchal organizations that can lead to discrimination against women (Ashcraft, 2000; Blair, Brown, & Baxter, 1995; Bullis & Glaser, 1992;

Calvert & Ramsey, 1992; Ferguson, 1984; Mumby, 2000; Mumby & Stohl, 1996).

Implicit in feminist approaches is the assumption that women have distinct ways of seeing the world ("women's ways of knowing") and of constructing meanings for it. Consequently, organizational dialogue may be transformed by women's voices. According to the feminist critique, however, most corporations are still structured on the basis of outdated societal and public norms and fail to account for women's needs (Buzzanell, 2000; Freeman, 1990; Mumby, 2000). One of the most significant differences between the feminist worldview and the male-dominated organization has to do with hierarchy. Although most contemporary organizations are hierarchical, women tend to think of organizations in terms of networks or webs of relationships, with leadership at the center of the web, rather than on top of a pyramid (Helgeson, 1990).

In contrast to traditional models, narratives by and about women tend to value

- Fluid boundaries between personal life and work life
- Relational aspects of work
- A balanced lifestyle
- A nurturant approach to co-workers
- . A network of relationships within and outside the organization
- Leadership as a web, not a hierarchy
- A service orientation to clients
- Work as a means of developing personal identity (Buzzanell, 2000; Grossman & Chester, 1990; Helgeson, 1990; Lunneborg, 1990; Trethewey, 2000)

Valuing women's voices in organizations means opening the dialogue to a different set of assumptions: Can we define *competition* as "doing excellently" instead of "excelling over" (Calas & Smircich, 1996)? Can we define *power* in a way that enhances, rather than diminishes, the power of everyone (Reuther & Fairhurst, 2000)? Can we value and seek diversity in organizations (Allen, 2000)? Can we view organizations as being responsible for social change (Marshall, 1984)? Can hierarchies be abandoned or reenvisioned as networks (Ferguson, 1984)? Can we learn to ask "whom does my work benefit" (Buzzanell, 2000)?

Alert readers will notice that women's ways of operating in organizations bear striking resemblance to more general prescriptions for leaders and managers! Specifically, there is a growing consensus that command and control does not work and that leaders must share responsibility, develop others, and build and maintain a network of relationships. What is fascinating is that few writers have been willing to characterize new leadership models as in any way "feminine"! One advantage of doing so is that it would allow us to see the masculine hegemony evident in traditional, purportedly gender-neutral organizations (May, 2000; Mumby, 2000).

Judi Marshall (1993) suggests that viewing an organization from a feminist perspective encourages us to examine four differences regarding power and interpretation:

1. *Male and female values.* In what is usually conceived of as an "archetypal polarity" (Marshall, 1993, p. 124), men are associated with agency (doing things), whereas women are associated with communion (relating to others). From an Eastern perspective, this relationship forms the yin and yang. Male values are associated with "self-assertion, separation, independence, control, competition, focused perception, rationality, analysis, clarity, discrimination, and activity. Underlying themes are a self-assertive tendency, control of the environment, and focus on personal and interpersonal processes" (Marshall, 1993, p. 124). Female values are associated with "interdependence, cooperation, receptivity, merging, acceptance, awareness of patterns, wholes and contexts, emotional tone, personalistic perception, being, intuition, and synthesizing. Underlying themes are openness to the environment, interconnection, and mutual development" (Marshall, 1993, p. 124). Although these polarities have been used to point to differences between men and women, Marshall sees "male and female values as qualities to which both sexes have access, rather than the exclusive properties of men and women, respectively" (1993, p. 125). She argues that "unmasking and contradicting the male positive/female negative values of this world has been a major feminist endeavor" (p. 126).

2. *Male-dominated cultures.* Marshall (1993) argues that "male forms are the norm to which organizational members adapt. Women copy these to gain acceptance and succeed in their careers" (p. 126). Female workers are typically judged according to male standards for job performance and are denied legitimacy for their home lives. Male dominance is viewed as a hidden power because it is perceived as the norm, goes largely unrecognized, and tends to be relatively stable and enduring. Language and imagery in business tend to reinforce and reflect this pattern. For example, it is still the case that competition between organizations is defined and discussed using war metaphors (e.g., hostile takeovers, plan of attack), which some women find either offensive or difficult to fully understand.

3. *Male-dominated organizations as high-context cultures.* Marshall (1993) draws on Edward T. Hall's (1973) distinction between high- and low-context cultures to characterize women's experiences in male-dominated organizations: Women "do not share much of the contexting that makes communication understandable. Nor do they have equal rights to engage in defining meaning within the patterns of communication that are experienced by men as low context because of their (women's) subordinate social position" (p. 127). Men transmit messages that carry implicit

(male-associated) meanings that women try to adapt to and understand. Women are required to learn to read the culture through a male-dominated, high-context lens and to monitor their communication and behavior accordingly.

4. *Women as communication.* According to Gregory Bateson (1972), "Being a woman is 'information,' in that it is 'a difference that makes a difference.'" In other words, just being a woman in an organization has meaning, even before you do anything. Marshall (1993) uses this idea to detail the following core issues of "women as information" in organizations:

Tensions about status. Women generally have less tension about status, which allows the male-dominated culture to read "female managers as secretaries, and so on" (p. 130). Women in nontraditional jobs disturb the hierarchy by "challenging people to innovate and to remodel old routines" (p. 130).

Public employment versus the private home. Here "men are largely identified with the public world and women with the private" (Marshall, 1993, p. 130).

Man-made language. Terms associated with women, such as *compassion, emotion,* and *empathy,* are devalued (Mumby & Putnam, 1993), and "women are often stereotyped and put in their place" (Marshall, 1993, p. 131).

Gender-differentiated discourse. Women tend to speak less often, for less time, and less loudly than men do, and their communication is evaluated on the basis of a male model.

Exclusion from men's informal networks and communication. Women in powerful positions are most often excluded, which has "significant impacts on their contributions to decision making and their abilities both to understand and to influence organizational cultures" (Marshall, 1993, p. 131).

Different patterns of thinking and valuing. Women tend to be more relational, contextual, and personal than men, all of which have major implications for the norms of speaking and listening in organizations.

Practically, a distinction must always be made between "women's actions" and "feminism" both in terms of subordination and resistance. With regard to subordination, at times women participate in their own oppression by relying on cultural recipes for "how women behave." In a study of a small business, women were quick to identify each other as catty, petty, and cliquish, and then seek to distinguish their own behavior as above or beyond all that. This kind of talk works to solidify the stereotype, and linking women "naturally" with cattiness makes these women complicit in their own subordination (Ashcraft & Pacanowsky, 1996).

Regarding resistance, we must be careful not to impose our own definition of what constitutes "real" resistance on others. In a study of poor, single mothers seeking help from social services, women lacking in much "legitimate" power nonetheless engaged in numerous effective forms of resistance. Some of these include parodying embarrassing confessional practices; fighting bureaucracy; playing games; and bitching. Over time, these small resistances often had significant positive effects, including changes in scheduling, monitoring, and decision making (Tretheway, 1997). Studies of flight attendants also reveal significant "hidden transcripts" of resistance, suggesting a balance between corporate control and self-determination (Murphy, 1999). A "hidden transcript" refers to language resources — knowledge, stories, and off-stage performances of power reversals — shared by lower-level or mid-level employees that are not articulated to management or to other power holders (Scott, 1990). One example of a "hidden transcript" that may be closer to your experiences as a student is the way in which humorous or derogatory caricatures of college professors are performed outside of class. The point of this resistance strategy is not to "get even" with the imitated professor (because the performance is *never* shown to her or him), but instead to regain a sense of personal equity by turning the power relationship upside down among other sympathetic students.

Feminist critical theory shows how exploited groups can challenge the hegemony of a dominant ideology by proposing different assumptions and definitions. Marshall (1993) suggests strategies for resisting the gendering of organizations. Derived from a dialogic model of organizational communication, the strategies are aimed at gaining voice, adapting to context, translating and screening out male-dominated forms of power, and challenging male assumptions about organizational communication. Buzzanell (2000), marking the emergence of the third wave of feminist thought, explains that there are three future directions for continuing the dialogue about the relationship between organizational communication and feminism:

1. *Sustaining tensions between binary oppositions.* One characteristic of ongoing feminist theories is the idea that we all need to learn to live and work with ambiguities and contradictions. However, this does not mean that feminists should abandon a critique of sameness/difference, inclusion/exclusion, or global/local dualisms that define and shape the experiences of working people. These tensions should continue to inform our research by teaching us how, for example, the seemingly benign essentialist admonition to "treat everyone the same" actually negates the important role of differences in our identities. Additionally, researchers must work to improve the ways in which issues of race, age, and class are seen to intersect with those of gender, so that our professional literature doesn't exclude the voices of minorities, older workers, or those who work for lower wages. Finally, the Eurocentric assumptions that currently influence feminist and organizational theories should be challenged by transnational issues and contexts.

2. *Exploring resistance.* Rather than simply describing resistance to forms of domination, new feminist thought should focus on the actual strategies

used by people to enact resistance in their daily lives. Studies suggest that hidden transcripts (Murphy, 1998), retelling or restorying events (Jovanovic, 2002), finding ways to preserve individuality and cultural identity within co-cultural exchanges (Orbe, 1998), and expressing silence (Clair, 1998) all demonstrate evidence of resistance to perceived (and real) forms of power at work.

3. *Promoting participatory discourse and alternative organizing.* At the intersection of gender and organizational structures lies a promising avenue of new research aimed at finding ways to make organizations more democratic. Studies indicate that workplaces can be more democratic by creating participatory stakeholder relations (Haas & Deetz, 2000), making more permeable boundaries between public and private spheres (Mumby, 2000), and co-constructing negotiation strategies and narratives about the experiences and meanings of working (Kellett & Dalton, 2000; Putnam & Kolb, 2000).

Feminist thought and research is producing the most significant shift in our current thinking about the relationship between communication processes and organizational power relations. Another — and parallel — shift is taking place in the value of organizational narratives to reveal sources of dialectical tensions, domination and resistance, and forms of alternative organizing. In the next section we explore one facet of organizational narratives in relation to our concern in this chapter for a critique of power.

Work-Hate Narratives

I hate my job. But I lie awake at night worried that I'll lose it. The company downsized and restructured. We went to teams, and I was "redefined" (they changed my job title). I'm no longer a manager. Now I'm a team member who shares facilitator responsibilities with other members of the team. I hate the job, but I feel powerless to change it. And given the economy, I'm not likely to find another job that pays as well. So I just grin and bear it.

The company I work for was bought by a Japanese conglomerate. I figured I might learn something new about manufacturing efficiency, and I did. I also kept my job, which was important. But no matter how hard I work I'll never advance to management. In America, if you work hard, you are supposed to get ahead.

I hate this company for what it's done to me and my family.

In a world in which work is often associated with one's identity and where making a living is a key to social status, sudden changes that negatively affect one's work status can be devastating. As companies struggle to keep up with the competitive pace, employee roles are continuously redefined, and many people have difficulty with the uncertainty. The preceding examples of work-hate narratives point to an insidious form of hegemony: a narrowly defined but pervasively enforced system that defines rational responses to circumstances beyond our control. In short, we are expected — or trained — to go along with (or even learn to embrace!) continual organizational changes.

Today, competition for well-paying jobs is intense, and people are expected to work harder to keep the (often multiple) jobs they have. In addition, advancement opportunities are more likely to be lateral in nature as the metaphor of "climbing the corporate ladder" continues to dissolve. As a result, as we have consistently pointed out, a clear distinction between the haves and the have-nots exists in almost every community in North America. Even more pronounced are worldwide divisions between a global northern hemisphere (of haves) and a global southern hemisphere (of have-nots) (Barnet & Cavanagh, 1994).

As general uncertainty and corporate hegemony increase, the likelihood of worker resistance also increases. Forms of resistance range from work-hate narratives (Goodall, 1995) to violence in the workplace. The work-hate narrative tells the story of the alienated, displaced, anxious, or angry worker. It can function as a therapeutic tool for relieving job pressure, assessing work-related situations, and regaining control over emotions. Work-hate narratives typically have two stages. In the first stage, the narrator's shock and surprise upon learning of the organization's changes combine with a lost sense of identity. Consider, for example, the following narrative of a middle-aged executive who was downsized:

> The first thing I felt [when] . . . I was fired was surprise — bone-rattling shock at finding myself, for the first time since the week I graduated from grade school, without a place in the world of work. My luck had been so good for so many years that I'd learned to think of it as something I had earned [or] . . . was owed. The idea that it could turn bad so abruptly was, for a while, impossible to absorb. I walked the streets in an almost trancelike state, as if I were on the bottom of the sea, cut off from everything, not like other people anymore. I started to daydream about walking through my front door . . . and seeing dozens of people — old bosses, old colleagues, the very people who had done this to me — leap out from behind the furniture and yell "Surprise! Surprise!" In my daydream they're wearing party hats. They explain how the whole thing had been part of some experiment, and how sorry they were to have had to put me through it. Ah well, I say with a smile, all's well that ends well. But each time I come home, they are not there. (Meyer, 1995, p. 39)

In the second stage of the work-hate narrative, the narrator is more accepting of the new circumstances but often expresses self-blame. In addition, intense envy of co-workers unaffected by the changes is common at this stage. Consider the following example:

> I am ashamed of . . . my feelings: murderous rage, envy, fear, and mostly, shame itself. . . . I am ashamed of myself for being out of work, for getting my family into such a fix, for allowing myself to become an "executive" in the first place and then letting the whole thing go so wrong. I am ashamed of myself for losing. . . .

Yet I'm jealous of anybody who still has the kind of job I used to have, of almost anybody who has a job, period. . . .

Calm down, I tell myself. Stop pacing. Find something sensible to do.

But I find that I can't do any such thing. (Meyer, 1995, p. 39)

We can imagine how this executive's narrative may turn out. On the one hand, if positive results come from the loss of identity and self-blame brought on by the changed circumstances, the story may become one of renewal or of "finding a new life." On the other hand, if the narrator's envy of others and internal rage are not balanced by hopes of a productive future, a less positive outcome is likely.

Remedies for these tales of woe brought on by sudden changes in people's work identity are part of the growing literature on managing organizational change (Kellett, 1999; Kellett & Dalton, 2000; Noer, 1993). However, work-hate narratives and, in extreme cases, workplace violence are evidence of the high stakes involved in organizational change — takeovers, restructuring, job redefinition, and downsizing. Work hate is further proof of the need to go beneath a superficial understanding of a "successful" economy to examine the kinds of trade-offs individuals must make to participate in this success. Above everything else, history teaches that human beings want to be free. Economic success in a capitalist society requires the surrender of part of some of these freedoms: control over our schedules, time with family, maybe even our honesty (Whyte, 1996). A critical approach challenges us to recognize the hegemony and consider the trade-offs.

Power, Negotiation, and Conflict

The critical approach to communication in organizations invites us to rethink the roles of power, gender, race, and class in all aspects of everyday work, but nowhere is the payoff as clear as in issues of organizational negotiation and conflict. Here again, we are witnessing a revolution in our understanding of how conflicts emerge, what issues may be relevant, and what effective communicators should be skilled in to negotiate this increasingly complex organizational terrain. To see how far our thinking has come, let's quickly review the idea of conflict in relation to previous theories of organizations and communication.

The classical approach views conflict primarily as a breakdown in communication between managers and employees whose real problem was simply an interruption in organizational efficiency. Because employees had little, if any, voice in decisions, conflict was usually marginalized or masked by managers who could fire anyone who disagreed openly with them. Conflict was basically viewed as warfare, and the optimal outcome was to trounce your opponent and claim victory. Power was the exercise of control and any "giving in" to demands was perceived as a weakness that could only lead to further trouble. Labor unions were created, in part, to force factory owners and managers to negotiate disputes and conflicts over working conditions and wages, with the threat of a strike by unionized workers a major source of resistance. What were perceived by managers as relatively minor issues — unfairness in the workplace, gender and racial discrimination, being required to do work that fell outside of a posted job description, or sexual harassment — were generally ignored or dismissed. Power was proudly held and control maintained by owners and managers who largely understood that their place in the organizational hierarchy entitled them to do so. For this reason, many conflicts could not be resolved or lessened by the principals, and third-party negotiators were brought in to negotiate a settlement.

The human relations approach differed considerably from the classical approach in that conflict as warfare was replaced with conflict as symptomatic of underlying interpersonal communication problems. Conflict was evidence of poor working relationships between labor and management, and diplomacy rather than warfare should be used to resolve it. Paralleling diplomatic theory in international relations, human relations approaches to conflict forwarded the radical notion that a "concern for the welfare of others" must be balanced with a "concern for the welfare of self" (Blake & Mouton, 1964). Managers were encouraged — largely due to the influence of the Hawthorne Studies — to listen to the complaints of employees, to have an "open door policy," and to seek compromise in conflict situations. From the 1930s through the late 1970s, generations of management trainees and business school graduates were educated to believe that "conflict styles" were choices to be made among five options (competition, collaboration, avoidance, accommodation, and compromise), and that compromise was best because both parties got something out of it and could, therefore, claim at least a partial victory. Organizational detente, however manufactured the consent, was the order of the era.

The human resources approach furthered the aims of improved relations between management and employees by positing that conflict was actually not an aberration to be avoided or compromised but something natural to human groups that could be used for mutual growth, organizational development, and learning. During this era of organizational thinking, bargaining and negotiation were added to the managerial repertoire of "conflict styles" to mediate disputes (Putnam & Pool, 1987). Additionally, distinctions were found between "distributive bargaining" (in which the goal is to maximize individual gains by withholding information) and "integrative bargaining" (in which the goal is to maximize joint gains through an open sharing of information). From a human resources perspective, integrative bargaining allowed for creative solutions through improved communication that fostered learning by both sides to the negotiation. As Putnam (1995) pointed out, this form of bargaining served as "a forum for identifying problems, clarifying misconceptions, signaling needs and interests, and negotiating the meaning of organizational events" (p. 196).

Organizational practitioners had come a long way from viewing conflict as open warfare, but there was still a lot to learn. Systems approaches revealed that conflict should be understood as part and parcel of a broader network of interdependencies, much as a pebble thrown against water produces wider and wider ripples and waves of motion. Rather than viewing conflict as an isolated local matter, researchers and practitioners learned to think of it as a surface reflection of deeper structural issues that in many cases are related to cycles of work activity, routine achievements, patterns of sense making, storytelling, and even seasonal pressures (Weick, 1979). Cultural approaches added to systems thinking by suggesting that the language used to frame and work through conflict was always culturally derived, and the metaphors used to frame the context for the conflict often were invaluable in helping employees and managers understand the power of what is taken for granted in shaping a culture's way of dealing with disputes (Geist, 1995; Neal & Bazerman, 1985; Smith & Eisenberg, 1987). This approach also opened an important pathway into international cultures that in turn has led to new research and theory on ethnic and racial differences in conflict management (Brett & Okumura, 1998; Shuter & Turner, 1997). Finally, the cultures approach identified narratives that emerge from conflicts as vital aspects of cultural storytelling that may also be used to identify oppositional dialectics and to open dialogues (Kellett, 1999; Kellett & Dalton, 2000).

Critical approaches to conflict begin with the idea that there are historical forces and structures of knowledge that have created our understandings of what causes conflict, how it is to be successfully negotiated, and what role power should play in these processes. To begin with, as Putnam and Kolb (2000) point out, the whole history of theorizing about conflict has been dominated by a masculine model that

> is gendered in that the qualities of effective bargainers (e.g., individuality and independence, competition, objectivity, analytic rationality, instrumentality, reasoning from universal principles, and strategic thinking) are linked to masculinity. Those attributes typically labeled as feminine (e.g., community, subjectivity, intuition, emotionality, expressiveness, reasoning from particulars, and ad hoc thinking) are less valued. (p. 80)

These authors forward an alternative model based on feminist critical practice that relies on "the co-construction of the situation and relationship through collaboration, the sharing of experience and emotion, dialogic interaction, and mutual understanding" (Miller, 2003, p. 198).

Postcolonial scholars further this lack of historical understanding of conflict by pointing out that "culture [is] a multiplicity of trajectories" (Shome & Hegde, 2002, p. 265). To begin to appreciate the power relations involved in organizing and circulating vast sums of capital — human, material, and financial — for the production and consumption of consumer goods and services requires a much deeper (and far more sobering) assessment of the politics of representation, oppression, identity (where issues of race, class, and gender are located), and agency. For example, "globalization" is often presented through mediated images that portray workers in developing countries in a series of benevolent images, thus creating a generalized representation of what is to count as "the story of globalization." This story leaves out important questions about whose interests are being served by corporate reliance on cheap labor and what are the social, financial, and political costs to these cultures and people. Viewed this way, disputes that emerge over meetings of the International Monetary Fund (IMF) or the World Trade Organization (WTO), or media accounts of a North Carolina textile apparel company closing all of its North American plants to move operations to South Asia, should be framed as part of a much larger and more complicated global organizational communication system that is, at its core, political.

Just as we have learned that there is no such thing as a neutral symbol, it is also true that there is no such thing as political neutrality when using communication to represent conflict in organizations that compete in global markets. From a critical perspective, the fact that this kind of knowledge has not typically been represented in, for example, textbooks like this one, is evidence of a power to authorize a version of history that effectively silences opposing political points of view. What critical approaches to conflict and negotiation provide us is an opposing point of view that brings to the foreground a story about the politics of power, which includes the power to define history that makes possible and legitimate the corporate colonization of the world's marketplaces, including our own marketplace of ideas. Conflict in the workplace is a manifestation of a deeper historical struggle, and its outcomes are likely to be much farther reaching than any localized negotiated settlement.

Pro-People or Pro-Profits?

The critical approach to organizational communication favors the individual or class of individuals and is, therefore, pro-people. Particularly in a growing economy, it is often criticized for not taking a pro-profits stance and for underestimating the need for companies to remain profitable in an increasingly competitive global market (see the ethical questions emerging from this problem in *What Would You Do?* 6.2). According to Stanley Deetz (1991, 1995), we need to defend individual freedom from corporate domination. He argues that corporate domination in U.S. society runs deeper than most of us recognize and that corporations have replaced governments as the main controlling force in people's lives.

What Would You Do? 6.2

FROM "THE ETHICIST" BY RANDY COHEN

In a letter to Mr. Cohen (*New York Times Magazine,* September 22, 2002), a reader from Fayetteville, Arkansas, writes:

> When I hire local teenagers to do odd jobs, I pay about what they'd earn at a fast food restaurant. I pay adults doing similar work at least twice as much and add a hefty tip, since they have families and basic living expenses. It's not the money but the message: I don't want the teenagers to think this might provide a lucrative career. Is this pay inequality ethical?

On a separate piece of paper or working at a computer, write out your response to this question before reading Mr. Cohen's response. Given what you've learned thus far about critical theory and work, what constitutes an ethical stance on this issue?

Here is Mr. Cohen's printed response:

> Two people doing the same job are entitled to the same pay. How they spend it — on rent or renting video games — is not your concern. It might not be about the money for you, but I assure you it is for your hires. They're not hauling around your boxes for the career counseling you provide.
>
> Looked at benignly, you're giving a bonus to an older worker to help him meet his financial obligations. Looked at less generously, you're penalizing a teenager for not having a couple of kids. Is that what you mean by "the message"? Are you prepared to fully embrace your pay plan? If an employee wants to buy a second TV or have a third child, will you give him a raise? When one of his kids grows up and leaves home, will you cut his pay? The history of this sort of paternalism is not heartening. Such thinking was once used to justify paying single women less than married men because while men had families to support, the women didn't "need" the money.
>
> The ethical solution is to pay what in your area is considered a fair wage for the job — not just what the market will bear, but a decent living wage — and offer it to whoever can do the job. That is, determine pay by the act, not the actor.

Now, given Mr. Cohen's response, think about how this answer might be used to critique some existing corporate policies about hiring workers in developing countries to do jobs for a lot less money than is paid to workers in the United States. How does Mr. Cohen's phrase "pay what in your area is considered a fair wage for the job" complicate your answer? Or does it? Where does the global become local?

Recall that the keys to control are (1) that it is hidden and (2) that people believe they have freedom of choice even though their options are actually quite limited. Thus, according to Deetz (1991), we believe U.S. society is democratic because we vote to elect our leaders, but there is little democracy or participation in the decisions that are made for us by corporations even though the issues profoundly affect our lives. Deetz calls this form of control the "corporate colonization of the life world," and he believes it will lead to the eventual breakdown of families, schools, and other social institutions. Such issues as childbirth, fashion, education, and even morality have been removed from the domain of the family and turned into externally purchased goods and services (Lukes, 1986). People's decisions about where to live and when to have children are increasingly based on career-related concerns. Alienation and loss of identity result when people can no longer turn to the social institutions (e.g., school, church, neighborhood) that once fostered a sense of belonging to a family or community. Modern education, increasingly concerned with training students for occupations, thereby reinforces the notion that corporate domination is both practical and acceptable. According to Deetz (1991),

> With such institutional domination in place, every other institution subsidizes or pays its dues for the integration given by the corporate structure, and by so doing reduces its own institutional role. The state developed for public good interprets that as the need for order and economic growth. The family that provided values and identity transforms that to emotional support and standard of living. The educational institution fostering autonomy and critical thought trains for occupational success. (p. 17)

Despite his sobering analysis, Deetz and others see positive change as possible in the current business world. Peter Block (1993), for example, argues that the ideal of stewardship should replace current notions of self-interest in workplace management. Workplaces could thereby operate democratically as places where employees make decisions together and share accountability for the outcomes of those decisions.

Similarly, Deetz (1995) outlines what he calls the "multiple stakeholder model" for balancing the corporation's profitability needs with society's needs for well-adjusted citizens (Figure 6.1). In this model, Deetz identifies "stakeholder groups" as including not only consumers, workers, investors, and suppliers, but also host communities, general society, and the worldwide ecological community. Deetz aims to demonstrate how business decisions influence all aspects of society and ecology. He thus assesses the worth of a business not only in terms of its profitability, but also in terms of how it uses resources (natural, human, technological, and so on) and how it affects the human community. In democratic societies, the public charter of private corporations gives people the right to perform such analyses. It also gives people the responsibility of ensuring that companies do not take from the collective welfare more than they give

FIGURE 6.1

Multiple Stakeholder Model of the Corporation in Society

STAKEHOLDER GROUPS	MANAGING PROCESS	OUTCOME INTERESTS
Consumers		Goods and services
Workers		Income distribution
Investors	Coordination →	Use of resources
Suppliers		Environmental effects
Host communities		Economic stability
General society		Labor force development
World ecological community		Lifestyles
		Profits
		Personal identities
		Child-rearing practices

Source: Stanley Deetz, *Transforming Communication, Transforming Business* (Cresskill, N.J.: Hampton Press, 1995), p. 50.

back in the form of products, services, and taxes. These "outcome interests," Deetz argues, must be balanced with stakeholder interests through a coordination of "workplace management." In other words, corporate managers and owners, employees, and citizens must all act responsibly to ensure that bottom-line concerns in corporations do not negatively affect society and the ecology of the planet.

Deetz's (1995) multiple stakeholder model attempts to balance global economic competition with a respect for the well-being of the planet and its citizens. As such, it raises critical questions about the potential consequences of a powerful economic elite and of decision making in the hands of multinational corporate and governmental leaders. How can this model be applied? Deetz (1995) outlines four steps toward workplace democracy in which shared decision making among stakeholders is crucial.

1. Create a workplace in which every member thinks and acts like an owner. The point of business is to be of service; this is best accomplished when every stakeholder becomes responsible for decision making and is accountable for the outcomes of those decisions both to the business and to society.

2. The management of work must be reintegrated with the doing of work. The cost of people watching other people work for the purpose of controlling what gets done and how it is done can no longer be seen as economically efficient. Moreover, it leads to bad decisions (i.e., decisions about how to do work are best made by those who actually perform it and will be rewarded by its outcomes) and to less accountability (i.e., "watched" people tend to resist domination by finding ways to slow down work processes or to goof off on the job).

3. Quality information must be widely distributed. To fully empower workers and the societies they serve, the current system of filling up the day with mostly meaningless memos, letters, faxes, and newsletters that only encourage control and domination should be replaced by bringing to the attention of workers "real" information about what is affecting the business and how the business is affecting society and the planet.

4. Social structure should grow from the bottom rather than be reinforced from the top. If the basic idea of a participative democratic workplace values the consent of the governed in the governance of everyday affairs, everything from routine office policies to limiting the terms of managers should be accomplished by ongoing negotiations among the multiple stakeholders. (pp. 170–171)

Although theoretically radical and difficult to implement, Deetz's suggestions move us toward a more democratic dialogue, or what he calls "constitutive codetermination" (p. 174). Similar strategies have been implemented by some companies in their new plants, such as car makers Saturn Corporation and BMW of North America. Indeed, Deetz's model may be easier to implement in new companies than in existing corporate and governmental structures.

In addition to the problems involved in putting it into practice, another limitation of critical theory's revision of existing practices is inherent in the suggestion that democracies are improved when power and decision making are more equally distributed. However, we contend there is no position that is not ideological. Hence, one group's view of the necessity for change tends to be countered by another group's belief that change is unnecessary. To assert the inherent "rightness" of one position is, by the very questions critical theorists have taught us to raise, at best naive and at worst elitist.

Critical Theory and Organizational Communication Research

In many respects, research from a critical perspective is similar to that of the cultural approach (see Chapter 5). To discover the deep structures of power, the investigator must look for details not only about what happens in the organization, and why it happens, but also how it is shaped by economic, political, and social circumstances and forces worldwide. From a critical perspective, the cultural approach moves in a useful direction by focusing on meaning and sense making, but it neglects to ask in whose interest certain meanings and interpretations lie. A critical theorist, then, gathers interpretive cultural data about race, class, gender, age, language, motives, and actions and makes judgments about the power relationships that exist in all aspects of organizing. This is a very subjective enterprise; not only can critical theorists be criticized for all of the same faults as cultural researchers (e.g., narrow samples and bias in selecting participants and events), but they can also be called "elitists."

Critical theorists have been classified as elitists because, in practice, they must be willing to argue that certain individuals or groups are oppressed but are unaware of their oppression. This is the most serious problem with asserting the existence of hegemony. In a marked departure from the cultural approach, critical theorists often maintain that people do not know their own minds (Clegg, 1989). Perhaps this is one reason why more recent critical studies of organizations openly embrace an advocacy role and political agenda, and why critical and cultural studies theorists often rely on passionate, highly personal experiences and arguments to make their cases. As critical studies of organizations increasingly find intellectual intersection with postcolonial and global studies of race, class, and gender, this advocacy role will continue to characterize research and theory. In his "Postscript" to a special issue of the journal *Communication Theory* devoted to postcolonial approaches to communication, Lawrence Grossberg elegantly explains why theorists will continue to take up the mantle of advocate:

> Postcolonial studies delivers the final blow to an illusory understanding of objectivity, which assumes that rigor requires the denial of all passion and the erasure of all political commitment. On the contrary, postcolonial research has demonstrated how much the modern practices of education and knowledge production are informed by the history of colonial power. Without renouncing the very possibility of rigor (as if its history were totally determining), postcolonial studies joins with the best work in communication studies in seeking to find more modest but still rigorous practices that will enable us to contribute, as intellectuals, to what is, in the end, always a political project. (2002, p. 370)

SUMMARY

Critical theory favors individual creativity over constraints on behavior. It seeks to expose corporate colonization, wherein corporations — particularly multinational ones — unobtrusively control much of our lives, from economies to systems of education and training. Similarly, feminism and hegemony reveal the cultural difficulties associated with opening up the organizational dialogue to diverse voices, as well as the potential gains in new organizing methods that might come from such a dialogue. Work-hate narratives, which reveal how individuals are affected by changes in organizations, underscore critical theory's emphasis on everyday practices as a source for understanding power and its consequences.

Until recently, critical theory has been less than successful at advancing alternative organizational arrangements for liberating employees from domination and allowing organizations to survive in the current economic system. While critiques of capitalism have value, critical theory is often criticized for not seeking a middle ground that would allow people in organizations to incrementally improve their lives (Carey, 1992). Focused on macroeconomic issues, critical theories lack an applied approach to the complex contours of organizational life. In this sense, most early attempts to apply critical theories to organizations have not led to real improvements. For example, in explaining how and why work-hate narratives occur, critical theory addresses neither remedies for them nor ways of confronting the hegemonic interests that contribute to and shape them.

Despite its limitations, however, critical theory plays three important roles in organizational communication studies. First, it reminds us that meaning is always inherently political. There are no neutral interpretations and no correct ideology. Second, critical theory points out that the greatest challenge to the hegemony of international corporate power is rooted in democratic alternatives to workplace design and participation. Given multiple bleak visions of our multinational, "megacorporation-controlled" future, we should actively pursue alternative models for promoting diverse participation in an open dialogue. Finally, the new questions about organizing posed by critical theory have encouraged theorists and practitioners to seek ways of fostering participative workplaces. Their work aims to transform controlling and potentially alienating work environments into more democratic and more profitable environments through use of the multiple stakeholder model.

The critical approach to organizing and communicating represents an important transition from the modern to the postmodern organization. Questions about the legitimacy of power tend to lead to further questions about the structure of the social order on which that legitimacy is based. In Chapter 7, we consider alternative forms of organizing that are emerging as a result of globalism and advances in technologies.

QUESTIONS FOR REVIEW AND DISCUSSION

1. What are the advantages and disadvantages of viewing organizational communication in terms of power?

2. How does ideology influence and constrain communication in organizations?

3. What roles do metaphors, myths, and stories play in maintaining and transforming existing power relations?

4. What are the main characteristics of the feminist approach to organizational communication?

5. What can be learned about "work-hate narratives" to help organizations prepare employees for change? What role should organizations play in helping employees transition through times of instability and change?

6. What can workplace democracy do to address some of the abuses of power by organizational members?

7. Compare the systems and cultures perspectives on organizational communication with an eye toward applying the lessons of a critical perspective. What lessons from systems and cultures approaches may be useful to understanding how power operates within organizations? What lessons may help improve companies' chances of becoming more open and democratic?

8. One of the criticisms of the critical perspective on organizations is that it is inherently "elitist." By assuming that there is only one "right" way to understand power — or gender — in organizations, effective dialogue on alternatives is diminished, if not silenced. What do you think about this charge of "elitist discourse"?

CASE STUDY I

The Brilliant Engineer

Carl McKnight is an electrical engineer with twenty-seven years of experience at a major aerospace firm in California. During his long career, Carl has played many pivotal roles in the company, particularly in its development of the space program. He is well respected by his peers and has received a number of awards from both the company and government agencies for his work.

Other than reading scientific journals and attending an occasional conference, Carl does not need to do much else to stay current in his field. He came to it as an electrical genius. Even in college he did not have to work as hard as other students to succeed.

Recently, however, Carl has sensed that his technical expertise seems to carry less weight. In the past, his colleagues regarded his role in designing a new satellite or spacecraft component as crucial. Now, however, his comments are often met with groans. Carl is not sure what to make of this change, but he suspects that it may be related to changes in what customers are looking for in electrical and aerospace design. Carl feels that the customers are too willing to forgo cutting-edge design in exchange for lower cost. He is offended because his expertise, in a sense, has become irrelevant.

ASSIGNMENT

Apply what you have learned in this chapter about critical theory and related concepts to envision a future for Carl McKnight. When responding to the following questions, be sure to address the connections among sources of expertise, sources of overt and hidden power, and processes of overt and covert communication.

1. From his manager's point of view, what plans should be made for Carl's future? How can he best be made a part of the changing situation?
2. From his peers' perspective, what is the best possible future for Carl?
3. From Carl's point of view, what has happened, and what should happen next?

CASE STUDY II

The Woman in Question

Shavonda McKay is a computer software developer who works out of her home in Raleigh, North Carolina, so that she can devote several hours a day to being a mom. As a private contractor, she acquires contracts to perform work for a variety of companies, both in the United States and in northern Europe. Some of the contracts are short-term and require her to work for only a few weeks or months. Others are longer-term and require a continuing commitment to a company.

One of her longer-term commitments is with a company located in Tampa, Florida. For two years she has produced work for them. This year, however, the Tampa-based company was acquired by a larger firm. Now, all employees, whether independent contractors or on-site workers, are required to attend a week-long session in Tampa twice a year. This places a hardship on Shavonda, as being absent from her home for a week means asking her former mother-in-law to keep her children, but she was willing to go along with it because of her continuing commitment to the company.

The first week-long session turned out to be a disaster. Because the new company is owned and operated solely by men, the schedule of events included boating outings for the men, while the three female independent contractors were relegated to "shopping trips" with the wives of the owners. Additionally, Shavonda discovered that her polite complaints about this gender inequity fell on deaf ears. In one instance, a manager informed her that "she could either go along with the program, or find other employment." Shavonda felt both harassed and put down because of her gender.

Two weeks ago, she received notice of the next week-long session. Scanning the schedule of events, she found, once again, that segregation by gender was the order of the day. What should she do?

CHAPTER 7

Alternatives to Hierarchy

In recent years, a number of new organizational forms have been identified, which . . . seem fundamentally different. . . . These new configurations are particularly interesting because of their dependence on communication. Moreover, the increasing prominence of new (or previously marginalized) forms may signal a changing relationship between communication and organizational structure.

— ROBERT D. MCPHEE AND MARSHALL SCOTT POOLE,
   "Organizational Structures and Configurations" (2001)

In this chapter, we continue our exploration of organizational communication theories that challenge accepted beliefs about the world of work. Strong external pressures such as the globalization of trade, the proliferation of "knowledge workers" (people hired on contract to perform specific tasks because of what they know how to do rather than because they have a specific degree or career path), a press toward interorganizational collaboration, employee resistance to arbitrary management practices, and a growing emphasis on continuous innovation have led companies to seek out alternatives to the hierarchical model of organizing. As we suggested in the previous chapter, attempts to organize using hierarchical, compliance-based practices today are doomed to fail, inasmuch as they lead to employee apathy, resistance, disloyalty, and mistrust (Cooper, 2002). Fortunately, a number of new organizational forms that do not follow hierarchical principles are now being developed and tested in forward-looking organizations around the world. In this chapter, we describe three of the most promising of these approaches, which draw upon three new metaphors for thinking about organizing: networks, narratives, and performances. We consider both the unique contribution of each new perspective as well as the commonalities among them.

Paradigms Lost

At least since the Industrial Revolution, the problem of effective organization has been mainly one of integration. As a company or institution grows, the main challenge is to keep it together, to ensure the effective and efficient coordination of people and parts (Kerr, 2000). While there are a number of ways to achieve integration in social systems (all of which involve communication), in practice the options have been limited by a widespread adherence to a mechanical model of organization that treats employees as isolated, fully replaceable cogs within a vast, impersonal machine. From this perspective, integration requires top-down control, and this control is exercised through hierarchy.

This traditional paradigm is familiar to most of us and involves the centralization of decision making, rigid division of labor, strict rules and policies, and the close guarding of business information. It works moderately well in a stable business environment with passive employees and less than demanding customers (Morgan, 1980), but none of these conditions exists today. The current business environment is complex, shifting, demanding, and highly fragmented. But if hierarchical control is no longer the best route to integration, what are the structural alternatives? Relatedly, how much structure does an organization really need to be effective?

Alternative Metaphors for Organizing

Three alternatives to thinking about organizations as hierarchies have emerged in recent years, each associated with a new metaphor designed to either usurp or add to the traditional hierarchical pyramid. These three approaches see organizations respectively as networks, narratives, and performances. Before describing each in turn, let us first identify what they have in common.

- All three approaches — network, narrative, and performance — emphasize the need for greater *fluidity and adaptability* of organizational structures.
- They all seek to *maximize participation* through decentralization of decision making and the widespread sharing of (and access to) information, often with explicit reliance on advanced communication technology.
- They all recognize the ongoing need to *renegotiate power relationships* within these emerging conditions.
- While they all recognize the ongoing tension between individual creativity and organizational constraint, they are each by their nature progressive and aimed toward *minimizing constraints* and maximizing both individual and organizational possibility.

- Each approach takes a cue from both systems theory and what has been called "postmodern" thinking in maintaining that there is *no one best way* — no single overarching framework — that applies equally well to all organizations, or even to the same organization in different areas or at different points in time.

In the next section, we take a closer look at the use of network language and thinking to refigure organizations and organizational theory.

Networks

As we describe further in Chapter 10, a communication network is defined as a collection of individuals who are connected or linked by their emergent pattern of interactions. Unlike formal structures, wherein reporting relationships (seek to) specify who talks to whom, communication networks appear as a byproduct of informal contacts, always emergent and after the fact. Moreover, they are relatively unconstrained in the form they may take, due to the fact that there is no "head" or "authority" insisting on or preventing particular linkages. Communication networks are fluid and emergent and serve an important role in the information flow of any social system.

Despite the obvious utility of networks and networking (long recognized as essential in sales and in job hunting, for example), few organizational designers of the twentieth century could articulate how they might one day be used as load-bearing structures for organizing. More recently, the enormous growth of the Internet, and especially the file-sharing protocols that followed (e.g., Napster, Kazaa), suggested otherwise. By the end of 2002, network forms were everywhere, from interdisciplinary care teams in hospitals to terrorist organizations like Al-Qaeda, powerful and diffuse at the same time. Analysts at RAND, a think tank with a long tradition of working for the U.S. military, go as far as to say that terrorism can only be stopped through "network-centric warfare" and that "it takes networks to fight networks" (Ronfeldt & Arquilla, 2001). The same may be true with regard to remaining competitive in business. Today, most organizations are "embedded to some extent in an emergent interorganizational communication network" (Monge & Contractor, 2001, p. 464). Network organizations are "spiders' webs spun from small, globally dispersed, ad hoc teams of independent organizational entities performing knowledge or service activities. They reshape themselves dynamically as customer requirements change or as the environment evolves" (Shockley-Zalabak, 2002, p. 233).

Scott Poole (in press) summarizes six essential qualities of these new organizational forms, focusing mainly on those consistent with a network or systems approach. According to Poole, new organizational forms:

1. Make use of information technology to integrate across organizational functions

2. Utilize flexible, modular organizational structures that can be readily re-configured as new projects, demands, or problems arise
3. Use information technology to coordinate geographically dispersed units and members
4. Favor team-based work organization, which emphasizes autonomy and self-management
5. Employ relatively flat hierarchies and reliance on horizontal coordination among units and personnel
6. Use intra- and interorganizational markets to mediate transactions such as the assignment and hiring of personnel for projects and the formation of interorganizational networks

There are a number of advantages to network forms. First and foremost, they are highly adaptable, both fast and flexible in response to changing conditions. Second, they encourage participation through the radical decentralization of decisions. Third, they are notoriously difficult to destroy. Lacking both a "head" and a "center," they repel all conventional attacks. In much the same way that viruses elude medical science through their continual shape-shifting, by their nature network forms of organizing have an increased chance of survival over their less flexible, more traditional counterparts.

Network forms also have some disadvantages. First, the decentralization of activity can lead to unproductive redundancy with groups (or cells) working at cross-purposes. Second, the distributed quality of decisions can create ethical problems, inasmuch as there are fewer overarching values, principles, and controls that apply to all members. For example, immediately before their indictments, Enron executives regularly received praise for how their senior management had "turned loose" their best people to aggressively pursue new opportunities. Third, employees today still have difficulty identifying with a network organization, and consequently these kinds of structures may be unlikely to engender much loyalty or commitment, unless there is an ideological cause or religious mission around which its members can rally, as in the case of al Qaeda or the Palestine Liberation Organization (PLO).

In a scant few years, and despite these formidable challenges, network forms of organizing have attained significant popularity across a range of industries (Monge & Fulk, 1995). They have succeeded in part due to parallel advances in communication technology, in the speed, reduced costs, and communal capabilities of electronic communication (Fulk & DeSanctis, 1995). Nevertheless, the network has not been the only metaphor receiving increased attention. Another alternative to hierarchy is narrative.

Narrative

Mechanical models of organizing often reduce communication to the flow of messages along pathways, with little genuine concern for the message content.

Network forms run the same risk of envisioning organization solely as the exchange of information and having little to do with language or the negotiation of meaning. With the exception of work on semantic networks (which attempts to add a shared language dimension), most discussions of network forms focus on existence, strength, and configuration of connections and on the substance of those connections. Narrative approaches offer a useful alternative in this regard.

What is sometimes called modernism by philosophers and cultural theorists is a set of ideas emphasizing individuality, rationality, science, technology, and the inevitability of progress. But numerous disturbing events in the twentieth century have led many to question this take on human life. After all, the Nazi death camps were organized in accord with strict scientific principles; and the technological triumph that was the H-Bomb proved both effective and supremely troubling, especially to those who designed it. In contrast to modernism, *postmodernism* is a set of ideas that challenges the singular domination of scientific thinking as a vehicle for human progress (Lyotard, 1984). Moreover, it rejects all grand narratives in favor of local storytelling — the ability of people everywhere to use resources at their disposal to make sense of their lives.

It is in this latter sense that a narrative perspective can have important implications for organizing. The narrative approach views identity — both individual and organizational — as fluid and socially constructed, pieced together from a range of sources available throughout the culture (e.g., families, friends, television, movies, sports). Seen this way, individuals are capable of engaging in a process of "re-storying" their lives, recategorizing and reframing their behavior in novel ways. For example, flextime and telecommuting have lately morphed into hotdesking and virtual officing; and job sharing is followed by a wholesale deconstruction (a critical taking apart) of the very idea of a "job" (read more about this in the section on "outsourcers" in the next chapter). Increasingly, people today are ignoring old categories and treating work as an occasion for *improvisation*, as a chance to question long-standing constraints and author new scripts for both themselves and their institutions.

In contrast to the rigid ways hierarchical models compel integration, organizational narratives promote integration by encouraging adherence to a common story. Organizational leaders exert influence on follower behaviors through storytelling, that is, by guiding employee sense making with their version of what they stand for and why they do the things that they do (Tichy, 1995). Organizational members live at the intersection of numerous competing narratives, and it is not at all assured that the one endorsed by top management — the "preferred" version that reflects the desired culture — will prevail (Gardner, 1998). In this sense, organizations are characterized by stories and counter-stories, cultures and subcultures; one's power has to do with one's degree of influence over framing and sense-making processes that are essentially co-constructive (Boje, 1991; Fairhurst & Sarr, 1996). Storytelling is not a neutral process (Mumby, 1988; Putnam & Fairhurst, 2001) and "narrative discourse is a mode of persuasion used to create and maintain a culture of obedience, to invent a credible history, and to exert covert control" (Putnam & Fairhurst, 2001, p. 110).

A revealing example may be drawn from higher education. The reputations of colleges and universities depend heavily on the narratives that circulate about them, which — for the most part — can have little connection to the educational experience. Moreover, a school's image largely drives its reputation, *whether or not it fairly represents its actual practices or investments*. This kind of cultural imagery is self-fulfilling to a point: Certain types of students seek out institutions known for challenging academics or athletics, and so on. Still, one has to wonder about the power of these stories to mask dramatic inconsistencies in class size, student resources, and quality of teaching. As a rule, these discrepancies are not brought to the surface because those attending schools with "good stories" have an incentive to perpetuate the myth — that is, the value of their degrees in the marketplace depends in part on their school's image and reputation.

Narrative forms of organizing have some distinct advantages. First, and contrary to what happens with network forms, narratives inspire identification and commitment. People have a basic need for sense making and will give themselves over to a good story. Multiple listeners can hear different things in the story at the same time. Second, narratives travel well; for a leader who makes an effort to do so, it is relatively easy to activate the grapevine and spread a message quickly. Third, significant organizational changes can be accomplished through narrative without necessarily doing much in the way of capital investment. For example, if a large number of employees can be convinced that "we are in a fight for our survival," this belief alone can be highly motivational.

The disadvantages of narrative forms are equally easy to see. First, you run the risk of words getting ahead of deeds, of being accused of "empty rhetoric" if organizational alignment doesn't accompany the new story. Second, there is a distinct lack of originality when it comes to the creation of organizational stories — people often choose boring, well-worn themes (e.g., first-time quality, 100 percent customer satisfaction) over newer, bolder ones. Hence the reliance on narrative can lead to a loss of distinctiveness when the narratives that are chosen are the same or similar across many organizations. Third, and finally, there are no stipulations or limitations concerning the moral or ethical value of a chosen narrative. The fact that millions of people buy into the story is still no guarantee that the story ought to be told.

An interesting example of this last point can be found in Taylor's (1990) insightful analysis of prevailing narratives at Los Alamos during the Manhattan Project, which produced the first atomic bomb. Taylor reports that project employees working in secret created a compelling story about their work, which was essential to the furthering of technological innovation and national interests. Lab employees were so convinced by this narrative that it was only after the bombs were deployed on civilians that dissenting views became known.

Thus far in this section we have provided two methods of organizational integration — networks and narratives — that eschew hierarchy and rely heavily on informal communication. The third and final section offers yet another language for thinking about organizing, that of performance.

Performance

Over a decade ago, organizational communication was described for the first time as a kind of cultural performance (Pacanowsky & O'Donnell-Trujillo, 1988). Central to this idea was the notion that organizations' sole existence comes from when they are being made and remade through interaction. Another way of thinking about integration, then, is as a kind of joint performance. This perspective takes the narrative approach and brings it to its feet, placing the *speaking body* front and center. A practical example of this approach is the Walt Disney theme park philosophy (they have a front- and backstage, and employees are "cast members") but it can be found in many service organizations. Employees work hard to perform their assigned roles, and managers conduct surveillance to make certain they are doing just that.

The importance of performance has been acknowledged before in research on organizational rites and rituals. Award ceremonies, annual parties, training sessions, and operational reviews are all occasions where the prevailing culture — complete with contradictions — is performed. While one can look at these events as extensions of key organizational narratives, there is a crucial difference. Specifically by involving people's bodies in joint activity, these performances are doubly reinforcing of prevailing views.

Much of the research on organizing as performance has been done in the service sector, specifically with regard to jobs that require emotional work. Studies of cashiers (Rafaeli & Sutton, 1987), flight attendants (Hochschild, 1993; Murphy, 1999), and nurses (Laine-Timmerman, 2002) use the language of performance to explain how employees are more or less successful at keeping to the "script," which in these professions implies a ritualized emotional display. And most prescriptive work on customer service takes a performative stance, encouraging employees to see customers as the audience and to respond with "scripted" responses.

An especially intriguing aspect of performance theory is the predictable sequence of events that comprises dramatic action. Following Victor Turner (1980), things get interesting when events don't follow the script, creating a "breach" that must be "repaired." Think of all of the organizational routines that one witnesses each day (e.g., boarding an airplane, ordering food at a restaurant, checking into a hotel, taking a business lunch, going to get the mail). Now think of what happens when a routine is violated, creating a breach. Generally speaking, any kind of violation creates strong feelings and leads the customer to expect some kind of repair (e.g., an apology or a refund). Notice what happens to your mood when a fast-food restaurant takes more than a minute or two to prepare your food. Organizational routines and scripted performances are most visible to us when they have been violated.

Some organizational performances create great emotional demands, as is the case with physicians who must tell someone that a loved one has died, or flight attendants who must keep a positive demeanor during bad weather or when faced with unruly passengers (Murphy, 1999). The performance lens is especially useful when thinking about organizational routines that are accomplished by multiple actors playing multiple roles. Part of what makes the flight attendant performance so challenging, for example, is the dramatic deference that must be given to pilots, and the constant need to balance a technical performance designed to ensure passenger safety with a hospitality-oriented performance whose purpose is to silence any thought that one's safety might be in question.

Joint performance always involves a balancing between scripted action and improvisation. Observing a cardiac resuscitation in an emergency room, one is impressed by the fluid overlapping of roles, how each person's training and experience have prepared them to play some part in this critical event. At the same time, if one looks closely, a range of verbal and nonverbal cueing behaviors become visible — people keeping each other in role, and on track, with the goal being a successful performance (which doesn't always mean a successful resuscitation — even if the patient is DOA, the team performs the resuscitation so that the family can be assured that "we tried everything"). Also, in the event that something doesn't go according to script — e.g., a sedated patient suddenly wakes up (!) — these actors become improvisors par excellence. Very often, such as when an orchestra makes a mistake in a performance, the recovery is so quick that the audience doesn't even notice, or notices but assumes that was how the piece was supposed to sound.

There is, in fact, a growing body of research comparing the work people do in organizations with jazz performance (Barrett, 1998; Bastien & Hostager, 1988; Eisenberg, 1999; Hatch, 1999). What this work emphasizes is that competent and even exceptional performance is much less about rigid controls than it is about creating structures that support without specifying. What this research also shows is that creativity and innovation can best arise in an atmosphere of mutual positive regard and a willingness to take risks.

Using a performance frame for thinking about organizing has several distinct advantages. First, it foregrounds the creativity latent in many organizational processes, and in particular the tremendous improvisational abilities shared by many organizational actors. Second, a performance approach forces us to recognize that organizing is always done before multiple audiences, who may protest loudly and even enter the performance if it doesn't meet their expectations. Third, there is a joy in pulling off a successful performance — however mundane — that people find to be emotionally fulfilling. A performance approach leads us to attend to the aesthetic quality of organizational life, the sensual nature of employee experience.

On the negative side, inauthentic performances can take a heavy emotional toll, leading to cynicism, anxiety, and depression. When employees have no say over their role or their lines, they may become equally or more alienated than factory workers who have no communicative responsibilities. They may become resentful that they are being asked to use their supposed "emotions" in this way. Second, a performance frame focuses mainly on the interaction to the exclusion of contextual factors such as compensation and work conditions, erroneously implying that these external factors can all be countered or coped with through improved performance. Third, and finally, what constitutes a "successful" performance is entirely relative to one's goals and interests — many financially successful musicians report how hard it is to continue to be creative when the audience (and hence the promoters) only want to hear the hits, over and over again. The ethical question is this: When is it best to follow the script, and when should you leave it?

A Postmodern Aesthetic

Earlier in this chapter, we identified some similarities among three emerging alternatives to hierarchy, highlighting how each is concerned with fluidity, participation, power, and possibility. But there is an underlying similarity — what might be called a postmodern aesthetic — that further reflects these new forms. A major aspect of this aesthetic is *challenge to established forms of authority*. As organizations have downsized and restructured, for example, the traditional model of organizing has been challenged by a political and economic aesthetic: team-based organizing made possible by advanced information technologies. Hierarchies have collapsed into teams and flat structures that differ considerably in their forms of decision making, information processing, and communication. The traditional distinction between managers and workers has been blurred as team facilitators and coaches have entered team-based organizations. At the same time, companies have demanded more of their employees' time by providing them with day-care services and home computers and fax machines. Here we see challenges to the authority of international date lines and even the routine separation between day and night.

These changes have not come without resistance. Consider the challenge many people in their thirties face when deciding whether or not to commit their lives to work. A growing number of people from this generation are questioning the assumption that people should work harder to acquire more commodities and toys, arguing that the near-obsessive dedication to making money more often than not leads to broken families, global conflict, and the further poisoning of the earth. Many people of all ages today are evolving a different work ethic, which goes something like this: Do more with less, value families over workplaces, and promote ecological awareness. Some of the potential implications of this changing worldview are explored in *What Would You Do?* 7.1.

A second aspect of the emerging postmodern aesthetic is a strong bias against unneeded structure. All of these approaches stress the use of the minimal amount of formal organization to get the job done. Inverting the traditional model, which assumed the necessity of structure and forced employees to argue for freedom, the new model assumes freedom and insists that structure be justified to prove its necessity. A common example arises around the issue of centralization. In accord with the postmodern aesthetic (and in dramatic contrast to the past) work is assumed to be temporally and geographically distributed unless there is a good reason to centralize.

A third aspect of the emerging aesthetic is an ethic of team-based collaboration in all things. Whereas traditional organizations were all about solo achievers, today's organization is all about creating great groups that can collaborate at a very high level. We can see the difference in sports teams, where even a handful of superstars is no match for a team that works. And we can see the difference in jazz bands, the members of whom set aside their egos in exchange for a transcendent level of collaboration (Eisenberg, 1990).

A fourth and final aspect of the postmodern aesthetic is a thoroughgoing disregard for boundaries. Within most organizations, this is evidenced in the pervasiveness of interdisciplinary teams for everything from product development to concurrent engineering to marketing. In some cases, these boundaries are also blurred for the customer, as is the case at the Senior Oncology Program at the Moffitt Cancer Center in Tampa, Florida. At Moffitt, older people with cancer are assessed and treated by a dynamic, interdisciplinary team of professionals representing every relevant specialty. The idea is that since life defies easy categorization, effective medical care must be structured in a way that can visualize the borders and connections between these arbitrary categories.

SUMMARY

We began this chapter with the notion that hierarchy no longer functions as it once did as a reliable means of integration in organizations. Changing environmental conditions have caused companies to seek out and experiment with new organizational forms, alternatives to the traditional hierarchical pyramid. Three forms in particular — network, narrative, and performance — have received a great deal of attention from both organizational communication scholars and practitioners.

With regard to network form, we begin with the assumption that most if not all organizations today must function within a broad interorganizational network in order to survive. We then describe what the structure looks like and

What Would You Do? 7.1

A Dilemma of Postmodern Ethics

The postmodern aesthetic is generally associated with situational ethics: There are no absolute standards for determining right and wrong. We must interpret ethical choices based on our definition and analysis of the context that produces the need for the choice and on our understanding of the potential outcomes of those choices.

Although this view of ethics is somewhat consistent with our interpretive approach to organizational communication, it suffers from a lack of ethical consistency. That is, without absolute standards of right and wrong, critics argue, we are too often left adrift on a sea of relativity. Furthermore, if we agree that contexts shape our interpretations of right and wrong, then it may be argued that a lack of information about a context can lead to alternative ethical conclusions. Put simply, how can we be held accountable for ethical decisions and actions that we take when we lack important information?

Furthermore, some radical postmodernists, drawing strength from the extreme left of critical theory, ask, Isn't the whole concept of ethics critically suspect? In their view, ethics refers to and is informed by a narrative of right and wrong. That narrative, created and used by the powerful, is meant to suppress the powerless by limiting how right and wrong can be analyzed and understood.

Finally, how can we resolve the ethical dilemma posed, on the one hand, by the postmodern advice to "trust the surfaces" when, on the other hand, it is viable to examine a situation for evidence of deep structures of power? Does ethics reside in surfaces, in structures, in both, or in some other formulation? Consider the complexity of this dilemma in the following scenarios:

1. You are called to an emergency meeting by your supervisor, who informs you that the company needs a press release to "justify" a recent toxic waste accident that it claims was not its fault. "This is just damage control," you are told, "and even though we don't have all the facts yet, we cannot afford to be made to look negligent by the media." How will you handle this situation? What are the ethical dimensions of the decision before you?

2. You discover that a co-worker has been reading your personal e-mail as well as the e-mail of others in the company. From your e-mail, the co-worker found out about your secret romance with

another company employee. The organization has a strict policy forbidding romantic relationships between its employees. Your co-worker has threatened to tell your boss about the romance if you report his reading of others' e-mail. How will you handle this situation? What ethical issues does it present?

the pros and cons of adopting a network approach. Next, our discussion of narrative returned us to some of the themes from earlier chapters such as the communication of culture and the hegemonic power of stories. Finally, we enumerated the characteristics, advantages, and disadvantages of taking a performance approach, highlighting the pervasiveness of improvisation in organizational life today.

QUESTIONS FOR REVIEW AND DISCUSSION

1. What are the advantages of a hierarchical approach to organizing? When is hierarchy absolutely necessary in contemporary society? Why?

2. Pick any product that you own or consume and trace its origins as far back as you can. What kinds of interorganizational networks and connections did you uncover in your search?

3. Review the literature your school distributes to potential applicants. Try to identify the narrative they are promoting for the school, and discuss how well that narrative aligns with your own experience as a student.

4. Reflect on a situation where you witnessed a breach in a performance, where things didn't go according to the script. Describe what happened, how you felt, and how well the organizational actors recovered.

CASE STUDY I

The Workplace of the Future

Scantel is the leading telecommunications company in Sweden, and until recently was an arm of the Swedish government. When it broke off from the state, the company had more than fifty offices in various locations around Sweden and many employees who had worked for the agency for all of their adult lives. In an effort to promote better coordination and integration, the company decided to consolidate all Scantel employees in one new location called Madru, located out in the country at the site of an old airport. Seeing this as a unique "green field" opportunity, senior management envisioned this new facility as "the workplace of the future," by which they meant it would be paperless and completely modular — there would be no permanent desks or offices, and employees would be encouraged to work anywhere, anytime, in accordance with their particular needs.

Employees began moving into Madru in 2001, and while the new concept seems to be working quite well, there have been some interesting tensions in the transition. More specifically, management had put a great deal of thought into the architecture of the space and the nature of the communication technology, but far less to the social, interpersonal, and identity implications of the move. So while the network infrastructure is strongly in place (so much so that they are simultaneously marketing the "Madru Solution" to other firms), employee narratives and performances are changing more slowly. For example, many employees remain unsure about the "real" motives behind the modularization of the workspace, and wonder how much of it was really about cost reduction. Also, employees from certain professions (e.g., law) are having some difficulties adapting to work in a radically open and paperless environment.

ASSIGNMENT

Imagine that you have been retained as a consultant to Scantel and asked to advise the company on how to best (and these are their words) "align peoples' perceptions of Madru with the physical and technological realities."

1. What communication issues are involved in making your recommendation?
2. How do the different metaphors raised in this chapter — network, narrative, performance — interrelate in this specific setting?
3. If Scantel could begin the project again, what if anything might you recommend it do differently?

CASE STUDY II

Designing a New University

In response to changing demographics, the state university system in Florida recently opened a new university on the Gulf Coast near Fort Myers. There has been much public debate about the nature and purpose of the project. The state sees it as an opportunity to address some long-standing problems in college education, as well as a way to bring current business practices into a university environment.

ASSIGNMENT

Using your knowledge of colleges and universities (and of education in general) and taking what you have learned about alternative organizational forms in this chapter, write or discuss your ideas for the successful design of this new university. Consider the following issues:

1. Given the changing nature of work and of organizations today, what can the university do to best prepare students for the future?
2. How should the university be structured in terms of administrative, business, and academic relationships?
3. What communication systems work best for students and faculty?
4. How should you structure the compensation and reward systems for university employees?
5. How can the physical layout of the university symbolize the commitment to postmodern principles? What other aspects of the physical environment should you consider?
6. How will globalization affect your plans for the future?
7. What type of information-processing systems will you develop for registration and advising? How will these systems differ from those in a traditional university?
8. How will you ensure that power and accountability are shared throughout the university?
9. What can be done to emphasize customer service in the university? Who are the "customers" in education anyway?

PART III

Levels of Analysis

CHAPTER 8

The Experience of Work

The future belongs to those knowledge workers who can make themselves understood to others who don't share their knowledge base.

— PETER DRUCKER, *Managing for the Future* (1992a)

Our goal in the first seven chapters of this textbook was to help you understand the evolving role of communication in organizations throughout history, emphasizing important theories and concepts. By now, you understand that there are many different ways of thinking about organizational communication, from the traditional (i.e., communication as an efficient means of conveying work-related information) to the contemporary (i.e., communication as a process of narrative sense making and joint performances across vast, dynamic networks). The remainder of the book goes in a different direction. Specifically, we explore the various organizational contexts or situations in which communication matters the most. This chapter, for example, examines how communication figures in how people make sense of their work lives. The following chapters pose similar questions regarding communication in work relationships, teams, technology, and the total business enterprise.

One question we often ask people in organizations is, "How is work different today from five years ago?" The responses come quickly and with remarkable consistency. The bursting of the dot-com bubble and subsequent decline in the stock market led to significant layoffs that have many people doing the work of two or more employees. At the same time, there is more focus on customer service than ever, and employees at all levels are increasingly expected to be accessible around the clock. Moreover, as we discussed in Chapter 1, the relationship between the individual and the organization has undergone a dramatic change. Blind loyalty is dead, and the "new social contract" between employers and employees dictates that employment will continue only as long as the relationship is mutually profitable. Everyone is looking for a better deal.

Management expert Peter Drucker (1992a) views today's revolutionary changes in the world of work and technology as signaling the dawn of a new age. He argues that just as humans evolved from hunters and gatherers to agriculturalists to urban industrialists, the current era involves another evolution — from the industrialist to the "new knowledge worker." According to Drucker, the new knowledge worker possesses four key characteristics:

1. A college education
2. The ability to apply analytic and theoretical learning
3. A commitment to lifelong learning
4. Good communication skills

The knowledge workers of today move through various kinds of work situations, some of which involve working for others in organizations and some of which include networked or team-based entrepreneurial activities. Today's students enter a world of work that routinely involves both working for organizations as well as investigating more independent, entrepreneurial options (Kotter, 1995). The first section of this chapter discusses the experience of work within organizations; the second section examines the experience of independent work outside of organizations.

The Experience of Work within Organizations

The experience of work within organizations is marked in part by each company's set of rules and expectations for employee attitudes and behaviors. Just as organizations may seek to control employees, they also provide resources that help make sense of life experiences. Since the Industrial Revolution, most people in the United States and Europe have survived financially by working for organizations. In exchange for wages, they have allowed at least part of their lives to be controlled by the company. The organization, in turn, has sought to elicit employee cooperation in working toward its goals. From the employee's point of view, the challenge has been twofold: a quest for individuation (personal achievement and distinction) and identification (membership in a larger community) (Burke, 1969; Cheney, 1983). Communication plays an important role in achieving individuation and identification; it is used symbolically to induce cooperation among people who, by their nature, respond strongly to symbols (Burke, 1969; Tompkins, 1987).

Even a cursory look at the corporate landscape reveals the enormous power organizations have over the lives of individuals. Although some of this power is overt, most of it is more subtle or hidden (recall our discussion of critical theory in Chapter 6). Rising competition and consolidation in most industries continue to make one's specific job prospects unstable. As a result, although most people today are confident of obtaining employment of some kind, they are challenged more than ever to design a career path or work life that makes sense over time.

Our examination of the individual's experience of work within an organization begins with a discussion of organizational assimilation, that is, how people come to organizations initially and how they learn to make sense of and incorporate the organization's values and goals with their own belief systems. From a communication perspective, our concern here is how the new employee enters the organizational dialogue and finds (or fails to find) a legitimate voice. In addition, the experience of work within organizations is marked by indicators of cooperation and resistance or stress. The indicators of cooperation include job satisfaction, job involvement, organizational identification, organizational commitment, employee empowerment, and worker productivity. Conversely, the indicators of resistance include stress, burnout, absenteeism, and turnover. The final part of this section explores new directions for the organization of work.

Assimilation: Entering the Organizational Dialogue

Assimilation is a process by which people learn the rules, norms, and expectations of a culture over time and thereby become members of that culture. We are all to some extent assimilated into a national and local culture. As children, we were taught by parents and others how to become members of a family, community, religion, or country. Thus, assimilation involves learning the rules that guide what members of a culture think, do, and say. Assimilation of its members is essential in any culture and begins at an early age. For example, in the United States, children learn much about American culture during dinnertime conversations with family members (Ochs, Smith, & Taylor, 1989).

In organizations, describing the assimilation process helps us understand how the new employee learns about and makes sense of the organization's culture (Jablin, 1987; Kramer & Miller, 1999). Although the employee's first week on the job is filled with surprises, over time the employee learns the formal and informal rules that govern behavior in the organization. This learning process has three broad stages: (1) anticipatory socialization, (2) organizational assimilation, and (3) organizational turning points or exits.

Anticipatory Socialization

Some of the lessons about the nature of work are learned long before the job begins. In the anticipatory socialization stage, people learn about work through communication. There are two forms of anticipatory socialization: vocational and organizational. The vocational type, which begins in childhood, involves learning about work and careers in general from family members, teachers, part-time employers, friends, and the media. Children and adolescents acquire a general knowledge of accepted attitudes toward work, of the importance of power and status in organizations (Jablin, 1985), and of work as a source of meaningful personal relationships (Atwood, 1990).

Later in life, the organizational type of anticipatory socialization involves learning about a specific job and organization. It takes place before the first day of work and is typically accomplished through company literature, such as brochures, personnel manuals, and Web sites, as well as through interactions between job applicants and interviewers. Through such communication, individuals develop expectations about the prospective job and organization. However, their expectations are often inflated and unrealistic due to interviewers' tendency to focus on positive aspects of the job and the company. In fact, because job interviews typically result in more information for the prospective employer than for the prospective employee, some researchers (Wilson & Goodall, 1991) advocate changing the nature of the interview to more closely reflect the model of dialogue discussed in Chapter 2.

Organizational Assimilation

The experience of organizational assimilation involves both surprise and sense making (Louis, 1980). As new employees' initial expectations are violated, they attempt to make sense of their job and the organization. "The newcomer learns the requirements of his or her role and what the organization and its members consider to be 'normal' patterns of behavior and thought" (Jablin, 1987, p. 695). For example, it is common for presidents and CEOs of companies to attend orientations for new employees and to deliver the message that their "door is always open" to employees who want to talk. In most cases, the employees who take this seriously are surprised by the likely reality that the president or CEO is either unavailable or unhelpful or that such conversations are not much appreciated by line and middle managers. After a few weeks, these employees come to make sense of "how things really work around here."

Newcomers' search for information carries a sense of urgency. Typically, new employees have some difficulty performing their jobs and getting along with others until they reach a level of familiarity. Potential sources of useful information for newcomers include (1) official company messages (e.g., from management, orientation programs, and manuals), (2) co-workers and peers, (3) supervisors, (4) other organizational members, including secretaries, security guards, and employees in other departments, (5) customers and others outside of the organization, and (6) the task itself. Newcomers thus attempt to "situate" themselves in an unfamiliar organizational context, but to do so they must first learn a great deal about how existing members define the organization's culture. To solicit the information they need, new employees tend not to rely on direct questioning because substantial risks may be associated with asking irrelevant questions. Instead, they use other tactics to solicit information about the organizational culture (Miller & Jablin, 1991; see Table 8.1). One of the more interesting of the tactics, "disguising conversations," involves making jokes about

TABLE 8.1

Newcomer's Information-Seeking Tactics

TACTIC	EXAMPLE
Overt question	"Who has the authority to cancel purchase orders?"
Indirect question	"I guess I won't plan to take a vacation this year." (Implied: "Do we work through the holidays if we don't finish the project?")
Third parties	To a co-worker: "I'm making a presentation to the president. Does she like it if you open with a joke?"
Testing limits	Arriving at work wearing casual clothes and observing others' reactions.
Disguising conversations	"That safety memo was sure a riot. Can you believe the gall of those guys?" (Waiting for reaction to see whether others also think it was funny.)
Observing	Watching which employees get praised in meetings and emulating those who do, paying attention to specific individuals.
Surveillance	Eavesdropping on peer conversations; paying careful attention at office parties; monitoring the environment for clues.

people, procedures, or activities and watching to see whether others think they're funny.

Over time, employees may evolve from newcomer status into full-fledged members of the organization (Jablin, 1987). This period of transition may or may not be lengthy, depending on the organization and the industry involved. In hotels and restaurants, for example, employees may feel like old-timers after only six months on the job, whereas in universities and professional associations, the transitional period may last nearly a decade. Of course, not everyone makes the transition to member. Either the organization or the individual may opt out of the relationship if there is a poor fit. Moreover, the assimilation process is rarely as neat as these "stages" make it sound; large organizations in particular often make room for numerous diverse voices and definitions of membership (Bullis, 1999).

During the transitional period of organizational assimilation, employees begin to differentiate between rules and norms that must be followed and those that can be ignored. Feeling more comfortable with the rules of the organization, employees begin to individualize their job, develop their own voice, and behave in ways that both conform to and transform the existing rules. For example, a new supervisor who makes minor changes in how work is delegated distinguishes his or her department from others in the organization. Whereas newcomer behavior focuses on discovering constraints, the transition toward assimilation is marked by a greater degree of creativity. The degree of balance between the two — and of the employee's satisfaction with his or her role in the organization — largely determines patterns of cooperation, resistance, and exit.

It is useful to apply to organizational assimilation the idea that all organizational communication comprises lists and stories:

> Lists are technical communication, progressive, public; and once shared they extend a power base. Stories are communications about personal experience told in everyday discourse. They reflect local knowledge, give coherence to group subcultures, change over time, and contain multiple voices. (Browning, 1992a, p. 281)

Competent members of organizations are able both to understand and to work with itemized lists, such as rules, procedures, and standard performance metrics, and to relate to stories that highlight informal understandings about an organization's politics and traditions. Lists are used to document and support official procedures, whereas stories can be either tools of resistance or instruments for maintaining the status quo.

Organizational Turning Points

In the course of one's engagement with an organization, much can happen that significantly changes the relationship. Research on organizational assimilation sometimes focuses on these critical moments, which have been called "turning points" (Bullis & Bach, 1989). Consider your experience as a student. The turning points in your experience probably include identifying with your college or university and its organizations or teams as well as choosing your major area of study. Together with other moments (some more positive than others), these turning points in your experience as a student have permanently altered your understanding and interpretation of the school and your membership in it. For example, you probably know students who are wholehearted supporters of your school's programs and teams and others who openly express more negative attitudes toward your college or university. In the same sense, employees come to understand their role in their place of work through organizational turning points. Examples might include receiving a favorable performance review, getting a long-awaited promotion, participating in genuine dialogue, or being unfairly criticized by a supervisor.

In addition to altering employees' perceptions of identification with the company, turning points can structure perceptions of career choices, job transfers, and even one's purpose in life. Turning points can change a person's life, influencing how the person sets goals, determines career paths, and makes the connection between work life and one's life course more generally (Fox, 1994).

Indicators of Cooperation

Cooperation, when present in the employee's experience of work, can have positive outcomes for both the individual and the organization. Indicators of cooperation include job satisfaction and involvement, identification with and commitment to the organization, and employee empowerment and productivity. Each of these ideas is discussed in turn.

Job Satisfaction

The most common indicator of cooperation is job satisfaction, sometimes called employee morale. Job satisfaction is measured by researchers and managers alike in their attempt to understand organizational climates. Not surprisingly, this focus on employee satisfaction originated in the human relations and human resources approaches to organizations and communication discussed in Chapter 3. Douglas McGregor, Frederick Herzberg, and Abraham Maslow have argued, in different but related ways, that a satisfied employee is one whose needs are being met. Employees have general levels of needs that correlate with degrees of job satisfaction:

- Level 1 needs include safe working conditions and sufficient pay, rewards, and equipment.
- Level 2 needs, which include supportive interpersonal relationships with co-workers and supervisors, contribute to employee morale and motivation (Richmond & McCroskey, 1979).
- Level 3 needs include opportunities for personal growth, such as those provided by challenging work tasks, greater responsibility, greater independence, and a clear career path for the future.

When all three levels of employee needs are satisfied, higher levels of job satisfaction are likely to result.

In some companies, basic job safety has the single greatest impact on employee satisfaction. Pressures to increase productivity and efficiency have been tied to the growing number of injuries sustained by workers in U.S. companies. In 1991, for example, twenty-five people died in a fire at a North Carolina poultry-processing plant with a history of negligent safety inspections; the emergency exit doors were locked (Baker, 1991).

A satisfied worker, then, is paid fairly, is provided with safe and pleasant working conditions, has supportive relationships with others at work, is challenged by his or her work, and has a significant degree of control over how tasks are performed. Although fair pay and pleasant working conditions can be costly for businesses, theorists generally agree that providing them leads to high levels of job satisfaction. In times of low unemployment, many companies make significant improvements in these areas in their efforts to attract and retain good people. Challenging work, on the other hand, only increases employee satisfaction when employees desire it (Loher, Noe, Moeller, & Fitzgerald, 1985).

There is disagreement about the productivity benefits of a satisfied work-force. Although researchers and managers have long hoped to prove that a correlation exists between job satisfaction and productivity, research studies do not in general support this conclusion (Loher et al., 1985). Instead, while productive workers tend over time to be happier if their productivity is recognized and rewarded, simply making unproductive workers happier through improved pay and working conditions has not been shown to increase their productivity. Put differently, an organization with high employee morale is as likely to have low productivity as it is to have high productivity because job satisfaction is not itself a key factor in determining levels of productivity.

Job Involvement

Job involvement, the degree to which employees personally involve themselves in their work and thereby satisfy personal goals, has been shown to have a direct, positive effect on worker performance and productivity. We are all familiar with people who display extreme levels of job involvement, from the person who "lives to work" to those who "work to live," seeking employment primarily to support their activities outside of work. These extremes are commonly found among workers today, even among high-ranking managers. As one engineering executive told us, "I come to work, put in my eight hours, get my paycheck, and go home to the things that really matter." For people who view work as a means to an end, there is an ongoing tension between making a living and making a life. At the other extreme are workaholics who feel at some level that their time at work is more invigorating, challenging, involving, and "functional" than their time at home.

Organizational Identification

Organizational identification is the overlap between an employee's values and those of the organization (Cheney, 1983; Tompkins & Cheney, 1985). It is accomplished through "the forging, maintenance, and alteration of linkages between persons and groups" (Scott, Corman, & Cheney, 1998, p. 304). "As members identify more strongly with the organization and its values, the organization becomes as much a part of the member as the member is a part of the organization" (Bullis & Tompkins, 1989, p. 289).

Organizational identification, the internalization of company values and assumptions by employees, can foster a sense of community (Bullis & Tompkins, 1989). However, it can also operate to control employee decision making. Specifically, it guides people toward "certain problems and alternatives" and thereby biases their choices "toward alternatives tied to the most salient identifications . . . [thereby] narrowing the decision makers' span of attention" (Tompkins & Cheney, 1985, p. 194). Identification can strongly shape interpretation in that the degree of employees' identification affects their definitions of what is real or taken for granted in any given situation. From a critical perspective, organizational identification exerts unobtrusive control over decisions.

Today, multiple identification targets are available to individuals, from job to profession to organization to work group. These identifications should also be expected to change over time. Many organizations have recently restructured their operations, replacing isolated departments with teams of people that are expected to be more flexible and creative in accomplishing work tasks. As a result of restructuring, identification may shift from the organization to the individual team or work group (Barker & Tompkins, 1994). Interestingly, the power of team identification in regulating individual behavior has been shown to be as strong as that of organizational identification. Regardless of its source, then, identification is an effective way to shape behavior through concertive control. Finally, while it may be tempting to imagine certain jobs as inherently more desirable targets of identification, research suggests otherwise. Notably, people in "dirty" jobs — butchers, undertakers, prison guards — develop elaborate ways of framing their work to ennoble and glorify it (Ashforth & Kreiner, 1999).

Organizational Commitment

Organizational commitment refers to dedication and support for the organization's goals and values. It encompasses both attitudes and behaviors, such as speaking positively or negatively about the company in public and stating one's intentions to remain with or leave the organization (Kiesler, 1971; Steers, 1977). High levels of commitment are to be expected from "traditional" workers who favor longevity, clear direction, and an explicit career path. It is much less likely among "emergent" workers who don't mind job hopping and prefer to be paid for performance (Murphy, 1999). Although organizational identification and commitment often go hand in hand, the link between commitment and job involvement is not as strong. Upon reflection, this makes sense: Employees can be highly committed to their company for a number of reasons but only minimally involved in their jobs.

Many factors contribute to a company developing a high level of commitment from its employees, such as generous compensation packages and well-timed promotions. Other more strategic factors like intensive orientation and training programs are geared explicitly toward creating commitment to the corporation. Still other factors operate from outside of the formal organizational structure; for instance, employees who dislike their work and managers may nevertheless remain committed to an organization within which they have many friends (Eisenberg, Monge, & Miller, 1983). Finally, commitment can vary by industry; in industries like software design, company commitment is typically low due to the high marketability of employee skills and the tendency to identify more with one's talents than with any particular company or job.

Employee Empowerment

In recent years, the tradition of company loyalty has eroded along with the dominating companies themselves. In their place, new, more competitively oriented firms encourage commitment by emphasizing the employee's contributions to company success. This trend toward employee empowerment is sometimes referred to as "high-involvement management" (Lawler, 1986).

The basic idea underlying high-involvement management is that people work best when they feel ownership over their work processes and decision making. Empowerment is what gives employees control over significant aspects of their work. There are many levels of employee empowerment, from one-time involvement in a specific project to self-directed work teams. Six levels have been identified, varying from limited to extensive employee empowerment:

1. Managers make decisions on their own, announce those decisions, and then respond to employees' questions.
2. Managers make decisions, but only after seeking employees' views.
3. Managers create temporary employee groups to recommend solutions to particular problems.
4. Managers meet with groups of employees on a regular basis to identify problems and to devise solutions.
5. Managers establish and participate in cross-functional problem-solving teams.
6. Ongoing work groups assume expanded responsibility for a particular issue, such as cost reduction (Osborn, Moran, Musselwhite, & Zenger, 1990).

In some cases, empowerment may be achieved through compensation schemes that afford employees ownership in the company. One compensation arrangement called "the Scanlon Plan" encourages innovation and gives all employees a share in company profits (Monge, Cozzens, & Contractor, 1992). This trend toward employee involvement suggests a modification of capitalist thinking in that it provides workers with greater control over the means of production.

When high-involvement management is successful, the workforce is highly committed and involved, and individual employees feel responsible for the company's success or failure. It also redefines the traditional "us versus them" division between managers and employees, favoring a "we're all in this together" attitude. However, high-involvement management is not easy to implement. The supervisory behaviors associated with generating employee empowerment are quite unlike those of traditional management. In some organizations, fear of negative repercussions remains a big obstacle to employees' speaking up and taking on more responsibility (Pfeffer & Sutton, 1999). Employees may also resist empowerment because they lack trust in management or are apprehensive about their new role and the greater accountability it brings. Empowerment requires the cooperation of both managers and employees. Organizations and supervisors can help create the conditions for empowerment (e.g., by providing reward systems and opportunities for cooperation and personal growth), but employees must be willing to accept empowerment in order for it to succeed. As Peter Senge (1991) points out, management cannot "impose" a vision on employees; rather, each member of the organization decides whether and when to "enroll" in that vision.

As tough as it is to cultivate today, a committed workforce offers benefits in today's competitive business environment. Committed employees not only work harder; they are also more likely to generate creative ideas about costs, quality, profitability, and schedules that benefit the company. Under conditions of employee empowerment, employees feel that the organization values their opinions and, therefore, that the work they do is significant.

Employee Productivity

From the organization's viewpoint, the most important indicator of cooperation is worker productivity. It is generally defined as the relationship between the outputs generated by a system and the inputs required to create those outputs (Campbell et al., 1988). Worker productivity has long been linked to efficiency, defined as the individual's ability to convert input into output within a specific time frame. More recently, however, our understanding of productivity has been broadened to include effectiveness as well, which is usually measured in terms of product or service quality. For example, the productivity of insurance adjusters may be measured by the total number of claims processed per day as well as by the accuracy of those claims; telephone operators by the number of calls taken per hour as well as by how well those calls are handled; and manufacturing assemblers by the amount of time it takes to make a product as well as by the amount of rework required to make the product acceptable to customers.

Although there have been great strides in recent years, most organizations continue to do a poor job of measuring individual worker productivity, except in the most routine jobs (see *What Would You Do?* 8.1). Moreover, productivity measures in terms of products and services can be ambiguous, especially when the product or service is not clearly defined (as is often the case for teachers and judges, for example) (Jacobson, 1992). While two decades of efforts toward achieving "continuous measurable improvement" have provided most workers with the tools to create and track quantitative measures of their productivity, such measures remain rare for white-collar jobs, where evaluation of productivity remains highly subjective.

Research on the relationship between communication — both quantity and quality — and productivity has been minimal. Some studies show a positive correlation, while others show a negative correlation or none at all (e.g., Papa, 1989). Part of the problem may be that wide ranges of factors are inconsistently

What Would You Do? 8.1

DEADBEATS ON NOTICE

In the following 2001 e-mail memo, the CEO of a Kansas City–based software development firm shared his frustration with his employees. After the memo was leaked on Yahoo!, the company's market valuation dropped 22 percent in three days. Here is the text of the memo:

> We are getting less than 40 hours of work from a large number of our K.C.–based EMPLOYEES. The parking lot is sparsely used at 8 A.M.; likewise at 5 P.M. As managers — you either do not know what your EMPLOYEES are doing; or you do not CARE. You have created expectations on the work effort which have allowed this to happen inside [the company], creating a very unhealthy environment. In either case, you have a problem and you will fix it or I will replace you.
>
> NEVER in my career have I allowed a team which worked for me think they had a 40-hour job. I have allowed YOU to create a culture which is permitting this. NO LONGER. You have two weeks [to change]. Tick tock.

Discussion Questions

1. Why did the CEO compose and send this e-mail? What do you think were his goals?
2. What assumptions does he make about communication and organizational change in the memo?
3. If you were a manager at this company, how would you react to this memo?
4. Why did the company's stock drop after the memo became public?
5. What are some alternative, more productive ways that this CEO might have dealt with his frustration?

---

defined by researchers as "communication" or "productivity." Certain types of communication, such as clear direction from supervisors and improved teamwork across related functions, have a positive impact on productivity, but other kinds of interaction that we would expect to improve productivity, such as supportive leadership, have been shown to have little impact (Scott, 1981). Still other kinds of communication, such as the boss who yells in anger, can raise productivity in the short term but have a negative effect over time.

Based on the available research, however, we can outline two alternative scenarios relating communication and productivity. The first, which is monologic, links communication to productivity by promoting a work environment in which simple tasks and clear performance measures allow continuous, measurable improvement. In this view, communication comes from the supervisor. While reminiscent of scientific management, this approach is still in use today, especially in manufacturing firms struggling to remain competitive.

The other potential association between communication and productivity is more dialogic. It emphasizes mutual, two-way communication between managers and employees working together to accomplish complex tasks (Figure 8.1). Here the relationship between communication and productivity is mediated by a sense of urgency. Sharing business information, encouraging employee participation in decision making, and providing employees with feedback about the successes and failures of their efforts lead to increased levels of identification, commitment, and involvement, which in turn increase worker productivity.

Indicators of Resistance

The indicators of resistance, when present in the employee's experience of work, can have a profoundly negative impact on both the individual and the organization. These indicators include stress and burnout, the causes of which are manifold. In this section, we group sources of stress into four areas — environmental,

FIGURE 8.1

A Dialogic Model of Communication and Productivity

Feedback about Results

Empowering Management

- Shares business information at all levels
- Eliminates status consciousness
- Solicits and uses employee input
- Supports teamwork
- Provides clear vision and direction
- Provides clear standards of accountability
- Makes decisions based on data
- Trusts employees

Source: E. Eisenberg and P. Riley, "A Closed-Loop Model of Communication, Empowerment, Urgency, and Performance," unpublished paper, University of Southern California, 1991.

organizational, job, and individual — and identify in each case the most likely causes of negative feelings. We begin with a brief definition of stress at work.

Stress and Burnout

Stress is on the rise in the workplace. The physical and psychological symptoms of stress can include chest pain, peptic ulcers, back pain, stomach problems, headaches, high blood pressure, anxiety, depression, and fatigue (Ray, 1987). Employee stress can cause serious problems in organizations, such as absenteeism, tardiness, sabotage, poor work quality, turnover, and dysfunctional conflict (Cooper, 1984; Hall & Savery, 1987; Quick & Quick, 1984). Of all forms of mental or emotional disturbances, depression alone affects an estimated 17.6 million Americans annually and twice as many women as men. In organizations it can lead to low productivity and morale, absenteeism, substance or alcohol abuse, poor work quality, high turnover rates, and even accidents. In addition, U.S. companies lose billions annually in lost working days due to heart disease alone (Ivancevich & Matteson, 1980). Finally, in the early 1990s the number of murders in the workplace doubled (Goodall, 1995).

Stress is marked generally by heightened feelings of anxiety, tension, or pressure. Job stress may be defined further as a psychologically disturbed response to work demands. Over time, a chronically stressed employee may become susceptible to burnout, which manifests itself as emotional exhaustion, depersonalization (or a negative attitude toward others, especially clients), and a weak sense of accomplishment as a result of work pressures (Maslach, 1982).

Environmental Stressors   Individuals in organizations have the least amount of control over environmental stressors, which are generated to a great extent by the national culture, intercultural difficulties, and the physical characteristics of the workplace.

1. *National culture.* A nation's prevailing beliefs about the nature and importance of work in people's lives can have a significant effect on job stress. Just as countries with insufficient safety laws promote sweatshops, low wages, and intolerable working conditions, a nation's attitudes about work play an important role in job stress. In Japanese society, for example, overworked employees use the term *karoshi* to refer to "death by overwork." The United States and Japan rank lowest in the world in the average number of vacation days per year. After one year of service, the typical U.S. or Japanese worker receives only ten vacation days, whereas in Austria, Brazil, Denmark, and Sweden, the average is thirty vacation days (Staimer, 1992). In Europe, a six-week vacation is the norm, and often it is granted by law (Rider, 1992). In addition, several industrialized nations have a four-day workweek. A country's values about the importance of work, expressed in policy statements and informal norms for behavior,

can contribute to job stress. However, employees often have little or no control over this form of environmental stress.

2. *Intercultural difficulties.* The stress associated with globalization is an undeniable fact of organizational life. A global economy requires people in organizations to travel more often. It takes time for even the most seasoned business traveler to understand the cultures, customs, and nuances of doing business in other countries. The business traveler today may encounter six sources of stress in unfamiliar cultures:

a. *Culture shock.* Entry into a new culture follows a predictable pattern. An individual first experiences euphoria (the new adventure is stimulating), disillusionment and frustration (the culture is too much unlike one's expectations or one's home culture), adjustment (the frustration begins to dissolve), and integration (one feels comfortable living and working in the culture). A similar adjustment period often accompanies the return home.

b. *The challenge of diversity.* Many companies today prepare business travelers for dealing with people in other cultures. Still, it can be a challenging task, particularly when unanticipated difficulties arise from subtle differences in cultural understanding. For example, when a Japanese businessman nods his head, he does so not to signal his agreement but to show only that he has heard what was said.

c. *Bias, discrimination, and prejudice.* Travelers may encounter religious intolerance, sexual discrimination, deep racial barriers, and other forms of prejudice that cause stress in their dealings and communication with others. Even routine activities may be affected, as one of our colleagues discovered when she attempted to have dinner alone in a restaurant during a visit to Turkey. After two police officers approached her, she learned that because only prostitutes dine alone in Turkey, her safety was in jeopardy. Similarly, visitors to the United States are often put off by the informality of American business and may feel insulted by the lack of respect shown for their status and position.

d. *Language barriers.* It can be extremely difficult for business travelers to interpret information conveyed in a foreign language. Even if travelers are fluent in the other language, colloquial expressions and subtle meanings within the language can present barriers to effective communication.

e. *Customs and taboos.* Although various books outlining the customs and taboos of doing business in other countries can help alleviate the stress of the business traveler, doing business abroad can be challenging, as the following brief list of cultural taboos indicates: Never refuse a cup of coffee from a businessperson in Kuwait; in Bangkok, when crossing your legs, make sure the sole of your foot does not point toward someone; do not remove your jacket in Japan unless your Japanese colleagues do so first; never help yourself to food at a banquet in China when you are the guest of honor; expect to wait patiently a half hour or more for an appointment with a Venezuelan businessperson; never discuss politics in Nigeria; do not offer your Saudi Arabian host gifts for his wife and children; plan on a two-hour business lunch in France.

f. *Physical stress.* Jet lag, feelings of dislocation, fatigue, and the difficulties of dealing with important problems at home or at the home office while abroad take a toll on the health and well-being of business travelers.

3. *Physical characteristics of the workplace.* The most common environmental causes of employee stress in the workplace are improper lighting, excessive noise, uncomfortable room temperatures, overcrowding, lack of privacy, and improperly designed tools and equipment (Altman, Valenzi, & Hodgetts, 1985). In the case of employees with disabilities, organizations that have neglected to modify their facilities to conform to the requirements of the Americans with Disabilities Act present unnecessary obstacles to job performance.

In a study of female clerical workers at a university, Greg Oldham and Nancy Rotchford (1983) point out that dark, nonprivate work spaces have several negative effects on employees:

a. Employees have poor interpersonal experiences due to excessive contact with other employees.

b. Employees feel that they have little control over their work and that their jobs lack significance.

c. The lack of privacy causes difficulties in concentration.

d. Employees are less satisfied with their work and are more prone to experience job stress.

The physical design of a company's offices can influence opportunities for interpersonal communication. In particular, work spaces that inhibit informal interaction, privacy, and control over a work area are most likely to cause employee stress. As a result, companies like Hilton use state-of-the-art design principles to build customer call centers that encourage friendly interaction and are bright, healthy, and pleasing to the eye.

Organizational Stressors   Some stressors are found within an organization's culture. More specifically, the organization's norms and expectations about social support, participation in decision making, diversity, and expression of emotion can be sources of job stress. Different types of organizational cultures affect individuals in varying ways:

A high-feedback, high risk-taking environment is one in which we are likely to find macho-type people who walk fast, talk fast, dress in modern-style clothing, compete with each other for promotion and salary, and live what can be thought of as a very fast life. Conversely, in a low-feedback, low risk-taking environment, we are likely to find people who follow the rules, do not make waves, write lots of memos to cover and explain their actions, and tend to live a very structured type of existence. Stress is an organizational culture problem for two reasons: (a) an individual who is mild-mannered may find him- or herself in a very stress-creating environment, and (b) regardless of the characteristics of the environment, even the most successful individuals may find the pressures of the situation to be extremely difficult. (Altman, Valenzi, & Hodgetts, 1985, p. 433)

Social Support   Although organizations and occupations differ in terms of their expectations about social support, providing employees with access to a network of support is critical to controlling job stress. Supportive interactions can be defined as those in which "co-workers are able to vent feelings, clarify perceptions, and mutually define the work environment" (Ray, 1987, p. 188). Most evident in stable social relationships, this type of communication with others at work can help alleviate stress as well as establish a sense of control. In contrast, an organization that isolates employees from one another (through incompatible schedules, poor physical layout, or strict limitations on informal interaction) restricts their access to social support and increases the likelihood of job stress (Ray, 1987).

Employees with poor support at work are less able to make sense of an uncertain work environment because they lack access to interpretive resources. As a result, they come to feel as if they have no control over the work situation, which, in turn, can lead to stress. On the other hand, supportive communication has been shown to "reduce one's perceptions of uncertainty [and thereby] help . . . develop a sense of perceived control over stressful circumstances" (Albrecht & Adelman, 1987, p. 24). Notice that unlike the earlier human relations focus on supportive communication and leadership, current research on social support also emphasizes the informational functions of supportive communication and the role that co-workers play in assisting one another in defining and making sense of their work environment.

Participation in Decision Making   Participation in decision making can help reduce stress and improve quality of work life by giving employees a sense of meaningful control over their work (Miller, Ellis, Zook, & Lyles, 1990). It also enhances employees' understanding of what the organization expects from its workers and how their efforts will be rewarded, thereby decreasing uncertainty and stress (Schuler & Jackson, 1986). However, organizations differ widely in terms of the amount of trust they have in employees' ability to make important decisions. At one extreme are organizations that take a scientific management approach, viewing employees as mere performers of managerial commands. At the other extreme are organizations that recognize the employee's expert knowledge of the job and the value of that knowledge in decision making.

Consider, for example, a decent but historically undistinguished university whose president announced some years ago that the school's new vision was to become a "top research university" by the year 2000. The vision was determined without consultation with faculty and staff, and consequently they were not in the least committed to its implementation. Moreover, the fact that the president would make such a pronouncement without broader participation held additional meaning for university employees: It said to them that he didn't much value their input. A good rule to remember is that people are more motivated to work toward a goal that they have had a hand in developing.

Organizations that do not value employee input tend to have high levels of job stress. They also tend to show their mistrust of employees' decision-making ability through electronic surveillance, time clocks, strict supervision, compensation policies, working conditions, and segregated parking lot arrangements. The indirect messages sent by these elements within an organization reflect the more explicit message of nonparticipation in decision making. An organization thus can affect the quality of its employees' work life by how much it values their input in important decisions. Competitive companies seek to create an organizational culture that encourages honest dialogue and eliminates fear of reprisal.

Diversity   How an organization deals with a diverse workforce can contribute to employee stress for minority employees. The number of women, Asian Americans, African Americans, and Hispanics in management positions has increased dramatically since 1970. Nevertheless, racism and sexism continue in corporations. According to a 1991 report by the U.S. Labor Department, women and minorities face numerous barriers to career development:

1. *Recruiting and hiring.* Companies may fail to inform recruiters of equal-opportunity requirements or of their desire to promote a diverse work-force.
2. *Succession and promotion.* Managers usually choose successors who are similar to themselves, and since most managers are white men, they tend not to promote women and minorities.
3. *Affirmative action.* Although the legal guidelines and restrictions of affirmative action are usually well known by human resources department personnel, managers who hire, fire, and promote employees are less aware of the guidelines. Moreover, changes in affirmative-action legislation at the state level have many managers confused about what to do. The problem is perhaps worst at the executive level; where job offers are made within a close informal network and records of hiring patterns are rarely maintained, diversity may suffer the most.
4. *Performance standards.* Managers may apply different criteria in evaluating men, women, and minorities. Minorities tend to be subjected to "tokenism," which involves being singled out for excessive scrutiny, which may lead to collapse under pressure. Women tend to be evaluated on the basis of inappropriate emotional standards. For example, their friendliness may be considered an important part of their job performance.
5. *Line management exclusion.* Most women and minority managers work in departments that support staff functions, such as human resources and

facilities, rather than in line management positions in production and engineering, for example.

For women especially, taking time off "from work to raise children or to pursue other noncareer interests does permanent damage to [their] earning power" (Silverstein, 1992, p. 1) and consequently can increase job stress. In many corporate cultures, women are regarded as less dedicated to their careers than men, and may be given less responsible jobs as a result.

Researchers attempting to identify the specific challenges faced by African Americans in the workplace have found that despite significant economic strides over the last twenty-five years, African American professionals face "more frustration and anxiety — even rage — than their less affluent counterparts" (*Tampa Tribune*, 1995, p. 122). This is due in part to a general inability to relax in a predominantly white workplace as well as to poor communication between blacks and whites. Whites tend to be distrustful of blacks who advance in the workplace, and those who advance into management may be held to a different standard of job performance. For example, a blunt white manager may be seen as being "decisive," while an African American counterpart may be seen as having "an attitude" (Jones, 1973). More recently, significant numbers of researchers have begun investigating the African American's experience of organizing; their findings are summarized in a groundbreaking new book (Nicotera, Clinkscales, & Wahler, in press).

Significant communication problems can ensue between members of cultures that on the surface may not appear to be all that different. For example, one of the authors of this textbook (Eisenberg) conducted a week-long communication training program for a Finnish paper manufacturer in which key communication differences were found in Americans and Finns. To the Finns, the Americans seemed superficial because they often restated the obvious in small talk, saying, "Have a nice day" and using the other person's name in conversation. To the Americans, the Finns appeared introverted and overly serious because they did not engage in small talk and seemed unwilling to use superlatives in conversation. Once these differences in cultural interpretation were exposed, however, communication between the two groups improved dramatically (Carbaugh, 1995).

An organization's attitude toward cultivating diversity is also expressed in its policy statements and accepted practices. For example, although gay and lesbian couples are usually denied health benefits for their dependent "spouse," some companies, including the Disney Corporation, recognize gay and lesbian "spousal equivalents" in their benefit packages.

Expression of Emotion   Certain industries and organizations tend to expect employees to hide their true feelings and display only those emotions considered appropriate at work (Rafaeli & Sutton, 1987). For example, flight attendants are expected to be cheery, funeral directors comforting, and bill collectors aggressive. An organization may reinforce these emotional expectations through its recruitment practices, socialization efforts, and systems of reward and punishment (Hochschild, 1979). As the pressure for improved customer service continues to increase, more companies are following the lead of Disney, Fidelity Investments, and Nordstrom in training their employees to manage their emotions with customers. While the organization benefits from these canned emotional displays through greater customer satisfaction and increased sales, their effect on individuals is less clear. Arlie Hochschild argues that emotional labor can even be detrimental to mental health. She uses an anecdote about flight attendants as an example:

> A young businessman said to a flight attendant, "Why aren't you smiling?" She put her tray back on the food cart, looked him in the eye, and said, "I'll tell you what. You smile first, then I'll smile." The businessman smiled at her. "Good," she replied. "Now freeze and hold that smile for fifteen hours." (Hochschild, 1983, p. 127)

Others argue that disguising one's real emotions at work is at times necessary and advantageous. A friendly food server, for example, is likely to receive more tips than one who does not disguise negative emotions. For physicians, some emotional detachment is absolutely necessary to personal well-being and professional success (Rafaeli & Sutton, 1987).

A sophisticated analysis of the relationship between the expression of emotion and stress among human services workers targeted the lopsided nature of the caregiver-patient relationship (Miller, Stiff, & Ellis, 1988). Caregivers, such as nurses, physicians, and social workers, must be careful to distinguish between two kinds of emotional communication: emotional contagion and empathic concern. When caregivers communicate empathic concern, they show concern for the other person, but they do not experience the same feelings as the patient. Emotional contagion — the experience of the patient's emotional turmoil — is more likely to lead to stress and burnout (Maslach, 1982). According to the study, effective caregivers develop "a stance in which concern for another can be held independent of emotional involvement" (Maslach, 1982, p. 262).

More recent observers have argued for seeing emotion as central to organizational life, and not simply in terms of emotional labor. According to Hochschild (1993), emotions at work today are more often seen as routine (not idiosyncratic), constructive (not disruptive), and central (not marginal). Contrary to Herbert Simon's (1957) notion of "bounded rationality," organizations must learn to tolerate and even appreciate "bounded emotionality," the appropriate use and display of emotions in the work context (Mumby & Putnam, 1993). Such a perspective endorses a work environment that rewards people who are passionate, tolerant of ambiguity, and committed to diverse goals and values, who seek a sense of community, and who use emotion as a spontaneous way to develop the critical relationships through which goals are accomplished.

A spate of recent studies illustrates the many ways in which emotion is a central part of contemporary work life. A study of 911 operators, for example, reveals that their job entails "double-faced emotion management," which means handling both their emotions and the callers'. Operators were found to cope with this demand through self-talk and gossip, both of which served to reinforce certain rules about how they were "supposed" to feel (Tracy & Tracy, 1998). Flight attendants must balance the emotional demands of service and safety and must do so through carefully orchestrated performances staged mostly for the emotional benefit of passengers. The ability to simultaneously comply with and resist the prescribed role is crucial to the maintenance of flight attendant identity (Murphy, 1998). Finally, hospital nurses must continually cope with potentially conflicting expectations for emotional display that tend to pit empathic care against professional demeanor. As a result, the emotional life of nurses is characterized by intense negative feelings associated with satisfying one expectation while violating another (Laine-Timmerman, 1999).

Job Stressors   In one respect, job stressors are created by organizations and their environments. For example, a restaurant chain that focuses on meeting customers' needs at the expense of employee participation in decision making is likely to create job stress. However, there are other dimensions of jobs that also affect stress, such as workload, role uncertainty, and job design.

1. *Workload.* Quantitatively, *workload* refers to the number of projects or processes an employee is responsible for completing within a given period of time. Qualitatively, *workload*, or *work overload*, can refer to either too much work or work that is too difficult. A new employee, for example, may have difficulty with the complexity of a task due to his or her lack of training or experience. This latter type of workload has been linked to a number of symptoms of stress (Miller et al., 1990). Like challenge, workload is also dependent upon an employee's ability (Farace, Monge, & Russell, 1977). Waiting tables in a busy restaurant requires physical coordination, a good memory, and interpersonal skills. A person lacking these skills would be unable to perform the job. However, an individual's level of ability does not necessarily remain constant. A college education, for instance, is intended in part to enhance skills and abilities in preparation for a career.

   Overload can be addressed in various ways. One method involves workload analysis. The number of hours required to complete a specific task is determined, and then the number of employees is modified to make the workload manageable. In addition, a work-flow analysis can be conducted to identify redundant operations within the overall work process and thereby balance the workload of all employees. For example, in a busy restaurant where it takes longer to prepare food than it does to seat customers and take their orders, it may be decided to seat customers at a slower rate in order to even out the workload in the kitchen or to hire support staff to take on some of the work of food preparation.

2. *Role uncertainty.* Employees who understand their role and responsibilities in the organization are better able to cope with work overload than employees whose role is marked by uncertainty and a lack of direction. Even simple jobs can be subject to role stress when the employee is given unclear or conflicting information about job duties. For example, department stores often hire young employees and provide limited training or explanation about anything beyond their immediate job duties. The result of this dearth of information is that they know what to do when everything goes perfectly but are stymied by anything out of the ordinary. Some employees develop role uncertainty from too much information. For example, a computer technician who works off-site at a client organization may get differing instructions from his client and the home office and feel torn between the two. Research has linked these types of role uncertainty to job stress (Miller et al., 1990).

3. *Job design.* The quality of the work experience can range from extreme boredom in an unchallenging job to extreme anxiety caused by overly challenging work and a fear of failure. University of Chicago psychologist Mihalyi Csikszentmihalyi (1990) has conducted numerous studies of how people experience work. This research shows that the best jobs fall midway between two extremes: They are varied and challenging enough to require close attention (i.e., not boring), but they do not demand more than the employee is realistically capable of performing (not overly anxiety-producing). When such a balance is achieved, the individual may even experience "flow" or "jamming" — a temporary loss of self-consciousness in the enjoyment of work performance (Eisenberg, 1990).

Research on employee work life has found that job design is an important factor (Altman, Valenzi, & Hodgetts, 1985). A specific set of job characteristics has been linked to an enriched work life — variety, task identity, task significance, autonomy, and feedback (Hackman & Suttle, 1977) — as illustrated in Figure 8.2. Job variety encourages employees to use multiple talents and skills, while task identity allows employees to complete a whole piece of work, such as a major auto subassembly or a financial transaction from beginning to end, rather than isolated parts or components. Task significance refers to the impact the job has on other people's lives. Autonomy is the degree of freedom or control employees have in scheduling and performing their work. Finally, feedback is the communication that employees receive about their work from others. This set of job characteristics values the employee's need for meaningful and responsible involvement in organizational dialogue. Jobs designed with these factors in mind are also likely to create among employees greater work satisfaction, motivation, and performance (Hackman & Oldham, 1975). When jobs lack these important characteristics, employee stress, burnout, absenteeism, and turnover can be expected to increase.

FIGURE 8.2

The Job Characteristics Model of Work Motivation

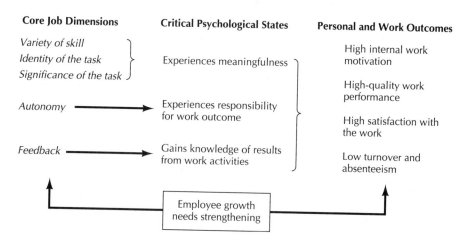

| Core Job Dimensions | Critical Psychological States | Personal and Work Outcomes |

Variety of skill
Identity of the task
Significance of the task

Experiences meaningfulness

Autonomy → Experiences responsibility for work outcome

Feedback → Gains knowledge of results from work activities

High internal work motivation

High-quality work performance

High satisfaction with the work

Low turnover and absenteeism

Employee growth needs strengthening

Source: Adapted from Richard Hackman and J. Lloyd Suttle, *Improving Life at Work: Behavioral Science Approaches to Organizational Change* (Santa Monica, Calif.: Goodyear Publishing, 1977), p. 129.

Here are several other suggestions for enriching the work experience:

1. *Combine tasks.* Employees' perception of task identity and variety improves when tasks are combined. For example, rather than having a car salesperson make the sale while someone else follows up on customer satisfaction, the two tasks could be combined to allow the salesperson to handle the entire transaction.
2. *Form natural work groups.* Greater task identity and task significance occur when people work in teams. For instance, rather than having a pool of typists, each one is assigned to a department's team of workers.
3. *Establish customer contact.* Autonomy and feedback occur when employees have direct contact with customers. One software company sponsors conferences for its users and encourages employees to attend. In this way they get to hear about the results of their work — both good and bad — directly from customers.
4. *Delegate decision making.* Employees at all levels of an organization should be involved in decision making and given greater discretion in determining schedules, methods, training, and the like. In addition, they should be provided with detailed financial and other information about

the overall effects of their decisions. Frito-Lay, for example, gives its employees on-line access to their own productivity levels via computer terminals.

5. *Open feedback channels.* All types of feedback — between work groups, from customers, and between managers and employees — should be allowed to flow unimpeded. In addition, employee performance feedback should be provided regularly, rather than just once or twice annually in performance appraisals (Altman, Valenzi, & Hodgetts, 1985).

Notice that most of these suggestions emphasize changes in communication that increase the individual's control over work processes.

Autonomy is perhaps the most important factor in reducing job stress and improving quality of work life because it encourages employees to feel effective, resourceful, responsible, and trusted by others in the organization (Jackson, 1983; Karasek, 1979; Luhmann & Albrecht, 1990). From a managerial perspective, autonomy may be fostered through "RAA delegation"; that is, by encouraging employees to accept more responsibility, authority, and accountability. Thus, when a supervisor asks a junior engineer to design a new product, the supervisor gives the engineer the responsibility and authority to accomplish that task. The junior engineer does not have to compete with others for resources or information and does not need to seek the supervisor's approval of each step in the design of the product. At the same time, the junior engineer is accountable for designing the new product in a way that meets the company's objectives and needs, and the supervisor is responsible for providing this information. Therefore, the junior engineer is responsible not only for the product's design, but also for meeting certain standards (e.g., of delivery and cost).

There is such a thing as too much autonomy. Failing to provide employees with important goals, guidance, and known constraints is both unfair and ineffective. Besides, most employees don't expect (nor want) complete control over and accountability for their day-to-day decision making. Instead, they want the opportunity to provide significant input into how their work gets done. New research suggests that not everyone wants this equally, however. Autonomy is most effective at reducing stress (measured as elevated levels of blood pressure) for people who see themselves as highly competent (i.e., have high self-efficacy). For those who feel incompetent, more autonomy can mean trouble, and this realization leads to increased, not decreased, stress (Schaubroeck & Merritt, 1997).

RAA delegation gives employees the authority to accomplish tasks as they see fit and holds them accountable for specific performance goals. In contemporary management, it reminds us of the need to manage the "loose-tight paradox" (Peters & Waterman, 1982) — encouraging employees' creativity while holding them accountable for results — which characterizes most organizations today. To balance creativity and constraint, organizations should avoid giving employees too much or too little autonomy; instead, they should strive to provide just enough autonomy to promote a positive work experience, high involvement, and productivity.

Of course, competitive pressures can work against empowerment and job enrichment in organizations. Some manufacturing companies, for example, use principles of scientific management to respond to the pressure to deliver high-quality products at low cost. Many organizations have responded to global competition by simplifying jobs and hiring less-skilled workers at lower wages. One manufacturing manager boasts that because it takes only three days to train unskilled workers to perform the assembly jobs, the company can hire people at the lowest possible wage. Nationally, manufacturing jobs have both declined in number and changed in nature — from an average of $14 per hour for complex assembly work to $7 per hour for repetitive work. Although organizations may believe these are as effective short-term business strategies, jobs that lack the key characteristics of variety, task identity, task significance, autonomy, and feedback can be expected in the long term to increase stress and decrease both motivation and productivity in the workforce.

Individual Stressors   Some causes of stress at work are unrelated to organizational factors or job design. Individual stressors may be caused by an employee's personality traits, personal life, or communication style.

Personality Traits   A workaholic typically regards the importance of the work experience as above all else, including family, friends, leisure time, and so on. Although workaholism sometimes emerges as a way of dealing with stressful events in an individual's personal life, it is more often associated with people who exhibit what are called type A personality traits. "In addition to competing with others, they constantly compete with themselves, setting high standards of productivity that they seem driven to maintain. They tend to feel frustrated in the work situation, irritable with the work efforts of subordinates, and misunderstood by superiors" (Burke, Weir, & Duwors, 1979, p. 57). In the long term, type A behavior is dangerous because it causes people to sacrifice all other life pursuits to their work goals.

Other research has focused on identifying those personality traits that help people cope with stress in more productive ways. For example, so-called hardy people are likely to view negative news and events as opportunities or challenges. They feel in control of their lives, welcome change, and, as a result, are better able to handle stress than their less hardy counterparts (Eisenberg, 1998; Kobasa, Maddi, & Kahn, 1982). A similar concept popular in business today is that of "emotional intelligence" (Goleman, 1995). A person's emotional intelligence quotient (or EQ) reflects the degree to which he or she can reflexively monitor and strategically deploy (exercise mastery over) his or her emotions. Most dysfunctional personality traits are related to low self-esteem. The quality of a person's work experience is highly dependent on his or her self-image and self-knowledge of such things as personal strengths and weaknesses and likes and dislikes. As Warren Bennis and Burt Nanus (1985) report in their classic study, great leaders know themselves well and feel confident in the face of others' criticism and advice.

One final aspect of personality that affects a person's work experience is patterns of attention (Larkey, 1984; March & Olsen, 1976). People tend to pay more attention to the past and future than to the present. At work, this may mean holding a grudge, regretting a business decision, hoping for a certain level of sales, or anticipating changes in the marketplace. However, in today's turbulent business world, it is more important than ever to attend to present-day issues and changes.

Personal Life   As you would expect, stressful events in an employee's personal life spill over to affect the work experience. Family problems, such as marital difficulties or a child's illness, can significantly increase an employee's level of stress. In addition, the stress of relocation commonly affects managers moving up the organizational ladder. Finally, financial problems, especially during difficult economic times, contribute to stress. Examples include overextended credit, unpaid bills, the cost of a child's education, or a laid-off spouse.

These sources of stress emphasize that the boundary between work life and personal life is highly permeable. People are only "partially included" in an organization (Weick, 1979). All employees, and especially those with families, must engage in a constant juggling act between work and home concerns. This act can take on many different forms. Communication researcher Jane Jorgenson (2002), for example, has been critical of the construction of work and home as "separate spheres." She argues instead that they very much intermingle in everyday life. Her studies of female engineers suggest that people devise many creative ways to make sense of these challenges, and that the engineers themselves actively resist the separate spheres division. Alternatively, sociologist Arlie Hochschild (1997) uses the notion of separate spheres to show how what once characterized "home" (intimacy, extended time together) now applies to work, just as aspects of "work" (efficiency, scheduling, goal setting) are now part of home life. The coming years will be marked by further efforts on the part of individuals and organizations to reconcile quality of work concerns with quality of life, which includes home and family.

Communication Style   Communication style also affects the employee's level of stress and quality of life at work. For example, people who are shy and afraid to communicate with others tend to experience more stress at work and are less likely to do well in many organizational settings than people who communicate more openly (Phillips, 1991). In contrast, competent communicators tend to be evaluated more positively and to achieve greater success at work (Monge, Bachman, Dillard, & Eisenberg, 1982).

Certain communication skills help employees cope with job stress. In a study of assertive versus argumentative communicators, it was found that assertiveness — the ability to state a position without attacking the other person — is associated with creating positive impressions in others and with improving the work experience (Infante, Trebing, Shepard, & Seeds, 1984). Argumentative communicators, in contrast, tend to be more aggressive and insecure, and they are less likely to be well regarded by others or to enjoy their experience at work.

The results of another study indicate that the ability to exhibit empathic concern inhibits stress at work (Miller et al., 1990). As noted earlier in the chapter, many jobs in the health-care field require empathic concern for the client's problems but a detachment from the client's emotional state of mind. This is a learned skill that is essential in jobs that make high emotional demands on employees.

New Directions for Work Organization

Various approaches to meeting the challenge of improving the experience of work have surfaced. One approach defines the problem as resulting from a general lack of coping skills among today's workers. In this view, increased job stress stems from the lack of knowledge about how to cooperate or the lack of desire to do so. By learning the strategies for coping with stress (Table 8.2), employees can improve the quality of their work experience (Sailer, Schlachter, & Edwards, 1982). Some of the more interesting coping strategies in Table 8.2, such as exercise and meditation, explicitly involve the body, which, like the emotions, has historically been a taboo subject in organizations.

Recognizing that it is hard for most people to initiate stress-reduction activities on their own, some employers have been creative in their attempts to reduce the stress in their work environment. Examples include nap and relaxation rooms (Nike), roving chair massages, shorter hours (SAS), and additional time off as a reward for good work (Dawson).

Most companies are also redesigning their reward systems to better meet the emotional needs of employees. As we have already revealed, companies increasingly pay for performance, which may lead to clearer expectations and a less conflicted work life. New studies show that "employees' top priority is gaining the flexibility to control their own time" (Conlin, 1999, p. 94). Consequently, organizations are providing greater modularization of jobs and flexibility in scheduling.

Then there is the intrinsic reward that comes from the work itself. Extensive research by Mihalyi Csikszentmihalyi (1990) and Charles Garfield (1992) links peak employee performance with certain social and psychological conditions, such as clear goals, regular feedback, and a sense of confidence. Furthermore, these conditions may not necessarily be met at the expense of profits; peak employee performance can be consistent with increased productivity.

TABLE 8.2

Strategies for Coping with Stress

Physical maintenance strategies
   Pay attention to diet and nutrition
   Get enough sleep
   Exercise
   Participate in leisure and recreation activities

Internal assistance strategies
   Learn relaxation responses
   Study biofeedback
   Meditate

Personal organizational strategies
   Plan to avoid stressful situations
   Delegate responsibility
   Choose to alter the work environment
   Engage in creative problem solving and decision making
   Set goals
   Manage time
   Restructure jobs
   Use self-assessment measures

Outside assistance strategies
   Consider psychoanalysis
   Seek stress counseling
   Take advantage of employee-development programs
   Employ behavior-modification techniques

Situational and support group strategies
   Participate in assertiveness training and role playing
   Develop supportive relationships
   Avoid substance abuse

Source: H. Sailer, J. Schlachter, and M. Edwards, "Stress: Causes, Consequences, and Coping Strategies," *Personnel* (July–August 1982) 59: 35–48.

In a related line of research, self-directed work teams are reported to encounter fewer obstacles to effective decision making and productivity (Wellens, Byham, & Wilson, 1991). The concept of self-directed work teams, however, has gained slow acceptance due to managers' concerns about the types of decisions these teams can and cannot be expected to make. At New United Motor Manufacturing, Inc. (NUMMI), a joint venture involving Toyota and General

Motors, self-directed work teams function successfully despite certain rules governing accountability, safety, and human resources. We discuss the responsibilities and actions of such teams in detail in Chapter 10.

Finally, Eisenberg (1990) identifies the preconditions and characteristics of "jamming" experiences, moments of seamless behavioral coordination that result in peak experiences for individuals and peak performance levels for the group. In practice, jamming requires proper staffing and risk taking. Staffing is key because a team is often only as strong as its weakest member. Risk taking is important for a team to let go of assumed controls and constraints and to set out in new directions. Under these conditions, people can give themselves over to the group and as a result achieve an enhanced individual experience.

The Experience of Work outside Organizations

A 1999 survey of California workers revealed that only one-third had traditional jobs, defined as single, full-time, permanent, day-shift work paid for by an employer on the employer's site. Both out of choice and necessity, many people now question the wisdom of dedicating their life to a single company. The new career path, which has been aptly called "Protean," is characterized by continuous learning, increasing challenge, and shifting identifications (Hall, 1996).

Several studies report a general trend toward a substantial workforce that is independent of organizations. Even before the attacks on the World Trade Center and the Pentagon on 9/11, Susan Dentzer, writing in *U.S. News & World Report* (1995) about "the death of the middleman," attributed the 34,000 job losses in the airline ticket industry to advanced technologies that permit travelers to review flight schedules and reserve and purchase airline tickets via computers. Similarly, automated teller machines (ATMs) have taken over most of the functions of bank tellers, and home loans can be secured over the Internet. Although these changes resulted in a dramatic loss of jobs in the early 1990s, the last year of that decade revealed a markedly different pattern. An expanding economy allowed those seeking corporate jobs to return to the workplace, although the jobs they found there were often more time-consuming and required more advanced skills. Most notably, many who left corporate America decided to go it alone, and they were steadily joined by even more people seeking greater autonomy and meaningful work. There has been an explosion of entrepreneurship in American society, creating an enormous amount of new wealth, particularly in high-technology industries.

Another source of optimism about the future world of work is related to the emerging organizations providing social services throughout the world. Some say that the largest growth in meaningful work is not in the public or private sector, but in an emerging "third" sector, which encourages forming or joining "soft-money-supported" volunteer organizations and agencies (Rifkin, 1995). In France, for example, third-sector organizations are the fastest-growing sector of that nation's economy. In Japan, most urban neighborhoods are governed by volunteers who manage everything from implementing safety and ecology standards to improving the quality of lives for the homeless and the poor. In the United States, where a massive volunteer sector already exists, the Clinton administration implemented a program in 1994 that provided money for a college education to people who dedicated two years of their lives to public service.

In many cases, working in the third sector does not mean working for free. It means that you are responsible for seeking out alternative funding to support your organization from private and public grant organizations and that you must demonstrate to those agencies your annual needs and accomplishments. An example would be heading a neighborhood community development corporation (CDC) responsible for bringing together multiple stakeholders and resources to envision and guide the future of the community. In jobs like this, you receive a salary or other forms of compensation for your work. You accept the responsibility for finding meaningful work and, in most cases, for supporting yourself while you do it. A major benefit is that you can choose work that is socially and personally meaningful. To a large extent, this type of work is communication-intensive.

Yet another reason for our optimism is that many people, particularly in affluent nations like the United States, are questioning the value of work in relation to their personal and spiritual lives (Fox, 1994; Goodall, 1996). After two hundred years of industrial growth, technological improvements, and capitalism, there are new concerns about the deterioration of our planet and the meaning of work in relation to a paycheck. New ideas about "stewardship" (Block, 1993), sustainability, and an "ecology of commerce" (Hawken, 1994) may chart a new direction for human labor and for how we define meaningful work (Handy, 1994).

Working outside of organizations as an outsourcer, entrepreneur, or independent contractor within the new global economy requires both self-reliance and capital. As a college student, you can prepare for the future by supplementing your education with the development of a specific set of skills. Others who have lost a managerial job can redefine themselves as independent workers.

Outsourcers: The New Economy

Although advancing information technology has contributed to a significant loss of jobs in nearly every industry, it has also created a new source of self-employment: the outsource service provider. Outsourcers are people who work for themselves, often from home via the Internet. In a widespread effort to reduce operating budgets, many businesses now use outsource service providers.

They save money by avoiding the costs of employee benefits (such as health insurance and pensions) and office space, thereby making better use of limited resources. In addition, competition among outsource service providers has meant that they can usually charge less for improved services.

As specialists who work for themselves, outsourcers tend to bear the financial burden of upgrading their skills, cross-training, and purchasing equipment. Although they pass along these costs to the businesses they serve, most companies still save money. The typical outsourcer earns more than if he or she had a similar job with salary and benefits in an organization. Many outsourcers also enjoy the flexibility of working at home, especially working parents who can reduce their child-care expenses while also spending more time with their children. In 2001, 19.8 million people performed at least some of their work at home, a figure that accounts for 15 percent of total employment in the United States. Of this number, four-fifths of these workers were in managerial, professional, or sales occupations (U.S. Bureau of Labor Statistics, 2003).

Outsourcers tend to provide what Peter Drucker (1992a) calls "knowledge work." Their services include a variety of managerial, secretarial, and technical tasks, computer documentation and training, and office equipment repair and maintenance. One outsourcer we know specializes in repairing and servicing laser printers; another develops on-line "help" systems for large-scale manufacturing firms.

A number of risks are associated with outsourcing. Businesses risk a loss of control over the services they no longer provide to themselves, although stiff competition among outsourcers tends to keep the service quality high. In addition, some U.S. businesses have turned to outsource providers in less-developed countries, thereby increasing competition among local outsourcers and lowering the fees that they can charge. This risk will continue to become more threatening to Americans who work at home as communication technologies advance. Finally, outsourcing presents a number of societal risks. Increasing numbers of U.S. workers lack health insurance and retirement benefits. The cost of health care alone has been identified as a potential threat to the financial health of the nation. Uninsured outsourcers may thus contribute to these risks to the nation's future economic health.

Self-Reliance: Developing a New Skill Set

To be self-reliant in the new world of work means being open to change and willing to work in fields you may not have considered before. Becoming a self-reliant worker is important for three reasons:

1. The new economy is a service economy, and the majority of its workers are service providers in a wide variety of specialties (from auto repair and physical therapy to systems engineering and investment banking).

2. The core of the new economy depends upon converging telecommunications and computer technologies.
3. More work involves single projects completed by teams. Although competitive companies have always used task forces to solve difficult problems, this trend is now evident in all industries. However, the task forces in the new economy are made up of independent specialists, rather than employees of organizations, who have experience in particular projects and proven records of success (Kiechel, 1994).

Furthermore, the new economy will require the college-educated adult to prepare for a lifetime of learning by developing a set of skills, including individual and team-based specialties. A skill set includes the abilities and experiences that a person brings to a potential employer, in such areas as project management, partnering, innovation in using new technologies, mentoring, documentation and training, editing, publishing, change management, telecommunications marketing, and developing a new client base. Skill sets are marketable to corporations, but they also give people the opportunity to go into business for themselves. Taking this idea to the extreme, current popular management literature encourages individuals to think of themselves as a brand; like Pepsi or Dell, "Dan Marino" and "Allen Iverson" have unique qualities for sale to the public.

The key to self-reliance is an understanding of the market relationship between one's knowledge and skills and the services one can provide to others. Although the number of traditional jobs within organizations will continue to decline, both the work itself and the skills needed to accomplish it will continue to exist. Those who develop a set of skills capable of providing needed services will be the ones most likely to succeed.

In many cases, a college education does not focus on developing a marketable skill set for the new global economy. As a college student, you will acquire knowledge, but you are not likely to gain the experience needed to define a skill set. Some colleges and universities are making progress in this area by involving students in company-sponsored internships and applied research projects, but most students will need to supplement their education with work experiences and additional individualized skill development. Depending on your interests, this can mean focusing on any one of a number of different things; for example, public speaking, technical writing, using specialized computer programs, or learning new languages. The point is that work will be available to people with talent, wherever they might be.

Walter Kiechel (1994) identifies what he calls the four "compass points" of a career in the new economy: (1) Be self-reliant (think of yourself as a business), (2) be a generalist (know enough about the various disciplines to be able to mediate among them), (3) be connected (a team player), and (4) be a specialist (an expert in some area). Similarly, the director of executive and workforce development at Sun Microsystems gives employees the following advice on assuming responsibility for their careers:

1. The overarching principle is to think of yourself as a business.
2. Define your product or service: What is your area of expertise?
3. Know your target market: To whom are you going to sell your product or service?
4. Be clear on why your customer buys from you: What is your "value proposition"?
5. As in any business, strive for quality and customer satisfaction, even if your customer is just someone else in your organization — like your boss.
6. Know your profession or field and what's going on in it: What does success look like in your area? Is your profession becoming obsolete?
7. Invest in your own growth and development, the way a company invests in research and development: What new products or services will you be able to provide in the future?
8. Be willing to consider changing your business or starting a new one. It isn't likely any more that you will have one career for your whole life (from Kiechel, 1994, p. 71).

Although communication students develop valuable process skills in areas such as team participation, leadership, written and oral communication, negotiation, and interpersonal relations, they typically lack technical expertise and project experience. Some technical expertise may be gained through course work in other fields of study and in off-campus seminars, while project experience may be found in internships and applied research opportunities on your campus that focus on completing real projects for actual customers. These supplements to a college education will help you to think of yourself as a business and develop a marketable skill set.

SUMMARY

The experience of work within organizations is marked by a process of organizational assimilation, by indicators of cooperation and resistance, and by new directions in improving the employee's work life. Communication plays an important role in organizational environments that value employee input and reduce employee stress through the creation of jobs with greater variety, significance, freedom, and control. A trend toward giving employees a greater voice in decision making is evident; it is likely to improve their work life and make organizations more productive.

The experience of work outside of organizations includes entrepreneurial ventures and outsourcing. In the new, service-oriented economy, a majority of workers will be outsource providers of specialized services. This will require the development of a marketable skill set and a commitment to a lifetime of learning. For people who have dedicated much of their life to working within organizations and who at midlife find themselves unemployed as a result of downsizing, redefining their work identity is necessary to meet the challenges of the new economy.

Of course, readying yourself for a successful work life is not simply a matter of going off somewhere and improving your communication skills. In our tumultuous times, effective communication is characterized by negotiation and dialogue, and it is the ability to use communication to forge productive work relationships (with customers, suppliers, co-workers, employees, partners) that is paramount. The role of communication in creating and sustaining such fruitful relationships is the subject of the next chapter.

QUESTIONS FOR REVIEW AND DISCUSSION

1. What are some indicators of job satisfaction? How closely related are job satisfaction and communication ability?

2. What are some indicators of stress and burnout? What can be done to reverse or avoid them?

3. What are the implications of an increasingly "outsourced" work world? How might you go about acquiring skills appropriate to such a working lifestyle?

4. How are the stages of organizational entry and assimilation similar to your own experiences of working?

5. In what ways are you prepared to work in a highly competitive global market? How can you better prepare yourself?

6. Why are negotiation and dialogue skills important to the experience of work in the twenty-first century? How might these skills contrast with those of traditional argumentation and debate?

CASE STUDY I

The Dilemma of the Empowered Dancer

Robin Reed is a twenty-two-year-old single mother and graduating senior at the University of Nevada. In addition to being an excellent student and loving mother, Robin is proud of the fact that she has worked hard to support herself and her three-year-old son and to put herself through school. She hopes to attend law school and someday to become a public defender.

Robin does have a problem, however. Since entering college, she has worked part time as an exotic dancer at Sparky's, a popular gentleman's club in Las Vegas, and she doesn't always feel comfortable telling people about her work. The few times she has disclosed her employer — once when a classmate recognized her at the club — she has found people to be very judgmental about what she does. And each time she talks to the people who care about her the most — her mother and her son — she feels forced to lie about what she does for a living.

For her part, Robin feels that stripping is a just a means to an end, no more degrading (and much more lucrative) than a dead-end job in retail or food service. She has read a good deal of feminist theory in her classes and feels torn between what these writers seem to want her to think — that she is complicit in the continuing oppression of women — and how she feels, which is powerful, resourceful, and strong.

Even so, the lying is starting to get to her, and she is increasingly anxious. She feels as if she is being forced to compartmentalize her life in order to survive. Robin feels comfortable in all of her worlds — at home, at school, and at the club. But problems occur when these worlds collide.

ASSIGNMENT

1. How would you characterize her emotional state at this time? What are some of the possible reasons she feels as she does? What might she do, if anything, about these feelings?
2. What moral or ethical questions is Robin facing? How would you counsel her if you were her friend? Her mother? Her fiancé?
3. What do you think of her analysis of power and oppression in the work she does? Is work of this sort always exploitative regardless of the worker's reported experience?
4. How does Robin's dilemma compare to other work situations people her age face? What, if anything, should she do about the growing feeling of compartmentalization in her life?

CASE STUDY II

Developing a Skill Set

Develop your own skill set. Review the skills you have acquired as a college student and through your work experiences, and consider how you might use those skills in the new service-based economy.

ASSIGNMENT

1. Evaluate your skill set. Identify any gaps in your experience, knowledge, and abilities. Create a plan for improving your skill set through experience and training seminars.
2. Compare your skill set with those of your classmates. Work together to create a plan for addressing the gaps or deficiencies within the skill sets.
3. Prepare a résumé that emphasizes your skill set.
4. Investigate the possibility of working as an outsource service provider for a local company. Use your skill set to determine how you can best prepare yourself to become an outsourcer for a company.

CHAPTER 9

Interpersonal Relationships and Organizational Communication

The people who insist on purely individual strategies and yet have to work in rapidly changing interdependent systems, like corporations and other organizations, are often struggling badly. They don't collaborate well because they haven't valued or developed that capacity. They need to see that teamwork is necessary, that strategic alliances are necessary, that cross-functional work teams are necessary, and that redesigning the corporation is necessary. All of those factors speak to the same reality: "if my end of the boat sinks, so does yours. And so we had better learn how to work together at a very high level of competence, not just give lip service to it."

— CHARLES GARFIELD, "Peak Performance and Organizational Transformation" (1999)

Whereas the previous chapter focused on individual sense making and the experience of work, this one highlights the importance of different kinds of relationships — both formal and informal — that develop in and around work. Just as the Industrial Revolution disrupted the extended family of the eighteenth and nineteenth centuries, the information revolution, combined with the recent emergence of a global economy, promises to transform organizations from physical places to virtual sites in cyberspace. (In fact, this has already happened with banks, libraries, car lots, bookstores, and florists, to name only a very few.) Although such a change makes some economic sense, its implications for human social life are not yet well understood. We know, for example, that humans are social animals and that social isolation is an important risk factor for heart disease and early death. What impact will the loss of face-to-face relationships at work — and the consequent impact on families and communities — have on individuals and society?

In the first half of this chapter, we describe the various kinds of interpersonal relationships that occur in and around organizations. Beginning with customers, we trace these various types of connections through supervisors, peers, and employees. In the section on relationships with employees, we spend a significant amount of time focusing on what makes for effective leadership. The second half of the chapter is organized around common obstacles to establishing satisfying work relationships, focusing on the nature and importance of boundaries. We examine how crossing national boundaries in global business affects the nature of work; how shifting physical boundaries, as occur in business travel, working at home, and new office designs, can challenge and transform taken-for-granted ideas about work life; and how crossing emotional boundaries — from office romance to outright harassment — affects the work environment. We conclude the chapter with a look at how obstacles common to interpersonal communication reveal themselves in organizational settings and how to move past them.

Interpersonal Relationships Are One Key to Success

Positive interpersonal relationships are crucial to the survival of individuals, teams, and organizations. To remain competitive, organizations must be flexible and open to new information. Strict rules and procedures that limit information flow are a hindrance. Instead, flexibility requires the development of responsive informal systems for sharing information and getting work done, along with social interaction that supports authentic dialogue and problem solving. Organizational success depends on the levels of trust and honesty that develop through ongoing communicative experiences among people who are willing to take risks and continually learn from one another.

Put differently, positive interpersonal relationships at work are no longer a luxury, but a necessity. More so than in the past, they are a prerequisite for effective job performance. Managers know that without positive work relationships, the work gets done slowly, poorly, or not at all. For employees, positive work relationships provide social support and a sense of identification with and participation in the organizational dialogue, which better enables them to anticipate change and to remain flexible. In contrast, people who are socially isolated at work feel insignificant and "out of the loop," which has negative effects on them and on the company as a whole. They may also be viewed by others as expendable inasmuch as they fail to build relationships with others that allow them to showcase their contributions.

This emphasis on relationships at work has its roots in the human relations movement, and more recently in the 1980s, when the primary focus of managerial work shifted from planning, organizing, and coordinating to communicating (Kanter, 1989). Managerial work today is much less about budgets and schedules than it is about building positive connections with colleagues that afford a high level of credibility and influence. The ability to influence others to behave in desired ways has in many cases replaced "the use of formal authority in relationships with subordinates, peers, outside contacts, and others on whom the job makes one dependent" (Keys & Case, 1990, p. 38). Because "positional authority" can no longer get the job done, a "web of influence" or a "balanced web of relationships" must be developed:

> Recently managers have begun to view leadership as the orchestration of relationships between several different interest groups — superiors, peers, and outsiders, as well as subordinates. Effectiveness at leadership requires balance in terms of efforts spent in building relationships in these four directions. (Keys & Case, 1990, p. 39)

Communicating with Customers

Researchers have known for some time that the most important communication most employees have is with customers. In an age of lean management and flattened hierarchies, it is more likely than ever that jobs will require direct customer contact and that customers will offer repeat business to a company only as long as the service meets or exceeds their expectations.

The Customer Service Revolution

Customers demand more from organizations today. Survival requires a revolution in the way most companies think about their customers. Two leading advocates of this revolution are Karl Albrecht and Tom Peters. These authors emphasize the importance of both hearing and responding to customers' needs and opinions.

According to Albrecht (1992), successful companies approach the customer service challenge by managing the customer's *experience*, rather than by just "doing things":

> [The] "doing things" mind-set seems to express an unconscious view of the customer as a nuisance. There is a powerful, unconscious tendency in most organizations to depersonalize and dehumanize the conception, discussion, and operation of the service delivery. Things are easier to deal with than humans, so we prefer to think of the people — both customers and employees — as just interchangeable elements of a big impersonal blueprint. (p. 35)

This point of view has found additional support in the notion of the "experience economy" (Pine, Gilmore, & Pine, 1999). From this perspective, all businesses today are essentially and inescapably in the "experience" business, even if they sell a well-defined product (like food, cars, or appliances). With the quality and price of most commodities becoming similar, businesses seek to distinguish their products through superior service (e.g., how the salesperson treats you, or what it feels like to call with questions to a toll-free support number). Here is a list of suggestions based in part on Tom Peters's (1987) blueprint for a customer service revolution:

1. *Specialize, create niches, and differentiate.* Specialization means tailoring a product or service to a clearly defined consumer audience. Products and services that appeal to a broad customer base are being replaced by those that target the needs of a more narrowly defined market. For example, network television is rapidly losing market share to cable channels, which more precisely target customers' interests. In the extreme, this has been termed "one-to-one marketing" and "mass customization" (Peppers & Rogers, 1996).

2. *Provide quality as it is perceived by the customer.* Organizations must be responsive to customer feedback about quality and must take action in response to the customer's perception of the product or service. Customer complaints should be seen as "gifts" in that they can provide useful feedback for improving the product or service.

3. *Provide superior service and emphasize intangibles.* Customers form positive or negative impressions of organizations based on their encounters (face-to-face or mediated) with service providers. Research suggests that intangibles — such as the accuracy, dependability, and interpersonal skills of service providers — outweigh other factors in determining customer satisfaction (Zeithaml, Parasuraman, & Berry, 1990). At the high-end department store Nordstrom, for example, gift wrapping is provided, merchandise may be returned for any reason, and salespeople are encouraged to use their good judgment in achieving their primary goal of outstanding customer service. Another example is a Florida-based software company called HTE, which sponsors an annual user's convention to obtain customer feedback on its products and uses this information to make improvements in product design.

4. *Achieve speedy responsiveness.* Because time is the customer's most precious commodity, a growing number of organizations are utilizing communication technologies to reduce the amount of time it takes to respond to consumers. At overnight-mail leader Federal Express, for instance, trucks are equipped with computers, and at Web retailer Amazon.com, "one-click" shopping makes shopping almost *too* convenient — click today, and the item arrives overnight at your door.

5. *Be an internationalist.* Cultivating relationships with domestic as well as international customers requires patience, empathy, and the ability to communicate with people from other cultures. In addition, global competition requires organizations to adapt their products or services to meet the needs of different cultures.

6. *Create uniqueness.* In a competitive market, an organization's product or service must stand out as unique, and employees must be able to articulate why it is unique. Both are easier said than done, and in some cases (e.g., air travel), many customers will ignore differences and shop for the lowest price in any case. Nevertheless, most marketing dollars are spent by companies aiming to distinguish their brand of shampoo, car, or college from their competitors' brands.

7. *Be obsessed with listening.* Listening to customers means respecting their opinions, recognizing their needs, avoiding distractions, paying close attention to their main points or concerns, and taking action on their complaints or suggestions. This listening doesn't happen automatically; the tendency is for people to avoid it. Consequently, successful companies institutionalize practices that ensure that customers' perceptions get heard somehow, through surveys, focus groups, and customer comment cards (Peppers & Rogers, 1996).

Communicating with Supervisors

The use of the word *supervisor* or *superior* in this section may seem strange given what we have said so far about the flattening of hierarchies and the growth of empowerment in contemporary organizations. Practically speaking, movement toward more participative structures has not eliminated the need for some degree of hierarchy and supervision. For this reason, it is still valuable to consider how one most likely develops a good relationship with one's boss.

In the past, employees were expected to be compliant, take direction, and speak mainly when spoken to. The movement toward greater participation and empowerment has led many employees to see their supervisor as a teammate, albeit one with the power to make tough decisions or to referee among differing points of view. Employees today recognize that they cannot count on superiors automatically to appreciate their opinions about work issues; instead, they must advocate for resources. The ability to advocate effectively begins with the recognition that superiors as a rule have different worldviews from their employees. One way that this difference has been described is as "semantic-information distance."

Semantic-Information Distance

The supervisor-employee relationship has long been studied by researchers interested in organizational communication. Most research suggests that supervisors spend about one-third to two-thirds of their time communicating with employees and that most of this communication is verbal in nature (Dansereau & Markham, 1987). Although this might lead you to think that supervisors and employees think about issues in similar ways, researchers have found instead that they hold different perceptions of organizational issues (Jablin, 1979). This gap in understanding, or semantic-information distance, is most notable in issues related to participation in decision making (Harrison, 1985) and basic job duties (Jablin, 1979). In addition, supervisors and employees tend to perceive communication differently. Whereas supervisors tend to believe that they communicate with employees more frequently and effectively than they actually do, employees tend to believe that supervisors are more open to communication than they actually are. Employees also tend to believe that they have more persuasive ability than their supervisors believe that they possess (Jablin, 1979).

A more recent study suggests that one area where semantic-information distance may be least is in employees' perceptions of the organization's social structure. (See Chapter 10 for a discussion of communication networks.) Supervisors and their subordinates tend to see social structure similarly, and this similarity is even greater when they are of the same gender or have acquaintances in common (Heald, Contractor, Koehlt, & Wasserman, 1998).

Some degree of semantic-information distance between supervisors and employees is the inevitable result of hierarchy. More important is the lack of awareness of these gaps in understanding. In other words, not only do supervisors and employees have different perceptions of key issues, but they are also likely to be unaware of these differences.

Is this a problem? Research on co-orientation provides one answer. *Co-orientation* refers to the degree of alignment of perceptions in a dyad. It includes (1) agreement (e.g., "How similar are our perceptions of this product?"), (2) accuracy ("How well do I understand how you perceive the product?"), and (3) perceived agreement ("How similarly do I think we perceive the product?") (Farace, Monge, & Russell, 1977). Surprisingly, even in the absence of high levels of actual agreement, the perception of agreement has been shown to have a positive impact on these relationships. Although a supervisor and an employee may disagree on an issue and be relatively accurate in judging the other's opinion, the perception of agreement by both employee and supervisor leads to a more positive evaluation of the relationship between them (Eisenberg, Monge, & Farace, 1984). Naturally, actual agreement is crucial in some situations, such as in the high-risk operations of air traffic control. In most other situations, however, it is equally and perhaps more important that the individuals in the relationship *perceive* themselves as being in agreement.

Upward Distortion

Whereas semantic-information distance is viewed as a natural outgrowth of organizational hierarchy, "upward distortion" is a purposeful attempt to create gaps in understanding (Roberts & O'Reilly, 1974). That is, employees may filter the information they give to supervisors, particularly when that information reflects negatively on themselves (Dansereau & Markham, 1987). There are four common types of upward distortion (Fulk & Mani, 1986):

1. Gatekeeping — some but not all information is passed on from subordinates to superiors
2. Summarization — emphasis is given to certain parts of a message
3. Withholding — information is selectively withheld from superiors
4. General distortion — entire messages are altered to suit the subordinate's motives or agenda

Ambitious, insecure employees are most likely to distort the information they communicate upward. Also, messages that reflect negatively on employees are most likely to be distorted. The motivation to distort information derives largely from the subordinate's perception of his or her relationship with supervisors. Employees tend to withhold information from supervisors they do not trust (Jablin, 1985) as well as from supervisors known to actively withhold information from employees (Fulk & Mani, 1986). Employees tend to distort information in ways that will please their superiors — that is, to tell them both what they want them to know and what they think superiors want to hear — and to convey information that reflects favorably on themselves (Krivonos, 1982).

As information is distorted on its way up the organizational ladder, the message received by senior management may be quite different from the original message. The ability of managers to do their jobs effectively depends on the quality of the information they receive from others, particularly from employees. Reducing the amount of upward distortion is thus important, but it requires managers to be open to (or actually solicit) interpretations and opinions about issues that may differ markedly from their own. Management by wandering around (MBWA) is one way to reduce upward distortion by getting managers more involved with employees and by rewarding questions, suggestions, and innovations. Like other programs, however, MBWA cannot succeed unless employees develop a trust of management and feel comfortable with conveying negative information. Once such trust is established, reliable upward communication can occur. Authoritarian management, by contrast, encourages both employee distrust and fear of repercussions and leads to the filtering of information.

Managing the Boss

Employees use a variety of tactics to establish and maintain positive relationships with superiors. One study of a government agency revealed that positive superior-subordinate relationships are characterized by a high degree of upward influence: Employees are happier when they feel that their boss listens and responds to their concerns (Waldera, 1988). In their *Profile of Organizational Influence Strategies* (1982), organizational psychologists David Kipnis and Stuart Schmidt identified six strategies for upward influence: reasoning, friendliness, assertiveness, coalition building, appealing to higher authorities, and bargaining. In addition, friendly ingratiation (making the superior feel important) and developing rational plans (reasoning) are commonly used to influence superiors (Kipnis, Schmidt, & Wilkinson, 1980). A more recent study (Kipnis, Schmidt, & Braxton-Brown, 1990) found that employees may choose from among four very different approaches to dealing with superiors:

1. Shotgun — the employee uses all available approaches
2. Ingratiation — the employee is friendly and warm
3. Tactician — the employee uses reason
4. Bystander — the employee avoids all approaches in general

Another study (Keys & Case, 1990) suggests that the tactical approach — i.e., rational explanation — is the most frequently used type of upward influence. As a rule, a rational explanation includes a formal presentation, analysis, or proposal. A host of other influence tactics, such as arguing without support, using persistence and repetition, threatening, and manipulating, have been deemed ineffective and are therefore rarely chosen by most subordinates (Keys & Case, 1990).

Positive upward influence may also be achieved through personal communication. More specifically,

> by encouraging discussion of non-work issues, subordinates solidify friendship ties with supervisors while presumably adding stability and predictability to the formal authority relationship. . . . A history of such contacts may work to the advantage of the subordinate, by reducing the perceived "riskiness" of upward influence attempts and other potentially threatening messages (e.g., complaints, protests). (Waldron, 1991, p. 300)

Naturally, some supervisors may not respond positively to these informal advances. Employees must learn to tailor their approach to their particular supervisor accordingly (Keys & Case, 1990).

Some observers envision the process of relating to superiors as one of "managing up." In this view, the subordinate role is perceived as a kind of performance designed to make the boss look good (Thompson, 1967). However, what works for one supervisor may not work for another. For subordinates to be successful at "managing up," they need to know their superior's professional and personal goals, strengths and weaknesses, preferred working style, and attitudes toward conflict. This information is invaluable in fostering relationships with superiors that accommodate their needs and leadership style (Gabarro & Kotter, 1980).

Some people — ourselves included — believe that the most critical skill required to effectively "manage" the boss is advocacy (Riley & Eisenberg, 1992). Based on principles of persuasion, effective advocacy entails learning how to read a superior's needs and preferences and designing arguments to accomplish goals. Unlike traditional views of superior-subordinate communication that emphasize subordinate compliance, advocacy emphasizes the following principles:

1. *Plan a strategy.* Impromptu appeals for resources or decisions are often ineffective. Think through a strategy that will work.
2. *Determine why the supervisor should listen.* Connect your argument to something important to your boss, such as a key company objective or a personal goal.
3. *Tailor the argument to the supervisor's style and characteristics.* Will your boss respond more favorably to statistics or a poignant story? To details or generalities? Adapt your evidence and appeal accordingly.
4. *Assess the supervisor's technical knowledge.* Do not assume that your supervisor has technical knowledge of the issue.
5. *Build coalitions.* Support your argument with the views of others in the organization.
6. *Develop your communication skills.* Even the best ideas may sound unconvincing if they are not articulated well.

Underlying these six principles is the fundamental idea that effective communication is always tailored to an audience. Employees should take into account their audience's needs when communicating with superiors.

Communicating with Peers

One of the benefits of having peers at work is that they can provide social support. However, because informal work group norms can enhance or inhibit employee morale and commitment, success increasingly depends on maintaining a web of influence not just up and down the hierarchy, but also with co-workers and peers. Three types of peer communication are common in organizations: within-group communication, cross-functional communication, and unstructured communication.

Within-Group Communication

Although we will discuss work teams in greater detail in the next chapter, most research on peer communication focuses on within-group communication. For example, various studies have shown that the use of humor among manufacturing workers helps boost morale (Boland & Hoffman, 1983; Roy, 1960). Human relations theorists emphasized the importance of informal group norms in shaping organizational effectiveness and the experience of work.

Interpersonal communication in groups or teams warrants special attention because these groups have become the basic building blocks of contemporary organizations. This is happening because tall hierarchies with extensive chains of command are too slow and are not sufficiently creative to remain competitive, and individuals working in isolation do not benefit from the multiple perspectives needed to solve complex problems.

Working in teams is hard. Too often, management assumes that team communication is both straightforward and unproblematic but nothing could be farther from the truth. As you will see in the next chapter, effective teamwork requires a mastery of facilitation skills, group process, and team member roles. Communicating effectively in teams requires a particular skill set that is not commonly found in the general population.

Cross-Functional Communication

Cross-functional communication occurs across departmental or functional boundaries. Not long ago, the traditional bureaucracies of U.S. automobile manufacturers led to a separation of functions into isolated "silos." Back then, engineering designed the automobile; manufacturing made it; and sales tried to sell it. Problems were commonplace due to the lack of coordination among the functions — for example, certain designs were difficult or impossible to build or to sell! Ford Motor Company revolutionized this process in the design of the Ford Taurus, using a process called "concurrent engineering." In concurrent engineering, all of the departments are invited to the design table. The result in the case of the Taurus was a car with half as many parts that was much easier and cheaper to build and sell.

Cross-functional communication among peers in organizations is important because it enhances the flow of work within and among departments. An increasingly competitive marketplace and rising customer expectations have encouraged organizations to see the need for effective communication across departments and functions. As a result, cross-functional work teams, through which the people who design, manufacture, sell, and service products or systems work together rather than in relative isolation from one another, have become more common.

Most organizations initially find it difficult to cultivate cross-functional communication among co-workers. Some employees still prefer to be left alone to perform their assigned task in their designated silo. What is more, this aversion to collaboration can be reinforced by professional divisions, in which department employees identify with a professional group with its specialized language and unique values (e.g., lawyers, engineers, physicians). Conflicts between engineering and manufacturing, or between sales and legal, for example, are common.

Various informal and formal strategies help organizations meet the challenge of cross-functional relationships. At informal gatherings like company picnics and sports leagues, accountants, engineers, assemblers, maintenance workers, and others have the opportunity to get to know one another. In addition, orientation programs, job rotation, and company tours help employees understand other departments' contributions to the overall work process. Two other effective methods for promoting cross-functional communication are managing the "white space" and cultivating internal customers and suppliers.

Managing the White Space in the Organizational Chart   Recalling systems theory, cross-functional communication encourages employees to supplement departmental loyalties with an awareness of how what they do fits within the total work-flow process. Although an organizational chart outlines functions and reporting relationships, most of the actual work takes place between functions, in what has been called the "white space" in the chart (Rummler & Brache, 1991). Managing the white space means first identifying, then analyzing and managing horizontal work-flow processes.

Anyone who has spent time in a large hospital has likely experienced the phenomenon of the white space from the standpoint of the patient. Traditionally, each hospital employee focuses on his or her functional specialty. Conversely, the patient experiences the hospital horizontally, as he or she is handed off or processed from admissions to risk management to nursing to physicians of various specialties to discharge. Quite often, patients end up "lost" between functions, perhaps in a deserted hallway waiting for radiology but far from their room. Worse yet, it may be hard to find anyone who knows how to help, since individual employees lack the big picture. Lately, as hospitals have recognized this problem, patients are increasingly assigned case managers who help them navigate the organization.

Cultivating Internal Customers   In addition to external customers, organizations increasingly recognize the importance of their "internal customers" — people within the organization who depend on the output of others in the same company to do their jobs. In a bureaucracy, employees function not as internal customers, but as independent entities who may be at odds and may compete for resources. Because they are generally unaware of their role in the overall work process, there is little incentive for considering the impact of their work on others. The notion of employees as internal customers is intended to address this problem. For example, a human resources (HR) worker supplies data on workers' compensation claims to a manager who is viewed as a customer of the HR worker's output. As a result, employees become more concerned with passing on high-quality work to their customers at the next stage in the work process.

Hewlett-Packard (HP) is one of many companies that cultivate the idea of internal customers to promote cross-functional relationships among employees in various departments. The positive results have included more frequent and effective communication among employees and greater commitment to the common goal of satisfying external customers. For example, a work-flow analysis of one of HP's distribution plants that was experiencing slow turnover in its accounts receivable (customers weren't paying their bills) resulted in the identification of a "weak link" between the department that recorded the order number and the department that mailed out the bills. Once the recording department was able to improve the accuracy of its numbers, the billing department (which was the internal customer) was more successful at doing its job, leading to a dramatic reduction in late payments.

Unstructured Peer Communication

Another form of interaction that is important to organizations is the unstructured communication that takes place in informal settings, such as in the mailroom, in a car pool, or during lunch. A valuable source of social support and identification, unstructured communication can also be a source of innovative ideas. Two employees who have no work reason to speak with one another can get together at lunch and devise an original idea. For this reason, some progressive companies now require employees to spend up to 30 percent of their time in work outside of their primary job in order to promote new ideas.

There are two potential difficulties with unstructured communication. The first is that it may support the company grapevine and can reinforce griping and the spreading of unsubstantiated rumors. The second is people's tendency to communicate with similar others. As a result, unstructured peer communication may fall along functional, gender, or ethnic lines. Effectively managing diversity in organizations can help overcome this limitation of unstructured communication.

Communicating with Employees

Various theories propose different approaches to communicating with employees. In classical management theory, downward communication is emphasized; it is formal, precise, and work related. Human relations theory stresses supportive communication, while human resources theory emphasizes the need for supervisors to involve employees in decision making. The systems and cultural approaches make no specific prescriptions about communicating with employees, whereas critical and postmodern theorists call for a radical leveling of power and authority among superiors and subordinates in which both are regarded as equally important to the organization.

No matter what their perspective, however, contemporary observers agree that effective communication with employees has at least four essential characteristics: It is open, supportive, motivating, and empowering. Each of these characteristics is discussed below. At the end of this section, we explore new directions in leadership from a communication perspective.

Openness

As a general rule, openness is a desirable goal in supervisor-employee relationships (Redding, 1972). The parties in an open communication relationship "perceive the other interactant as a willing and receptive listener and refrain from responses that might be perceived as providing negative relational or disconfirming feedback" (Jablin, 1979, p. 1,204). Openness has both verbal and nonverbal dimensions. Nonverbally, facial expression, eye gaze, tone, and the like contribute to degrees of open communication (Tjosvold, 1984).

Studies conducted by W. Charles Redding (1972) and his many students at Purdue University reveal a positive correlation between a supervisor's open communication and employees' satisfaction with the relationship. The researchers identify five key components of an open communication relationship:

1. The most effective supervisors tend to emphasize the importance of communication in their relationships with employees. For example, they enjoy talking at meetings and conversing with subordinates, and they are skilled at explaining instructions and policies.
2. Effective supervisors are empathic listeners. They respond positively to employees' questions, listen to suggestions and complaints, and express a willingness to take fair and appropriate action when necessary.
3. Effective supervisors ask or persuade, rather than tell or demand.
4. Effective supervisors are sensitive to others' feelings. For instance, reprimands are made in private rather than in public work settings.
5. Effective supervisors share information with employees, including advance notices of impending changes and explanations about why the changes will be made.

Other researchers suggest that openness plays a more complex role in the superior-subordinate relationship and that its effects are not always this easy to predict. Eisenberg argued that depending on the context, openness can have dramatically different outcomes (Eisenberg & Witten, 1987). For example, a supervisor may use openness in indiscreet or insincere ways or as a way to intimidate employees. Although supervisors should strive for open communication with employees in appropriate contexts, openness should not override other concerns, such as confidentiality and ethics. For example, it may be highly inappropriate for a supervisor to disclose reservations he or she may have about the performance of one of his colleagues. Instead, the supervisor ought to share this information with the proper audience and in the proper context — that is, with his or her supervisor. Problems can arise when open communication is viewed ideologically and indiscriminately as a moral mandate for full and honest disclosure, without sensitivity to the communicative context of the situation (Bochner, 1982; Eisenberg, 1984).

Supportiveness

Research suggests that supportive communication with employees is more useful to supervisors than openness. According to the theory of leader-member exchange, or LMX (Graen, 1976), supervisors tend to divide their employees into two types and to form very different relationships with members of each group. The two types of relationships are (1) in-group relationships, which are "characterized by high trust, mutual influence, support, and formal/informal rewards," and (2) out-group relationships, which are "characterized by . . . formal authority [and] low trust, support, and rewards" (Fairhurst & Chandler, 1989, pp. 215–216). In-group relationships develop over time, tend to be more trusting, and are characterized by a greater willingness by supervisors to delegate important tasks (Bauer & Green, 1996). In general, in-group relationships are associated with greater employee satisfaction, performance, agreement, and decision-making involvement as well as lower turnover rates than out-group relationships (Graen, Liden, & Hoel, 1982; Liden & Graen, 1980; Scandura, Graen, & Novak, 1986).

There is also evidence to suggest that having a positive in-group relationship with one's supervisor leads to better integration into important social networks (Sparrowe & Liden, 1997) as well as enhanced feelings of perceived organizational support, which in turn strengthens commitment and performance (Wayne, Shore, & Liden, 1997). (See *What Would You Do?* 9.1.)

Communication researchers Gail Fairhurst and Theresa Chandler (1989) extended LMX theory in an examination of actual in-group and out-group conversations involving a warehouse supervisor and three subordinates. Their analysis reveals some consistency in the communication resources deployed by those in each type of relationship. The in-group relationship is characterized by influence by mutual persuasion (in which both parties challenge and disagree with each other frequently) and greater freedom of choice for subordinates. In contrast, the out-group relationship is marked by the supervisor's authority, a traditional chain of command, little freedom of choice for subordinates, and a disregard for their suggestions.

A more recent application of the leader-member exchange model to co-worker communication revealed how an employee's privileged relationship with a supervisor affected that employee's relationship with peers. In most cases, the employee's co-workers engaged in communication aimed at making sense of the preferential treatment, made judgments about the unfairness of the in-group relationship, and experienced a general erosion of trust in management (Sias & Jablin, 1995). Although the leader-member exchange distinction focuses on broad issues of trust and support, it does not prescribe open communication as the sole means for attaining supportive relationships. Instead, supervisory communication is viewed as an ongoing attempt to balance the multiple and competing relational, identity, and task goals (Dillard & Segrin, 1987; Eisenberg, 1984). Moreover, certain types of communication may ensure employee compliance

What Would You Do? 9.1

MANAGING THE SUPERIOR-SUBORDINATE RELATIONSHIP

Major Ramone Martinez recently completed a management workshop on empowerment and has a new perspective on his role as an active listener at work. Ramone, who works for the U.S. Army, believes that he has always been a good listener but that the workshop has sharpened his skills. He is eager to put those skills to good use.

Captain Eileen Davis works for Ramone in the procurement department of the U.S. Army. She and Ramone have long shared a close professional relationship. Recently, however, Ramone has more actively sought to engage Eileen in conversations that are characterized by his attentive listening to her comments. This has made Eileen feel even closer to Ramone and more willing to share information.

As a result, Eileen decided to share some personal information with Ramone that she had kept secret for fear of losing her job: She is a lesbian. Homosexuals are not allowed to be open about their sexual orientation in the military, but Eileen felt she could share her secret with her friend and confidant, Ramone.

Ramone now finds himself in the midst of an ethical dilemma. On the one hand, as a supervisor he is obligated by the military's code of conduct to report the information about Eileen to his supervisors. On the other hand, Ramone feels responsible for encouraging her to share the information with him. If he had maintained some emotional distance in the relationship, Eileen would not have confided in him as she did.

Exercises

1. Divide the class into two groups. One group will develop arguments in favor of reporting Eileen; the other group will develop arguments for the opposite action. After the arguments are presented to the class, try to resolve the competing arguments by agreeing on a course of action.
2. Discuss this issue in relation to the material presented in this chapter on the importance of effective interpersonal communication between superiors and subordinates. Then discuss it in relation to the material on maintaining emotional boundaries at work. Is there a way to resolve the inherent contradictions between these two ways of framing the issues?
3. Using what you have learned in this course thus far, how do you think Ramone can best respond to this dilemma?

but may also be demoralizing to employees. For example, a supervisor who insists on managing "by the book" despite employee extenuating circumstances (e.g., personal or medical emergencies) can create a negative work climate. Effective supervisors, in contrast, strive to communicate in ways that simultaneously show concern for the relationship, demonstrate respect for the individual, and promote task accomplishment. Unfortunately, limited data exist on how one might practically achieve this complex balance in actual superior-subordinate communication.

Motivation

Motivation can be defined as "the degree to which an individual is personally committed to expending effort in the accomplishment of a specified activity or goal" (Kreps, 1991, p. 154). Although various other factors contribute to employee motivation (see Chapter 8), our focus here is on how supervisors encourage or discourage employee motivation through their communication with subordinates. Their communication can function in two ways to motivate employees: Managers can (1) provide information and feedback about employees' tasks, goals, performance, and future directions and (2) communicate encouragement, empathy, and concern. In both cases, however, the motivating effect comes from the manager's ability to endorse particular interpretations of organizational issues through communication (Sullivan, 1988).

The four best-known theories of employee motivation involve goal setting, expectancy, equity, and compliance gaining.

Goal-Setting Theory   Goal-setting theory maintains that because employees' conscious objectives influence their performance, supervisors should assist employees in developing goals that are motivating (Locke & Latham, 1984). Some of the most important findings of this research are as follows:

1. Set clear and specific goals. Clear goals have a greater positive impact on performance than do general goals.
2. Set goals that are difficult but attainable. They will lead to higher performance than will easy goals.
3. Focus on participative rather than assigned goals.
4. Give frequent feedback about the goal-setting and work processes.

Although goal-setting theory is not a communication theory per se, most of these findings deal with communication. To wit, to be motivating, goals must be clear and specific, must be set through a dialogue with employees, and must be the subject of performance feedback. Feedback is especially important to employee motivation because it helps employees both to see how they're doing and how their efforts contribute to the success or failure of the company. Employees who receive such feedback from supervisors tend to be more satisfied, perform better, and are less likely to leave the company than those who do not receive feedback on their work (Jablin, 1979; Parsons, Herold, & Leatherwood, 1985).

An ingenious field experiment supports the importance of goal setting and feedback in shaping employee performance. Eighty Air Force employees who repaired electronic equipment or distributed materials and supplies took part in the study. Productivity measures were compiled for the nine months before the study. For five months, employees were given monthly feedback on their productivity. For the next five months, employees working in groups set difficult but attainable goals for themselves. During this five-month feedback period, productivity improved by an average of 50 percent over the initial nine-month baseline. Improvements in morale were also recorded (Pritchard, Jones, Roth, & Steubing, 1988).

Feedback on goals can take many forms, but to be effective it must be frequent and specific. Annual performance reviews have been shown to be ineffective in influencing employee behavior (Ilgin & Knowlton, 1980). Such infrequent reviews encourage managers to focus on negative behavior that was noticed but not discussed throughout the year. Performance management should ideally be an ongoing, everyday conversation, since the best time to give feedback about employee performance is as soon as possible after it has occurred.

Not all supervisory feedback, of course, is negative. Tom Peters and Robert Waterman (1982) argue that successful managers give formal or informal recognition for a job well done. Management guru Ken Blanchard famously encouraged supervisors to "catch their employees doing something right." Generally speaking, positive feedback has been shown to encourage job satisfaction, identification, and commitment among employees (Larson, 1989).

Recently, some companies have made feedback part of certain jobs through the management of information systems. At Frito-Lay's snack food factory in California, for example, computer terminals are located in the packaging areas so that machine operators can access feedback on their daily performance, including the amount of raw material used, the number of hours an assembly line was not working due to repairs, and the number of person hours worked. According to one operator,

> People have more pride in their work now. We go to the computer at the end of the day and see how much we made or lost. If the numbers are good, we feel proud because we know we did it. If the numbers aren't good, we get with our team members and figure out what went wrong. Before, we seldom even saw the numbers. It's no wonder we weren't very interested in the business. (Grant, 1992, p. D7)

As this example shows, clear goals and immediate feedback are important in the increasingly popular shift from feedback from interpersonal communication to feedback from computer-accessed data.

Because many supervisors do not provide enough feedback, subordinates may actively seek it out (Ashford & Cummings, 1983). It is hard to do a job without knowing how you are doing. At the same time, it can be tricky to ask for feedback. Not unlike what happens to newcomers (see Chapter 8), employees seeking feedback from a supervisor can be "faced with a conflict between the need to obtain useful information and the need to present a favorable image" (Morrison & Bies, 1991, p. 523). In a marked departure from times past, when seeking feedback was seen as a sign of weakness, effective performance today requires constant communication in all directions. Consequently, even when a supervisor does not provide sufficient feedback to an employee, the employee is making the right move in seeking it out.

Expectancy Theory   Expectancy theory makes three assumptions about employee behavior:

1. Employees perceive a relationship between a specific work behavior and some form of payoff or reward; that is, the behavior is viewed as instrumental to obtaining the reward.
2. Each reward or positive outcome is associated with a value (or valence, in the language of the theory) that reflects how much the individual wants the reward.
3. Employees develop expectations about their ability to perform the desired behavior successfully (Vroom, 1964).

Employee motivation increases when outcome valences are positive, expectancies are high, and outcomes are clear. Under these circumstances, the employee desires the reward or outcome, feels capable of performing the desired behavior, and has a clear understanding of what will be rewarded as a result of that performance. For example, one resort manager who in the past had a serious absenteeism problem now bestows quarterly rewards of free weekend trips upon employees who have records of perfect attendance for the three-month period. It's fair to say that everyone likes a free vacation, and that it is possible with some extra effort to have a perfect attendance record in most quarters. The existence of the program has been well communicated, and employees know what it takes to get the free trip. One could well argue that this manager's approach works because it meets all three criteria of expectancy theory.

Generally speaking, the expectancy model has been shown to benefit individuals and organizations by increasing employee motivation and improving the quality of the work life (Steers, 1981). In addition, because expectancy theory demands clear communication of performance outcomes, communication plays a key role in its successful implementation.

Equity Theory   In a different approach to employee motivation, equity theory examines the role of perceived inequities in the reward-to-work ratio (Altman, Valenzi, & Hodgetts, 1985). Employees who feel that they receive fewer rewards than their co-workers for performing comparable work are not likely to be motivated to perform their jobs well. Judgments of equity and perceptions of fairness are shaped by communication. In particular, the communication of superiors can affect subordinates' perceptions of equity. For example, a supervisor who takes the time to explain long-range plans for an employee's development helps the employee put present differences in position and salary into meaningful perspective.

Equity theory highlights the often subjective nature of employee performance evaluation and rewards. Although supervisors may strive to establish supportive relationships with employees, and organizations may be structured in ways that make identification and cooperation likely, employees may still lack motivation if they perceive themselves as underrewarded for their efforts. As in Herbert Simon's (1957) conceptualization of employee decision making (discussed in Chapter 3), the judgments and decisions that lead to variations in employee attitude and performance are subjectively determined by factors in the social environment.

Compliance-Gaining Theory   Informal compliance-gaining tactics may help motivate employees to perform. Supervisors who encourage employees with positive feedback are most likely to achieve task compliance and subordinate satisfaction (Daniels & Spiker, 1991). An investigation of the informal strategies used by superiors to influence subordinate behavior revealed that managers explain tasks or delegate assignments more often than they give orders (Keys & Case, 1990). They also tend to convey confidence, encouragement, or support in their attempts to influence employees, and to use reasoning and facts to suggest the merits of a new procedure or a desired behavior. In addition, managers often attempt to gain compliance by regularly soliciting employees' ideas (Keys & Case, 1990).

However, these informal tactics of influence may be ineffective when dealing with chronically poor performers. In a study of the compliance-gaining strategies used by bank managers, the researchers note a discrepancy between how administrators claim to deal with employees and what they actually do:

> Branch and personnel administrators in the banks we studied advocated the use of the punitive approach only after the problem-solving approach repeatedly failed. Yet, in the field, we find that the punitive approach predominates from the start for many, [while] the problem-solving approach is used by some but is quickly abandoned. (Fairhurst, Green, & Snavely, 1984, p. 289)

Current research on compliance-gaining tactics suggests that supervisors who rely on traditional lines of authority and punitive approaches are less effective motivators than supervisors who use a variety of influence tactics tailored to the needs and personalities of individual employees as well as to the specific goals involved. Indeed, setting clear goals, articulating ways of achieving them, and providing immediate feedback are an important part of the supervisor's job.

From a communication perspective, conveying the right combination of these messages helps to motivate employees.

Empowerment

Definitions of empowerment vary considerably from the sharing of power and decision making with employees, through delegation, to enabling and motivating employees by building feelings of self-efficacy. As illustrated in Figure 9.1, the empowerment process enhances feelings of self-efficacy by identifying and removing conditions that foster employee powerlessness (Conger & Kanungo, 1988). Furthermore, to feel empowered, an employee must also feel capable of performing the job and must possess the authority to decide how to do the job well (Chiles & Zorn, 1995).

Empowerment requires the manager to act more like a coach than a boss by listening to employees' concerns, avoiding close supervision, trusting employees to work within a framework of clear direction, and being responsive to employee feedback. An organization committed to empowerment encourages employees to take on ever-increasing responsibilities that utilize their knowledge and skills. A study of W. L. Gore & Associates (Pacanowsky, 1988), the company that invented the fabric GORE-TEX®, identified six rules for empowering employees:

1. Distribute power and opportunity widely.
2. Maintain an open and decentralized communication system.
3. Use integrative problem solving to involve diverse groups and individuals.
4. Practice meeting challenges in an environment of trust.
5. Reward and recognize employees to encourage a high-performance ethic and self-responsibility.
6. Learn from organizational ambiguity, inconsistency, contradiction, and paradox.

Notice that these rules focus on providing the resources and opportunities for creating an environment in which subordinates become empowered by taking greater responsibility for their work.

Organizations (and departments within organizations) vary in their degree of empowerment (Ford & Fottler, 1995). Degree of empowerment is a direct result of how decision-making authority is defined. A distinction exists between the employee's control of job content (how the job gets done) versus job context (the conditions under which the job gets done, including goals, strategies, and standards). For example, it is increasingly common for line employees to have considerable say in the scheduling and tools they use to accomplish their work (job content) but still quite rare to have input into things like mission, strategy, and organizational structure (job context). What is of greatest importance is for managers and employees to maintain clear agreements about the expected degree of empowerment in order to avoid misunderstandings that can foster resentment and mistrust.

FIGURE 9.1

The Five Stages of the Empowerment Process

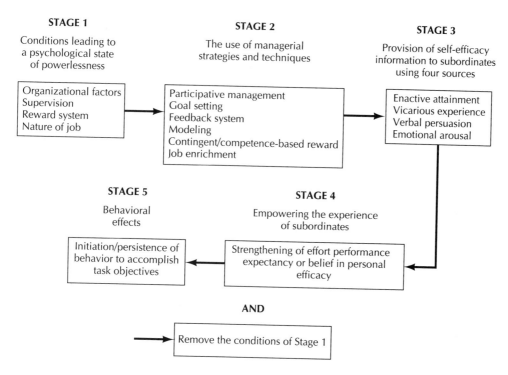

Source: Adapted from Jay Conger and Rabindra Kanungo, "The Empowerment Process: Integrating Theory and Practice," *Academy of Management Review* 13 (1988): 411–482.

New Directions in Leadership

Leadership is among the most studied phenomena in organizational behavior. Contemporary researchers define leadership as a system of relationships through which individuals motivate followers to perform desired behaviors (Hollander & Offerman, 1990). However, the history of theories on leadership reveals a growing emphasis on the importance of interpersonal relationships and communication. In a way, current thinking about leadership draws together many of the isolated supervisory behaviors discussed earlier.

Early theories of leadership maintained that certain people were born with leadership skills or traits — you either had them or you didn't. As a result, much research went into identifying "natural born leaders." By the late 1940s, however, a different idea emerged: situational leadership. This theory held that "situations varied in the qualities demanded of leaders, so those qualities were appropriate to a particular task and interpersonal context" (Hollander & Offerman, 1990, p. 180). Thus, for example, different types of leaders were believed to be more suited to the start-up phase of a high-tech company than to the management of a mature government agency.

Over the past few decades, researchers have shifted their focus from leaders, to followers, to the leader-follower relationship. In this view, sometimes called the "transactional" approach, followers' perceptions of a leader determine the leader's success or failure (Calder, 1977). Although the transactional approach considers the importance of communication in leadership, it assumes that the needs and desires of followers are fixed.

In contrast, the transformational leader seeks to transcend the bounds of routine follower behavior to offer the possibility of a new vision for the organization. This theory recasts leadership mainly as the management of meaning (Bennis & Nanus, 1985). In addition to setting goals and focusing on tasks, transformative leaders help followers interpret organizational events and make sense of the world of work in general. Management theorist Karl Weick (1980) argues that contemporary leaders are nothing if not evangelical: They must invent positive ways to communicate with and inspire others to action.

Put another way, recent research on leadership emphasizes the importance of positive relationships with potential followers and the willingness to exert one's influence gradually over time. An increasing number of authors advise would-be leaders to profess ignorance and avoid decisive action in favor of bringing others' initiative to the fore (e.g., Sample, 2001). Most contemporary metaphors for leadership are closer to an orchestra conductor than they are to a factory foreman.

Among the new metaphors guiding organizational studies is spirituality (Fox, 1994; Goodall, 1996; Spretnak, 1991). Transformational leaders often draw inspiration and techniques from spiritual leaders, movements, and events. Since the Industrial Revolution, however, managers have replaced leaders, and their concerns differ (Table 9.1). For example, leaders tend to define organizational realities and visions, whereas managers implement those visions. In addition, managers specialize in getting the most from workers, but leaders specialize in giving of themselves to others. Managers divide tasks that have been envisioned by leaders, whose actions are driven by a sense of deep purpose and conviction. Although managers and leaders may both be engaged in spiritual work, their tasks and approaches to the work often differ.

Two leadership metaphors with connections to spirituality that have enjoyed recent popularity are that of the steward (Block, 1993) and the servant (Greenleaf, 1998). In contrast to the traditional notion of a leader as strategic

TABLE 9.1

The Management/Spiritual Leadership Model: The Functions,
Interests, and Concerns of Management and Leadership
and Their Spiritual Basis

MANAGEMENT	LEADERSHIP	SPIRITUAL BASIS	LEADER AS
is mostly concerned with:	*is mostly concerned with:*		
Goals and objectives	Vision	Covenant	Sense maker
Honesty	Integrity	Dharma (truth)	Moral architect
Priorities	Values	Virtue	Values steward
Plans and strategies	State (of mind)	Equanimity (inner peace)	Yogi
Getting	Giving	Service	Servant
Management of people	People's energy and heart	Spiritual awareness	Guide
Organization structure/sense of team	Organization culture/ sense of community	Unity/(cosmic) oneness	Whole maker
Error correction	Acknowledgment	Gratitude (basic belief)	Optimist
Problem solving/ decision making	Presence	Inner/higher power	Warrior

Source: Jack C. Hawley, *Reawakening the Spirit in Work: The Power of Dharmic Management* (San Francisco: Berrett-Koehler, 1994), p. 168.

and self-motivated, both of these concepts envision a leader whose values are closely aligned with those of the organization and who sees subordinates as trustworthy and cooperative given direction. Steward and servant leaders are hard to find and may only emerge through a unique combination of personal disposition, trusting ownership, and a positive local culture (Davis, Schoorman, & Donaldson, 1997).

In Japan, leadership skills are referred to as "warrior spirit" and are associated with the idea of a life of service to work. In the West, and particularly in the United States, the new spiritual dimension of work — and especially of leadership — is in part a response to the troubling questions about loyalty, security, natural resources, and meaning posed at the end of the organizational age (Fox, 1994; Goodall, 1996; Rushing, 1993). As contemporary organizations deal with increased competition, the most successful companies survive because their leaders are effective communicators. They know how to inspire employees with honesty and optimism. Effective leaders treat the business problems of today as problems that affect each worker's whole being — their minds, bodies, hearts, and spirits.

Learning Leadership Skills

The Center for Creative Leadership (CCL) in North Carolina surveyed 45,665 leaders in business, industry, and government to discover how people acquire leadership skills (Moxley, 1994). The survey revealed that a variety of experiences and the ability to accept and meet challenges are most important in developing the skills of effective leadership. More specifically, experiences that provide the following are noted:

1. A change in the scope and scale of a job
2. The opportunity to introduce a new product or to start a new project or business
3. A "fix-it" opportunity, such as being called on to solve a problem
4. A task force opportunity that is important to the organization, yields positive results, and encourages communication with senior managers
5. A line-to-staff move that involves negotiating with, influencing, and motivating others

According to the survey, challenging assignments also involve learning new skills, but they are marked by a need to deal with difficulties or obstacles. Examples include working with ineffective supervisors and with difficult employees. Other examples include surviving business failures, career stalls (e.g., losing a job or not receiving a promotion), and personal traumas that indirectly affect the work life. Through experiences like these, people learn how to confront and overcome challenges to their work and work identities.

Leadership and Organizational Effectiveness

Three attributes of leaders have been linked to overall organizational effectiveness: (1) certain innate skills, (2) the ability to lead others, and (3) good communication skills (Moxley, 1994).

The innate skills of leadership include resourcefulness, decisiveness, optimism, and determination. A person who possesses these innate skills is able to adapt well to change, take appropriate action in response to change, and use these experiences to learn how to make good decisions. The ability to lead others encompasses various skills aimed at balancing sources of creativity and constraint in organizations. Examples include delegating work tasks effectively among employees, establishing appropriate developmental or learning climates, dealing with difficult employees fairly, fostering a team-based orientation toward work, and hiring talented staff members. Finally, the communication skills of leaders include the ability to be straightforward but flexible, to build and mend relationships with followers, to maintain a balance between one's work and personal life, to possess self-awareness, and to express compassion and sensitivity in order to make others feel comfortable in their relationship with the leader (Moxley, 1994).

Another way of thinking about the personal orientation leaders bring to situations is in terms of emotional intelligence (Goleman, 1998). Similar to Bennis's notion of "self-management" and Senge's "personal mastery," leadership today requires individuals to be secure and skilled enough in handling their own emotional reactions so that they may deal effectively with others. The most critical dimension of emotional intelligence is self-awareness, defined as

> the knowledge of one's own abilities and limitations as well as a solid understanding of factors and situations that evoke emotion in one's self and others. Equipped with this awareness, an individual can better manage their own emotions and behaviors and better understand and relate to other individuals and systems. (Cavallo & Brienza, 2002, p. 1)

Along with the growing realization that one's emotional makeup is key to leading others is newfound respect for the importance of emotional reactions — often called intuition, or gut feel — in effective decision making. Today's business environment rarely if ever offers prospective leaders all the data and alternatives needed to make a decision; consequently, the best decision makers are exquisitely aware of and can make sense of their bodily, emotional reactions to situations. According to his son, international financier George Soros, who has made billions in currency speculation, changes his position in the stock market when his back starts killing him. Much decision making today is like successful hitting in baseball — if you have to think about it, you're already too late. Instead, effective leaders must learn to trust the wisdom of the body, the things you know only through experience.

There is also reason to believe that effective leaders are good storytellers (Gardner, 1996). Stories help recruit new followers, cultivate identification, and adapt to uncertainty and change (Stewart, 1998; Tichy, Pritchett, & Cohen, 1998). Stories can carry the company culture, or they can reveal conflict and contradiction. Stories can motivate employees to move in a specific or even a new direction. In every case, the leader's challenge is to promote adherence to their preferred narrative by employees who are constantly bombarded with alternative frameworks and explanations.

Because some aspects of leadership skill are innate, not everyone will respond well to leadership development and training (e.g., if they do not adapt well to change). More companies today are conducting leadership assessments on their employees first to gauge their potential for becoming leaders. With this information, better decisions can be made about how to invest money and time in leadership development.

All three sets of leadership skills rely heavily on communication. Research suggests that an organization can create leaders by satisfying their needs for varied and challenging experiences as well as by allowing enough time for people to develop leadership skills (Moxley, 1994). Organizations need to resist the temptation to make specialists out of people, focusing instead on providing employees with a variety of experiences and challenges. Furthermore, organizations must recognize that leadership skills take time to develop and that moving employees from one job to another too quickly is counterproductive. Leadership training is time-consuming because the ability to confront and meet new challenges develops gradually over time. The CCL research suggests that promotions and training programs, for example, cannot substitute for or reduce the amount of time it takes to develop leadership skills through varied and challenging work experiences (Moxley, 1994). Instead, training programs are effective only when employees can bring to them the knowledge and skills they have gained over time and an ongoing desire to learn.

Obstacles to Interpersonal Relationships I: Working the Boundaries

In this last part of this chapter, we explore obstacles to forming positive relationships in organizations and discuss how communication may play a role in confronting those obstacles. In our view, there are two general categories of obstacles to communication between and among people at work: (1) the cultural, physical, and emotional expectations we have for relationships and the perceived violations to boundaries that we expect to see maintained in the workplace, and (2) the interplay of relational dialectics, conflict, and dealing with difficult people on an everyday basis. Specifically, in this initial section we are concerned with cultural, physical, and emotional boundaries to open relationships in the workplace.

Cultural Boundaries

Although most research on work relationships assumes that people share a similar cultural understanding, an important distinction has been made between results-oriented and relationship-oriented cultures (Varner & Beamer, 1995). In a results-oriented culture like the United States, it is assumed that work and communication at work are governed by the management of objectives — that is, identify a goal, then work systematically to achieve it. Anything that gets in the way of achieving that goal is perceived as a problem, and measurements of success are based on the results of goal achievement.

In contrast, a more relationship-oriented culture exists in many other countries of the world (Varner & Beamer, 1995; Victor, 1994). In Japan, for example, maintaining *wa*, or harmony, in relationships with others is a primary concern, and in Spain and Mexico, businesspeople do not conduct business until they have had the opportunity to get to know one another. Chinese business depends significantly on informal networks of relationships called *guang-xi*. Whereas Asians tend to value the means to an end more than the end itself, the French find the American preoccupation with measurements (of everything from job satisfaction to performance) peculiar and even humorous.

Effective intercultural communication depends on an awareness of and sensitivity to the many differences between results- and relationship-oriented cultures. Three areas of cultural understanding are especially important: knowledge, achievement, and universal issues.

Ways of Thinking and Acquiring Knowledge

Unlike American culture, which views knowledge as being rooted in concepts, other cultures place greater value on knowledge that is gained from firsthand experience (e.g., many Latin American countries) or from intuition (e.g., followers of Taoism, Hinduism, and Buddhism). Cultural differences can influence not only what one knows, but also how one comes to know it. Thus, in Asian, Latin American, and southern European cultures, learning comes less from asking questions than from receiving information from teachers and significant others. Moreover, whereas Western cultures view scientific knowledge as separate from religious faith, many non-Western cultures do not make that distinction. In addition, ways of thinking in most Western cultures are based on the cause-and-effect reasoning that derives from scientific inquiry, whereas in China and many other non-Western cultures, logical thought is based on an appreciation of the yin and the yang (opposites that are not mutually exclusive).

Ways of Doing and Achieving

The American's preoccupation with doing and achieving things in life can seem odd to people from cultures that value silence, serenity, peace, and stillness in life. Similarly, the ways in which tasks are done can vary by culture. Tasks tend to be completed sequentially in results-oriented cultures and simultaneously in relationship-oriented cultures. In America, uncertainty and shyness are viewed as obstacles to achieving success, but to most non-Westerners, our communication model of uncertainty reduction can seem inappropriate or rude, and throughout most of Asia, where quietude is prized, frequent talkers are mistrusted. In addition, whereas westerners believe that planning is a key to achieving success, in many Buddhist, Taoist, and Hindu cultures, people are born with *karma*, or destiny, that they learn from and deal with to achieve success. Similarly, some Asians believe in *feng shui* or geomancy, wherein the arrangement of buildings, earth and rocks, offices, doorways, windows, and the like is determined by *chi*, the spiritual forces that govern the universe. At Hitachi's Greenville, South Carolina, plant, for example, about $150,000 was spent on installing large rocks in front of the plant to attract the spirits that reward harmonious business practices. Cultures throughout the world have their own ways of expressing their belief in fate. In India, astrologers routinely function as business consultants; in Taiwan, during "ghost" month, people avoid making business decisions because they believe that such ill-timed decisions are doomed to fail; and in the United States, most hotels and office buildings do not have a thirteenth floor.

Ways of Thinking about Universal Issues

Cultures also differ in their understanding of universal issues, such as life and death, divine powers, nature, and change. A compelling example of these kinds of differences can be found in the current international debate about genetically altered food. Europe, and Great Britain in particular, has taken a strong stand against such practices, and at present there is no European market for bioengineered foods. By contrast, there has been comparatively little organized resistance in the United States. Perhaps this reflects cultural differences in how people view risk, technology, and nature.

In the United States, immigrant and guest workers may possess different cultural understandings, values, and beliefs in addition to speaking a different language. Furthermore, guest workers may be the target of racism and discrimination in nations where political sects still hold hostile attitudes based on old animosities. Managers and team leaders must be knowledgeable about world politics and religions to deal effectively with these issues.

Nonverbal Dimensions of Culture

When doing business at home, most American businesspeople know that the nonverbal communication of English-speaking people is as important as the spoken word. Similarly, the nonverbal dimensions of intercultural communication are both important and culturally specific. Although some international firms provide intercultural training programs for business travelers who will deal with the verbal and nonverbal dimensions of communication, most companies do not invest enough of their resources in such training. This is surprising because the subtleties of nonverbal intercultural communication can often mark the difference between what is considered appropriate (respectful) and inappropriate (rude or insulting) behavior.

Americans, for example, use various nonverbal behaviors — eye contact, head nodding, body posture, movement, and other gestures — to show respect for people with power and wealth (Scott, 1990). Americans tend also to be relatively abrupt and to accept abruptness from superiors. Respect for authority in Japan is expressed nonverbally by the depth of a bow, for example (Barnlund, 1994). In Norway, it is bad form to raise your voice or to touch the person to whom you are speaking.

American businesspeople who fail to respect the nonverbal customs of other cultures create the impression that they are disrespectful or arrogant. Among the many nonverbal dimensions of intercultural communication, tone of voice and eye contact are perhaps the most important. Speaking softly among Asian people shows respect for the value they attribute to harmony in relationships. Accepting the brash communicative style of Germans shows respect for the value they attribute to assertiveness. Finally, looking directly into a Japanese person's eyes for lengthy periods will be seen as inappropriate and aggressive.

Negotiating a Middle Ground

Although generalizing about another culture is helpful, individual differences must also be taken into account. New intercultural thinking suggests that an appreciation for the middle ground of negotiated meanings can improve the interpersonal relations among people of goodwill in business dealings. Appreciating the need to adapt to another's culture is balanced with a recognition of the person's individuality. When people from different cultures have only *cultural* expectations for one another, miscommunication is likely to occur.

Here again, we confront the formidable challenges of intercultural communication in business relationships. Dealing effectively with these challenges involves finding productive ways to communicate with others whose understandings and values may differ considerably from your own.

Physical Boundaries

The movement of people from farms into the cities during the Industrial Revolution contributed to the idealized image of a business as a "place." Work was less a process than a locale, a building (or set of buildings) with an address. Enormous efficiencies were created simply by locating employees in one place. Over time, the introduction of new communication technology (the telephone!) permitted even more people to crowd into the same square footage, this time stacked on top of one another in skyscrapers.

As companies pursued customers outside of their home cities, an important change began to take place. Company leadership was faced with the challenge of staying coordinated across geographic distance and changing time zones. At first, the preferred solution was employee travel, as employees were anxious to meet and shake the hands of co-workers in remote locations. Still, there were considerable problems in timing and distortion of messages that persist in some businesses today. If significant numbers of employees are geographically distributed, the organization has the additional challenge of promoting a common vision and culture across disparate regions.

Today, communication technology allows knowledge employees to access their "desktop" anytime, from all over the world. Organizations are less physical places and more like complex intersections of biological and symbolic information. Consequently, a large number of people work in off-site locations or telecommute from home. Unfortunately, connectivity is not the only issue in making physically dispersed companies successful. Telecommuters sometimes struggle to create an efficient home environment, remarking that in retrospect, the "commute" served as quiet time for role transition. Critical theorists argue further that telecommuting (and variations) is an invasion of home by work, continuing a trend toward the corporate colonization of all aspects of our lives (Deetz, 1991).

Our point is that while technology proponents may boast of perfect connectivity anytime, anywhere in the world, most businesses today are still struggling with how to make this a practical reality. Often, people without regular opportunities for face-to-face communication feel ignored and diminished by those who do. Differing time zones and a lack of understanding of national and regional cultural differences often lead to misunderstandings.

The emergent model for dealing with companies that seem increasingly virtual is to create an intranet site for all employees to access. This intranet contains all of the critical top-down business, product, and financial information and is updated constantly. In addition, state-of-the-art phone and e-mail systems are necessary to support the informal contacts that employees make on a daily basis. Finally, in the end there is no substitute for targeted face-to-face communication, both from the top or cross-functionally among key experts and functional leaders.

Emotional Boundaries

Most organizations seek to foster close interpersonal relationships at work but discourage romantic and sexual relationships. However, "sex is like paperclips in the office: commonplace, useful, underestimated, ubiquitous, [and hardly] appreciated until it goes wrong" (Jones, 1972, p. 12). Intimacy in work relationships can range from flirtation to full-blown romance. Classical management theorists view any type of fraternizing among workers as a source of inefficiency. Some — but not all — companies have explicit policies that limit on-the-job relationships. In a typical case, a well-known clothing chain prohibits intimate relationships between its managers and its employees in the same store: If love blooms, one of the two has to leave. At the state universities where we work, department chairs are not permitted to supervise their faculty spouses. Given the high rate of intermarriage in academia, this means that many alternative reporting structures must be found (e.g., a faculty member can report directly to the dean). The University of North Carolina recently accepted the resignation of a tenured faculty member who was engaged to be married to a student because, the board argued, the university must serve as a moral leader in the community.

Romantic Relationships at Work

Organizational psychologist Robert Quinn (1977), the first to study why employees establish romantic relationships with others at work, identified three underlying motives: love, ego, and job. Employees motivated by love have a sincere desire to find a long-term companion or spouse, whereas those motivated by ego are looking for sexual excitement and adventure. Employees with job-related motives may pursue a romance with the hope of gaining more job security or power.

Related research further suggests that social stereotypes about why people form romantic relationships at work — that is, as a way to gain power or as an ill-advised fling — are overly simplistic (Dillard & Miller, 1988). In one study, only 14 percent of the romantic relationships surveyed included a woman with job-related motives and a man with more power in the organization. In contrast, 59 percent of the relationships studied were marked by partners motivated by love or by a combination of love and ego (Dillard & Segrin, 1987). (Pairings of powerful women with less powerful subordinate men have received little attention in the research literature.) Jim Dillard and Katherine Miller (1988) thus conclude that the motivation underlying organizational romance is often more complex than society typically assumes. They also point out that the consequences of such relationships are not always what we might expect. Rather than negatively affecting productivity, careers, and workplace environments, romantic relationships may lead to improved performance when employees attempt to overcompensate for others' negative expectations.

Negative perceptions and interpretations by others, however, can create problems for romantic partners at work. Even after a romance has ended, co-workers may cling to negative perceptions about the motives, character, or performance of the involved parties. Whether or not the relationship has in fact affected their work performance, co-workers may assume that it has.

Boundary Violations: Harassment and Sexual Harassment

In discussing relationships thus far, we have been emphasizing welcome relationships among consenting adults. However, relationships also may be a site for *discrimination* through the use and abuse of power. When such abuses occur, they are called "harassment." Harassment is one form of communicative behavior that degradates or humiliates people. Based on the federal Equal Employment Opportunity Commission (EEOC) guidelines, harassment includes:

- Slurs about sex, race, religion, ethnicity, or disabilities
- Offensive or derogatory remarks
- Verbal or physical conduct that creates an intimidating, hostile, or offensive work environment
- Creating conditions that interfere with the individual's work performance

One type of harassment that is prevalent in the workplace is sexual harassment. Sexual harassment refers to any type of verbal or nonverbal communication that interferes with someone's work. According to the Civil Rights Act of 1964, additional legislation in Congress, and federal, state, and local court rulings, there are two forms of sexual harassment, quid pro quo and hostile work environment:

1. Quid pro quo ("this for that") harassment is based on the threat of retaliation or promise of workplace favoritism or promotion in exchange for dating or sexual favors. Recently, this principle has been interpreted to include suggestions and innuendoes as well as explicit quid pro quo comments.
2. Hostile work environment harassment is sexually explicit verbal or nonverbal communication that interferes with someone's work or is perceived as intimidating or offensive. It is important to note that the behavior doesn't have to be intentional to create or contribute to a hostile work environment. Off-hand remarks or casual displays of sexually explicit materials count as harassment. So do remarks that the sender may think of as "compliments."

The EEOC reports that between 1990 and 1996 harassment suits jumped 150 percent (see <http:www.eeoc.gov/stats/harass.html>). Sexual harassment suits occur between persons of the same sex as well as persons of the opposite sex. Sexual harassment has become so prevalent in the United States that most for-profit and nonprofit organizations, government agencies, and schools have implemented policies, mandatory seminars, and workshops to train employees in how to recognize harassment and prevent it. However, while sexual harassment is clearly recognized as a problem in the United States, it is not always viewed similarly in other countries and other cultures. Latin and Mediterranean cultures, for example, do not regulate physical contact or suggestive language usage in the workplace. As a result, cultural misunderstandings can and do take place. Once again, we see that our assumptions about the meanings of communicative acts are, in fact, culturally derived.

Women are usually the targets of sexual harassment by men because "as a group [women] have less formal and informal power than men in organizations, confront more obstacles on their path to developing organizational power, and have fewer opportunities to acquire organizational power through activities and alliances" (Bingham, 1991, p. 92). Commonplace in organizations, sexual harassment is the unacceptable behavior of men who cling to outdated notions of a male-dominated society and organizational status quo. It is crucial to understand that sexual harassment is not a personal problem, rather, it is an organizational problem. It is management's responsibility to create a work climate that reinforces appropriate boundaries between employees (Cleveland & McNamara, 1996).

In a special issue of the *Journal of Applied Communication Research* (Wood, 1992), a rich and complex assortment of firsthand accounts of sexual harassment on the job reveals a disturbing trend: Most often experienced initially by teenagers and students working a first job, sexual harassment may thereafter be accepted as normal or ordinary behavior. This may explain why many women tend to avoid reporting instances of sexual harassment to superiors, to underestimate their importance, or to be uncertain about identifying such behaviors (Clair, 1998). As a result, sexual harassment remains outside of mainstream communication in organizations, and women participate in both their own subjugation and the perpetuation of the male ideology.

In fact, male ideology has been cited as a major factor in the sudden reported increase in cases of male-on-male sexual harassment (Talbott, 2002). These cases demonstrate that "macho" male cultures contribute to hostile work environments for men as well as women, even in cases where no sexual favors were involved. In one particularly vivid case, a male sales manager for a Chevrolet dealership in Denver, Colorado, routinely grabbed the genitals of male salesmen to make them flinch, addressed them as "little girls" or "whores," and simulated masturbation when male employees talked. If a male employee failed to make a sale, he was asked "if he used tampons . . . or had to squat when he urinated" (Talbott, 2002, p. 54). Even within a male-dominated car sales culture where "being raunchy" may have been accepted practice, the dealership was indicted, paid a $500,000 fine, and promised to implement sexual harassment training for all employees. The two managers who were the perpetrators of these actions were fired. Clearly, in the findings of the EEOC in this case, it was the organization's responsibility to create a positive working environment and the existence of a dominant male ideology was not an acceptable defense.

Just as the Chevrolet case demonstrates graphically, dealing successfully with the problem of sexual harassment requires defining its characteristic behaviors more precisely. Once defined, this information can be used to raise employees' awareness and potentially change their abusive behavior. The following specific behaviors are considered sexual harassment:

- Inappropriate verbal comments, even those defended as compliments (e.g., "I wish my wife was as pretty as you")
- Inappropriate nonverbal gestures, such as outlining body parts or eyeing someone up and down
- Inappropriate visual displays or objects (e.g., posters or calendars depicting nude women or men)
- Terms of endearment (e.g., "sweetie," "dear," "honey")

- Inappropriate physical acts, such as patting, fondling, stroking, or standing in a doorway to obstruct someone's passage through it
- Asking for or implying that someone must submit to sexual advances as a basis for continued employment or advancement in the company

In addition, Tamaki (1991) outlines a series of strategies for dealing with sexual harassment: (1) Confront the harasser, (2) report the behavior to a supervisor or to the human resources department, (3) keep a written record of the offenses, and (4) confide in supportive colleagues, family members, and friends. If the harassment continues, the employee may request a formal investigation by the department of fair employment and housing or by the EEOC or the employee may file a lawsuit. Although the 1991 Anita Hill–Clarence Thomas hearings made the public aware of the difficulties of proving sexual harassment, legal awards for victims of sexual harassment at work are now quite common, especially when written records and support from others in the organization are provided as evidence.

Shereen Bingham (1991) offers a communicative approach to managing sexual harassment in the workplace. She argues that direct confrontation with a harasser is complicated by multiple risks, including losing a job, receiving an unfavorable recommendation, being demoted, losing interest in the job, and so on. Bingham suggests that various responses — assertive, nonassertive, and even aggressive — may be appropriate in certain circumstances. Most observers agree that assertiveness helps to confront a harasser in a direct but nonthreatening way. However, assertiveness may also be interpreted as a rejection of the other person, which practically speaking may cause the victim to "win the battle but lose the war." It may be more effective to temper assertiveness with "apparent" empathy when responding to a sexual advance.

Finally, the entrance of male-on-male sexual harassment cases has further complicated the concept of "hostile work environment" among legal scholars (Talbott, 2002). The idea was first introduced in the 1980s under the assumption that sexual jokes, vulgarity, and macho displays of dominance offended women because women are, as legal scholar Rosa Ehrenreich puts it, "uniquely vulnerable to men" (cited in Talbott, 2002, p. 55). However, as recent male-on-male harassment cases have documented, some men are clearly also vulnerable to other men and offended by coarse behavior. Another problem is that some men are victimized by male-on-male sexual harassment because they are gay, but sexual orientation is not covered by Title VII of the Civil Rights Act of 1964. As law professor Deborah Zalesne argues, "[If] your *harasser* is gay, you stand a good chance of winning a same-sex harassment case. If *you* are gay, you lose" (cited in Talbott, 2002, p. 57). For these and other reasons, the theoretical framework of sexual harassment law is currently undergoing revisions on a case-by-case basis. In the meantime, some victims of sexual harassment have found that they can successfully bring charges under existing tort law, civil rights laws, and other federal and state statutes.

There can be no doubt that sexual harassment is a crime. Organizations should design educational programs for employees to help them understand sexual harassment, as well as offer strategies for dealing with it in particular situations. Workshops, films, and literature may be used to make employees more aware of the types of behavior that constitute sexual harassment in the workplace. Firms that operate with public monies are especially concerned with this issue. Responding effectively to sexual harassment requires paying close attention to ways of communicating appropriately at work.

Obstacles to Organizational Communication II: Relational Dialectics and Relational Conflict

In this section we will describe obstacles to organizational communication that emerge from patterns of everyday communication. These obstacles often emerge as conflicts that derive from misunderstandings and misperceptions about relationships we engage in with each other at work or from having to deal with people we cannot seem to get along with.

Relational Dialectics

One of the most interesting analytic tools to emerge in the relational communication literature in the past decade is the intriguing concept of "relational dialectics" (Baxter & DeGooyer, 2000; Baxter & Montgomery, 1996; Rawlins, 1994). A dialectic refers to the "interaction of two opposing arguments or forces — called *tensions* — operating within the boundaries of the same relationship" (Goodall & Goodall, 2002, p. 181). For example, in interpersonal relationships there are at least three major sources of relational dialectics (Baxter & Montgomery, 1996):

1. *Autonomy-Togetherness dialectic* refers to the opposing forces of *wanting to be with* a relational partner and *needing to be alone* (Rawlins, 1994). At work, this dialectic can help us understand how expectations for and perceptions of interpersonal closeness and distance — as well as the emotional work required to construct, deal with, or repair them — contribute to relational tensions that can produce organizational conflicts.

2. *Novelty-Predictability dialectic* refers to the opposing forces of achieving a comfortable pattern of interaction or routine and, at the same time, desiring newness or change in a relationship. In the workplace, managing the tensions produced by this naturally occurring dialectic can lead to creativity and dialogue (Baxter & DeGooyer, 2000) or can contribute to interpersonal stress and organizational dysfunction.

3. *Expressive-Protective dialectic* refers to the opposing forces that often inform decisions about how much information we share with relational partners, colleagues, and co-workers. For example, revealing personal information may serve as an important marker of a close bond between team members working on a project, but that same personal information may also become the source of organizational gossip.

Appreciating the dialectical complexities of relationships is important because it provides us with insight into relational conflicts at work as well as further testimony to the centrality of dialogue as a way to deal with those conflicts. If we learn to think of a dialectic as the interaction of opposing forces that are naturally at work in all human relationships, then the role of communication in promoting relationships based on mutuality and growth becomes even clearer. After all, communication is where the work of balancing self-interest and mutual growth is accomplished, and dialogue is "more concerned with discovering than disclosing, more interested in access than in domination" (Anderson, Cissna, & Arnett, 1994, p. 2). By using communication to access dialectical tensions and discover the perceptions they create in relationships, we can promote healthy dialogue about what is really going on in our relationships and discourage misperceptions, hurt feelings, and a buildup of silences that may hide unhealthy resentments (Kellett, 1999; Kellett & Dalton, 2000).

Working through Relational Conflict

Conflict refers to "the feelings or perceptions of imbalance that arise in a relational setting" (Goodall & Goodall, 2002, p. 182). Equity theories suggest that individuals who find themselves in imbalanced or inequitable relationships will seek to restore equity using a wide range of communicative activities (e.g., trading eye-for-an-eye, asking for an apology, engaging in escalations of verbal combat, spreading rumors or gossip about the wrongdoer, withdrawing into a strategic silence, or withholding information or affection) or *psychological* activities (e.g., forgiving the transgression mentally, finding an excuse for the untoward behavior, or feeling superior because you don't react negatively). Motivational theories suggest that individuals' responses to conflict may be a reflection of their psychological need to withdraw, accommodate, compromise, or avoid/postpone it (Johnson, 1993), but that these strategies all represent less than optimal ways of working through problematic situations or with difficult people.

While the inequitable effects and personal motivations of conflict partners are experienced relationally, the conflicts themselves often "point to underlying tensions in organizational structures, processes, and changes" (Kellett & Dalton, 2000, p. 120). For example, deeper meanings hidden in layers of organizational politics (Cheney, 1995), differing departmental perceptions of what the "real issues involved" are in a dispute (Mumby, 1993), and underlying tensions created by strict codes of conduct shaped by organizational culture themes (Smith & Eisenberg, 1987) all may contribute to organizational conflicts. Additional tensions may erupt into conflict when employees and managers fail to be aware of, to be sensitive to, or to recognize how gender, race, class, age, and sexual orientation issues figure into the social construction of relationships at work (Bullis & Stout, 2000; Mumby, 2000). Following the tragic events of 9/11, another potential layer of complication has been added to our understanding of organizational conflict — fear of random terrorist acts may lurk beneath the surfaces of business interactions with persons who do not share our background, culture, language, color, religion, or values (Ellis, 2002; Goodall, 2002).

Using dialogic skills to negotiate the complex communicative, relational, and psychological dimensions of conflict offers us the opportunity to achieve resolution of differences and the restoration of equity without giving up (withdrawing, avoiding/postponing) or giving in (compromising, accommodating). In management and negotiation literature, this strategy is termed *win-win* (Fisher & Ury, 1981). At the core of a mutually beneficial outcome to conflict, dialogic skills promote inquiry over judgment and encourage the mutual exploration of deeper, systemic causes. Dialogic skills require asking questions, such as:

1. Where is this conflict actually coming from? What is our problem?
2. How is this conflict being managed, both organizationally and relationally?
3. How are other people at work reacting to it? How are their reactions playing into our conflict?
4. How is our conflict affecting other people's organizational relationships and functions?
5. How is our conflict and its outcome likely to be manifested in subsequent organizational practices? (adapted from Kellett & Dalton, 2000, p. 129)

Asking these questions and creating a space for dialogue should lead to relational understanding and ultimately to relational learning. When the conflict emerges from — and reflects — broader organizational issues, the result should be systemic understanding that contributes to organizational learning (Senge, 1991).

SUMMARY

This chapter covered a wide range of topics, each in a different way emphasizing the growing importance of interpersonal relationships in successful organizing. Specifically, we suggested that there are, for most employees, four primary audiences for organizational communication: customers, supervisors, peers, and employees. We then described the communication challenges associated with each relationship. Our extensive discussion of communication with employees focused on the changing nature of employee motivation and leadership. Finally, we described common obstacles to building interpersonal relationships in and around work, focusing on the effective negotiation and maintenance of cultural, physical, and emotional boundaries.

QUESTIONS FOR REVIEW AND DISCUSSION

1. Why are responsive informal systems of communication between and among supervisors, peers, and employees important keys to business success?

2. What is the relationship between the "experience economy" and tenets for effective communication brought about by the customer service revolution?

3. Describe how the evolution of participative work structures has changed the nature of effective interpersonal relations with one's boss or superiors. What strategies can employees use to "manage the boss"?

4. Describe cross-functional communication, and relate this concept to effective communication with peers on work teams and in small groups.

5. Why do you think the concepts of openness, supportiveness, and motivation are important in relation to communication between supervisors and employees?

6. Discuss the ideas of steward and servant in relation to current practices in leadership communication. Describe how communication functions in each of them.

7. How do intercultural differences influence perceptions of effective interpersonal relationships at work?

8. Discuss the concept of relational boundaries as a way of thinking about the role of emotions in interpersonal communication at work.

9. List and explain the major sources of harassment and sexual harassment in the workplace.

10. Using the material provided in this chapter, list the dialectical tensions in at least one of your work or school relationships. Does understanding these tensions help you see more clearly the reasons for conflict in your relationship? Can the idea of dialogue help you address them?

CASE STUDY I

The Total Empowerment Program

Lovitt International is a medium-size electronics manufacturer. Although it is located in the Midwest, it is owned by the French-English conglomerate Sagem-Lucas. Lovitt uses multinational work teams to design interchangeable parts for electronic ignition systems. The parts, which meet international standards, are marketed to various automobile manufacturers, including Nissan, Volkswagen, Peugeot, and Ford.

The company has been relatively successful. Recently, however, it has experienced some problems attributed to communication issues, such as difficulty in coordinating its team-based operations and difficulty meeting customers' deadlines. Lovitt also has introduced a new program, called "total empowerment" (TE), which is aimed at creating self-directed work teams, giving employees the power to make decisions about their work, and making employees more accountable for the results of their work. The TE program also includes an incentive plan: a 60/40 split in bonuses that is divided between team and individual members according to their performance ratings. However, team members have received little or no training in how to accomplish the objectives of the new TE program, other than an initial meeting with the senior managers who initiated it and a company party to celebrate the new endeavor.

The TE program, though designed to empower Lovitt employees, has instead led to a number of unexpected problems. Difficulties between employees from different cultures, for example, have emerged. American workers believe that their nonnative counterparts neglect to share information with teams and facilitators, while Latino, Cambodian, and South African employees feel that their American co-workers neglect to convey information clearly and tend to express a "superior attitude" in general. In addition, team leaders are dissatisfied with the way the program has been implemented as well as with its lack of recognition of their complex role in the distribution of incentive bonuses.

Many Lovitt employees view the company's move toward empowerment as a short-term management fad. Others believe it is merely a way for the company to demand more of them for less. Still other employees, particularly those with strong cultural ties to England or France, argue that genuine participative decision making is not possible in a top-down

(continued)

bureaucracy. Moreover, they argue, a number of competitors failed in their attempts to introduce similar innovative programs involving self-directed work teams.

ASSIGNMENT

You are the communication training specialist retained by Lovitt International to design workshops aimed at improving employee communication and ensuring the success of the TE program. Using what you have learned in this chapter about the role of communication in establishing good interpersonal relationships at work, design the Lovitt workshops. Also consider the following issues:

1. In your analysis of the situation at Lovitt, what are the key problems?
2. How can you best address those problems in a series of workshops?
3. How can you design the workshops to encourage team members' commitment to the TE program? What kinds of experiences will team members need to have in order to understand and learn from the empowerment process?
4. In addition to workshops, what other solutions will you propose?

CASE STUDY II

Sexual Harassment of a College Intern

Kate Mowry is a junior majoring in communication studies at a large university in the American Southwest. As part of her program of study, she enrolled in a three-credit internship program sponsored by her department. She was placed with a local public relations firm and told that her duties would be to work closely on a project with a team of PR professionals. Kate looked forward to this opportunity to gain some practical work experience that would show her how to apply the theories and techniques she acquired through her course work.

On her first day at the PR firm, she was assigned to work with a senior PR analyst named Reggie Davis. She introduced herself to him and couldn't help but notice how he gave her body the "once over." *Men*, she thought. *They're the same everywhere!* She quickly dismissed her thoughts when Reggie began explaining to her what her duties and responsibilities would be. As she came to understand it, she was basically being assigned to work with Reggie on this project. "We'll work closely with each other," he said, smiling. "You don't have any problems with that, do you?"

"No," she replied brightly. "I'm looking forward to it."

According to the terms of her internship contract, she was supposed to put in ten hours of work a week at the PR firm, keep a diary of her experiences there, and write a five-page project report that summarized her experiences in the internship. Dutifully, Kate showed up at the firm on a regular schedule, did all of the work assigned to her, and tried to get along well with everyone. Soon she became known as a hard worker, and she felt she was definitely making a good impression on the team.

Reggie's attitude toward her work was less positive than that of his coworkers. Where they would praise her, he would find immediate fault with her work. Several times he suggested that she stay after hours so he could show her "how it is done *right*." Fortunately for Kate, she always denied his requests for after-hours instruction. She had a class, or she had a date, or she needed to study for an exam. With each denial of his request, he became more insistent.

One afternoon, Reggie invited Kate into his office for a chat. After discussing how she could improve her work, he indicated that she could be considered a candidate for permanent employment after her internship,

(continued)

"if you do the right things for me." She asked what she would need to do, because the opportunity to work full-time in a PR firm was very appealing to her.

"Well," Reggie began, "you can begin by respecting me as a man, not just as your boss at work." When she asked him what that meant, he replied, "I think you know exactly what that means. I'll be watching you to see if you do." Then, after gently touching her face with the palm of his hand, he dismissed her.

By now Kate realized that Reggie's attention toward her was not entirely based on her potential as an employee. She also realized that he would be turning in a grade for her contributions to the project at the end of the semester. She knew that if she dropped out of the internship program now, she would delay her graduation by at least another term, something she could not afford to do. On the other hand, she also had no interest in Reggie as a person, and she feared him as a supervisor. What should she do?

ASSIGNMENT

1. Discuss the major issues related to sexual harassment that are apparent in this case. For each issue, describe what Kate should have done or what she still could do.
2. Do you think there is a way for Kate to resolve this issue with Reggie? If so, how? If not, why not? Use what you have learned in this chapter about effective interpersonal communication at work to answer these questions.
3. Assuming that Kate has been keeping a diary of her work experiences, what relationship might this document have to her filing a formal case against Reggie?
4. Assuming that Kate cannot resolve this situation herself, who should Kate report this problem to? Reggie? Reggie's boss? Her internship coordinator at the university? The EEOC official in her region? A lawyer?
5. Assume for a moment that you find yourself in a similar situation while interning for credit in your program of study. What rules and regulations does your institution have regarding sexual harassment?

CHAPTER 10

Communicating in Teams and Networks

The sudden burgeoning of teams is in part a product of the complexity of our world, which demands radically more effective means of integrating what bureaucracy has split apart.

— GIFFORD PINCHOT AND ELIZABETH PINCHOT, *The End of Bureaucracy and the Rise of the Intelligent Organization* (1993)

Real networks are self-organized. They offer a vivid example of how the independent actions of millions of nodes and links lead to spectacular emergent behavior.

— ALBERT-LASZLO BARABASI, *Linked: The New Science of Networks* (2002)

The drive to organize comes from the realization that no single individual, or for that matter no pair of individuals, is sufficient to achieve complex goals. Moreover, when people seek to make sense of their work lives, they tend to identify with larger groups (e.g., my department, my division, my building). This chapter builds on the prior two chapters by addressing communication that occurs in teams and networks. Today, most work that goes on inside organizations utilizes a team approach, whereas work that takes place outside of organizations (e.g., entrepreneurship, outsourcing, or consulting) relies even more heavily on networks and networking. If knowledge is power, such power is inevitably exercised in webs of relationships.

Teams

What Is a Team-Based Organization?

Most American employees now work in some form of team-based organization. The importance of *teamwork* has long been appreciated. Filene's, a Boston-based department store, introduced the concept of teamwork, which referred to a general ability to work together across different departments and functions, in the United States in 1898. Today's emphasis on teams goes beyond teamwork, or simply working together. A team-based organization is one that has restructured itself around interdependent groups, not individuals, as a means of improving work processes and providing better quality and service to customers.

Team-based organizing differs sharply from bureaucratic forms of organizing. First, consistent with the human resources approach, in team-based companies every employee is seen as possessing valuable knowledge that must be widely shared for the benefit of the whole. Teams are composed of employees from a variety of organizational functions (e.g., sales, manufacturing, engineering) to maximize the cross-functional exchange of information. In a bureaucracy, a hierarchical chain of command distinguishes managers (as "thinkers") and workers (as "nonthinkers"), emphasizing the need for division of labor and close supervision. Team-based organizations, in contrast, encourage informal communication and view all employees as capable of making decisions about how to manage work tasks. In the most progressive team-based organizations, supervisory work is conducted by self-managed work teams. Employees thus become "knowledge workers" dedicated to self-improvement, positive results, and productive collaboration:

> In the conversion to postbureaucratic organizations, teams form the basic unit of empowerment, small enough for efficient high involvement and large enough for the collective strength and the synergy generated by diverse talents. Within teams people can take wide responsibility for one another, for the organization, and for the quality of their products and services. (Pinchot & Pinchot, 1993, p. 194)

The current interest in work teams is rooted in both the Hawthorne Studies (which attest to the importance of informal groups; see Chapter 3) and European experiments with autonomous work groups (Kelly, 1992). Research in Europe and Scandinavia has been on the forefront of these new forms of organization, beginning with the development of the sociotechnical school in the 1950s (Trist, 1981). This school of thought maintained that organizational effectiveness depends upon a proper blending of technical and social factors at work and stressed the importance of communication and collaboration. One study of British coal miners, for example, emphasized how communication processes optimize social and technical systems. In this study, there were clear indications of higher productivity and job satisfaction among those workers who were given more control of their jobs. Eric Trist's studies also indicated that organizations with workers who were more involved in the operation were better equipped to respond to changing markets and political conditions — something that large and rigid organizations found difficult (Wellins, Byham, & Wilson, 1991).

Types of Teams

Despite widespread enthusiasm for team-based organizing, definitions of what constitutes a team remain ambiguous. However, all groups in an organization are not necessarily sufficiently *interdependent* to be classified as teams. A collection of working people may be a committee, a task force, or an ad hoc group. Teams, in contrast, generally fall into these three categories or types: project teams, work teams, and quality-improvement teams. Depending upon the location of its members, any one of these types may also qualify as a virtual team.

Project Teams

Project teams, which help coordinate the successful completion of a particular project, have long been used by organizations in the design and development of new products or services. For example, a project team might include software and hardware engineers, programmers, and other technical specialists who design, program, and test prototype computers. A project team might instead be assigned to address a specific issue or problem. For example, a savings and loan recently charged a project team made up of representatives from all the major areas of the bank with the task of developing ways to bring in new business.

Project teams may struggle because people lack the communication skills needed to collaborate across significant functional divides. Collaborative behaviors are hard to learn, hence while many project teams are "formed with great optimism, few are managed for success" (Jassawalla & Sashittal, 1999). Management must actively work to build a sense of real collaboration, by increasing commitment to team decisions, and to demonstrate a deep caring about team outcomes and accomplishments.

A special type of project team exists within matrix organizations, which are characterized by dual reporting relationships. Imagine a large matrix (like an expanded tic-tac-toe board) where the columns represent organizational functions like research and development, sales, production, and information services. Imagine also that the rows represent particular projects or product lines, like shampoo, conditioner, and hair mousse. In a matrix organization people's "home" departments are their functions (e.g., a chemical engineer would reside in research and development), but they are also assigned to a project team responsible for producing a particular product. This results in most employees reporting to two different supervisors. Although this form of organizing was very popular over the last few decades, it is less common today due to the ambiguities that can result from having multiple supervisors.

Work Teams

A work team is a group of employees responsible for a "whole" work process that delivers a product or service to a customer. For example, one such work team at a California aerospace company is responsible for all metallizing of components in the company. The team resides together, outlines its own work flow (e.g., the steps for applying metal coatings to parts), and is engaged in making ongoing improvements in the work process (e.g., making the metal coating as thin as possible). Such teams have been found to aid an organization's efficiency. Federal Express, General Electric, Corning, General Mills, and AT&T have all recorded significant productivity improvements after incorporating work teams (Wellins, Byham, & Wilson, 1991). Kodak reportedly reduced its turnover rate to one-half of the industry's average and improved its handling of incoming customer calls by 100 percent after reorganizing into work teams. Similarly, Texas Instruments Malaysia managed to boost employee output by 100 percent and cut production time by 50 percent after moving to a team-based approach.

Successful work teams are supported by a commitment to empowerment. Because they are given the discretion and autonomy to make decisions and to solve problems, empowered teams are not frustrated by a lack of authority to implement their ideas and solutions. More generally, a group can do a better job of managing its resources when it understands the big picture, has the authority to adapt to changing work conditions, and feels that its work is meaningful and has an impact (Churchman & Rosen, 1999).

In practice, of course, work teams differ in degree of empowerment, as indicated in Figure 10.1. Lower levels of empowerment are indicated by "housekeeping" responsibilities (such as conducting meetings) and cross-training responsibilities. As empowerment increases, the team assumes responsibility for the continuous improvement of work processes, the selection of new members, the election of a team leader, and capital expenditures. At the highest level of empowerment, the self-directed work team is also responsible for performance appraisals, disciplinary measures, and compensation (Wellins, Byham, & Wilson, 1991). This type of self-directed work team is not yet common but is becoming more prevalent today.

For teams to succeed, the company reward system has to recognize the contributions of both the team *and* its individual members. Organizations continue to struggle with the challenges posed by evaluating and rewarding teams whose members contribute unequally to the whole team. Similarly, differences in the knowledge and skills of team members can cause some members to work harder than others and, therefore, to be more deserving of rewards for their efforts. The empowerment process may involve an employee stock ownership program (ESOP) to encourage team members' motivation and dedication to the team approach: "I will be motivated to do my best because the fruits of my labor are now visibly mine." ESOPs vary in structure — stock may be purchased by employees or given as a benefit — but they all share a common principle, which is

FIGURE 10.1

The Empowerment Continuum of Work Teams

Degree of Empowerment

• Making Compensation Decisions
• Disciplinary Process
• Team Member Performance Appraisal
• Product Modification and Development
• Budgeting
• Facility Design
• Equipment Purchase
• Choosing Team Leaders
• Vacation Scheduling
• Cross-Functional Teaming
• Hiring Team Members
• External Customer Contact
• Managing Suppliers
• Continuous Improvement
• Quality Responsibilities
• Production Scheduling
• Equipment Maintenance and Repair
• Training One Another
• "Housekeeping"

| Team Level | Level 1 20% | Level 2 40% | Level 3 60% | Level 4 80% |

Responsibility/Authority

Source: Richard Wellins, William Byham, and Jeanne Wilson, *Empowered Teams* (San Francisco: Jossey-Bass, 1991), p. 26.

getting shares of the company in the hands of its employees. Many line employees at Home Depot and Microsoft, to offer two very different examples, have become rich from employee stock. Companies create ESOPs with two very different sorts of intentions (Harrison, 1994). The first approach is limited to seeing the stock as a financial benefit but is not tied to any increased opportunities for participation on the part of employees in company decision making. The second approach is ideologically motivated, with greater employee involvement accompanying equity (stock) participation. Not surprisingly, it is this latter form of ESOP — stock plus greater employee involvement — that has the most dramatic positive effects on employee motivation, identification, and commitment.

One potential barrier to the effectiveness of work teams is union agreements, which may prohibit cross-training or may specify rules that conflict with self-management goals. For example, some union rules specifically limit the extent to which one classification of worker can "cover" for others in their absence. Where these conditions exist, there must be sustained collaboration between unions and management to establish rules beneficial to both parties.

As we discussed earlier, managers sometimes resist the move to empower self-directed work teams (Tjosvold & Tjosvold, 1991). For managers and supervisors, team-based organizing requires a fundamental change in their role, from operational expert or overseer to coach or facilitator. The ability to oversee an empowered work team has become an increasingly important management skill. It requires the supervisor overseeing a team to

- act as a facilitator, keeping the group on track while respecting a free exchange of ideas
- be hard on rules, agenda, goals, and accountability but soft on the means by which the team chooses to organize itself and do its work
- communicate extensively with others to keep the team informed of the work of other teams and of the organization as a whole

Effective managers of work teams create a climate for honest and supportive dialogue and possess the necessary communication skills to do so. The considerable challenges involved in such an undertaking are reflected in *What Would You Do?* 10.1.

Quality-Improvement Teams

Popular in organizations in the 1980s, informal problem-solving groups called "quality circles" met voluntarily to address work-related issues on a weekly basis (Kreps, 1991). Quality circles have since been replaced by quality-improvement teams whose goals are to improve customer satisfaction, evaluate and improve team performance, and reduce costs. Such teams are typically cross-functional, drawing their members from a variety of areas to bring different perspectives to the problem or issue under study. In theory, a quality-improvement team uses its diverse talents to generate innovative ideas.

Some organizations have taken a novel approach to creating quality-improvement teams. For example, in a program called Work-Outs at General Electric, which was initiated by CEO Jack Welch in 1989, management selects forty to one hundred employees to attend a three-day conference (Stewart, 1991). A facilitator divides the employees into five or six smaller groups, and each group works independently for two days to identify problems with the company and to prepare a presentation to senior management regarding recommended changes. On the third day, the panel of senior managers is confronted

What Would You Do? 10.1

THE DILEMMAS OF MIDLEVEL MANAGEMENT IN FOSTERING EMPOWERMENT

Fred Myerson is a midlevel manager trained in the traditional approaches to management. His company has shifted to self-directed work teams, including an intensive employee empowerment program. Fred is now a "coach" responsible for facilitating work teams. He is dedicated to making the program work.

However, Fred recently encountered a problem that the empowerment training seminars did not address: how to diplomatically handle unworkable ideas from work teams without discouraging them from contributing new ideas in the future. In addition, Fred does not want to create the impression that he is resisting change, but he also cannot isolate himself entirely from the decision-making process. He has been an effective manager in the past, but he feels less effective in his role as team coach.

In Fred's opinion, he has three bad options: (1) pass along what he perceives as unworkable ideas (thereby supporting the empowerment program but violating his ethical responsibility to the company); (2) ignore the proposals he considers unsound (thus behaving unethically toward the work teams by undermining their empowerment); or (3) argue against the unsound proposals (thereby creating the impression of himself as a control-oriented manager, disempowering the work teams, and discouraging them from contributing innovative ideas in the future).

Discussion Questions

1. How can Fred most effectively deal with both the problem and the ethical dilemmas it poses?
2. Given what you have learned thus far about teams in organizations, what other options might Fred consider?

by each group and its proposals, and the managers must agree or disagree with each proposal or ask for more information (in which case, the group agrees to supply it by an agreed-upon date). One vice president describes the experience in this way: "I was wringing wet within half an hour. . . . They had 108 proposals, and I had about a minute to say yes or no to each one" (Kiechel, 1994, p. 70). This is but one dramatic example of how organizations are using teams to encourage creativity and to open the dialogue between managers and employees.

Virtual Teams

In response to a dynamic global economy, many organizations have found it advantageous to maximize their geographical reach and become immersed in a wide range of local cultures. This makes good sense, because, as discussed earlier, companies ignore cultural differences at their own peril. Unfortunately, the geographical distribution of employees creates predictable communication difficulties associated with time and space, and may result in misunderstandings and disagreements. Fortunately, a range of technological tools has evolved to support these groups of people who work together across time and space in what are called *virtual teams*.

A superficial analysis of virtual teams can identify likely problems to watch out for, such as language barriers and differences in work customs and habits. But deeper consideration reveals that all virtual teams engage in a developmental process that builds a negotiated order — a shared set of practices or microculture that emerges among members (Gluesing, 1998). Some of the items that are typically up for negotiation include division of labor, sequencing of activity, and the nature and regularity of outcome assessment. In addition, virtual teams must work out more mundane but still vexing issues surrounding the use of listservs, intranets, e-mail, and document transfer. This team development process is social and involves the development of mutual respect and trust (Baba, 1999).

Pamela Shockley-Zalabak (2002) conducted an important study of an international, self-managing, virtual team created by a technology company seeking to do a better job of meeting customer needs. She describes the functioning of this team over a two-year period as "protean," inasmuch as it operated with "rapid fluidity" and was characterized by "minimal form." Moreover, this research revealed some of the challenges associated with these kinds of structures. Two years into this experiment, while the members of this team most clearly did not want to return to hierarchy, they did express a strong desire for more structure, in the form of better processes and clearer work rules. While the idea of geographical boundaries was no longer relevant, a new kind of boundary was important to the team. Specifically, "Boundary as guide, sense of place, commitment, relationship, and shared meaning [amidst continuous change]" (Shockley-Zalabak, 2002, p. 249). Future studies of virtual teams will shed more light on the pragmatics of succeeding with this new organizational form.

Communicative Dimensions of Teamwork

In 1987, a very large manufacturing organization in Saint Louis was facing significant financial losses. The company president decided that the cause of his problems was employees' working at cross-purposes, not looking out for the good of the whole. His solution was to charge his head of "quality assurance" with restructuring the entire organization — 40,000 people — into teams over a twelve-month period.

One of the authors of this textbook (Eisenberg) was working with this quality manager at the time and pointed out that while one could certainly rename departments "teams," simply calling a group a "team" did not make it one. A group becomes a team through the kinds of communication it displays over time and the resulting feelings of trust and interdependence. More specifically, there are five communicative elements of team interaction that are essential to consider: team roles, norms, decision-making processes, management of conflict and consensus, and cultural diversity. The following sections address each of these elements.

Roles

Inherent in teamwork is the need to achieve a balance between the diverse goals of individual members and those of the entire team. Although individual member behavior can vary significantly, members tend to enact typical communication roles (Goodall, 1990c). According to the classic typology, the three broad types of communication roles are the task, maintenance, and self-centered roles (Benne & Sheats, 1948). In performing the *task* role, the team member summarizes and evaluates the team's ideas and progress or initiates the idea-generating process by offering new ideas or suggestions. In the *maintenance* role, the team member's communication seeks to relieve group tension or pressure (e.g., by telling jokes or by changing the subject of a conversation) or to create harmony in the group (e.g., by helping to reconcile conflict or disagreements) (Shockley-Zalabak, 1991, pp. 189–190). Enacting the *self-centered* role, the team member seeks to dominate the group's discussions and work or to divert the group's attention from serious issues by making them seem unimportant. Unlike the positive effects of task and maintenance roles, the self-centered role is almost always considered inappropriate and unproductive.

H. L. Goodall has identified two other roles, the prince role and the facilitator role. The prince role is exhibited by group members who view themselves as brilliant political strategists and the world as a political entity. In the facilitator role, a team member focuses on group processes (e.g., following an agenda and maintaining consensus in decision making) for the benefit of the team, while refraining from substantive comments on issues.

Some people both serve on teams and facilitate team communication, playing different roles in various group situations. A training manager, for example, may act as a facilitator if during a team meeting the conversation sways off-topic. At the same time, the manager may suspend the facilitator role by offering information or opinions relevant to the discussion. Two other roles played by team facilitators — sponsor and coach — can help organizations ease the transition to a team-based approach. A sponsor who is not a member of the team and who has significant power in the organization is responsible for keeping the team informed of organizational developments, removing obstacles to effective teamwork, and advocating on behalf of the team for access to necessary resources. A coach, typically a former supervisor and a respected team member, is responsible for helping the other members acquire the cross-functional skills needed to accomplish team-based tasks. Coaching is especially important to team success because it addresses the specific problems associated with transitioning from a classical management approach to a team-based one. In addition, a coach teaches team members how to ask for coaching and thereby how to deal with errors, weaknesses, or deficiencies in ways that promote the team's performance.

Norms

Norms are the informal rules that "designate the boundaries of acceptable behavior in the group" (Kreps, 1991, p. 170). For example, team members may be expected to attend meetings on time, to prepare for meetings in advance, and to distribute the meeting's agenda by an agreed-upon deadline. Norms about conflict may express an intolerance or an acceptance of disagreement. Some observers attribute Motorola's success to its norm about conflict, which encourages team members to engage in loud debates at meetings (Browning, 1992b). Taking a different tack, a software company CEO insists that no one should ever kill a new idea. He instead encourages "idea angels" who are charged with saying something positive about any new idea that is brought up. 3M's success has been linked to a similar approach to innovation. 3M lives and dies by a norm that says, in effect, "when in doubt, try it."

Team norms, which are shaped by the national and organizational culture as well as by personal agendas, influence member roles. At a large U.S. bank, for instance, where the organizational culture is generally intolerant of conflict, work teams tend also to avoid conflict by focusing on maintaining group harmony and relieving tension and by deemphasizing summary, evaluation, and the motivation to take action. Norms are enforced informally through members' approval of them as well as by the dominant organizational culture.

Decision Making

Decision making by teams is generally more productive than decision making by individuals. Teams get more people involved in the decision-making process and generate more information and ideas. In addition, the act of participating in decision making makes team members more aware of important issues, more likely to reach a consensus, and better able to communicate about issues with co-workers. Team members are also encouraged to think, solve problems, and thereby to become more responsible and productive.

Unlike the classical management approach, which separates the tasks of making decisions from implementing them, the team-based approach gives employees control over decisions that affect their work and has been shown to decrease job stress. Moreover, "the more complex and challenging the issues under evaluation, the more powerful the outcomes of decisions, and the greater the number of people affected, the better groups are for making the decisions" (Kreps, 1991, pp. 173–174).

Group decision making also poses a number of problems. In what is called the "risky shift phenomenon," a team may tend to make decisions that involve more risks than decisions made by individuals because of perceived safety in numbers (Cartwright, 1977). In addition, strong-willed or verbose team members may dominate conversations, intimidate others, or manipulate team decisions to benefit themselves in an effort to gain power or to improve their image. Groupthink, a well-known problem associated with team decision making initially identified by psychologist Irving Janis (1971), occurs when team members go along with, rather than evaluate, the group's proposals or ideas. According to Janis (1971),

> In a cohesive group, the danger is not so much that each individual will fail to reveal his [or her] objections to what the others propose but that he will think the proposal is a good one, without attempting to carry out a careful . . . scrutiny of the pros and cons of the alternatives. When groupthink becomes dominant, there is also considerable suppression of deviant thoughts, but it takes the form of each person deciding that his misgivings are not relevant and should be set aside, that the benefit of the doubt regarding any lingering uncertainties should be given to the group consensus. (p. 44)

A number of strategies for dealing with groupthink are consistent with our ideal of promoting organizational dialogue:

1. Encourage team members to voice their objections and to evaluate others' ideas.
2. Encourage team members to remain impartial and, therefore, to maintain objectivity in decision making.
3. Use more than one group to work on a problem to generate a variety of proposed solutions.
4. Encourage team members to discuss the team's deliberations with people outside of the group to obtain feedback.
5. Invite outside experts into the group to obtain their input and feedback.
6. Make one team member responsible for ensuring that the team explores all sides of an issue.
7. Divide the team into subunits that work independently on a problem and then report back to the team.
8. Arrange a special meeting after a consensus has been reached to give team members the opportunity to discuss any doubts or concerns that remain (Gibson & Hodgetts, 1986).

Decision making by teams also requires team members to face the challenge of sorting through multiple interpretations of a problem or issue to find the single best recommendation or course of action. Members who are intolerant of others' perspectives may find this task especially challenging. For this reason, extensive research has been conducted on identifying effective decision-making strategies.

Aubrey Fisher's (1980) model of group decision making sees decisions as the product of four stages:

1. Orientation
2. Conflict
3. Emergence
4. Reinforcement

In the orientation stage, the members of a newly formed team get to know and trust one another. Their communication tends to focus on clarifying the team's purpose and function and on reducing tension and uncertainty. After the orientation stage, communication about tasks inevitably initiates the conflict stage, as team members express and debate different ideas, perspectives, positions, styles, and worldviews, forming alliances and coalitions in the process. A team that manages the conflict stage well will emerge with a diverse assortment of perspectives and valuable information that it uses to move toward a single position. In the emergence stage, coalitions give way to a working consensus as a delicate balance of compromise and negotiation is worked out. Emergence involves moving toward action, and determining how to implement the decision. Finally, the reinforcement stage is marked by a strong spirit of cooperation and accomplishment among team members (Fisher, 1980).

Teams that skip the orientation phase for whatever reason may never truly feel comfortable as a group, inasmuch as members know one another only as roles, not as people. They may also lack direction. Teams that avoid the conflict stage — mainly through cowardice in the face of difficult conversations — run a decided risk of groupthink, of agreeing on a course of action before exploring all of the available information or alternatives. Teams lacking in communication skills often fall apart at the emergence stage, as group members find it impossible to work together and agree on a common direction. Many teams don't survive to experience the reinforcement stage.

Other studies of team decision making challenge the stage models proposed by Fisher and others by suggesting that most teams follow a less linear path toward decision making. These writers believe that group decision making is more varied and complicated than these models suggest (e.g., Poole, 1983; Poole & Roth, 1989). Seen this way, teams experience periods of disorganization that are unpredictable, tend to go through cycles and to repeat stages multiple times, and may engage in activities (e.g., managing tasks and establishing work relationships) in a haphazard rather than a coordinated fashion. In many cases, stages do not occur in an orderly or predictable pattern.

Similarly, the *punctuated equilibrium model* suggests a new way of viewing the group decision-making process (Gersick, 1991). If trust is lacking in the group, or if members' differences are significant, the team will be unable to function. Some members may withdraw, while others may assert their power over the rest of the group. Drawing on similarities across various fields and subject areas (e.g., individuals, groups, organizations, academic disciplines, and species), this model offers three concepts related to group development: (1) deep structure, which is the set of assumptions and performance strategies that the team uses to approach the problem; (2) the equilibrium period, during which the team works within the established framework without questioning its fundamental approach to the task; and (3) the revolutionary period, when the team examines its operating framework and reframes its approach as a basis for moving forward. Note that the three concepts do not apply to all teams. At a point about halfway between a team's inception and a predetermined deadline, the opportunity to embark upon a revolutionary period arises. Whereas successful teams regard this potential crossroads as an opportunity to examine their basic assumptions, unsuccessful teams bypass the revolutionary period altogether, ignoring the opportunity for self-examination and proceeding on the basis of their initial assumptions.

Other important contributions to our understanding of effective group decision making include the argument that effective teams give more attention to the group process (i.e., the procedures used to solve problems) than do ineffective teams (Hirokawa & Rost, 1992). Referred to as "vigilant interaction theory," this theory holds that successful teams focus on four areas of self-assessment: (1) the nature of the task, (2) the standards for evaluating various decision options, (3) the positive aspects of the various options, and (4) the negative qualities of the various options. The theory claims that "group decision performance is directly related to a group's efforts to analyze its task, assess evaluation criteria, and identify the positive and negative qualities of alternative choices" (Hirokawa & Rost, 1992, p. 284).

Finally, in a sustained effort to apply communication technology to group decision making, *group-decision support systems* (GDSSs) are used to give teams access to various decision-making tools (Poole & DeSanctis, 1990). For example, software that creates an electronic display for input and accepts input from all group members, and software for problem solving, decision analysis, and expert systems, can help teams make better decisions (Contractor & Seibold, 1992). This kind of technology is increasingly available to assist in the operation of all kinds of teams, both colocated and virtual.

Conflict and Consensus

Conflict occurs among members of organizations and teams largely because people in different positions of power pursue different interests. Here we are concerned with teams as sites of conflict and with team-based strategies for achieving consensus. Team conflict may occur among members who come from different fields or professions, such as in a cross-functional project team, or between line workers (who work directly with the product or service) and staff teams (who provide behind-the-scenes support). It may also occur as a result of perceived inequities in group member status or productivity, personality differences, or other work-related problems.

Conflict is defined as "the interaction of interdependent people who perceive opposition of goals, aims, and values, and who see the other parties as potentially interfering with the realization of these goals" (Putnam & Poole, 1987, p. 552). In organizations, conflict most often arises from the acquisition and use of resources. Like other types of communication, conflict changes or evolves over time and is unpredictable. It also takes place in the interdependent relationships among people who depend on one another to some extent for resources.

Attitudes toward conflict in organizations have changed significantly since the 1950s, when overt conflict was viewed as counterproductive and to be avoided. By the 1970s, however, some recognition of the benefits of conflict had emerged, such as its role in generating different ideas and perspectives (and thereby helping to avoid group think) as well as in facilitating the sharing of information. Studies have found that some degree of team conflict is essential to achieving high levels of productivity and effective communication (Franz & Jin, 1995). An absence of conflict over an extended period of time is more likely a sign of group stagnation than of its effectiveness. The constructive role of conflict is mostly understood today, although it remains difficult to realize in practice.

Research on conflict in organizations includes classical management studies that view conflict as a breakdown of communication (Hunger & Stern, 1976) and cultural studies that define it as a dispute over different perspectives of organizational realities (Smith & Eisenberg, 1987). Most research on the cycles and escalation of conflict has been approached from a systems perspective (Putnam & Poole, 1987), whereas critical theorists view conflict as reflecting deep imbalances of power in the organization and society (Mumby, 1993).

Because team conflict is inevitable, we are most concerned with how team members handle it. Broadly distinguished as emphasizing either a "concern for self" or a "concern for others," conflict style is also marked by degrees of assertiveness and cooperation (Kilmann & Thomas, 1975). Collaboration, which is generally seen as the most effective conflict style, emphasizes high assertiveness combined with high levels of cooperation. In contrast, compromise is considered less effective in resolving conflicts because neither party's preferred solution is adopted. Collaboration is more likely to lead to a novel solution that satisfies both parties. In addition, accommodation may at times be effective, but in most conflict situations, it is counterproductive, causing stress for the team member who accommodates others and undermining the team's ability to generate creative ideas.

Unfortunately, there is often a significant gap between individuals' expressed or preferred conflict style and how they behave across a variety of conflict situations. For example, while supervisors' strategies for dealing with problem employees reflect their styles when the conflict first surfaces, over time they tend to use more coercive strategies regardless of their expressed conflict style (Fairhurst, Green, & Snavely, 1984). The supervisor's tendency to use increasingly coercive compliance-oriented strategies generally takes less time for men than for women (Conrad, 1991). Therefore, because multiple situational factors and goals affect conflict strategy selection, conflict style is not always a good predictor of communication behavior (Conrad, 1991).

A team's commitment to collaboration and consensus, however, involves ongoing communication and results in good decisions with long-term impact. Consensus does not mean that all team members agree with a decision but that they feel that their views have been adequately considered by the team. "If there is a clear alternative which most members subscribe to, and if those who oppose it feel they have had their chance to influence, then a consensus exists" (Schein, 1969, p. 56). Naturally, people agree to a group consensus with the understanding that their point of view will be accepted at least some of the time, or they would most likely leave the group. Consensus reflects an overarching belief that in the long haul, "all of us are smarter than any one of us." Effective conflict management through consensus thus means accepting the inevitability of differences and being committed to an ongoing dialogue that is open to alternative perspectives and that encourages creative decision making.

Cultural Diversity in Teams

As corporations make greater use of intercultural teams in response to global competition, researchers are increasingly concerned with the effects of cultural differences on team member communication. In one such study, communication scholar Charles Bantz (1993) reports on his experiences as a member of a ten-person intercultural research team. Starting with four well-accepted dimensions of cultural diversity — power distance, uncertainty avoidance, individualism, and instrumentalism or expressivity (Hofstede, 1983) — and four difference factors — language, norms, status, and politics — he offers the following conclusions:

> The range of difficulties generated by the diversity in a cross-cultural research team [leads] to a variety of tactics to manage those differences. The tactics include . . . alternating leadership styles across time and tasks; agreeing on long-term goals, while continuing to negotiate shorter-term goals; building social cohesion; [ensuring that] longer-term goals [meet] individual needs; alternating task and social emphases; maintaining social support by engaging in confirming communication even when disagreeing; adapting to language difference[s] by slowing down, checking out, restating, and using more than one language; discussing work schedules; using varying conflict modes across different issues; discussing group procedures; initiating social discussion of work life to ascertain perspectives; and responding to political differences. While . . . tactics vary, [the] four [most] common [ones are] (1) gather information, (2) adapt to differing situations, issues, and needs, (3) build social as well as task cohesion, and (4) identify clear, mutual long-term goals. (p. 19)

He also points out that "awareness of cultural differences is necessary, but not sufficient for the accomplishment of cross-cultural team research" (Bantz, 1993, p. 19).

Negotiation is one key to managing intercultural team differences. The following four phases in the negotiation process occur in all cultures (Varner & Beamer, 1995), but the amount of time devoted to each phase and its relative importance may differ:

1. *Developing relationships with others.* For the members of a newly formed intercultural team to develop productive work relationships, they need to be given sufficient time to explore long-term team goals, build trust, and adapt to cultural differences. In most cultures, candid answers to questions mark the beginning of a productive relationship, even when the required answers may be perceived as self-disclosing. However, face saving is just as important to members of Asian and African cultures as candidness is to other cultures. Therefore, it is wise to avoid insensitive remarks, to express tolerance of others' goals and values, and to respect the status that others enjoy in their native culture.

2. *Exchanging information about topics under negotiation.* Honest or frank disclosures are one way to generate trust among members of an intercultural team, but information exchange may also be enhanced by responding to questions with other questions that open up the team dialogue. Questions can be used not only to access information and to clarify ideas, but also to call bluffs, to show interest in another's ideas, to control the direction of a conversation, and to address controversial issues in nonthreatening ways. The types of exchanges generated by such questions help team members adapt to their cultural differences while also communicating with trust and openness. Team members also become more aware of how culture plays a role in the answers generated by questions; for example, "Why?" questions are answered with explanations of cause and effect in Western cultures, but they are answered more generally through stories, personal narratives, and cultural myths in non-Western cultures.

3. *Recognizing multicultural techniques of persuasion.* Rational arguments are considered persuasive by members of many cultures, but different perspectives on what is considered rational, and different ways of communicating rational arguments, can pose difficulties in intercultural teams. It is thus recommended that teams focus more on gaining information than on persuading and that team members respect their cultural differences when persuasion is necessary. For example, using *I* is less persuasive than the more inclusive *we*, and using such words as *must*, *should*, and *ought* may be viewed as arrogant by members of non-Western cultures.

4. *Emphasizing the role of concession in achieving agreement.* Most cultures appreciate the value of fair exchange, including the value of concession in

gaining agreement. In general, concessions are best expressed as "if" comments (e.g., "We can deliver those services if your suppliers can meet this schedule"), rather than as directives (e.g., "We can deliver those services but your suppliers must meet this schedule"). However, while Americans tend to emphasize the importance of concessions in the form of a well-executed plan, such as a business contract, Asians tend to emphasize the same principles in a different form — in their informal relationships with others. Thus, for example, an American businessperson may be surprised when an Asian businessperson does not observe the stipulations of a signed contract. A contract is considered binding in American culture, but in most Asian cultures, a contract may be superseded by informal relationships. Similarly, an American conducting business in Finland may be surprised to learn that formal written agreements are often considered unnecessary because verbal agreements are executed with trust.

Team Learning

Successful team-based organizations foster an environment that values and rewards team learning (Pinchot & Pinchot, 1993; Senge et al., 1994). MIT management and systems experts Peter Senge and colleagues (Senge, Roberts, Ross, Smith, & Kleiner, 1994) define team learning as "alignment" or the "functioning of the whole":

> Building alignment is about enhancing a team's capacity to think and act in new, synergistic ways, with full coordination and a sense of unity [among] team members. . . . As alignment develops, [members do not] have to overlook or hide their disagreements to make their collective understanding richer. (p. 352)

Senge and colleagues (1994) go on to suggest that team learning transforms the following skills of "reflection and inquiry" into "vehicles for building shared understanding" (p. 352):

1. *Balancing inquiry and advocacy.* Teams need to balance inquiry (i.e., asking questions that challenge the existing assumptions and beliefs about work) with advocacy (i.e., stating opinions and taking action). Neither inquiry nor advocacy should control the team's learning process. Figure 10.2 identifies various types of inquiry and advocacy commonly used by teams.
2. *Bringing tacit assumptions to the surface of team dialogue.* Senge and colleagues (1994) suggest that because "we live in a world of self-generating beliefs which remain largely untested" (p. 242), our beliefs appear to be the truth, the truth seems obvious to us, and the evidence for our beliefs is limited to the data we select from our experience. A team that learns to question these assumptions moves down the "ladder of inference" revealing the motivations behind our beliefs (Figure 10.3). As the team

FIGURE 10.2

Balancing Inquiry and Advocacy

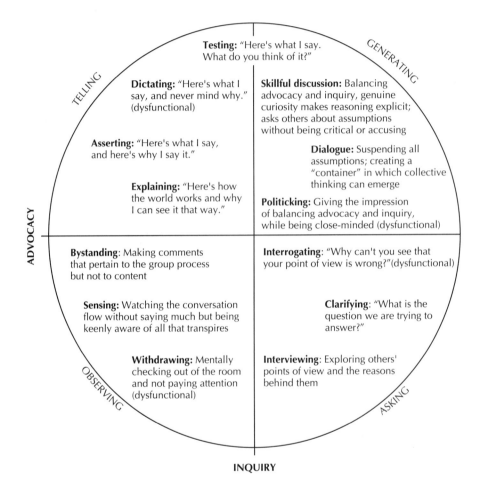

Source: Peter Senge et al., *The Fifth Discipline Fieldbook* (New York: Currency Doubleday, 1994), p. 254.

brings tacit assumptions to the surface of its dialogue, it discovers the role of those assumptions in the development of beliefs and conclusions.

3. *Becoming aware of the assumptions that inform conclusions.* Once assumptions have surfaced, it is beneficial for teams to reflect on how these particular beliefs give rise to interpretations of events that support specific

FIGURE 10.3

The Ladder of Inference

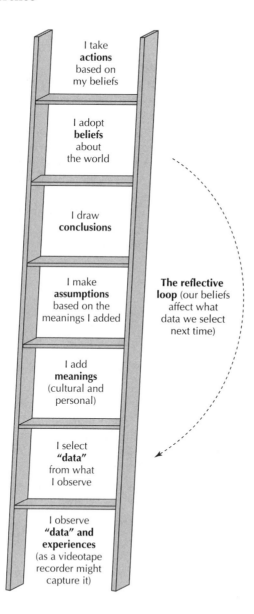

I take
actions
based on
my beliefs

I adopt
beliefs
about
the world

I draw
conclusions

I make
assumptions
based on the
meanings I added

**The reflective
loop** (our beliefs
affect what
data we select
next time)

I add
meanings
(cultural and
personal)

I select
"data"
from what
I observe

I observe
**"data" and
experiences**
(as a videotape
recorder might
capture it)

Source: Peter Senge et al., *The Fifth Discipline Fieldbook* (New York: Currency Doubleday, 1994), p. 243.

conclusions about work processes, employees, or customers. Making these connections explicit makes them easier to change. Conclusions, then, are filtered through members' assumptions and beliefs, which are unobservable and highly personalized. This is what makes the generation of new ideas challenging. However, by counteracting these abstract influences on the thought process, teams can promote creative thinking.

Dialogue is important to team learning. According to Senge and colleagues' (1994) model of the "evolution of dialogue," shown in Figure 10.4, team dialogue moves initially from invitation to conversation to deliberation. From deliberation, the dialogue may follow a path to discussion or to suspension and dialogue. Team learning thus encourages members to think about dialogue as allowing the "free flow of meaning," unencumbered by logical analysis (e.g., skillful discussion) or debate. People from Western cultures may find it difficult to learn the speech and listening skills associated with this type of dialogue because of the value they place on rational argument. In addition, such dialogue challenges many of the assumptions of traditional communication in organizations. The objective is not to argue a point effectively but to balance inquiry with advocacy in ways that contribute to the knowledge of the team as a whole.

In the transition to a team-based approach, therefore, the organization not only must help employees cope with change, but also must help them learn new ways of communicating. This is a formidable challenge that requires a commitment to training and team learning.

A Retreat from Teams?

Ideally, self-directed work teams help contemporary organizations deal with the pressures of global competition and help promote autonomy, responsibility, and empowerment in the workforce. In practice, however, the ideals of the team-based approach are often not realized by organizations.

In one recent example, a small airline tried to implement self-directed work teams but found that decision making was hindered by disagreements among team members. For example, the mechanics were frustrated by other groups' unwillingness to defer to them on all safety issues. This company's experience reveals the importance of the following factors in successful team formation:

1. Teams are only as good as their members; the careful selection of members is thus essential.
2. Teams must be sufficiently trained in group decision making and communication.
3. Only some decisions can be assigned to teams: those involving a significant challenge where the outcome affects many people. Simple tasks with limited impact are best assigned to individuals.
4. Some members of a team have more expertise and experience than do other members; therefore, all members do not contribute equally.

FIGURE 10.4

The Evolution of Dialogue

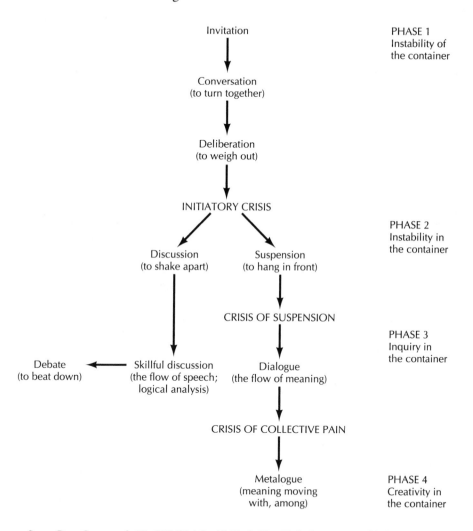

Source: Peter Senge et al., *The Fifth Discipline Fieldbook* (New York: Currency Doubleday, 1994), p. 361.

Ford, Procter & Gamble, and Honda have found that teams require too much time to make decisions and tend to shield their members from taking responsibility (Chandler & Ingrassia, 1991). Why are teams failing at these companies? Teams may fail because they suggest a radical reframing of traditional power relationships in organizations that managers, in particular, may resist. Employees may also tend to view teams with skepticism, at least initially. If employees are empowered by the team approach, they become its strongest advocate. More often, however, management does not follow through on its promise of empowerment, and teams inevitably fail. Finally, teams fail when management neglects to define the types and functions of the teams it seeks to establish (Drucker, 1992b). As a result, teams do not have a clear understanding of their function in the organization. A highly empowered, cross-functional team that does not receive strong leadership support is likely to fail.

Networks

As indicated at the outset of this chapter, contemporary organizational communication has expanded rapidly from face-to-face teams to real and virtual networks of people across multiple locales organized for a common purpose. Although networking has always been key to business success, defined communication networks — groups of individuals who may be identified as sharing regular lines of communication — have emerged as a primary mode of organizing in the new economy. Networks are as a rule emergent, informal, and somewhat less interdependent than teams. Networks matter because regular contact between identifiable groups of people, whether they be scientists or political action groups, can play an important role in establishing access to information and in the quality and direction of decision making.

Within organizations, the concept of a "network" has emerged as a result of researchers' enduring interest in the structure of organizational groups. Human relations theorists recognized that small groups do much of the important work in organizations. The pattern of communication among group members, called the group's "communication structure," is affected by many factors. For example, management may design a group in a way that hinders its communication, or employees with low status in a group (e.g., newcomers) may be less willing to communicate freely than those with high status. Formal lines of authority and rules about communication may also restrict the flow of information in a group. These investigations into communication structures have led to the idea of communication networks.

Types of Networks

Small-Group Communication Networks

Early research on communication structure focused on examining small-group communication networks (groups of five people) to determine the effects of centralized versus decentralized networks on decision making. In a well-known example,

> a small number of individuals are placed in cubicles and allowed to communicate only by means of written messages passed through slots in the cubicle walls. The slots connecting each cubicle can be opened or closed by the experimenter, so that different communication patterns can be imposed on the interacting subjects. . . . A typical task presented to groups of individuals placed in these networks is to provide each individual with a card containing several symbols, only one of which is present on the cards of all subjects. The task is . . . completed when all participants are able to . . . identify the common symbol. (Scott, 1981, pp. 148–149)

Four types of small-group communication networks were typically studied: the circle, wheel, chain, and all-channel networks (Figure 10.5). The circle and all-channel networks are highly decentralized, whereas the chain and wheel are centralized. It was found that centralized networks are more efficient than

FIGURE 10.5

Small-Group Communication Networks

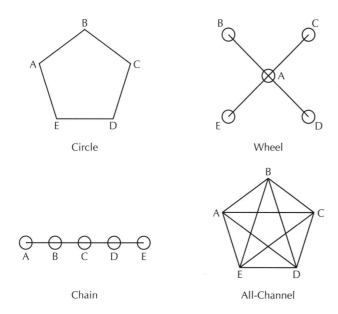

Circle   Wheel

Chain   All-Channel

Source: W. Richard Scott, *Organizations: Rational, Natural, and Open Systems* (Englewood Cliffs, N.J.: Prentice-Hall, 1981), p. 8.

decentralized networks, as reflected in the speed with which they can complete a task (Leavitt, 1951). Further investigations, however, reveal that centralized networks are not necessarily superior to decentralized networks:

> As tasks become more complex or ambiguous, decentralized net[works] are usually superior to centralized structures. . . . Formal hierarchies aid the performance of tasks requiring the efficient coordination of information and routine decision making whereas they interfere with tasks presenting very complex or ambiguous problems. . . . Specifically, hierarchies impede work on the latter by stifling free interactions that can result in error-correction, by undermining the social support necessary to encourage all participants to propose solutions, and by reducing incentives for participants to search for solutions. (Scott, 1981, pp. 149–150)

This early research also yielded some interesting findings about small-group decision making. For example, when a group faces a routine task or a tight deadline, participation by and input from all members is not expected. In contrast, when a group faces more complex issues or problems, a more open dialogue promotes member satisfaction and better solutions.

However, many critics argued that the experimental small-group networks studied had little in common with actual groups in organizations (Farace, Monge, & Russell, 1977). In fact, research interest has recently turned toward what has been dubbed "bona fide groups" in organizations, groups that really function that way "in the wild." Examples of bona fide groups are surgical teams and juries. Early research suggests that these "real" embedded groups act in more contradictory and disorderly ways than was ever anticipated by laboratory studies (Sunwolf & Seibold, 1998).

Emergent Communication Networks

The most powerful groups in organizations are those that emerge from the formal and informal communication among people who work together. These groups are referred to as "emergent communication networks."

The current focus on communication networks in organizations stems from a general acceptance of systems theories, which emphasize the connections between people and the relationships that constitute an organization. In terms of communication networks, researchers examine those relationships that emerge naturally within organizations as well as the groups and member roles associated with them (Rogers & Kincaid, 1981). Formal networks and emergent networks coexist in organizations, and each is best understood in the context of the other (Monge & Contractor, 2001; Monge & Eisenberg, 1987). For example, although new employees may rely on a copy of the formal organizational chart to understand reporting relationships and the structure of departments, over time they realize that the actual communication relationships among employees do not precisely mirror the organizational chart. Departments with no formal connections may nonetheless communicate in order to manage the work flow, and salespeople working on different product lines may share common experiences at lunchtime. A great deal can be learned about an organization's culture by identifying the discrepancies between informal emergent networks and the formal organizational chart.

Early research on emergent communication networks investigated the so-called organizational grapevine. The term *grapevine* dates to the Civil War, when telegraph wires strung through trees resembled grapevines (Daniels & Spiker, 1991). This term has since come to mean the persistent informal network in an organization, sometimes referred to disparagingly by management as the "rumor mill." In reality, most of the time the rumors are true; important information travels quickest through informal channels. Building on Chester Barnard's (1938) observations about the value of informal communication, Keith Davis (1953) argued against the standard party line, which encouraged managers to suppress the rumor mill, and instead supported the importance of such communication to the health of an organization, both as a source of information and for bolstering a sense of belonging. Subsequent research has shown that informal communication on the grapevine is as a rule more efficient and accurate than the formal dissemination of information (Hellweg, 1987).

Researchers and managers alike seek to identify the paths of informal communication and the structure of informal networks in order to understand the distribution of information and informal power in organizations. Complex network analysis techniques have been used to "map" the emergent communication networks of an organization (Monge & Eisenberg, 1987). In one such effort, employees are asked to participate in a survey to determine how often they engage in informal communication with co-workers and to identify the topics of their conversations.

Communication Networks

Analyses of communication networks are used to examine the structure of informal, emergent communication in organizations, sensitizing us to the tendency of individuals to forge new linkages, apart from formal rules or boundaries. Informal communication in organizations is fluid and in a constant state of change. Whereas formal reorganizations may occur only infrequently, informal reorganizations occur continuously (Monge & Contractor, 2001). In studying emergent communication networks, we are concerned mainly with overall patterns of interaction, communication roles, and areas of communication content.

Patterns of Interaction

As illustrated in the sample communication network shown in Figure 10.6, a number of informal groups, or cliques, emerge as a result of communication among people in organizations, both within and across departments or functions. Communication networks vary in density, which can be determined by

FIGURE 10.6

A Sample Organizational Communication Network

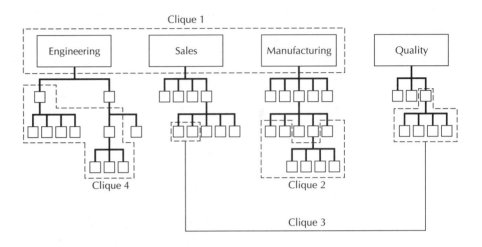

dividing the number of communication links (reported communication contacts) that exist among all organizational members by the number of possible links. For example, a professional association is a low-density network because communication among its members is infrequent, but the kitchen crew of a restaurant is a high-density network in which most or all members communicate regularly with one another. Similarly, formal hierarchies are less dense than more progressive organizations that encourage employee participation and communication.

Research suggests that dense organizational networks have considerable influence over whether other employees adopt a new idea or technology. In a study of elementary schools and administrations, it was found that personal relationships play a key role in the development and acceptance of new ideas when cliques form to focus on those ideas (Albrecht & Hall, 1991). These close connections help people overcome feelings of uncertainty and make them more likely to accept and adapt to change.

The density of an organizational communication network can have some less obvious implications for organizational effectiveness. For example, we get less new information from people we work with every day than we do from people we know but contact less often. These infrequent contacts are called "weak ties," and they can be very helpful for surfacing new perspectives and helpful people, as often happens in job hunting or recruiting (Granovetter, 1973).

When all members are closely connected, the risk of groupthink greatly increases. Communication researcher Michael Papa (1990) makes a similar point about network density in his study of an insurance company: "The more diverse an employee's network [is], the more coworkers he or she talk[s] to about [a] new technology, and the more frequently he or she talk[s] about [it], the more productive that employee [is] likely to be using the new system" (p. 361). In addition, Karl Weick (1976) notes the benefits of loosely coupled systems (less dense networks in which decisions and actions can occur independently) as sources of organizational flexibility, adaptation, creativity, and competitiveness.

A study of a community church found that "joint involvement in focused activities" is crucial to the development of networks of relationships (McPhee & Corman, 1995, p. 133). In addition, people who are frequently involved in joint activities are also likely to be well connected in the communication network.

Finally, some researchers use what they call a "network approach to participation" to redefine the notion of empowerment (Marshall & Stohl, 1993). According to this view, empowerment is a "process of developing key relationships in the organization in order to gain greater control over one's organizational life" (p. 141). An employee's personal communication network affects the experience of empowerment, involvement, and participation at work.

Communication Network Roles

A communication role in a network determines a person's influence on the flow of information. Well-connected individuals in an organization tend to be the most influential (Brass, 1984) and the least likely to leave. Four types of communication roles occur in networks: the isolate, group member, bridge, and liaison. Isolates have little contact with others in the organization; they work alone either by choice or because their jobs require them to be structurally or geographically isolated from other employees (e.g., salespeople or service technicians who travel constantly). Group members communicate mainly within an informal clique, which may at times involve communication with a departmental, professional, or demographic grouping (e.g., an accounts receivable specialist or a member of an advertising team). Bridges (who are also group members) have significant communication contact with at least one member of another informal group (e.g., a human resources representative dedicated to serving a particular department), and liaisons have connections with two or more cliques but are not exclusive members of any one group (e.g., mediators or facilitators who are not themselves part of a team; some senior managers specializing in cross-functional initiatives like quality or strategy).

Recent developments in information technology have reduced the felt isolation of many jobs by connecting them through various forms of electronic communication. Research has not yet been conducted on whether these types of connections can substitute for face-to-face contact. In our experience, some people are more likely to seek out and to even thrive under relatively solitary conditions. Moreover, isolation within the organization does not necessarily mean a lack of connection in the field or profession; in the new economy, a person's network of connections outside the organization (both personal and professional) may be far more important than organizational communication networks.

Within organizations, liaisons can be the dominant interpreters of the organizational culture. As key communicators with tremendous influence on the direction of the company, they are able to transform any message into an interpretation that is consistent with their beliefs and to pass that interpretation quickly throughout the company (and at times to customers and the community). When organizational improvement efforts fail, it is most often a result of the improper mobilization of liaisons.

Any attempt to analyze network communication roles in an organization may be a sensitive issue for employees, who do not always perceive their degree of communication contact with others in the same way. For example, a subordinate might report having daily contact with a superior, whereas the superior may claim to have no communication with the subordinate. Differences in status or perception may also cause employees to respond in ways that reflect not actual but expected communication roles, reporting contact only with people they "ought" to communicate with at work. In addition, employees may be reluctant to participate in a network analysis because the results may reflect negatively on them. For example, in our analysis of network roles in a professional association, a department head who was identified by subordinates as an isolate was dismissed from the organization. Consequently, it is critically important to collect and handle network analysis data with an awareness of the political implications of various findings. Network structures should not be shared with top management or the public without first considering the possible impact on employees who participated in the study.

Content Communication Networks

Emergent communication networks develop around specific topics, or content areas, of communication (Farace, Monge, & Russell, 1977). Each content area is regarded as defining a separate network; for example, a bank may have a social network for communication about personal matters and a task network for discussion of work duties. Someone who is an isolate in one network may be a bridge or a group member in another. We have all known people who are "well connected" when it comes to gossip but less so with regard to business updates and company strategy.

Moreover, the identification of multiple types of communication content contributes to our understanding of the relationships between people in networks. Thus, for example, two people who communicate about only one topic — say, task issues — are said to have a uniplex relationship, whereas people who communicate about two or more topics — say, personal issues, task issues, and new ideas — are said to have a multiplex relationship. Multiplex linkages have been identified as sources of social support and organizational innovation (Albrecht & Hall, 1991; Ray, 1987).

The content of communication networks takes on added significance when we consider it in terms of the sense-making process. In an attempt to extend the cultural approach to organizations, one of the authors of this textbook suggested that analysis of "semantic" networks (in which people hold similar interpretations of key organizational symbols or events) may be useful (Monge & Eisenberg, 1987). The same network measures may be applied (e.g., bridge, group member, isolate, and liaison), but in this case they would refer not to the presence or absence of communication, but to overlapping interpretations of key cultural symbols. Individuals who are in the mainstream with regard to employee values and beliefs would be group members; those holding radically different interpretations would be isolates. Measures of network density would also apply. In a dense semantic network, for example, there is shared meaning about major organizational issues. This approach has been successfully applied to the analysis of perceptions of organizational missions and value statements (Contractor, Eisenberg, & Monge, 1992; Peterson, 1995).

Interorganizational Communication Networks

Employees communicate with co-workers within the organization as well as with customers, suppliers, and others in different organizations or institutions. In an advertising agency, for example, account managers interact with people from various newspapers and television stations, and in a university, the gifts and development staff communicates with alumni, accountants, attorneys, and local officials. Communication networks thus cross organizational boundaries.

Interorganizational communication networks are the enduring transactions, flows, and linkages that occur among or between organizations. Such networks vary in terms of their openness, density, and interdependence. Tightly coupled or highly interdependent interorganizational networks are sensitive to environmental jolts that affect whole industries (e.g., in the deregulated airline industry, a minor change introduced by one carrier, such as reduced fares, significantly affects all others).

As discussed in Chapter 4, open-systems theory affords great significance to an organization's environment. Some researchers regard organizational environments as consisting mostly of networks of other organizations. The complexity of this network of interorganizational relations varies, and highly complex interorganizational environments require great vigilance and skill to manage. Put differently, an organization's environment is a kind of "nested box problem," where each network exists within a larger network, ranging from one's division, to one's industry, nation, and the world (Perrow, 1986).

Organizations participate in interorganizational communication networks in various ways. Two organizations are said to be *vertically integrated* when one builds parts or provides services that the other needs for its delivery of a product or service. For example, Pratt & Whitney manufactures aircraft engines for sale to Boeing. In contrast, two or more companies are *horizontally integrated* when their customers are passed from one to the other in the service cycle. An example of this is the connections between a cancer screening clinic, a hospital, and a hospice center.

One of the authors of this textbook developed a typology of interorganizational communication that is useful in sorting out different kinds of linkages (Eisenberg et al., 1985). Specifically, there are three types of network linkages for the exchange of materials and information: institutional, representative, and personal. An institutional linkage occurs without human communication, as in the automatic transfer of data between companies. A representative linkage exists when people from various organizations meet to negotiate a contract, plan a joint venture, and the like. A personal linkage occurs when members of two organizations communicate privately. However, it may be difficult to distinguish between personal and representative linkages when people meet informally without any intentions of discussing business but do discuss business with significant results. The various types of linkages may also change over time; for example, two companies planning to engage in a joint venture may initially host luncheons or dinners intended to make people more comfortable with each other personally. Later, representatives may be identified to work out the details of the plan, part of which may include the automatic transfer of data between the organizations.

Interestingly, one efficient way of sharing information across organizational lines is not through overt communication but by hiring employees from other companies. Ideas about management, marketing, structure, communication, and employee treatment are "imported" through personnel changes. In some cases, new employees who bring both their technical ability and their interpretive framework to organizations can help promote needed change. For instance, when Hughes Aircraft Company hired a former IBM executive to serve as its CEO, the company's emphasis shifted from engineering to business and financial management. In other cases, however, new employees' previous experience may become an obstacle to initiating change.

In the contemporary economic environment, organizations are most likely to turn to strategic alliances — such as mergers, acquisitions, and joint ventures — to enhance their financial status and political power. Most companies recognize that they need to narrow the scope of their services by coordinating their activities with those of other organizations. Especially common among highly specialized health-care providers (e.g., transplantation centers), strategic alliances are increasingly seen in higher education, where universities can no longer afford to offer a wide array of programs, as well as among companies engaged in international business. Similarly, high-technology organizations are investing in joint research and development ventures in order to cut costs and improve the collective work of scientists.

Recent studies show clearly the advantages of interorganizational participation for organizations. A study of 230 private colleges over a sixteen-year period showed that "well-connected" schools were better able to learn from and adapt to changing environmental conditions (Kraatz, 1998). A ten-year study of more than four hundred hospitals in California showed that hospitals were more likely to adopt service innovations when they were linked to their peer institutions (Goes & Park, 1997). Perhaps there is safety in numbers! Smaller companies may be especially well served by interorganizational relations. Such partnerships (like the Kentucky wood manufacturers network) have been shown to be associated with more process improvements, enhanced company credibility, and access to important resources (Human & Provan, 1997).

Interorganizational communication networks can be difficult to manage. For example, scientists from one organization may be reluctant to share their best ideas with scientists from another organization. Formal interorganizational alliances are risky because they require a good deal of trust, a willingness to give up autonomy, and the juxtaposition of potentially incompatible organizational cultures. Many mergers and acquisitions in recent years have been problematic because the organizational partners brought different levels of formality and different attitudes toward employees to the alliance.

Like multidisciplinary groups, interorganizational communication networks are potential sites of dialogue. As interorganizational cooperation across organizational, industrial, and national boundaries increases, the challenges of communication will become greater. In particular, ways of promoting productive dialogue among diverse networks will become increasingly important.

The Networked Society

Within only a few years, our understanding of what constitutes a network has changed considerably, from the connections among people within a single organization — such as a hospital, manufacturing plant, or school — to the connections among people in a global society. During this short time, we have seen tremendous growth in both network marketing and in computer networks on the World Wide Web.

Communication networks have also been transformed by the World Wide Web, through which people engage in on-line communication with others around the world. Significant changes in communication behaviors have been noted, especially in information seeking and relational development. For example, computer users post questions on Internet bulletin boards and receive responses within hours from people around the world. In search of meaningful relationships, millions of computer users participate in thousands of virtual gathering places, sharing real or apparent disclosures in pursuit of intimacy.

Network marketing and computer networks have significantly contributed to the emergence of a global networked society. The implications of such a society on our relationships and communication with others are yet to be understood. Some critics mourn the demise of local communities, whereas others envision an electronic global village that provides people with instantaneous access to information and other people worldwide. We will return to some of the potential effects of technology on communication in Chapter 11.

Creativity and Constraint in Teams and Networks

Team-based organizations face the challenges of balancing creativity and constraint in group relationships and of productively dealing with diverse interpretations. The members of a newly formed team are typically anxious about their role in the group and struggle to find a voice for themselves in the context of the group. This can be a formidable challenge during the orientation phase of a team's development.

During the conflict and emergence stages, members attempt to articulate their perceptions creatively, but their efforts are heavily weighted with constraints (e.g., "We tried that, and it didn't work" or "Management will never take our proposal seriously"). Other constraints can be useful in promoting team effectiveness, such as meeting times and places, agendas, and problem-solving procedures. In general, however, team members' ability to function as a group depends on their skill in balancing the creative contributions of individual members with the constraints imposed by the group as a whole.

Networks both within and among organizations are notable for the speed with which creative new ideas can be diffused among large groups of people. Mostly independent of the usual constraints, such as formal positions and hierarchy, informal communication networks encourage innovation and collaboration. Nevertheless, over time networks may acquire a relatively stable structure that can act to constrain future communication. In some countries (particularly in Asia), informal connections among large corporations largely dictate the flow of business among these companies.

SUMMARY

Teams and networks within and among organizations create and respond to norms, decision-making processes, cultural differences, and conflict and consensus. In team and network communication, different cultures, languages, and interpretations make communication complex and miscommunication likely. Communication across networks is also greatly enhanced by the advent of electronic communication channels.

Project teams, work teams, and quality-improvement teams play critical roles in the high-involvement organization. Team member communication roles and cultural communication processes characterize team contexts within and among organizations, and team learning occurs through dialogue.

The role of communication networks in our global society continues to expand. In organizations, small-group networks include the circle, wheel, chain, and all-channel. The more powerful emergent networks (grapevines, cliques, and loosely coupled systems) emerge from the formal and informal communication among people in organizations. Interorganizational networks include institutional, representative, and personal linkages. Network communication is affected by patterns of interaction, communication roles, and content areas. Network marketing and computer networks (e.g., the World Wide Web) have contributed to the emergence of a networked society.

QUESTIONS FOR REVIEW AND DISCUSSION

1. List and explain the types of teams used in today's organizations. What are the advantages and disadvantages of taking a team-based approach to organizing?

2. What is a communication role on a team? What types of roles are available to team members? Discuss the advantages and disadvantages of using a diverse array of roles in a team-based situation.

3. What makes for an effective team? What role does conflict play in team effectiveness?

4. What are communication networks? What characteristics do communication networks share with organizational teams? How does a communication network differ from a team?

5. Why do electronic networks complicate our understanding of communication? How might they be advantageous to teamwork?

6. Why is being well connected in a variety of networks important during times of economic and social change? What are the potential costs of not being well connected during these times?

7. How do new network forms affect the way an organization thinks about growth and expansion? What effect does this new way of thinking have on the nature and challenge of competition between organizations?

CASE STUDY I

The Networked University

Like most social institutions, for most of their history universities have been associated with specific towns or locations, and it would be hard to conceive of them otherwise (e.g., how about moving the University of Southern California to Nevada, where the property taxes are lower?). At the same time, schools wishing to compete in a global marketplace have gradually expanded their offerings worldwide, establishing campuses in Europe, Asia, and elsewhere. And they offer a significant number of degrees on-line through distance education.

Still, most of these institutions continue to retain an attachment to a particular locale. Recently, private institutions like the University of Phoenix have emerged on the higher education scene without these preconceptions. They set up shop wherever potential customers (students) congregate, and they offer highly flexible degree programs that require very little in the way of physical presence in a classroom.

ASSIGNMENT

Imagine that you are the education reporter for the *New York Times*, and you are writing a feature article on the changing landscape of higher education in America.

1. Knowing what you do about organizational communication, what would you say are the main reasons for the emergence of these types of schools at this time in history?
2. What will be the main advantages and challenges of building a corporate network of schools like the University of Phoenix?
3. Finally, what should be the reaction of more traditional, place-oriented schools to the introduction of these new competitors?

CASE STUDY 11

The Networked Community

BACKGROUND

Founded in 1913, Fleeberville is an average American city of 1.5 million people with typical urban problems. The city is located on a large, spring-fed lake in a mountain setting just north of Atlanta, Georgia, and industrial pollution has over the years become a serious problem there. Traffic on the two major highways gets worse every year, as does the rate of violent crime. The software companies that dominate the local economy are downsizing, and the remaining jobs require extensive technical expertise. The result has been an expanding underclass, much of which has been forced to seek public assistance. People with resources have increasingly isolated themselves from the city as a whole, and gated communities and private schools grow more numerous each year. Meanwhile, basic city services and public schools are in decline.

ASSIGNMENT

Imagine that you are an activist, community organizer, and communication expert who has recently decided to make Fleeberville your permanent home. You intend to put down roots, start a career, get married, and raise children there. However, for many reasons, you feel that the city must embark on a path of self-renewal.

You observe that many citizens seem to care about the city, but isolated efforts to improve things (e.g., clean up the lake, clothe the homeless, sponsor a school) don't appear to be very effective. Knowing what you do about systems, teams, networks, and organizing, how would you approach the problem of making Fleeberville a better place to live?

1. What actions would you begin with, and whom would you contact for help?
2. What patterns of communication would you encourage, and how ought they to change over time?
3. How would you deal with existing groups who feel uniquely responsible for determining the future direction of the city?
4. What teams and networks would you build to promote such a massive effort, and how would you prepare these groups for the challenges?
5. How would you evaluate the success or failure of your efforts?

CHAPTER 11

Managing the Total Enterprise: Communication and Strategic Change

Purpose is the statement of a company's moral response to its broadly defined responsibilities, not an amoral plan for exploiting commercial opportunity.

— Christopher Bartlett and Sumantra Ghoshal, "Changing the Role of Top Management: Beyond Strategy to Purpose" (1994)

For an organization or institution to succeed over time, senior managers and boards of directors must take a "bird's eye" view of the total enterprise, both to see what it looks like from the outside and to determine how it is perceived by various publics, partners, and competitors. Nevertheless, the temptation to not engage in this activity is great. Not only is it hard to find the time to speculate about the future when dealing with the crisis of the day, but honest talk about how others see you can be hard to take. Still, those possessing the discipline to think strategically — i.e., to make a conscious choice about organizational values, niche, and direction — invariably end up ahead of the game both financially and in terms of employee loyalty and morale.

But the game doesn't end there, of course, because no strategy works forever. Consumer tastes, market conditions, and countless other factors alter the organizational landscape on a daily, if not hourly, basis. What made sense yesterday may no longer make sense today. The only way of dealing with this dynamic environment is to encourage dialogue and learning, i.e., to sponsor and stage regular conversations about the appropriateness of the current strategy and the possible alternatives.

This chapter begins with a detailed discussion of strategic positioning as a communication issue, followed by a description of strategic alignment, the process of bringing organizational systems in line with the strategy. Central to these systems is the management of human resources in all its dimensions, from selection, to training, to individual and organizational development. The next section goes into more depth about these important details. The conclusion broadens our view by looking at organizational learning more generally, encompassing basic skills, technology, and morality.

But success begins with strategy. Contemporary organizations must position themselves effectively in the social and economic landscape. Positioning involves selecting a strategy or purpose that distinguishes the organization from its competitors. In addition, the strategy must be effectively communicated to employees, who use it as a guide to decisions, and to customers, who use it to judge the company's image or reputation.

Positioning the Organization

Competitive Strategy

Strategy is of critical importance to the long-term success of a business. A competitive strategy is a clear statement of why customers should choose a company's products or services over those of competing companies. Simple descriptors such as *cheapest, fastest, most reliable, friendliest*, and *best quality* are typically used in the expression of a company strategy. In addition to communicating a strategy, however, a company must ensure that all aspects of its business reflect the strategy.

Despite the importance of strategy, few organizations actually have one, relying instead on their success with a particular product or service (typically introduced before the competition's). However, contemporary organizations that lack a strategy are seriously at risk in today's highly competitive global market. At this writing, a number of companies are struggling for position in the computer industry. Compaq and IBM, in particular, are watching customers flock to Dell, which in 2002 booked close to $18 million in on-line sales a day. Fast-food restaurants like Checkers are also struggling to carve out an identity in an industry saturated by giant brands like Subway.

As an example of how a competitive strategy works in practice, let's suppose that you own a new fast-food eatery that serves, among other foods, hamburgers stuffed with mashed potatoes. After your first six months in business, your customers are only beginning to warm up to the idea of stuffed burgers. However, as a local business owner, you have been invited to attend a reception hosted by the city's chamber of commerce, providing you with a special opportunity to promote your fast-food business. You dress appropriately for the event and bring your business cards with you. More important, you prepare what you will say about your business to others at the reception, keeping in mind that it should take only about fifteen seconds to explain what you do and why your business is worthy of their attention. They, in turn, will be able to convey the same brief message to others later on, and it is your job to ensure that they want to do so. If you succeed in both respects — if your message is memorable and distinct — your company has a competitive strategy.

As competition continues to increase in today's business world and as the markets for products and services become more specialized, competitive strategies must adapt to these changes by targeting market niches and a more narrow consumer audience. In publishing and broadcasting, for example, both large and small companies now provide magazines and news programs that cover highly specific topics in order to target specific market segments. For example, few people know that the largest television station in Los Angeles in terms of viewership is the Spanish-language station. Very small companies sell specialty products like food or dietary supplements by mail or via the Internet. Similarly, following a trend called "narrowcasting," cable television companies typically offer a number of channels that focus exclusively on sports, comedy, news, women's issues, or home shopping programs. Large companies may pursue two or more strategies to target multiple market niches; for example, to appeal to an older audience, MTV created its VH1 channel, Honda created its Acura model, and Gap introduced Banana Republic.

For communication specialists, crafting a competitive strategy involves close attention to message design. Thus, for instance, an effective strategy for your hypothetical potato-stuffed burger restaurant would likely focus on its uniqueness: "The only place in town with potato-stuffed burgers!" However, your strategy would be successful only if a niche market existed — or could be created — for your product. In the first case, pent-up demand can be identified for a product or service, so that its introduction is met with understanding and appreciation ("We've always needed a good coffee shop on this side of town"). In the second, niches can quite literally be created for novel products and services (e.g., bottled water, minivans, or the Sony Walkman). The customer remarks, "I never knew I needed that until I saw it!"

A company that does not narrow its focus and attempts instead to target broad markets (e.g., "We serve potato-stuffed burgers, fresh-squeezed juices, and deli sandwiches at the lowest prices") is not likely to be able to serve the demands of all consumer markets or to distinguish itself as unique in any one market.

Developing a strategy for a new company often begins with the founder's intuition about the potential demand for a product or service. The next step is careful analyses of the target market, of the business environment (which includes potential customers, stakeholders, and community and government agencies), and of the existing competition. Competitor analysis is especially important in identifying whether a similar product or service is offered by other companies in nearby or remote locations or if any past attempts to offer the product or service have failed. In formulating a competitive strategy, then, the prospective business owner must consider not only the potential demand for a product or service, but also how the company's strategy will be received by various publics. A serious objection by any one group can threaten the survival of the business.

Put another way, strategy is a compelling story, a "teachable point of view" about where the company is going and how it will get there (Barry & Elmes, 1997; Tichy, Prichett, & Cohen, 1998). The power of a strategy to motivate employees and to attract customers is largely dependent upon whether the strategy makes for a compelling narrative. Moreover, company leaders no longer have a monopoly on telling their stories: The Web in particular has encouraged the proliferation of "anti-sites," Web sites dedicated to trashing various businesses for poor quality, service, or community relations. This makes it even more challenging for companies to tell a coherent story to the public.

Types of Business Strategies

There are two basic types of business strategies: those that emphasize lowest cost and those that focus on differentiation (Porter, 1980).

Adopting a lowest-cost strategy involves a commitment to offering a product or service at the lowest possible price. Examples include discount appliance stores, no-frills airlines, and manufacturers of generic products. These companies emphasize their lowest-cost products or services in order to target consumers motivated by that strategy. To reach that consumer market, however, the strategy must be communicated effectively. Among the disadvantages of a lowest-cost strategy is the need to reduce operating costs in order to maintain a cost advantage. In a competitive global market, it may be difficult for such companies to manage the high costs of labor and materials.

A more popular business strategy is differentiation, which involves highlighting the unique or special qualities of a company's product or service. For example, a company may be the most reliable, have the quickest delivery time, or offer the most comprehensive warranty service in the business. In the automobile industry, Volvo highlights safety (at least traditionally — they have been making some moves lately toward better styling), whereas BMW highlights performance. Differentiation is a highly communication-based strategy in that its success depends less on *actual* differences among competing products and more on the company's ability to create the *perception* of its product as unique in some way.

Developing a successful strategy can be as simple as noticing an unfilled niche in a particular market. For example, a physician might notice that a community's residents do not have access to medical care on weekends and may choose to address that need. The owner of a car rental company may respond to consumer demands for hourly rentals with a strategy that incorporates both daily and hourly rates. In most cases, however, developing a successful strategy is more difficult and complex because multiple businesses often compete within the same market (e.g., three Los Angeles supermarkets seeking to become the lowest-cost leader conduct ongoing comparison studies to assert their superiority). Similarly, in the battle among leaders in the overnight package delivery business, various strategies are used to compete within the same market. Federal Express differentiates its service as being the most reliable, whereas the U.S. Postal Service emphasizes lowest cost. Although the major long-distance phone carriers — AT&T, Sprint, and MCI — claim to offer the highest quality service or the lowest possible cost and tend often to dispute each other's claims, their prices are actually quite similar.

Strategy is especially important in highly cost-sensitive industries with low brand loyalty, such as in the airline industry. Following deregulation, relatively small airlines entered the marketplace and offered fares on major routes that were significantly less than the fares charged by major carriers. A fare war ensued; airfares continued to drop, but so did profits. Many of the small lowest-cost airlines failed, taking a few major carriers with them. The survivors, scrambling for a way to encourage brand loyalty, settled on frequent-flyer programs. Airfares increased, and the carriers developed differentiation strategies to entice consumers (e.g., "the most on-time departures" and "the best food").

In developing a differentiation strategy, a company chooses the most competitive aspect of its operation. This does not mean that the company is without other positive attributes, but it does mean that the company generally does not communicate them to the public as competitive advantages. At Nordstrom, for instance, customer service is highlighted even though the company is also concerned with cost, quality, and other factors. More than any other attribute, Nordstrom believes its customer service is what most differentiates it from competitors.

The following is a comprehensive list of business strategies adopted by many familiar companies (Robert, 1993):

- Product- or service-driven companies, such as Boeing and Ritz-Carlton, strive to provide the highest-quality products or services in the business. They continually focus on how to improve their products or services as well as their work processes.
- Market-driven companies offer a wide range of products to a specific group of consumers. For example, Johnson & Johnson sells its products to doctors, nurses, patients, and parents. American Express Financial Advisors now target affluent individuals and sell their ability to handle all of their financial needs. Companies like these must engage in ongoing market research and must strive to cultivate consumer loyalty.
- Production-capacity-driven companies, such as airlines, make substantial investments in facilities and equipment and aim to have them running at

full capacity at all times. They engage in market research to meet customers' needs and demands; they also offer special incentives (e.g., reduced fares or discounted vacation packages) to increase business during slack periods.

- Technology-driven companies, such as 3M, Hughes Aircraft, Sony, Gore, Amgen, and DuPont, own or specialize in a unique technology. For example, DuPont invented nylon; the other companies on the list have each filed thousands of patents. Such companies invest a considerable amount of money in research and development.
- Sales- and marketing-driven companies, such as Mary Kay and Tupperware, provide a wide range of products or services to customers in unconventional ways, including door-to-door selling, home shopping club sales, and Internet sales.
- Distribution-driven companies, such as Wal-Mart, United Parcel Service, Home Shopping Network, food wholesalers, and Internet-only businesses like Amazon and eBay, have unique ways of getting their products or services to the customer. Some may also push a variety of products through their distribution channels. Such companies strive to maintain a highly effective distribution system.

The overriding factor in strategy development is a keen awareness of the related industry as a whole as well as its potential for change or improvement. Before air travel was made possible, people crossed the oceans on ships. With the advent of passenger air travel, however, transportation companies offering ocean passage were threatened with obsolescence. Some of them survived by redefining their strategy: Instead of providing transportation, some changed their strategy to providing entertainment on cruise lines. Similarly, McDonald's, a leader in competitive strategy, is not in the food business. People go to McDonald's for comfort, security, predictability, and safety, which is for the most part reflected in the location and cleanliness of its restaurants and in its rigid standards for food worldwide. Recent financial problems are at least in part the result of some franchisees losing sight of this strategy and allowing these factors to slip. It seems that when faced with the loss of cleanliness and predictability, people will happily buy their burgers elsewhere. Having closed hundreds of stores, McDonald's is now engaging in a worldwide campaign designed to convince customers that they will try harder to provide a positive, service-oriented environment.

Strategy and the Business Life Cycle

Strategy changes as an organization progresses through what might be called the "stages of the business life cycle" (Kimberly & Miles, 1980). Strategic and communicative challenges also differ at each stage.

At "birth," a new company is concerned mainly with developing a strategy and finding a niche. The company secures financial backing and makes an initial foray into the marketplace.

In "childhood," the company's major challenge is managing its growth and development. In its pursuit of multiple opportunities, the growing organization may be distracted from its basic strategy or may lack the discipline needed to maintain a focus on its competitive advantage. Effective leadership can help counteract these problems.

When the company reaches "adolescence," it typically encounters stiff competition. As a result, the original strategy no longer functions as a competitive advantage, and the company must work to change or fine-tune it accordingly. This may require paying special attention to both internal communication (to streamline processes, cut costs, and develop new competencies) and external communication (to remind customers of why the company's product or service is superior to those of its competitors).

In the final phase of the business life cycle, "maturity," the company faces the difficult challenge of renewal — of letting go of the old business in favor of a new one, while also maintaining a position in the marketplace. The biggest success story of this sort in recent years has to be Abercrombie & Fitch, which almost overnight went from appealing to well-off, mature, world-travelers to fashion- and price-conscious teenagers! Efforts by J. C. Penney and Sears to upgrade their inventories and appeal to a broader market are other examples. Honda, which entered the world market in the 1970s with the tiny Honda Civic, is known for its strategic excellence. Since the 1970s, Honda has focused not on a particular product but on the customers who purchased the early Civics — baby boomers buying their first car. Transforming and upgrading its products to match those customers' needs, Honda introduced the Prelude and Accord as these young adults moved into their thirties, and the upscale Acura line as they moved into their forties and became more affluent. Honda's strategy is thus tied to satisfying a well-defined market segment.

The failure, or "death," rate in most industries is quite high. Failure can occur at any point in the life cycle, and in fact few start-up companies make it past their first two years, largely because they are undercapitalized. In recent years, many small businesses have either gone under or been sold to larger corporations because of the critical lack of available talent from which to choose.

Strategic Alignment

A company may communicate a strategy such as "environmentally friendly" or "superior customer service," but if customers and employees do not see evidence of the company's claim, the strategy will be unconvincing and ineffective. Therefore, in addition to communicating the strategy to various internal and external publics, the strategy must be reflected in various other aspects of the organization. Strategic alignment, then, refers to the process of modifying organizational systems and structures to support the competitive strategy. This may affect such areas as job design, levels of authority, job training, reward systems, and staffing, among many others.

In the absence of strategic alignment, a business can neither accomplish its strategy nor create the desired image. For example, a print shop that claims to have the lowest prices in town but pays its employees above-average wages is not likely to achieve success. Similarly, a company that claims to be responsive to customers would be unable to implement that strategy if its automated phone system did not give customers the option of speaking with a service representative directly.

Successful strategic alignment is difficult because it forces the company to consider the relationship between its strategy and its internal systems. In addition, strategic alignment is complicated by employees' reluctance to see themselves as part of a system and by managers' tendency to make decisions in isolation rather than based on the company's strategy. Companies that overcome these obstacles to strategic alignment, pursuing a carefully chosen strategy, are more likely to achieve success.

The Original 7-S Model of Strategic Alignment

The original 7-S model of strategic alignment, developed by members of the consulting firm McKinsey & Company, is shown in Figure 11.1. According to this model, strategic alignment involves the following seven factors:

- *Strategy.* Strategy provides a common purpose for all employees and stakeholders. It discriminates the company from its competitors.
- *Superordinate goals.* More specific than a company's mission statement, superordinate goals — such as obtaining a return on an investment or winning a specific contract — must flow logically from the company's strategy. Some authors have argued that the best route is for firms to develop "big hairy audacious goals" (Collins & Porras, 1994).
- *Structure.* The formal reporting relationships as prescribed by the organizational chart should reflect the company's strategy and should symbolically represent the company's values. A team-based organization or an inverted chart with the customer at the top of the pyramid are two common examples of meaningful organizational structure.
- *Systems.* The flow of information through various media (e.g., telephones and computer systems and meetings), the formal systems of operation (e.g., management information systems), the informal operating procedures (e.g., cultural practices), and the informal connections among people (e.g., emergent networks) should all be aligned with the company's strategy. Systems are relevant to communication in that they deal with the distribution of information throughout a company. Certain strategies can be used only with certain types of systems. For example, a

FIGURE 11.1

The Original 7-S Model of Strategic Alignment

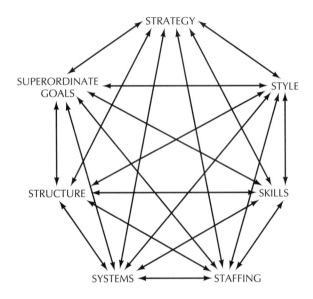

Source: R. D'Aveni, "Coping with Hypercompetition: Utilizing the New 7-S Model," *Academy of Management Executive* 9:3 (1995): 48.

quality manufacturing strategy would require a control system to identify and correct defects immediately.

- *Staffing.* Here, the company's strategy is reflected in its hiring practices,
  in its job assignments, and in its workforce generally. Companies that
  promote from within and those that have technical as well as managerial
  career paths are two examples of approaches to staffing that may support
  a specific competitive strategy.
- *Skills.* Employees' technical and interpersonal skills should be used in
  ways that promote the company's strategy. A company striving to differentiate itself as a leader in customer service would need employees with
  excellent interpersonal skills.
- *Style.* Both management style and organizational culture (how a company
  perceives and treats its employees) can contribute to the success or failure
  of a business strategy. A company that strives to be competitive but that
  routinely permits its employees to miss deadlines is not likely to survive.

The strategic alignment process is best approached by thinking of the organization as a communication system. In this way, we see how the information in each subsystem reflects and affects the whole organization. In an organization that is out of alignment, decisions in one system are made without considering their potential effects on other systems. Over time, even the best organizations' systems usually drift out of alignment as internal functions become outdated and as external developments in technology and market demographics necessitate internal change. In addition, employees are highly sensitive to alignment problems; that is, if the company claims to promote trust and empowerment, employees are likely to voice their objections if their actual decision-making participation is limited. At Disneyland, for example, employees objected to what they perceived as inconsistencies between the company's strategy — "The happiest place on Earth" — and its treatment and compensation of employees (Smith & Eisenberg, 1987).

The strategic-alignment process begins with the development of a strategy, preferably one that focuses on reliable information about the future and that aims to reinvigorate the company. Once a strategy is formed, it must be translated into superordinate goals so that it can be communicated to all employees. Structure is examined next, to determine whether it supports the strategy. For example, in the process of transitioning from a government business to a commercial supplier, a major electronics company sought to become a customer-driven firm (unlike its competitors). However, the company's existing structure, characterized by vertical lines of expertise and authority and minimal cross-functional communication, would not support its new focus on customer relations. The company thus decided to modify its structure by creating a centralized customer service office to act as an interface for customer communication, a repair center designed to meet customers' needs, and cross-functional teams to promote effective communication.

An analysis of systems typically occurs at this point in the strategic-alignment process. In our example, the electronics firm found that its existing voice-mail system kept customers on hold for too long, so it made changes to ensure that customers could reach a service representative within a reasonable amount of time. In addition, the company's past experience with military projects and lax schedules meant that group meetings would need to focus on addressing work issues more expediently. With the help of the human resources department, the company's chief decision-making groups worked together on creating a greater sense of urgency in its informal systems.

Staffing, skills, and style are the final considerations in strategic alignment. The electronics firm recruited employees with the technical and communication skills needed to enact the proposed strategy. Managers and employees in the customer service offices were trained in how to cultivate new customer-oriented styles of working and communication with openness and empathy. Employees who were less open to this change were reassigned to positions that were less visible to customers.

In most cases, strategic alignment is accomplished gradually; a management team focuses on each stage of the process before proceeding to the next stage. Sometimes, however, large-scale strategic alignment may be attempted, as in the case of total quality management (TQM). In pursuing the strategy of total quality, a company may simultaneously redefine its objectives (superordinate goals), overhaul its organization (structure), fire managers from the "old school" (style), recruit new managers with skills better suited to the redefined structure (staffing), and train all employees in empowerment, teamwork, and other areas (skills). However, as a large-scale intervention, strategic alignment is only rarely successful. In addition to the difficulties associated with maintaining a focus amidst rapid change in multiple areas, employees tend to react negatively to change that is radical rather than gradual. They may become suspicious of the company's intentions, worry about losing their jobs, and be less willing to commit themselves to the program's success. Another problem associated with TQM occurs when a company focuses mainly on winning external recognition for its efforts. The Malcolm Baldrige National Quality Award, for example, is given by the U.S. government to companies for excellence in total quality management. Winning the award provides a company with excellent publicity and some powerful advertising copy. However, in the case of a Florida utility company that pursued TQM to win the award, its efforts led to internal havoc and a worse complaint record than that of several other Florida utilities (Sashkin, 1991).

Finally, strategic alignment is not an issue just for corporations and government agencies. Smaller not-for-profit companies and nongovernmental organizations (NGOs) are also challenged to define their strategy in such a way that they send a consistent message and focus their efforts through alignment. A familiar example is environmental activist organizations like Greenpeace, which must be vigilant in communicating a clear and consistent focus both proactively and in response to external challenges.

Human Resources

The shift from local industries to global knowledge work has fundamentally altered the essential elements of business. Whereas in the past enormous capital expenditures went into buildings and materials, today the two most critical parts of any successful business are people and technology. Increasingly, work can be done anywhere, anytime, and the work of an organization may even be done by people not on the payroll — outsourcers and subcontractors. Technology is addressed in the next section; this section deals with the human resources that are the core of any successful enterprise.

Talent

Many chief executive officers are quick to minimize their role in their company's achievements and are anxious to celebrate the accomplishments of their people. This makes good sense. The primary role of the CEO and the senior management team (with some direction from the board of directors in the case of public and nonprofit companies) is to develop competitive strategy and to communicate it in a way that focuses and motivates the rest of the organization. Their other key role is to develop organizational systems (e.g., recruiting, reward, development, and communication) that support the acquisition and retention of talent.

When manufacturing was dominant and the machine model at its peak in America, hiring was done unsystematically, and nepotism and other forms of favoritism were common. With the rise of bureaucracy in the mid-twentieth century, many companies began to understand the importance of attracting and keeping good workers. They established personnel departments to provide a consistent focus on policies affecting employees. Shifting emphases toward employee participation and innovation resulted in further transformation from personnel departments to departments of human resources. As discussed in Chapter 3, the name itself reflects a willingness to see employees as having valuable knowledge that can serve as a resource for the organization's success.

Over the past few decades, human resource management has grown as a credible and highly sophisticated discipline of its own. Whereas in the past salaries, benefits, and training were treated as an afterthought and shaped by the opinions of line managers with little or no knowledge of research on attracting and developing talent, today most large companies have a senior vice president of human resources who reports to the president or CEO and has input into strategic decisions. Recent developments have made the wisdom of this shift even more apparent. At a conference of the five hundred fastest-growing companies in 1998, a large percentage of entrepreneur-founders were seen looking for people to buy their companies. The most common reason they gave for wanting to cash out was their inability to attract and retain sufficient talent.

Research shows that companies that treat people as their most important asset are also the most profitable. In one award-winning study of 968 companies across all industries, it was revealed that "a one standard deviation increase in the use of (high performance practices) was associated with a 7.05 percent decrease in turnover and, on a per employee basis, $27,044 more in sales and $18,641 and $3,814 more in market value and profits, respectively" (Huselid, 1995). By "high-performance practices," the researchers counted such things as self-managed teams, employee empowerment, pay for performance, extensive training, extensive information sharing, and a purposeful reduction in attention paid to status differences (Pfeffer & Veiga, 1999).

Companies in highly competitive industries are always seeking skilled employees at all levels. Those that can afford to do so are trying new approaches, such as recruiting abroad, building employee housing, providing huge incentives to current employees who refer a new hire, and even hiring groups of friends. One progressive firm, Warner-Lambert (now part of Pfizer), has a director of talent management who defines her job as attracting the best and the brightest and then "protecting" them from the organization while they learn the culture and find their feet. Once integrated into the company, she sees her further responsibility to "re-recruit" star performers to ensure that they don't leave to join the competition.

What we would consider progressive human resources management has many aspects, but three key components have everything to do with effective organizational communication. These components are targeted selection, performance management, and training and development.

Targeted Selection

Particularly in times of full employment, there is a tendency to minimize job qualifications and to fill positions with anyone who seems minimally competent. Although this might get the company through the week, it is a losing strategy in the long run. The new employees are set up to fail, and fail they will, angering and alienating customers along the way. A much better approach is for senior management to have sufficient discipline to identify a unique competitive strategy (see earlier discussion) and to define job qualifications in ways that support that strategy. Although this may seem obvious, it is difficult in practice: Think of all the companies you patronize as a customer whose mission is customer satisfaction but whose frontline employees lack the knowledge or the motivation to satisfy anyone other than the most routine customer! When jobs are created in a conscious way, each job comprises critical dimensions, such as word-processing skills, strategic thinking, oral communication, and tolerance for ambiguity. Successful organizations spend lots of time analyzing jobs to ensure that they support the company's strategy.

A good reason for careful job analysis and the identification of key job dimensions is that clear job descriptions communicate to everyone — managers, current job incumbents, and applicants — what is expected of them. Targeted selection is a systematic job-interview process through which selected company experts assess job candidates on the key dimensions of each job. At the end of a search process, the interviewers meet to pool their data and make an informed choice. Employees selected through targeted selection are, with few exceptions, immediately capable of making a contribution to the company's performance.

Performance Management

Just as key job dimensions are directly in support of company strategy, *performance management* is a name for any system that tracks and gives feedback to employees about how well they are accomplishing objectives tied to each of their key dimensions. For example, if skill in computer programming is a dimension, an objective might be to write three new programs without error each month. Managers and employees can track against these performance standards and record both the number of programs accomplished and the number of errors. Deviations from objectives can be easily brought to the surface and addressed.

It is this last step — using the performance-management system as a basis for a conversation with employees — that is both the heart of the system and the most difficult to achieve. When the system works, it can provide uncanny alignment between individual jobs at any level and organizational success in the aggregate. However, in the absence of any system, managers go by "gut feel" and in most cases play favorites based upon personal relationships, not real productivity. With a performance-management system in place, everyone knows what is expected of him or her, and performance is relatively public (at least to one's manager). A difficulty occurs, however, because most people avoid stressful communication situations that are potentially conflictual. This is why so many employees report that they are late in getting performance feedback, if they get any at all. The worst-case scenario occurs when cowardly managers leave employees a copy of their review with a note that says, "Call if you have any questions." This is unacceptable and defeats the purpose of performance management, which is designed to make both managers and employees accountable for open communication about results.

In the days before human resources departments, feedback on employee performance was either highly informal, annual, or nonexistent. Today's best thinking suggests that performance management is an ongoing conversation that every manager ought to have with employees, during which strategy is reinforced, objectives are reviewed, results are revealed, and gaps are examined. Failure to perform to standard can mean many things other than employee incompetence, including understaffing, inadequate tools, or poor planning. Quite often, it is the result of inadequate employee development and training.

Training and Development

In one form or another, employee training has always been a part of the function of management. Businesspeople have long recognized that there are benefits to identifying the best practices in performing any given job and then communicating these practices systematically to employees. Even Frederick Taylor, inventor of the time-and-motion study, placed a heavy emphasis on training, inasmuch as scientific management could help identify the best ways of doing things that could (and should) be taught to everyone.

Training is much simpler when the job requirements stay roughly the same over a long period of time. What is especially challenging today is that the knowledge and skills to be taught are evolving at blinding speed, making last year's training potentially obsolete. For this reason, the notion of isolated training sessions has been replaced in almost every successful company with a focus on ongoing employee development and the facilitation of continuous learning.

There is further recognition that such development efforts cannot be "one size fits all." Employee-development programs are increasingly tailored to fit the interests, learning styles, locations, and even schedules of targeted employees. Like customers, employees want education that is "just in time, just for me." For this reason, companies are designing highly flexible and modular development centers or "corporate universities" that offer a dazzling array of learning opportunities through a range of media. The underlying idea is that the best time to "teach" someone something like Lotus Notes or supervisory skills is when they most want or need to learn it.

Progressive companies tie training and development efforts to their performance-management systems. Job analysis shows the key dimensions in which an incumbent must excel to succeed at the job; performance management tracks how well the employee is doing along each dimension. At this point, a manager can use the performance-management conversation to coach employees about development opportunities in or outside of the company (much education is outsourced these days) that specifically target their areas of below-average performance. Senior managers can use summary performance data to target entire departments or regions for certain kinds of development, such as customer service or time-management training.

There is one last piece of the puzzle that, when applied, can turbocharge the whole human resources function. Tying employee performance to clearly defined rewards — compensation, benefits, advancement, recognition — rationalizes the system for employees. Rather than being busywork that has little to do with "my real job," the business of filling out tracking forms and meeting with managers to discuss performance becomes central to each employee's work life. Targeted selection ensures that people are hired who have a chance of performing the needed functions; performance management tracks their success and provides specific feedback on where they must improve; development and training provide opportunities for continuous learning in those areas; and employees are rewarded for consistently doing the things that, by design, support the company's strategy.

The best employees will get frustrated and quit if they lack appropriate tools to perform their jobs effectively. Interestingly, this problem is compounded in companies with performance-management systems because employees are acutely aware of their accountabilities and are given incentives for meeting their goals.

Organizational Development

Any progressive human resources practitioner will tell you that no amount of training can substitute for enterprise-wide efforts to transform and sustain a new kind of organizational culture. For this reason, the best and brightest HR professionals have over the years been drawn to the subfield of organizational development (OD), which deals with the facilitation of strategic systems change. In practice, this usually amounted to senior management enlisting the help of their internal human resources staff — or hiring an external HR consultant — to assist in promoting a particularly challenging organizational change. The occasion for such an initiative varied, from mergers to reorganization to downsizing.

In every instance, the decision to involve an OD professional — many of whom have backgrounds in communication — reveals some important realities about the nature of strategic change in organizations and institutions. Having been involved in many of these initiatives ourselves, we will state these realities as three core "lessons" we have learned in approaching the strategic change process using a communication lens.

1. *People still want to be inspired.* Particularly in the wake of the old social contract, it is important to remember that people still look to work as a potential source of meaning in their lives, and a compelling vision or strategy can provide this. The flip side of this lesson is that you can't force people to change to meet a schedule — people enroll in a change when they are ready.

2. *People are more likely to support something they helped to create.* Another key principle of change management is that employees must be given sufficient information and opportunities for dialogue if one expects them to support the new direction. Much of what OD practitioners actually do is facilitate these conversations.

3. *Actions still speak louder than words.* The strategy can be inspiring and the dialogues far-reaching, but if the nonverbal behaviors of management conflict with the espoused direction, the change effort is dead in the water. This is the hardest part of alignment for an OD professional to address, since it implicates the judgment of senior management.

Organizational Learning

In our rapidly changing world, learning organizations have a distinct advantage. Composed of people who not only profit from past mistakes, but also question the assumptions that led to those mistakes, learning organizations are well equipped to deal with continuous change (Argyris & Schon, 1978; Senge, 1991; Steier, 1989).

Learning Basic Skills

Most organizational practitioners, educators, and politicians agree that the U.S. educational system does a mediocre job of providing students with even the most basic job skills. The U.S. labor secretary's Commission on Achieving Necessary Skills identifies three foundational abilities and five learning areas as essential to success in the workplace (Table 11.1). One important foundational ability is the ability to think, to reason, and to make decisions. This ability in turn supports each of the learning areas, such as the ability to troubleshoot and to work with advanced technologies. Other examples of specific details discussed in the commission's categories are creativity and learning how to learn, sociability, skills in teamwork, negotiation, and giving and receiving feedback. In addition to negatively affecting people's quality of life, widespread deficits of basic skills pose a threat to the business world. Quality and customer service suffer in any industry that depends on an inadequately skilled workforce. In an attempt to address this problem, many food outlets have resorted to equipping

TABLE 11.1

Necessary Workplace Skills

THE FOUNDATIONAL ABILITIES

Basic: Reading, writing, mathematics, speaking, and listening

Thinking: Creativity, making decisions, solving problems, seeing things in the mind's eye, knowing how to learn, reasoning

Personal qualities: Responsibility, self-esteem, sociability, self-management, and integrity

LEARNING AREAS

Resources: How to allocate time, money, materials, space, and staff

Interpersonal: How to work on teams, teach, serve customers, lead negotiations, and work well with people from culturally diverse backgrounds

Information: How to acquire and evaluate data, organize and maintain files, interpret and communicate, and use computers to acquire and process information

Systems: How to understand social, organizational, and technological systems; monitor and correct performance; and design improved systems

Technology: How to select equipment and tools, apply technology to specific tasks, and maintain and troubleshoot technologies

Source: U.S. Labor Secretary's Commission on Achieving Necessary Skills, June 1991.

cash registers with pictures of food items rather than monetary figures. Similarly, a growing number of manufacturing firms are redesigning complex, good-paying positions into simple, low-paying, dead-end jobs. The result is a downward spiral of quality, service, job skills, wages, and employee self-esteem.

One proposed solution to these serious problems is to establish workplace literacy programs designed to teach basic skills to employees. These programs, which are offered by private companies, public agencies, and corporations themselves, vary widely in their focus and intensity. For example, some programs focus on job-related language skills, while others teach a broad array of basic skills that are useful in work and personal situations. In addition, the programs vary in terms of length (from forty to four hundred hours). Some training programs are sensitive to employees' different needs; others make no such distinctions.

The most successful programs thus far are those initiated and taught by the companies themselves. At American Honda and General Motors, for instance, databases are used to match employees' level of education and skill with job opportunities. However, such programs are rare, and even when they do exist, they cannot adequately address the underlying problems in the U.S. educational system. "The share of the nation's economy invested . . . in education and training, children's programs, infrastructure, and civilian research and development has plummeted 40% since 1980. America ranks behind all its major competitors in each of these categories" (Tyson, 1991, p. D2). Although a tremendous amount of effort will be directed at teaching basic skills to employees of the twenty-first century, without major changes in the educational system and in the nation's spending priorities, those efforts will do little to solve the problem.

Taking a broader view, however, even skills training may not be sufficient in helping the unemployed and working poor to participate in an expanding economy. Social philosopher Earl Shorris (1997) has argued that it is not job skills — but the ability to know about and reflect on questions central to all human existence, about life and death, right and wrong — that is the genuine portal to a better life. To test this hypothesis, Shorris assembled a team of star college teachers (including some Nobel Prize winners) and began offering a course in the humanities to economically disadvantaged adults in New York City. The twenty-eight-week course, dubbed "The Clemente Project," was sponsored by Bard College and included instruction in such topics as moral philosophy, art history, and American history. Thus far, the results have been encouraging. There is a big difference between teaching someone about specific business tasks and having them consider work behavior as it might have been seen by Aristotle. An old saying states, "If you give someone a fish, they eat for a day, but if you teach them to fish, they will never go hungry." The Clemente Project, now being tried in many cities around the country, is one attempt to teach "fishing" to the most disenfranchised members of our society.

However it is addressed, we must be sure to factor into our thinking about the future of work the "grotesque gap" that exists in income and living standards around the world. Consider this statement from the United Nations Human Development Report (July 12, 1999) on the problems with thinking of development solely in terms of financial markets:

> The richest nations of the world have 20% of the population, but 86% of the income, 91% of its Internet users, and 74% of its telephone users. . . . When the market goes too far in dominating social and political outcomes, the opportunities and rewards of globalization spread unequally and inequitably — concentrating power and wealth in a select group of people, nations, and corporations, marginalizing the others. The challenge is not to stop the expansion of global markets. The challenge is to find the rules and institutions for stronger governance . . . to preserve the advantage of global markets and competition but also to provide enough space for human, community, and environmental resources to ensure that globalization works for people, not just for profits. (Longworth, 1999, p. 16)

Learning New Technologies

Today, regardless of its positioning in the marketplace, every organization must utilize some form of communication technology. In the 1950s and 1960s, organizational researchers emphasized the importance of face-to-face communication between supervisors and employees and among co-workers. Although face-to-face interaction is still important in today's organizations, advances in communication technology — from computer networks and facsimile transmissions to voice mail and e-mail — have overcome some of the limits of face-to-face interaction, especially those associated with speed, geographic distance, and processing capacity. As a result, organizations can no longer function effectively without the use of some type of communication technology. Furthermore, implementing a new technology significantly affects work processes, employees' productivity and work life, and the character of interpersonal and power relationships.

Types of Communication Technology

Two broad categories of communication technology are currently available to organizations:

- Computer-assisted communication technologies include the various methods of image transmission, including facsimile (fax), videoconferencing, e-mail, voice mail, Web sites, and personal digital assistants. These are widely used both within organizations and with customers as part of the massive development of global electronic commerce (e-commerce).
- Computer-assisted decision-aiding technologies include on-line management information systems, group decision support systems, information-retrieval database systems, and expert systems or programs that provide technical information. Traditionally used as tools internal to the organization, these technologies are now offered to customers as well.

Computer-assisted communication technologies are designed to enhance the speed of communication as well as the ability of people to communicate regardless of their geographic location. E-mail, for example, allows people to receive computer messages that may be retrieved at a later time. Other popular computer-assisted communication technologies include voice mail, voice messaging, answering machines (sometimes connected to personal computers), audioconferencing, and cellular phones. The recently introduced personal digital assistant (PDA) contains a pager, a fax, and a telephone and allows the user to send image, voice, or text messages (typed or handwritten) from a hand-held unit.

Computer-assisted decision-aiding technologies are designed primarily to provide easy access to hard-to-find information needed to make decisions. For example, a company may use market data accessed via an external database to decide whether it should introduce a new product. Internally, a sales manager may access information about last quarter's sales to decide whether the company's salespeople would benefit from a proposed training program. Information on virtually any topic is available on-line. Far from taking the place of humans, research shows that, in practice, the systems that simply support decision making but leave final decisions to the user are more successful than systems that substitute machine decisions for human decisions or that significantly curtail the user's freedom of action (Turnage, 1990).

An especially useful decision-aiding program is the search robot or "bot," which allows computer users to direct a search for information based on their personal preferences. For instance, a bot user might input information about a desired vacation itinerary (e.g., location, price range, and other preferences) and have the computer shop for and book the trip. Bots extend consumer reach by searching obscure and hard-to-find sources of needed information.

Effects of Communication Technology

The potential effects of communication technology are multiple and varied. Contemporary observers usually support one of four major views on the subject: utopian, dystopian, neutral, and contingent.

From the utopian view, information technology serves to equalize power relationships at work by bridging time and space, thereby improving both productivity and work life. Proponents of this highly optimistic view "see the computer as freeing employees to work on more challenging tasks by taking over the routine aspects of jobs, thus increasing productivity and competition and creating more employment in the long run" (Turnage, 1990, p. 171).

In contrast, the more pessimistic dystopian view sees communication technology as benefiting an economic elite and — through the modification and loss of jobs — as causing such problems as downsizing (particularly among middle managers), the lowering of work skill requirements, and physical and mental disorders (Braverman, 1974; Cohen, 1985). Proponents of the dystopian view range from extremists, sometimes called "Luddites," who advocate a return to simpler times, to moderates, who suggest that a technology's consequences be considered. For example, many people today are frustrated with the increased amount of communication that has come with easier access to technology. In a survey of a diverse group of employees, respondents reported significant levels of overload due to the proliferation of electronic media. Indeed, the average Fortune 100 worker sends and receives 178 e-mail messages daily (Dunham, 1999). In contrast, there are those with little or no access to technology who, in the dystopian view, are fast becoming the have-nots in a growing "digital divide" (Dunham, 1999). (See *What Would You Do?* 11.1.)

The neutral view of communication technology holds that it has no significant effects on human behavior and that people can be expected to behave in predictable ways whether they use a traditional telephone or a computer to communicate. Proponents of this view believe that the potential effects of technology on communication and behavior are exaggerated by utopians, dystopians, and others.

The contingent view of communication technology is best supported by research. From this view, the effect of a given innovation depends on the context or situation in which it is adopted. For example, the health hazards associated with video display terminals (VDTs) — which include radiation exposure, headaches, eyestrain, sleeplessness, anxiety, and repetitive-motion disorders — may be more the result of how an organization uses the technology (e.g., long working hours and poor design of workstations) than of the technology itself (Smith, Cohen, Stammerjohn, & Happ, 1981; Steelman & Klitzman, 1985).

Another example is the computerized monitoring of employee productivity, wherein the frequency and speed of work are measured and stored by the computer and are reviewed by management. The productivity of approximately 6 million U.S. workers is now monitored electronically, and the telephone and airline reservation industries are leaders in the use of this technology (Turnage, 1990). Employees' reactions have been mixed; although some employees consider electronic surveillance to be an invasion of their privacy, others believe that it is useful in giving good performers greater recognition for their efforts (Bell-Detienne, 1992).

Most communication technologies, though designed for specific uses, take on other functions related to the individual user's needs (Poole & DeSanctis, 1990). The telephone answering machine, for instance, was designed to receive and record incoming calls; however, some people also use it as a call-screening device. Similarly, medical information systems designed to help physicians keep track of patients' prescriptions, diagnostic testing, and treatments are now used by pharmacists as well (Aydin & Rice, 1992).

A significant amount of research has been conducted on computer systems designed to support group decisions. These so-called group-decision support systems (GDSSs) allow teams to retrieve obscure facts or other hard-to-find

What Would You Do? 11.1

SURFING SICKNESS

The following message appeared on the Internet in 1995.

TO: Internet addiction support group

SUBJECT: Literally got sick, surfing

I got on the Net . . . because I was convalescing from back surgery. Previously, being physically active, I had no time for the PC or the Internet. Initially, I spent only thirty to forty-five minutes on the PC, twice a day, exploring various bbs and doing infantile Net explorations. Then one night I woke up in the middle of the night and went on-line. I rationed myself to one hour for surfing. I needed reading glasses to focus on the screen. Sitting close enough to focus with my glasses caused me to strain my back (less than one week after surgery). After five and a half hours on the Net, my back ached from bending, my head ached from the eye strain, and I was nauseated from the distorted images I was processing visually. I remained disabled and sick in the stomach, pained in the neck and leg, and with a throbbing headache for at least twenty-four hours. . . .

My wife was disgusted with me. I couldn't believe I'd stayed on the Net so long. Since that time I have lost hundreds, maybe even thousands of dollars in unearned income due to unfinished proposals and projects. . . . I [have] lost rapport with friends and associates, missed deadlines on discount travel and airfares, [and been late] to appointments. . . . I've spent countless hours typing out messages like this to people I don't know and will probably never hear from. I've typed out more letters and messages since my back surgery . . . than in my entire life before then. My own kids since then have received no more than two or three notes from me in the snail mail. They won't get on the Net so I won't even write to them.

My back surgery was so successful that after a few weeks I could do anything. . . . And yet I still gravitate to the PC several times a day. My wife is annoyed that my office here at the house is stacked with months of snail mail and other projects I used to do on a regular basis. I'm annoyed, too.

But it's too much fun writing to you, whoever you are.

Discussion Questions

1. Do you know someone who is an overly involved Internet user? Why do you think this problem occurs? Is it a personal problem or one that affects society as a whole?
2. In what ways do face-to-face communication and on-line communication differ? How might these differences affect employees of organizations moving toward distributed types of work? What effect might they have on the organization's culture?
3. What advice would you give to the person who posted this message?

information instantaneously via a computer database. In addition, GDSS allows team members to communicate via multiple channels, thereby improving the distribution of information in the organization and promoting team members' involvement.

The successful implementation of a communication technology takes into account the social and political aspects of the organizational environment in which it will be used. The "rational" use of communication technology is "subjective, retrospective, and influenced by information provided by others" (Fulk, Schmitz, & Steinfeld, 1990, p. 143). The authors of one study conclude,

> There is no such thing as pure technology. To understand technology, one must first understand social relationships. . . . Everything about the adoption and uses of media is social. . . . Logical expectations for the adoption and use of the new media are rarely met. The pragmatics of technological communication must always be understood in the context of motives, paradoxes, and contradictions of everyday life. (Contractor & Eisenberg, 1990, p. 143)

Table 11.2 identifies six important considerations in the analysis of a communication technology.

Synchronicity and Media Richness

Two particular aspects of communication technology are of special interest to communication scholars: synchronicity and media richness. *Synchronicity* refers to the capacity of a technology to allow for two-way communication. For example, a telephone is synchronous, but an answering machine allows the telephone to become asynchronous. Similarly, while most e-mail is asynchronous, the proliferation of chat rooms on the World Wide Web and instant and text messaging has created more possibilities for synchronicity. Both synchronous and asynchronous communication have their particular advantages. For instance, certain requests and work tasks are best approached via two-way communication, whereas other tasks may be well communicated and performed through asynchronous channels (e.g., when busy people communicate across time zones). However, asynchronous communication can lead people to make more contacts than they can reasonably handle (Gergen, 1991). This is why many people in high-status or high-visibility jobs sometimes avoid using voice mail and e-mail systems.

Media richness refers to the number of multiple channels of contact afforded by a communication medium (Daft & Lengel, 1984). Each channel roughly corresponds to one of our senses; consequently, face-to-face communication is classified as most rich because it simultaneously allows for speech, nonverbal communication, vision, smell, and touch. Using this definition, a letter would fall at the low end of the media richness scale, inasmuch as it only allows for verbal exchange. Videoconferencing is a richer medium than teleconferencing, but it still leaves out important channels that people want. In addition, people

TABLE 11.2

Six Concerns in the Analysis of Communication Technology

1. *Humans are agents.* Accept the fact that "humans are reflexively monitoring what goes on in a particular social system, that they are motivated by wants and aspirations, and that they have the power not to perform the prescription laid down by systems designers" (p. 312).

2. *Tacit knowledge should be respected.* "People know more about their lives than they can put into words. People do know how to handle practical affairs without being able to explain fully what they are really doing" (p. 312).

3. *Understanding is partial.* "There are always unacknowledged conditions for and unintended consequences of people's behavior" (p. 313).

4. *Technology is politically ambiguous.* Although a technology can be used to promote dialogue and to improve individual quality of life, the same technology can also be used to constrain, limit, and control.

5. *Informal communication must be acknowledged.* "Informal informing is an organizational fact. . . . It is necessary to understand how formal information is mediated through various more or less structured patterns of informing" (p. 313).

6. *Counterrational decision making should be acknowledged.* "The rational model is not a viable way of understanding the intricacies of modern business management. On the one hand it is questionable that decision-makers cognitively are able to cope with the complexity and amount of information needed to make rational decisions, and on the other hand, it is probable that all sorts of political and social pressures are called upon in everyday management" (pp. 313–314).

Source: Jan Mouritsen and Niels Bjorn-Andersen, "Understanding Third-Wave Information Systems," in C. Dunlop and R. Kling, eds., *Computerization and Controversy: Value Conflicts and Social Choices* (San Diego: Academic Press, 1991), pp. 308–320.

are often quite strategic in choosing how rich a medium to choose, depending upon their goals. Most of us have on occasion left an uncomfortable message on someone's answering machine because we couldn't "face" their response.

Secrecy and Privacy

The primary benefit of communication technology — the radical expansion of connections between people and institutions — is also its main liability. Every connection leaves traces that can be followed and exploited by others for personal gain. Issues of privacy, secrecy, and copyright in computer-aided interaction are currently being debated in courts around the world. In most companies, for example, managers have access to employees' e-mail messages. Major credit card companies follow consumer spending patterns very closely, including where transactions are made by clients. The effects of electronic surveillance on people's right to privacy is already a major issue.

Mediated Interpersonal Communication

With the widespread use of telephones, fax machines, computers, and overnight delivery services, many interpersonal work relationships are routinely conducted by people who never actually meet face-to-face. The result is a new hybrid of social relationships that we call "mediated interpersonal communication." Mediated forms of written communication are popular, particularly in international companies. For example, at Ryobi, a Japanese manufacturing firm with several U.S. subsidiaries, more money is spent on faxes than on any other form of communication. The same is true of many Asian-owned firms that operate in the United States, where culture demands strict adherence to procedures and an ongoing flow of information about work processes. However, at Sagem-Lucas, a French and British partnership with U.S. subsidiaries, appointed representatives are sent to the United States for several weeks to become acquainted with business colleagues and the local culture. The representatives report back to the company's headquarters in Europe, where their on-site observations become the topic of internal memos, faxes, and computer-based communication.

Similar patterns of mediated communication are found in U.S. companies. For many companies, real offices are being replaced by virtual ones. A virtual office, with most of the usual functions of an office, can be literally anywhere the user can gain access to a modem. A 1994 study of fourteen hundred distributed workers in the United States reveals that more than 50 percent are males earning in excess of $45,000 per year, only 34 percent have graduate degrees, and about half their work time is devoted to interacting with customers and coworkers. In addition, desktop computers, modems, and multiple phone lines serve their communication needs, while their productivity is up to 20 percent higher than that of nondistributed workers. Distributed workers also tend to experience less job-related stress (Grantham, 1995).

Emerging Technologies

Biotechnology

Over the past two decades, enormous amounts of time and money have been invested in biotechnology, which is the purposeful creation or modification of genetic material (DNA) for commercial applications. The new biotechnologies are "already reshaping a wide range of fields, including forestry, agriculture, animal husbandry, mining, energy, bioremediation, packaging and construction materials, pharmaceuticals, medicine, and food and drink" (Rifkin, 1999, p. 11). For example, pharmaceutical companies have developed gene therapies to treat certain diseases; supermarkets sell genetically altered produce that has a longer shelf life; and the U.S. Army is implementing a gene bank to facilitate the positive identification of soldiers. The Human Genome Project, a worldwide effort by scientists to identify the biological roots of human diversity, has already "mapped" the more than one hundred thousand genes that make up a human being. Microsoft's CEO, Bill Gates, has said that in the information age, "biological information is probably the most interesting information that we are deciphering and trying to decide to change. It's now a question of how, not if." Most futurists agree that we have entered the new "bioeconomy" (Davis & Davidson, 1992) or even the "Biotech Century" (Rifkin, 1999).

Extraordinary benefits await organizations that rethink their products and services in light of this new context. Recent research has identified genes that may lead to cures for stubborn diseases like asthma, hemophilia, and diabetes. Oil spills may be far less disastrous due to the development and use of petroleum-eating microbes. Individuals' personal lives may be made simpler and safer by the consolidation of personal health and financial records either on "smart cards" that are carried or in silicon chip implants like those that already aid in the recovery of hundreds of lost pets each year. One leader in this arena has been Motorola, whose tag line "digital DNA" nicely expresses the "wetware" interface between biological and nonbiological information. Motorola produces a handheld DNA scanner that reads blood samples in seconds. This is an example of how new technology will radically transform entire industries, in this case the laboratories that take days or even weeks to do a similar analysis.

The stakes are high and have important implications not just for individuals, but for nation-states. In an agreement between Merck Pharmaceuticals and the government of Costa Rica, for example, Costa Rica agrees to send small parcels of biological samples (e.g., bushels of twigs, packages of ground-up caterpillars) to Merck for possible use in research and development. For any product that Merck develops from a Costa Rican sample, the country receives a percentage of the pharmaceutical company's profits. The arrangement is interesting in other respects as well. It suggests, for instance, that a country "owns the rights" to its biological resources. Once Merck identifies a biological specimen that can be developed into a product, the company does not need any additional material from Costa Rica to manufacture the product. Based on the genetic code found in the original sample, scientists can recreate or synthesize the material, which suggests that Costa Rica is selling not biological resources but biological information that provides the clues for genetic engineering.

There are good reasons to fear the misuse and abuse of these powerful technologies. Moral and legal challenges to biotechnology are already under way throughout the world. For example, the European Union (EU) has been united in its boycott of genetically altered organisms in its food supply, dubbing it

"Frankenfood." In the world of medicine, a businessman named John Moore found that his body parts had been patented by the University of California at Los Angeles (UCLA) and licensed to the Sandoz Pharmaceuticals Corporation. During treatment for a rare cancer, doctors found that Moore's spleen produced a blood protein that encouraged the growth of white blood cells that fight cancer. UCLA created a "cell line" from Moore's spleen tissue and patented its invention, which could be worth billions of dollars. When challenged, the California State Supreme Court held that although Moore should have been informed of the potential economic benefits of commodifying his tissue, the cell line itself was indeed the property of UCLA and that Moore had no rights to it! An underlying question is whether anyone should have the right to patent life (and reap the profits) or whether the gene pool ought to remain an "open commons" to be used by present and future generations (Rifkin, 1999).

Virtual Reality

The term *virtual reality* (VR) describes a family of technologies that allows a user to experience "immersion" in imaginary worlds in strikingly realistic detail. For example, one type of virtual reality requires the participant to wear a device, such as wraparound goggles or a headset, that can simulate a realistic scene (such as a battlefield, ballfield, or crime scene) as well as adjust the sensory input based on the user's command (e.g., by moving the hands, head, or feet). This type of virtual reality is now used in some pilot-training programs to simulate flight conditions.

Two familiar precursors to virtual reality are computer-aided design (CAD) and holography. CAD allows engineers, graphic artists, and others to work with their drawings in a three-dimensional computerized format. CAD also permits the movement or rotation of objects in the computer-generated diagrams, which eliminates the time-consuming task of drawing several versions of a building's floor plan or a graphic design by hand. Holography is also an advanced form of image projection whereby three-dimensional scenes appear on a flat surface or are suspended in the air in front of the viewer (as in some video games and on some of the rides at newer theme parks like Universal Studios' "Islands of Adventure" in Orlando, Florida). Holograms are used in engineering and design and are beginning to appear in education, where, for example, holographic images of three-dimensional molecules spinning in space will appear suspended in air in the chemistry classroom. Many well-known movies, like *Star Wars: The Phantom Menace*, make extensive use of computer design to create apparently three-dimensional, simulated worlds that "feel" increasingly real.

The huge advances that have been made in wireless communication technology, which allows people to move away from screens and into situations where all of their senses can be engaged, are enabling the development of virtual reality. Other potential uses of virtual reality include "driving" a virtual car as a student driver or "walking through" a virtual prehistoric scene during science class. In entertainment, education, health care, and other areas, numerous applications of virtual reality will be forthcoming.

For communication scholars, the transition from e-mail communication to multiuser domains is especially interesting. Multiuser domains (MUDs) are virtual "places" in cyberspace where computer users can "gather" to meet and interact (see <http://www.activeworlds.com> for a popular example). MUD environments are often rendered in great detail, and in the wild world of the World Wide Web, users select special names, or "avatars," to represent themselves in these spaces. Qualitative research on these environments suggests that people put them to complex and varying uses, from making new friends to establishing a separate and in some ways more "real" identity than they experience in their physical bodies (Markham, 1998). Organizational intranets will likely move in this direction, expanding possibilities for rich interaction among groups of people who are not colocated.

Our examination of new technologies suggests a number of recommendations for students of communication. First, become as computer literate as possible. Second, even if you are not interested in science per se, gain a working knowledge of anatomy and biology through either formal course work or outside reading. Many of the issues that have in the past been considered squarely within the domain of the humanities and the social sciences — such as mood, personality, and human interaction — are increasingly taking on biological components. In addition, complex biological systems are increasingly being used as models for designing organizations, and manufacturing shop floors in particular. Finally, be open to an expanded notion of communication that involves not only symbols and meaning, but also genes and DNA. The "wetware" interfaces between mechanical and biological systems (e.g., voice-recognition systems, security systems that scan the iris) will be a primary source of innovation in the coming years.

Moral Dimensions of Organizational Communication

The growing concerns about communication ethics and ecological responsibility will continue to be important in the future. In both cases, communication plays a key role in facilitating moral judgment.

Communication Ethics

Ethical issues are not new to organizations, and many business schools and corporations require their students and employees to receive formal training in ethical decision making. Why? Because, since 1985, more than two-thirds of

Fortune 500 firms have been convicted of serious crimes, ranging from fraud to the illegal dumping of hazardous wastes. In addition, employees who make poor business decisions also tend to take unethical actions aimed at covering up their mistakes.

Indeed, most business decisions involve ethical choices, and communication is at the heart of any ethical dispute (Redding, 1991). Moreover, as some scholars argue, theories of human communication tend to assume that people tell the truth, but in many cases, they do not. In our culture, for instance, "telling white lies" and "stretching the truth" are more or less condoned. In pursuing a career or searching for a job, we are advised to paint only positive portraits of ourselves and our past employment experiences. (See *What Would You Do?* 11.2.)

One could even argue that "the ethic of personal advantage" has led to a general lowering of the standards of business ethics (Mitchell & Scott, 1990). Associated with the ethic of personal advantage are "(1) a present versus a future orientation; (2) an instrumental as opposed to a substantive focus (i.e., the ends justify the means); and (3) an emphasis on individualism contrasted with community" (pp. 25–26). In addition, the capitalist system has created a culture of denial in which businesspeople remain generally unconcerned about the effects of their activities on others. Although ethics education can strive to build moral character, at some point our society will need to address the underlying problems of the business culture. As an alternative to the typical business ethics course, which through problem solving and case studies teaches "rules" of ethical conduct, management theorists Terrance Mitchell and Richard Scott (1990) suggest that "moral discourse" may be a more fruitful enterprise:

> Moral discourse is a process of rhetorical engagement by students and professors in free and open forums of conversation and debate. One tries to persuade others of the truth of his or her point of view on moral issues. In the process, widely divergent opinions are expressed and each individual is exposed to alternative propositions about values. The whole point is to provide knowledge of moral options and the opportunity to choose among different value systems. . . . The function of ethics courses should be to instill an open, moral, loving, humane, and broadly informed mentality, so that students may come to see life's trials and business's ethical challenges as occasions to live through with integrity and courage. (p. 29)

Ecological Responsibility

The deterioration of our physical environment (deforestation, acid rain, toxic waste) and the rapid depletion of natural resources are the results of our inability or refusal to see the world as an interconnected system (Hawken, 1994; Mitchell & Scott, 1990). Cancer rates in areas known for industrial pollution are on the increase, and many by-products of human industrialization threaten the health of people and of the planet. Intentionally or not, business organizations are sometimes among the most thoughtless enemies of nature. More generally,

What Would You Do? 11.2

WHO'S RESPONSIBLE?

Recently, a federal court ruled against a manufacturer of oil pipelines for showing a blatant disregard of environmental standards in the construction and installation of its product. The judge added that her decision was meant to "put the entire pipeline industry on notice" that there will be significant consequences for future abuses of the land.

An interesting wrinkle in this and many similar cases is that the complainants in the lawsuit are not content to seek damages from the offending company. They are filing criminal charges against the owners of the company, which could lead to significant financial penalties and even jail time.

Discussion Questions

1. What is your opinion on the ethics of prosecuting owners and senior managers for the wrongdoings of their companies?
2. If you were to start a business of your own, would your opinion be any different?
3. Does the global nature of the economy and of many companies affect your opinion on this issue?

the "dark side" of global business is a felt lack of connection between people and families, local communities, bioregions, other species, the earth, and the cosmos (Spretnak, 1991). Moreover, it is when people feel least connected to others that they become most capable of violence.

We are beginning to understand that the exploitation of our natural resources will create an unsustainable world if limits are not imposed. Making a shift from our present hyperexpansionism to a more sane, humane, and ecologically safe world in the future will likely mean reevaluating our most basic assumptions about what constitutes a good life (Robertson, 1985). Echoing an aspect of ecofeminism, one aspect of this reevaluation may involve elevating various forms of "caring labor" — parenting, nurturing, teaching, helping — that have been devalued by our market-driven, expansionist system (Rose, 1983).

The United States has a significant role to play in the pursuit of a sustainable ecological future. At a worldwide climate summit held in Kyoto, Japan, in 1997, many countries put pressure on the United States to agree to an aggressive plan to reduce production of dangerous "greenhouse gases" over the next twenty years. The United States refused to cooperate, saying the plan was not feasible (the U.S. Congress agreed), and said they would come back to the parties with an alternate plan, which they have not as yet done. At the same time, national leaders are reluctant to do anything that might further depress a faltering economy, and while more environmentally friendly business practices are clearly desirable, they can be expensive.

Another factor affecting the future of life on earth is the size and behavior of military forces around the globe, notably in the United States but also in North Korea and the Middle East. The trade-offs involved in maintaining a military-based economy are enormous; the money allocated to developing and manufacturing a single intercontinental ballistic missile in the United States could instead feed 50 million children, build 160,000 schools, or open 340,000 health care clinics (Sivard, 1983). While for a time it appeared that the end of the so-called "Cold War" with the Soviet Union would permit a significant reduction in the size and cost of the U.S. military, other threats have prevented this shift in resources to occur.

Most decisions about ecological issues also involve significant economic and personal trade-offs. The twenty-first century will be marked by increased concern about how our choices will affect the well-being of the planet and ourselves. In one sense, the movement toward sustainability is rooted in systems theory in that both recognize that survival depends on attending to the needs and requirements of the whole. According to Charlene Spretnak (1991),

> The ecologizing of consciousness is far more radical than ideologies and strategies of the existing political forms. They often try to tack ecology onto programs born of instrumental rationality, scientific reductionism, and the modern belief that further advances in the manipulation of nature for human ends will deliver a future filled with peace, freedom, and goodwill. It seems quite unlikely that political versions of democracy that are steeped in these values of modernity [and] that have proven so deficient can serve as the vehicles for transformation . . . into our new relationship with the entire Earth community and our own potential. It is already clear that visionary, political developments lag behind the ecological and spiritual awakening. Increasingly, moral authority lies less in official position than in wisdom, in an experiential sense of the interrelated nature of our reality. (p. 229)

SUMMARY

Successful organizations have strategies. There are two general types of competitive strategy: lowest cost and differentiation. To succeed, a company must select its strategy carefully and then purposefully align its systems and structures to reflect that strategy. Competitive strategies are only as good as how they are communicated. When employees truly understand the big picture, they are most likely to work in ways that support the overall direction of the firm.

Management of human resources has become a highly sophisticated discipline that addresses how companies can best attract and retain talented employees. Targeted selection is the general label for the conscious selection of employees with abilities that support the company strategy. Performance management is the system by which employee accomplishments are measured and discussed. Organizational development and training is made available to employees to support continuous learning. To be successful, a company's human resources function must be well integrated and become part of the corporate culture through its inclusion in regular conversations about results and improvement.

Learning has become the new watchword for organizational effectiveness in the twenty-first century. The world changes so quickly that companies must continually be willing to question their assumptions about reality. Organizations and the people that populate them must continually learn new skills and new technologies. Communication technology serves both to bring additional knowledge to the organization and to permit more and better connections among employees. It is fundamentally changing every aspect of business, including the introduction of e-commerce. At the same time, technology has many unintended consequences for the quality of employees' work life. Simply because a company can do something hardly means that they should. As the power of companies expands due to technology and global reach, we must always remember to make the connection to what matters most, our moral purpose for organizing.

QUESTIONS FOR REVIEW AND DISCUSSION

1. Why is it important to take a "bird's eye" view of an organization in charting its future?

2. What happens to companies that are not consciously positioned in the marketplace, or to those whose employees are unaware of their companies' positioning?

3. Which elements of strategic alignment seem the most challenging, and why?

4. In what ways does the HR department contribute to the successful implementation of company strategy?

5. Which industries seem likely candidates for transformation through the adoption of virtual reality or biotechnology?

6. How can decisions about communication, organizations, and society affect the ecology of our planet?

CASE STUDY I

Advertising and the American Way of Life

According to one study (Jhally, 1998), the average North American is exposed to more than 3,500 advertisements a day. Consider the number of commercial messages that you are bombarded with — everything from media images, Internet "banner ads," billboards, radio jingles, and print ads to designer labels on clothing. One effect of living in a media-rich environment is the increasing lack of public space available for noncommercial messages. Think about important public health information campaigns, antidrug messages, or open expressions of disagreement (or agreement) with public policies or governmental actions. Another effect is the increasingly visceral nature of the images and the content of the advertisements themselves — more naked bodies, louder volumes, more "in-your-face" messages. According to Sut Jhally and his associates at the University of Massachusetts at Amherst, these two effects combine to squeeze out public dialogue about important issues related to global problems, such as the demise of the ecosystem.

Let's assume that you are part of a public interest organization, funded as a nonprofit enterprise, whose task is to come up with strategy for gaining public awareness of the relationship of unmonitored global capitalism and the rapid demise of the rain forests.

ASSIGNMENT

Using what you have read in this chapter about strategy, human resources, and technologies, as well as your experiences and knowledge on the topic, answer these questions:

1. Describe what your business strategy would be, and how that strategy can help you align your resources and technologies to develop a successful campaign.
2. Think about how you would manage such an enterprise. What important questions and issues should you raise about the implementation of your business strategy? What human resources issues can you think of? What technology issues?
3. Using your business strategy as a framework, develop ideas that can be translated into vivid images and powerful messages about the environment and that are capable of gaining the attention of audiences already overexposed to mediated messages. Come up with an advertising campaign capable of maximizing your strategy, resources, and technologies.

CASE STUDY II

Hacked Off

Computer hackers consistently pose threats to Internet users as well as to commercial, public, and governmental computer files and systems. By "hacking into" company or government files or by inserting computer viruses into these systems, hackers can do major harm in a very short period of time. One of the more recent hacking ventures involved the creation of "zombie" computers that flooded Internet sites with junk messages, effectively shutting them down for business for three days. Losses were estimated to be in the tens of millions of dollars.

One of the outcomes of computer hacking has been an increased need for security from such attacks. In an effort to reduce the possibility of internally generated viruses and security breaches, many firms have developed strict policies against employees using e-mail or the Internet for anything other than business reasons. Companies sponsoring such policies often hire specially equipped surveillance outsourcers to monitor the content of company e-mail, thus creating privacy issues for employees. Other companies forbid employees from removing company computers or software from the premises, thus reducing the ability of some employees to work off-site or at home. In an unprecedented case in 1999, a former director of the Central Intelligence Agency was called on the carpet for taking his laptop home because it contained some secret and top secret files. Clearly, the rapid expansion of — and now dependence on — computer technologies in business and government has created unprecedented challenges to the management of organizations.

Balancing the legitimate needs of users with the legitimate rights of an organization to protect itself is a delicate activity. Based on your reading in this chapter as well as your own experiences, how would you go about establishing a fair and equitable policy about the use of technology in the workplace?

ASSIGNMENT

1. How should a business strategy be used to guide the development of a technology policy?
2. In what ways would the 7-S model be useful in helping you develop such a policy?
3. What input should you seek in developing the particulars of such a policy?

(continued)

4. How important do you think the language of the policy will be to its successful implementation?
5. What steps should you take to ensure the successful implementation of the policy?
6. How would you assess the effectiveness of the policy?

PART IV

Applications

CHAPTER 12

Working with Integrity: Organizational Communication as Disciplined Practice

What is the true secret of happiness?
When you are hungry, eat.
When you are tired, sleep.

— ZEN SAYING

How should we think about and prepare for the future? What have you learned from this book and by participating in this course that can be applied to your work? The study of organizational communication theory can be a worthwhile pursuit in and of itself if you plan to become a university professor, but most students choose working lives outside of the academy. For them, the historical, cultural, and theoretical study of organizational communication is useful mainly as "equipment for living" (Burke, 1989), which means that to be of value it should translate easily from theory to practice.

This chapter offers a guide to making this translation. As we said at the outset, it is not our intention to provide a set of "right answers" about organizational communication — since these are always contingent and have a tendency to change — but instead to help you to develop a more *conscious* approach to the choices you make about communicating in organizations, as well as an awareness of the likely consequences of those choices. Put another way, our primary aim is to encourage the practice of "mindfulness" (Goodall & Goodall, 2002) that draws upon what you have learned about communication for the purpose of living and working with integrity. Mindful communication practice offers productive and rewarding ways to balance the desire for individuality and creativity with organizational and social constraints.

Conscious Communication and Mindful Communication Practices

Mindful and Mindless Communication

While many people believe that communication is mostly a conscious activity, studies have demonstrated that this is not the case (for a comprehensive overview, see Langer, 1998; see also Motley, 1992). In fact, communication and cognition researchers believe that most of us behave mindlessly most of the time. This is because we rely on forms of talk that are easy to perform and whose likely outcomes are well known to us.

An advantage of being able to speak mindlessly is that the brain reserves energy for more challenging situations (King & Sawyer, 1998). The disadvantage is the tendency to get "locked into" rigid habits of mind. Physicist and dialogue theorist David Bohm (1980) underscores this tendency in his distinction between thinking and having thoughts. Most of the time, we mindlessly draw upon the stories we have been told throughout our lives to make sense of new situations (i.e., we "have thoughts"). The risk in doing this is that we will misapply what we believe that we know. Alternatively, "thinking" involves genuine reflection on the nature of the situation and a conscious choice of appropriate frameworks. Unlike having thoughts, thinking implies a willingness to listen and be open to beliefs beyond what one already knows. Thinking is crucial in true collaboration and innovation, and is the essence of authentic dialogue (see Chapter 2).

Consider, for example, the following mindless exchange known as *phatic communion:*

> "Hello, how are you?"
> "Fine. And you?"
> "Good. (Pause) So what's new?"
> "Not much. And you?"
> "Same old same old. (Pause) I have to get back to work."
> "Yeah, me too."
> "See you later — "
> "Okay, see you later."

Phatic communion is a form of small talk that helps us appear social and gives the impression that we are interested in others. However, it also shows disregard for each other because nothing that is said really matters to either person. Regular reliance on these kinds of routines may prevent us from finding newer, more interesting, and ultimately more satisfying conversations at work.

Another form of mindless communication uses a *script*. Scripts are routine exchanges of talk delivered in rote fashion, something like reading well-rehearsed lines in a play. We typically use scripts at work when we engage in what we consider to be routine and unimportant interactions, such as selection and performance appraisals; dispute resolution sessions; and everyday conversations (i.e., "shooting the breeze") on well-known subjects with familiar co-workers. Scripts are played out automatically as if our communication is guided by formulas rather than by creative engagement or spontaneity.

We do not deny that all of us engage in phatic communion and scripts at one time or another. Nor do we question the importance of mindless communication much of the time. We are, however, concerned about how effective we become in our work and home lives when we *rely too much* on these forms of mindlessness. Stephen Covey's *The 7 Habits of Highly Effective People* (1990) advocates that to be successful requires becoming more goal-oriented, focused, and strategic in our dealings with others. His prescriptions for success in the workplace prompt us to become more conscious of our communication and more reflective about the outcomes we wish to achieve.

Becoming More Mindful

A mindful approach to organizational communication enables us to understand talk "as a mental and relational activity that is both purposeful and strategic" (Goodall & Goodall, 2002, p. 50).

Elaine Langer (1998) found that when we become more conscious of our communication we become more mindful, and that when we become more mindful we will likely become more ethical as well. We will learn to recognize that we are responsible for our communication goals, our communication choices, and our performance relative to achieving them. We are less apt to act thoughtlessly toward others.

But how can people become more mindful in their communication? Research has shown that we "naturally" become more mindful under the following conditions (Motley, 1992):

- There is a conflict between perceived message goals.
- Undesirable consequences are expected from the use of a particular message strategy.
- There are time delays between messages and mental processing difficulties, such as interpreting the meaning or intention of the message.
- Communication situations are particularly troublesome or unique.

In other words, we naturally become more mindful when we sense potential danger, are confused, or perceive a negative outcome. However, when those things happen we also become more attuned to our surroundings, more alert, and more focused on the situation. We become more creative and rely less on scripts, or at the very least think carefully before selecting a course of action. We become conscious of how we are being perceived and attended to by others and we are more likely to interpret the messages of others meaningfully. To become more mindful in the workplace requires (Goodall & Goodall, 2002):

- Analyzing communication situations and developing strategies for accomplishing goals informed by the organization's culture; power relations among participants; and differences in message interpretation derived from race, ethnicity, and gender.
- Thinking actively about possible communication choices as well as the potential organizational, relational, and personal outcomes of those choices.
- Adapting our messages in a timely and thoughtful manner when we seek to inform, amuse, persuade, or otherwise influence listeners and audiences.
- Evaluating the feedback or responses we receive as an indication of how successful we were in accomplishing our purpose.

Mindful communication requires discipline and everyday practice. It begins when we catch ourselves behaving mindlessly and decide to become more conscious of our interactions. It improves as we find that by not using phatic communion or scripts as much, we see new possibilities in our relationships with others. It provides us with a more ethical foundation for building trust and behaving authentically with others, which, in turn, encourages others to act with greater integrity toward us. And becoming more conscious as a communicator affords us one additional, crucial benefit: It promotes learning.

Conscious Integrity

Integrity is a mindful state of acting purposefully to fulfill the promises you make to others. It is a term that we associate with honesty, openness, commitment, and trust. It is also a term we associate with women and men who consciously make choices about treating others fairly and equitably, and who understand that in today's turbulent business and social environment those who lead have obligations to those who follow them as well as to the bottom line and stockholders.

As we go to press with this new edition of our book we have some excellent examples of people who have done just that. *Time* magazine's "Person of the Year" for 2002 was, for the first time, shared by three brave women: Cynthia Cooper (WorldCom), Coleen Rowley (FBI), and Sherron Watkins (Enron). Each of them "blew the whistle" on unethical or irresponsible actions in her respective organization. Each risked her job and reputation to do what she believed was right for her co-workers and her company's stakeholders. In the case of Watkins, it also meant standing up for the interests of a nation. Each woman made a conscious choice to act in the best interests of others, regardless of the cost to themselves. Because these women were willing and able to speak up, their organizations were given a valuable opportunity to learn from past mistakes and create a better system going forward.

Another person who acted with integrity was Aaron Feuerstein, the owner of Massachusetts fabric maker Malden Mills. He chose to keep his 3,000 employees on the payroll and rebuild his company after a devastating fire that destroyed three company buildings. Feuerstein, the grandson of the founder of the company, said that he never considered shutting the business down after the fire. He believed that his employees deserved to be treated well because without their dedication and hard work the company would not have grown. He made a conscious decision to honor his commitments to them even though it represented a huge personal loss for himself.

Our list could go on, but the point we are making is a simple, yet potentially profound one. Rather than being an abstract aspect of character, integrity is a core business principle that requires mindful, disciplined communication and considerable courage to enact.

New Logics of Organizing

You will recall that in Chapter 7 we discussed "alternatives to hierarchy." Philip Tompkins and Maryanne Wanca-Thibault (2001) provide an interesting and subtle account of the prospects for organizational communication in the future that underscores the importance of thinking through organizational issues in new ways. Their analysis suggests that one major accomplishment of organizational scholars has been the identification of key processes, relationships, issues, and challenges that define the basic facts of work: leadership and followership, structures and networks, the creation and interpretation of messages, communication media and channels for communication. Those basic facts — the basic *grammar* for organizational studies, if you will — are least likely to change.

What *has* changed is the underlying logic of organizing. More specifically, the "old" logic of organizational communication rested solidly on a seemingly bedrock principle that assumed hierarchies of all kinds were "givens." One of the consistent themes in our book has been the need for new, non-hierarchical and empowering ways of thinking about communication in organizations. Another "old" logic that seemed incapable of challenge even a generation ago assumed that the world of work revolved around men — and, in particular, white men. Consider how dramatic the changes to how we think about and perform communication at work have been based on our new understandings of — our new logics for thinking about — diversity in the global workforce. Time and space have collapsed, and new technologies have emerged that facilitate the operation of global organizations. And more than likely, the dominant organizational forms will change again (and likely more than once) in your lifetime.

And how can one prepare for that?

Management as Poetry

One way to become more conscious of alternative logics is to rethink the ways in which we assume distinctions between and among categories. For example, Ian Lennie in *Beyond Management* (1999) suggests that if we understand managing as "that activity of meaningfully organizing ourselves in everyday life" (p. 1) then we ought to consider poetry as fundamental to improving how we accomplish that in organizations. He argues that poetry is a balancing of order and chaos made sensible through interpretations of language, and it is difficult *not* to see that same process of sense making as essential to managing an organization (Whyte, 1996). In so doing, we consciously alter the way we logically organize managerial tasks, seeing them less driven by a literal language and technical rationality and more driven by a language of story and metaphor.

Communication as Discourse, Voice, and Performance

Three new metaphors — "discourse," "voice," and "performance" — are currently at the forefront of organizational thinking (Jablin & Putnam, 2001, p. xii). Each of these terms, when joined with organizational communication, reveals new logics to guide both organizing and organizational research.

Discourse invites us to examine organizations as texts, and to bring to such examinations the well-developed logic of literary and conversation analyses. As we have seen in the Lennie example above, thinking of what we say and do in a literary way opens up new possibilities for finding creative solutions to age-old organizational challenges.

Voice invites us to think of who has the right to speak in organizations and to consider what a "chorus of diverse voices" or "singing solo" may implicate in relation to the logics of power and suppression at work. Here again, by "thinking outside the box" we broaden our understanding by bringing to it a new language of music.

Performance asks us to consider dramatic enactment as a new way of thinking about coordinated activities, storytelling, and collaborative practices in organizations. We can also understand issues of identity as performances of self and teamwork or group work as an ensemble performance (Murphy, 2002). By employing the logic of dramatic enactment to understand life at work, new thinking can be encouraged.

Viewing organizational communication through the lens of these metaphors puts us in a mindful state, makes us more aware of the language we use to represent and evoke organizational experiences, and prepares us for the likely changes in dominant organizational forms in our lives. Becoming more conscious of the language we use to represent and evoke organizational experiences will undoubtedly be a key factor in continuing to learn new ways to solve old problems. Acquiring sensitivity to language, and being able to think with it, only occurs when you are in a mindful state.

Mindfulness, Integrity, and the Experience of Work

In Chapter 8 we detailed the factors that contribute to our experience of work, both inside and outside an organization. We discussed the organizational socialization process and the reasons why living with the tensions and sources of stress at work can lead to ill health, burnout, and a lack of commitment and loyalty to employers. We indicated that learning how to manage stress at work involves identification with the mission and values of the company; active involvement in decision making and feelings of empowerment; and the ability to balance home and work lives. All of these processes benefit from mindfulness and conscious communication.

We have also found it useful to incorporate the wisdom of the Dalai Lama into our thinking about work. In a widely circulated Internet message about achieving "Good Karma" in the new millennium, the Dalai Lama offered some practical advice that we believe is useful to consider. Regardless of your spiritual orientation we feel his insights help put the experience of work into a broader experience of living well. Here are some excerpts from his statement, "Instructions for Life in the New Millennium":

1. Take into account that great love and great achievements involve great risk.
2. When you lose, don't lose the lesson.
3. Follow the 3 *R*'s: *R*espect for the self; *R*espect for others; *R*esponsibility for all of your actions.
4. Not getting what you want is sometimes a wonderful stroke of luck.
5. Learn the rules so you can know how to break them.
6. Don't let a little dispute injure a great relationship.
7. When you realize you made a mistake, take immediate steps to correct it.
8. Spend some time alone each day.
9. Open your arms to change, but don't let go of your values.
10. Remember that silence is sometimes the best answer.
11. Live a good, honorable life. That way, when you get older and think back, you will be able to enjoy it a second time.

12. A loving atmosphere in your home is the foundation for your life.
13. Share your knowledge. It is a way of achieving immortality.
14. Be gentle with the earth.
15. Once a year go someplace you have never seen.
16. Judge your success by what you had to give up in order to get it.

Taken together, these recommendations underscore the importance of positive interpersonal relationships and openness to new experiences and to learning, personal growth, and happiness.

Cultivating Interpersonal Integrity and Relational Mindfulness

In Chapter 9 we discussed interpersonal communication in the workplace. In that chapter we addressed the factor most directly associated with organizational success: your ability to cultivate positive working relationships. Whether your position inside or outside the company involves communicating with customers, clients, patrons, donors, bosses, employees, and/or peers, there is no doubt that interpersonal integrity and relational mindfulness form the core communication competencies in your workplace.

In one sense, this should be fairly easy to do, right? The bottom line for most business relationships is contained in the DWYSYWD formula (Do What You Said You Would Do). In other words, follow through on your interpersonal commitments and make sure your company does the same thing.

However, like the Zen saying at the opening of this chapter suggests, this is easier said than done (we would be willing to bet, for example, that you occasionally stay up even when you are sleepy). Bruce Hyde (1995) asks his students to keep track of their verbal commitments over the course of a week, and to try to honor each one (which he calls "being your word"). Not surprisingly, the students are shocked by how often they fail to follow through on their commitments. In organizations, the question of follow-through is complicated by the fact that things and people change, and expectations for what is really promised by a slogan such as "provide the best customer service possible" can be open to various interpretations. Fortunately, understanding that conscious communication places a strong value on listening to others and trying to adapt your messages to them encourages all of us to become more mindful in our embodiment of organizational values, slogans, and commitments.

It is important to *establish expectations* and to *be mindful of boundaries* for relationships at work (Goodall & Goodall, 2002, pp. 170–172). This means applying what you have learned about organizational cultures as well as interpersonal relationships to your unique work environment. Each organization has evolved standards for communication practices among peers, subordinates, superiors, and customers that newcomers must acquire as part of the organizational socialization process. Learning the expectations and boundary standards will also help you behave ethically in all aspects of your job. Why? Because contrary to popular opinion when it comes to workplace communication, the ends don't justify the means. Behaving ethically means, as Gandhi put it, living with the profound understanding that "means are ends in the making."

Ethical behavior in the workplace is achieved on a solid foundation of core communication values. Communication is, after all, the primary means by which relational ends are attained. For example, in North American business cultures, the organizational values associated with ethical communication practices include (from Harshman & Harshman, 1999, p. 30):

- Trust one another
- Treat each other with respect
- Recognize the value of each individual
- Keep your word
- Tell the truth; be honest with others
- Act with integrity
- Be open to change
- Risk failing in order to get better
- Learn; try new ideas

These values echo the timeless wisdom of the Dalai Lama. See what you think of the relationship between these core ethical values and the National Communication Association's Credo for Ethical Communication (1999):

NCA Credo for Ethical Communication

Questions of right and wrong arise whenever people communicate. Ethical communication is fundamental to responsible thinking, decision-making, and the development of relationships and communities within and across contexts, cultures, channels, and media. Moreover, ethical communication enhances human worth and dignity by fostering truthfulness, fairness, responsibility, personal integrity, and respect for self and others. We believe that unethical communication threatens the quality of all communication and consequently the well-being of individuals and the society in which we live. Therefore, we, the members of the National Communication Association, endorse and are committed to practicing the following principles of ethical communication.

- We advocate truthfulness, accuracy, honesty, and reason as essential to the integrity of communication.
- We endorse freedom of expression, diversity of perspective, and tolerance of dissent to achieve the informed and responsible decision-making fundamental to a civil society.
- We strive to understand and respect other communicators before evaluating and responding to their messages.

- We promote access to communication resources and opportunities as necessary to fulfill human potential and contribute to the well-being of families, communities, and society.
- We promote communication climates of caring and mutual understanding that respect the unique needs and characteristics of individual communicators.
- We condemn communication that degrades individuals and humanity through distortion, intimidation, coercion, and violence and through the expression of intolerance and hatred.
- We are committed to the courageous expression of personal convictions in pursuit of fairness and justice.
- We advocate sharing information, opinions, and feelings when facing significant choices while also respecting privacy and confidentiality.
- We accept responsibility for the short- and long-term consequences for our own communication and expect the same of others.

As we pointed out in Chapter 9, no matter how ethically we behave, we will inevitably encounter conflict. Behaving mindfully, however, can help us think through conflict. From research done by Peter Kellett and Diana Dalton (2000), we learn that conscious communication in times of relational conflict teaches us to ask (and answer) the following questions:

- *Where does the conflict come from?* Who and what is producing the disagreement? Is there a history of disagreements between the communicators?
- *How is the conflict being managed?* Who avoids it, and who wants to engage in it? What goals are sought by the participants?
- *How do other people react to the conflict?* Is it perceived as "something new" or "nothing new"? What negative work-related consequences can be associated with the conflict? What personal consequences follow from it?
- *How does the conflict affect key organizational functions?* How does it influence productivity? How does it influence openness? Honesty? Learning? Dialogue?
- *How does the conflict manifest systemically in other organizational practices?* Are stress levels higher for those with similar conflicts? Are discussions routed around the key participants? Is there a loss of potentially important feedback? Are denial and blaming strategies spread to other conflicts? If the conflict is gender, class, or race based, are other work relationships negatively impacted? If so, how?

In our global business environment, the idea of interpersonal effectiveness extends to global relational communities. The idea of a "global community" necessarily includes diversity, and with it come possibilities for distortion or misunderstanding based on a lack of a common or even a shared language, and vastly different beliefs about appropriate communication, face-saving, self-disclosure, and silence. This means that in addition to mastering the rules, boundaries, and expectations of *our own* organization's culture, it is vital to learn about the rules, boundaries, and expectations for *other nations'* business cultures.

One important idea to help you become more mindful of cultural differences is the distinction between *individualist* and *collectivist* cultures. Individualist cultures, such as the United States, revere the individual person and expect people "to make their own decisions, develop their own opinions, solve their own problems, have their own things, and, in general, learn to view the world from the point of view of the self" (Samovar, Jain, & Porter, 1998, pp. 73–74). Persons from individualist cultures value democratic relationships and distrust status and hierarchy as ways of informing how they should treat each other. By contrast, collectivist cultures, such as the dominant culture of China, revere the common good over self-interest, value group and family identity over individual achievement, and tend to respect vertical status hierarchies. These differences between individualist and collectivist cultures are so deep that they ask us to question our fundamental assumptions about communication. So what should we do to behave more mindfully, more consciously, when communicating in a global relational community?

Arthur Bell and Gary Williams (1999) suggest that mindful communication in a global business environment begins with the coproduction of a "transaction culture":

> When you and your own cultural background come into contact with persons of another culture, something new emerges — a middle ground, called a "transaction culture." In this new middle ground, sensitive and often unstated rules and understandings guide behavior. That is, if a member of Culture A interacts with a member of Culture B, neither the cultural rules of A nor those of B are the sole guide for behavior. Instead a mixed set of rules — middle Culture C — develops for the purposes of interaction. (pp. 452–453)

We discussed in Chapter 9 the nature of gender differences in the workplace, with particular emphasis on problems caused by sexual harassment. Indeed, behaving more mindfully, and communicating more consciously, helps us avoid giving offense to others as well as passively accepting it from others. It reinforces our perceptions of other's needs and sensitivities, and it helps us learn how ask for, and to give, honest and productive feedback.

Thinking Together: Mindful Dialogue in Relationships, Groups, Teams, and Networks

One of the most important lessons of living more mindfully and communicating more consciously at work is the idea of "thinking together" (Bohm, 1996) rather than "having thoughts individually." This is because when we think together we are truly engaging in a dialogic process.

In the West, dialogue is often depicted as a "peak experience" for humans (Goodall & Kellett, in press; Maslow, 1994). This is because it is experienced as a rare event between or among persons born to highly individualistic cultures. Our pride in "thinking for ourselves" is too often manifested as a *fear* of engaging the most intimate, deep, spiritual, or profound thoughts of others. We confuse honest attempts at self-disclosure with a hidden desire to move a relationship to what may be perceived as an inappropriate or unwarranted romantic level. Some of us may also believe that if we listen carefully to what others are really saying, we may be influenced to change our minds, something that people reared to be "self-sufficient" often avoid at any cost. Increasingly, one of the problems of democracy is the fact that too many people are unwilling to engage the ideas of others who differ from them.

Dialogue, as we have repeatedly observed, is based on a profound willingness and ability to engage differences without judgment. But it is also far more than that. It is also a cultivated, conscious ability to value the thoughts, passions, and actions of others who differ from us, and to work with those ideas, feelings, and behaviors in new ways. This is what Bohm means by "thinking together." The point of the mindful engagement of dialogue is to produce thoughts that neither party in a relationship, nor any participant in a group, team, or network, could have produced alone.

As you studied in Chapter 10, the promise of groups, teams, and networks may only be fulfilled if the members of those collectivities learn together, speak and listen together, and move forward in new and creative ways. In order to accomplish such collective, dialogic action, each member must actively *choose to think together and to consciously suspend the judgmental self from the process*. Echoing the words of the Dalai Lama (but with an intentionally different spin), "judge your success by what you had to give up to get it." In this case, what "you had to give up" to become successful was the judgmental self and an over-reliance on mindless communication.

Applying What You've Learned

As communication consultants, one of the best lessons we've learned about wrapping up an intervention is an activity called: "What Will You Do Monday Morning?" Much of what you have read here mirrors what we offer our for-profit and not-for-profit clients, in that we teach them a new vocabulary for addressing their problems and offer them tools for solving them. On Monday morning they return to their old jobs as newly minted organizational communicators, duly armed with new ways of thinking about, and thinking together about, issues as they arise at work.

Before we let them go we ask them to work together on one or more of the following four scenarios. Each scenario — or "caselet" — depicts a typical organizational dilemma and asks them to provide (1) an analysis of the situation based on what they have learned with us, and (2) alternative plans to address or resolve the difficulty. Now that you have been educated to approach organizational life in a uniquely prepared way, we think this exercise will be valuable for you as well.

King Dick

Richard is a senior vice-president of technology for a large multinational firm specializing in athletic sportswear. Richard is a man driven by his own vision of perfection — to be the best at everything he does. This admirable motivation to succeed and competitive spirit has made him a local sports celebrity, with amateur awards and first-place trophies in golf, tennis, hockey, and billiards. It also has been a significant force in his meteoric rise from entry-level computer technician, at twenty-three, to senior vice-president at the still youthful age of thirty-nine.

As he rose in the company, the company invested in him. At first they sponsored trips to management seminars, but as his strong motivation to "be the Man" led him further and further up the corporate ladder, they also provided Richard with access to the world's leading authorities on organizational leadership. Always, whether during retreats or seminars, Richard made a point of being heard, of proving that he was the one who had the answers and should, therefore, be in charge.

Moving up from middle management of computer resources into his first senior level job as Director of Global Networks, he confronted three new challenges. First, he had never operated as the leader of a group or of a network before. However, his track record of success in team sports combined with his stellar ratings in seminars marked him as capable of learning this aspect of his new job quickly. The second challenge was that his position was truly one that required constant contact with clients, customers, and support technicians in India, Ireland, Spain, France, Indonesia, and Mexico. Richard, like many North American men, does not speak any other languages, nor had he traveled extensively to any of those countries. The third challenge is harder to define. Richard is, as we said, a driven man, a competitor, and a consistent winner. He does not handle defeat well, probably because he has experienced it so rarely in his adult life. So when things don't exactly work out the way he planned, he explodes. In one recent meeting of his increasingly quiet, cowering managerial staff, he harshly interrupted a young woman, Tatiana, who was trying to explain why the backup systems failed a recent security test, with the question: "Do you want *me* to solve this problem *for* you? I can solve it, apparently unlike you or your half-witted staff, but I will guarantee you that neither you nor your half-witted staff will *enjoy* my solution. But you will all have to live with it. So, I ask you again, Tat, DO YOU WANT ME TO SOLVE THIS PROBLEM FOR YOU?"

You have been retained by Richard's company as an organizational communication and leadership consultant. Your job is to work with Richard to improve his leadership communication skills. It's Monday morning — what do you do?

Miss Elizabeth

Elizabeth Peters is a woman in her mid-fifties with almost twenty years of seniority in a retail store that is part of a prominent national chain and is located in a suburban shopping mall in the southeastern United States. She is currently an assistant manager of the store after having been repeatedly turned down for promotion to store manager for reasons she associates with a sexist and racist superior in the regional corporate office. Her views of her manager are not shared by anyone who works with her, nor are they shared by his superiors at the corporate office.

Miss Elizabeth, as she demands to be called, is a technically proficient employee with a long list of customers, usually women "of a certain maturity" who can easily afford to spend large sums of money on clothing and accessories in the store. She guards her list of "preferred customers" and regularly hides new shipments from other sales associates so that she can provide them to her own customers. Partly for this reason, she also produces an annual level of sales far superior to anyone else's. A few years ago, when a former manager threatened to let her go because of her "uncooperative attitude," Miss Elizabeth made a few phone calls and had her manager removed instead. She clearly has friends in high places.

She is also a widow who lost her much older insurance broker husband to a heart attack. Prior to losing him the two of them were hailed as community leaders because of their wide-ranging charitable activities and support of the local community theater. In those days, she had been a leading actress who had previously been a beauty queen, and he had been an adoring theater-goer with no wife and deep pockets. When her husband died, she discovered that the life insurance policy he had written on himself barely paid off their splendid house in one of the better parts of town and did not insure a future for her that would be without work. That is when she became an assistant manager, and that is when she used her contacts in the community to build her solid client list.

You have recently assumed the position of manager of the store. A week did not pass before each one of the sales associates had drawn you aside to complain about Miss Elizabeth. At first you sensed a conspiracy among the younger employees to get rid of Miss Elizabeth, and told them that you believed in giving everyone a fair chance to prove herself. In staff meetings for the first month you couldn't help notice that Miss Elizabeth arrived late, left early, and mostly attended to her client list during your talks. When you asked her to perform a routine task, such as changing the clothes on a display or opening the store on a Saturday, she politely but firmly refused, suggesting that "perhaps this is the sort of task that ought to be relegated to someone with less seniority." At first you went along with her because she was, well, significantly older than you, and because she seemed so confident that hers was the better way. This is your first management position and you have been out of college for only two years.

In short order you lose three valuable employees. Each one clearly stated that they were leaving the store because they couldn't put up with Miss Elizabeth any longer. You called the regional corporate office and asked for advice from your mentor, who warned you that Miss Elizabeth was a legendary sales leader and that no matter what, you could not fire her. She advised that you needed to find some other way to solve your personnel problem. It's Monday morning — what do you do?

Phone Rage

You are a customer service representative for a financial group whose clients are brokerage houses. It's a good job and pays well but has a downside. In this case, the downside is a client named Mr. Roberto Santini, Esquire, a senior stockbroker with a law degree and an MBA from Columbia University, a bachelor's from Princeton, and a war record from the Persian Gulf that includes a Silver Star and a Purple Heart. You know all of these things about Mr. Santini because he makes a point of dropping them into his phone conversations as if to repeatedly emphasize his natural superiority over you.

Mr. Santini is also very rich and powerful. His firm's account is vital to the success of your company and his happiness and relative satisfaction with the company is primarily *your* responsibility. Your co-workers often joke that you are, in fact, not a customer service rep, but "Santini's slave." You can't really deny it, but you would like to find a way to work with Mr. Santini on a somewhat more equitable and professional basis. If you can't, chances are very good that you will be forced to leave the company and, in the current economy, finding another job with what would only be a mediocre (if that) reference from your boss is unlikely.

And Santini, *Mr.* Santini, clearly understands this to be the case.

The phone rings, as it always does, ten minutes prior to the opening of your business day. But this is Mr. Santini, and Mr. Santini can call any time of the day or night and it is your job to deal with it.

"Hey *jackass*, you there?" This is Mr. Santini's usual opening gambit. He never calls you by your name.

"Yes, Mr. Santini, I am here. And my name is Li." Inside, you seethe with anger. If your father knew someone talked to you like this, he would find the man and kill him. Which is precisely why you never mention this abuse at home.

"Yeah, *whatever*, jackass. So what do you have for me?" Santini's tone is visceral and bold, without a hint of respect.

So you run the numbers for him, just as you always do. From time to time he interrupts with some abrupt question, but by and large he just listens. Santini listens like other people speak — the absence of voice on his end of the phone feels like the presence of power. After you run the numbers for him, you ask, simply, "Will there be anything else, sir?"

Santini laughs. It is a dry laugh, full of menace. "You sound about the right age to enjoy this, jackass, so here's a fairy tale for you. Consider it a gift. Once upon a time, back when I was a tank commander on the second day of the Gulf War, we spotted a group of retreating enemy soldiers on the other side of a dune. They were scared shitless. So you know what I did?"

"No, Mr. Santini, what did you do?"

"I pointed my cannon at them and gave the order to fire." He paused, and the dry laugh came over the line again.

"Why did you *do* that, if they were retreating?"

"Because they were the enemy and because they were retreating," he said. "I never had any respect for a coward."

"Why are you telling me this?"

"Because, jackass, I think *you* are a coward, too."

There was a click and the line went silent.

You can't afford to lose this job, nor do you feel that you should have to be the one to back down in this situation. At the same time, you feel that you can't take much more of this abuse. After a long weekend of stewing in anger, it's Monday morning — what do you do?

Whistle While You Work?

You are a public relations spokesperson for a major pharmaceutical company located in the northeastern United States. The company has made over-the-counter drugs for relief of headache pain and muscle aches for nearly thirty years. By and large, your relationship with the company has been very positive and you enjoy working as their spokesperson. You have applauded their efforts to provide free drugs to state nursing homes and day-care centers with tight budgets.

But recently something has come up that you feel isn't being handled correctly. Three teams of research scientists, in separate studies funded by this pharmaceutical firm, have discovered that people who take their best-selling pain reliever for prolonged periods of time often have "rebound syndrome," which is what the scientists are calling the propensity of the human brain to lose its natural ability to recognize pain signals as a result of exposure to the active ingredient in the pain reliever. For about a year the senior public relations officials have maneuvered around this issue by suggesting that the studies are "preliminary," and the findings "inconclusive."

But this is not what the research scientist in charge of one of the studies has told you in confidence. And you suspect he told you such sensitive information to impress you because he wants to date you. His claim is that the evidence is overwhelming but that the company is keeping it quiet because this would effectively end sales of this drug and seriously reduce profits for the foreseeable future.

It's Monday morning. What should you do?

Conclusion

Working with integrity is important to the well-being of individuals, organizations, society, and the planet. As we have shown in this concluding chapter, working with integrity means refusing to rely on old scripts and making informed choices about how you think, communicate, and act.

Working with integrity is primarily enabled by your willingness to learn how to think together and to discipline yourself to the habits and practices of mindful communication. In this way, working with integrity asks you to apply the lessons of balancing creativity and constraint through dialogue. It asks you to respect others and to respect yourself, to reach out to others while standing your ground. It asks you to live and work honorably, by accepting full responsibility for not only what you say and do, but for your human connection to the world outside your room and to people whom you have never met who nevertheless are now — and will always continue to be — affected by the choices you make, the decisions you reach, the words and actions you offer to the world.

Thank you for allowing us into your reading life. Thank you for inviting us into your ongoing conversation about communication, organizations, and the future we will make out of them.

A Field Guide to Studying Organizational Communication

Many students enrolled in an organizational communication course are required to write a term paper. Usually, the paper involves applying concepts from the course to ongoing communication processes within an organization. In most cases, when presented with the requirement to write a paper of this sort, students ask for more specific guidelines — the practical how-tos — of studying organizational communication.

For this reason, we have prepared the following practical field guide to studying organizational communication. The use of the term *field guide* is intended to evoke an *ethnographic* approach to collecting data, analyzing it, and writing the paper. (For an extended discussion, see Goodall, 2000.) An ethnographic approach uses

- *Naturalistic observation* of everyday communication episodes and events as the primary source of data
- *Participant-observer interaction and interviews* to collect stories, accounts, and explanations for the events and episodes observed
- *A critical/historical framework* for developing key questions, problems, and issues to pursue through observations and interactions with employees
- *A narrative format* for describing and analyzing the data

In short, what we describe is a way of doing field research in an organization for the purpose of finding and telling the story of one or more of its everyday communication practices.

Finding an Organization to Study

One of the axioms of organizational ethnography is that you must "*know* where you are" (Goodall, 1994, p. 176). This means (in academic-speak) that all knowledge is *contextually derived*; it also means that it is a good idea to study an organization within the community in which you live. Why? Because chances are pretty good that access to the organization will be easier to acquire (e.g., friends and family members may work there, you may have had summer employment or an internship there, you may know someone who knows someone, etc.). Additionally, you will probably have a basic understanding of the history and role of the organization within the community, which will come in handy when you write the paper. If you are not a local and don't have personal contacts that can provide access to the organization for the purpose of conducting a communication study, ask your instructor for advice and guidance.

Approaching an organization for the purpose of doing a study is always problematic. Many for-profit companies and government agencies strictly limit access to employees and usually have no interest in allowing students from the local college or university to hang around observing people, interviewing employees and managers, and otherwise disrupting their work. Some companies even have regulations against it — and no company or agency is required to let you inside.

For these reasons, it is a good idea to develop a professional relationship with the organization you want to study before requesting permission to do a communication study. The more the people you contact trust you, the more they learn to see you as a serious person, the more likely it is that they will cooperate with your goals. To facilitate your professional relationship, we recommend the following:

- Write a one-page proposal detailing the purpose and time frame for your study, the methods of data collection that you plan to use, and the anticipated results. Your instructor can provide you with examples from prior student projects.
- Offer to provide the organization with a copy of your final paper. Agree that nothing you discover or write about will be disseminated to the public without prior written approval by the company.
- Always arrive at any appointment on time, dressed in a professional manner appropriate to the standards of the organization you want to study, with a prepared list of questions to ask and a way of recording or keeping notes of the interview.
- Never directly interfere with ongoing organizational work. Make your observations as unobtrusively as possible; schedule interviews for times convenient for the interviewees.

Framing Your Study

To write a proposal for the study, you will first need to develop a research question and ground your study in the current research literature. These writing processes are called "framing a study" because, like placing a photograph within an appropriate frame, they allow you to place your *story* within a larger academic or professional *narrative*.

There are three major resources for locating information that might help you frame a study. First, as a student, you are part of a college or university that has resident experts in just about every aspect of life. Locate an instructor with research expertise in the general area that interests you. Arrange to interview her or him to find out what the current thinking is on the general topic you have selected. Be sure to ask what the two or three best articles are on the subject, and then go to your library and check them out. For example, let's assume you want to study the specific organizational practices associated with building and maintaining a learning organization. Chances are good that someone in the communication department or the business school will be able to help you find resources to frame a study of a learning organization.

The second resource is the library. Using the references provided in this book — as well as any additional ones provided by your instructor and local university experts in the subject area — you should be able to conduct library research on most topics relevant to organizational communication. If the library research process is unclear to you, contact your library for information about the research librarian most able to assist you with finding information about your topic.

A third resource is the Internet. By accessing on-line search engines like ProQuest and typing keywords, you can search a variety of databases for information. You may also join an Internet-based chat room or bulletin board where your topic is being discussed. Professional academic organizations typically sponsor such Internet activities and research sites. We recommend beginning your search by visiting the American Communication Association research site <http://www.americancomm.org/> or the National Communication Association research site <http://www.natcom.org>. You may also find relevant information by checking out the home pages of organizational communication scholars, who sometimes provide links to rich research resources relevant to their specialties.

After reading the available research on the general topic you plan to pursue, you should be able to articulate some of the questions that are of concern to scholars and professionals. Adapt these questions to the organization you plan to study and to the purpose of your paper.

Framing your study *before* you enter the organization for observations and interviews provides you with an important way to limit what you are looking at and asking questions about. You have to know what you are looking for in order to find it. However, as any ethnographer will tell you, surprises and setbacks will occur. You may find that the initial research question you posed doesn't really get at the meaning of the interactions you observe and participate in, or you may discover that you cannot complete all of the interviews you had planned. These are not necessarily problems, but they may be challenges. You may need to modify your research question. Settle for fewer interviews. Find other people to talk to. You may even need to reframe your study in light of what you find is *really* happening.

Ten Assumptions about Doing Field Research[1]

Organizational field researchers are interested in telling the stories that make up everyday organizational life. As such, they rarely are interested in issues typically associated with managerial notions of efficiency. For example, rather than asking how a particular routine can be streamlined or reengineered to improve the efficiency of an operation, field research asks how that particular routine came to be a routine and what it requires (mentally, morally, physically, culturally) of a person or group to accomplish it. Other characteristics of field research include:

1. Field research is *qualitative* in nature. The quality of it is largely dependent upon the insights discovered by the researcher. By contrast, many worthwhile organizational studies are *quantitative*, which means that they derive their conclusions from facts that are amenable to statistical tabulation and analysis. Field research, being qualitative, derives insights from close observation of actual, ongoing, communication processes. Conclusions are generalizable; insights are contextual.
2. Field research begins from theoretical assumptions and conceptual underpinnings but is more generally dedicated to providing documentation for the *moral and ethical* knowledge of working. For this reason, many contemporary ethnographic studies of organizations focus on issues of power and strategic control, as well as on race, age, and gender.
3. Field research assumes that every organization is as unique as an individual human fingerprint. One way to think about this is that people are

[1]Some of the material contained in this section is adapted from a working paper developed by Michael E. Pacanowsky, "An Idiosyncratic Compilation of the Twenty-Seven Do's and Don'ts of Organizational Culture Research," unpublished paper, Department of Communication, University of Utah, 1986.

not understood as "types," and activities and practices are not reducible to "behaviors."

4. What people at work *say* and *do* are the substance of who they are (at work) and what your study should be about. By comparison, think of what you are studying as an exercise in observing and documenting a television sitcom about work. What is the setting? Who are the characters? Where do they come from? What are their dreams? What do they think about their jobs? About each other? What do they talk about? What clothes do they wear? And so on. You might want to practice your skills by observing and analyzing just such a television show.

5. Remember that you won't be watching a television show when you enter an organization. These aren't actors performing rehearsed scripts written by someone else. That is a major difference, and one that ultimately matters. You are studying ongoing life — *real* life. In real-life studies, expect a lot of empty spaces between the meaningful interactions. Don't expect conflicts to be solved in thirty minutes or less. People won't be as funny as they are on television, nor are they working out a predetermined theme. The theme, the thing you are studying, the story you are trying to find and tell about, emerges gradually from disparate places and people. *You* are the scriptwriter.

6. Don't neglect the places — the *contexts* — and their influences over the interaction. As Marshall Sahlins, a famous anthropologist, once put it, "A culture is the meaningful order of persons and things." Don't forget to observe *things*. Describe them. Ask people to comment on their meanings, *here*.

7. There is no such thing as "an organization." In real life, there are only "organization*s*," which means that every person you observe and talk to will have a slightly different take on what "reality" is. The farther you move away from a particular group of people who interact regularly and have tacitly agreed to see reality in similar ways, the more different and complex "reality" becomes.

8. You aren't going to find any one truth. At best, you will find many copresent and conflicting truths. That is why field researchers learn to think (and write) about life as a "plural present" (Goodall, 1991a, p. 320). If you doubt this statement, ask the same question three levels up the organization's ladder from where you are locating your study, and then three levels below it.

9. You are studying the *particulars* of human actions. Pay close attention to details. Nuances of speaking, of gesturing, of touching, of *not* saying something, all count. You are looking at what is said and done, what is given or foregrounded, but you are searching for what is unspoken, not done, withheld, and in the background, in the depths of shadows only the actors know.

10. Write down *everything* you observe and hear. You never know what will end up being important. Tape-record or videotape what you are allowed to record. Write out your notes and transcriptions the same day you take them (or else you lose 83 percent of the meaning), and write them out in story format. That is how, when, and where you will ultimately find the story line.

How to Study Naturalistic Communication in an Organization: A Basic Process Outline with Commentary[2]

We have found that it is very useful to instruct students to take field notes on their observations, interviews, conversations, and personal reflections on the meanings of people at work. Taking field notes is akin to keeping a diary, but instead of writing about your family and your love life, you write about your working life. In a notebook or on your computer, describe the events of your day, make theoretical and practical connections to what you are reading and thinking about, and try to use the writing process to help you figure out how to connect the dots that gradually emerge from your study.

To help you take field notes, here is a list of people and things, activities, symbols, and events that occur and have some meaning in most organizations. This list may help you isolate field note entries and organize your research.

- Begin in the parking lot. Begin early. Watch the cars file in, and note where they park. Make notes on the kinds of vehicles that individuals drive. At lunchtime, observe who drives the gang from work, and where they go. If possible, join in on their lunch conversations. Watch when they leave work in the afternoon or late evening. Who leaves last? Why?
- Phone the public relations department, and ask for a company tour. Explain that you are doing research on similar types of companies in the area. Listen carefully to what the official version of the company is during the tour, and collect as much written documentation as possible. These resources will become important to you later.

---

[2]The following outline will not apply equally to all organizations or be appropriate for all classes in organizational communication. Some advisories provided here will fit the place you want to study; some won't. We recommend limiting your study to a particular work group, team, or department, but your instructor may want a larger-scale study. Depending on your instructor's preferences, you may also want to conduct a quantitative study, in which case all of the information in this appendix may help you create material from which you develop hypotheses to test via surveys or experiments.

- Research the financial standing of the company if it is publicly held. How is it doing? How does it compare to other companies in the industry? Do a keyword search for the local newspapers in your library to see what kinds of stories have appeared about the company and about its people in the past year or so. These details can become useful as a way of understanding the evolving context of the interaction.
- Make a chart of all the people (or the department) you plan to include in your study, and note their organizational relationships to one another. Ask yourself how your understanding of organizational hierarchies may inform what you are observing.

Using what you have read in this book about classical theories of organization and communication, what kind of organization would you say this is? Do you see Frederick Taylor or Abraham Maslow lurking about? Is this more like a Theory X or a Theory Y company? Are elements of all of the classical theories evident here? If not, why not? If so, what does this suggest to you about theories of organizing or about this place?

Now think about this group or department as a system or as part of a system. Draw or describe the group's interactions accordingly. Think about the organization of feedback among members of the group. Think about access to and distribution of information. Listen to their accounts of "how things are around here," and see if Karl Weick's "retrospective sense making" helps you understand them. Keep applying ideas from what you read to what you are seeing, hearing, and attending to.

Now do the same sort of thing with your knowledge of organizational cultures, by assuming that these people are part of a culture. They *are* part of a culture, so this shouldn't be too difficult.

Ask questions about leadership and power. Who is in charge here — *really* in charge? How do you know that? What is it about this person's communication, manner, style, or attitude that conveys this to the people here? Perhaps there is no one leader. How is leadership shared? What does that mean, in terms of exchanges of talk, every day? In either case, how are individuals' control needs being met? How are they negotiated? What conflicts exist? How do you know this? What happens to inform your evaluations and your judgments?

- Using what you have learned about the study of power, how would you describe its uses and abuses in this locale? Is power linked to gender? To race? To age? To beauty? Are there different forms and expressions of power? Is power related to expertise? If so, how? If not, what is it related to?
- Given that all organizations exist within a global economic structure and have dealt with issues of reorganization, downsizing, team-based organizing, flattening hierarchies, information technologies, and other concepts associated with the rise of the postmodern, what *stories* are told

here about all of that? Are there heroes and heroines? Villains? Legendary mistakes? Bits of good fortune? What do these people talk about when they talk about the future? Are there active company training programs? What do people say about them? Are they preparing for a lifetime of employment with this company?

- You want to find as much as you can about each individual's personal experience of work. Review the material in Chapter 7, and then see what you can observe, discover, or otherwise find out about the organizational socialization process, about signs of organizational identification, satisfaction, and burnout. What stressors do people routinely deal with? How do they deal with them? Is there any difference between what they say and what you observe? What can this mean?

- What are the relational contexts for communication among this group or in this department? What has your reading about communicating with superiors, subordinates, and peers taught you to look for? How do members of this group or department gain compliance? Set goals? Establish and maintain equity in everyday conversations? How are employees from different national or ethnic cultures treated? Are there accounts of sexual harassment? What is the company's "official policy" about dating co-workers or managers? Are there stories that support the policy or that contradict it? What about workplace romance? Can you examine office humor, cartoons that are displayed on desks, or graffiti in restrooms for evidence of the "unique sense of place" here?

- How are work groups, teams, and networks organized in this organization? What systems of problem solving and decision making are employed? What is the influence of information technology on their operation and functions? What have you learned from reading about groups, teams, and networks that seems to apply directly to what happens here? What doesn't apply? For example, do you find evidence for the concept of team learning or interorganizational networks?

- You want to attune yourself to the ways in which the overall vision, mission, and core values of the organization play out in everyday discourse and interactions. Are the workers familiar enough with the organization's vision, mission, and values to talk openly about them? Do they try to consciously apply them to their everyday work habits? Where are the deviations? Why are there deviations? Are the deviations a sign of resistance or perhaps only of ignorance? How does this group or department handle crises? How do individual members' identities figure into the image of the firm? Trace the uses of technology in this organization. Are there stories about the introduction of new technologies? What lessons were learned about technology that are practiced today? How are the members of this department preparing themselves for continuing demands for technological skill and knowledge? How has the availability of laptop computers, cell phones, pagers, and the like changed their working and personal lives? How do they feel about this?

- What is the role of communication consulting and training in this group or department? Is there an overall company plan for training and development, or is it left up to the individual workers? What kinds of issues or problems are managed by the group or department, and what kinds of issues or problems require the assistance of a professional consultant? How satisfied are the employees with past consulting interventions? What stories do they tell? How do the members describe the future of this company or agency? Do their metaphors suggest particular scenarios?

- Remember, you are studying everyday communication in this organization. How are you defining *communication* for the purposes of your study? What counts as communication? What doesn't? How valuable is our definition in your study? Can you see communication as the moment-to-moment working out of the tensions between individuals' desire for creativity and the organization's need for constraint (order)? When you examine your field notes with this definition in mind, what is accounted for? What is left out?

- If you are still having trouble deciding how to tell this story, go back over your notes and look carefully at the metaphors used by employees and managers. Many organizational scholars believe that people live and interpret their lives through the linguistic lenses of their daily metaphors. What metaphors do you find in their talk? What metaphors do you see in their actions and activities? What does the presence of these particular metaphors suggest are their binary opposites? Are the binary opposites places where you can also make sense of the unsaid, the unspoken, the covered up, or the neglected?

- When you write your account, include as many particulars — reports of conversations and observations of actions, clothes, cars, and gestures — as you can. These are your primary sources of evidence for the case that you are making. Remember that it is a case that *you* are making. You are ultimately responsible for what you say. Your views will not necessarily be the views of the people you have observed, of your instructor, or of this textbook. Write what you have lived through, what you have experienced, in the course of doing your research.

- Make sure you follow the style guide (APA, MLA, Chicago, Turabian, etc.) appropriate to your instructor's requirements.

Typical Organization of a Paper Based on Field Study Methods

Research reports typically follow an established pattern. Below we offer one you can use to organize your paper.

Title page
   Title of the paper
   Your name, class, and instructor
   Date
   Academic integrity statement (optional)

Abstract
   Brief description of the purposes of the study and its conclusions

Introduction
   Narrative orientation to the company, team, or department studied
   Statement about the specific purpose of the study
   Literature review (focusing on the specific topic area)
   Research questions
   Description of method chosen to answer the questions

Body
   Narrative account of the organization's communication organized *linearly* over time from initial observations through final conclusions and *topically* by communication issue or question raised
   Analysis and interpretation of the field study via research questions

Conclusion
   Review of the study, purpose, method, and major insights
   Link or contribution of this study to current literature on the topic
   Conclusion and suggestions for future research

References

Good luck! Studying and writing about organizations and communication can be an interesting and rewarding activity. It allows you to really work with concepts, apply them to ongoing processes of communicating and organizing, and find meaning in otherwise everyday occurrences. It will enrich your educational experience.

References

Adams, J. (1980). Interorganizational processes and organizational boundary activities. In L. L. Cummings & B. Staw (Eds.), *Research in organizational behavior* (Vol. 2, pp. 321–355). Greenwich, CT: JAI Press.

Adorno, T., & Horkheimer, M. (1972). *Dialectic of enlightenment*. New York: Herder and Herder.

Ahrne, G. (1990). *Agency and organization*. London: Sage.

Albrecht, K. (1992). *The only thing that matters: Bringing the power of the customer into the center of your business*. New York: HarperBusiness.

Albrecht, T., & Adelman, M. (1987). *Communicating social support*. Beverly Hills, CA: Sage.

Albrecht, T., & Hall, B. (1991). Facilitating talk about new ideas: The role of personal relationships in organizational innovation. *Communication Monographs, 58*, 273–288.

Allen, B. (2000). "Learning the ropes": A Black feminist standpoint analysis. In P. Buzzanell (Ed.), *Rethinking organizational & managerial communication from feminist perspectives* (pp. 177–208). Thousand Oaks, CA: Sage.

Altman, S., Valenzi, E., & Hodgetts, R. (1985). *Organizational behavior: Theory and practice*. New York: Academic Press.

Alvesson, M. (1993). *Cultural perspectives on organizations*. New York: Cambridge University Press.

Anderson, J. (1987). *Communication research: Issues and methods*. New York: McGraw-Hill.

Anderson, R., Cissna, K., & Arnett, R. (1994). *The reach of dialogue*. Cresskill, NJ: Hampton Press.

Argyris, C. (1957). *Personality and organization*. New York: Harper & Row.

Argyris, C., & Schon, D. (1978). *Organizational learning: A theory of action perspective*. Reading, MA: Addison-Wesley.

Arquilla, J., & Ronfeldt, D. (1997). *In Athena's camp: Preparing for conflict in the Information Age*. Santa Monica, CA: Rand Corporation.

Arquilla, J., & Ronfeldt, D. (2001). *Networks and netwars: The future of terror, crime, and militancy*. Santa Monica, CA: Rand Corporation.

Ashcraft, K. (2000). Empowering "professional" relationships: Organizational communication meets feminist practice. *Management Communication Quarterly, 13*, 347–392.

Ashcraft, K., & Pacanowsky, M. (1996). "A woman's worst enemy": Reflections on a narrative of organizational life and female identity. *Journal of Applied Communication Research, 24*, 217–239.

Ashford, S., & Cummings, L. (1983). Feedback as an individual resource: Personal strategies of creating information. *Organizational Behavior and Human Performance, 32*, 370–398.

Ashforth, B., & Kreiner, G. (1999). How can you do it? Dirty work and the challenge of constructing a positive identity. *Academy of Management Review, 24,* 413–434.

Atkouf, O. (1992). Management and theories of organizations in the 1990's: Toward a critical radical humanism? *Academy of Management Review, 17,* 407–431.

Atwood, M. (1990). *Adolescent socialization into work environments.* Unpublished master's thesis, University of Southern California, Los Angeles.

Axley, S. (1984). Managerial and organizational communication in terms of the conduit metaphor. *Academy of Management Review, 9,* 428–437.

Baba, M. (1999). Dangerous liaisons: Trust, distrust, and information technology in American work organizations. *Human Organization, 58*(3).

Baker, B. (1991, October 6). Safety risks: The price of productivity. *Los Angeles Times,* pp. 35–36.

Bakhtin, M. (1981). *The dialogic imagination* (C. Emerson & M. Holquist, Trans.). Austin: University of Texas Press.

Bakhtin, M. (1986). *Speech genres and other late essays* (C. Emerson, Trans.). Minneapolis: University of Minnesota Press.

Bales, K. (2000). *Disposable people.* Berkeley: University of California Press.

Banta, M. (1993). *Taylored lives: Narrative productions in the age of Taylor, Veblen, and Ford.* Chicago: University of Chicago Press.

Bantz, C. (1993). *Understanding organizations: Interpreting organizational communication cultures.* Columbia: University of South Carolina Press.

Barabasi, A. (2002). *Linked: The new science of networks.* Cambridge, MA: Perseus.

Barge, K., & Little, M. (2002). Dialogical wisdom, communicative practice, and organizational life. *Communication Theory, 12*(4), 375–397.

Barker, J., & Tompkins, P. (1994). Identification in the self-managing organization: Characteristics of target and tenure. *Human Communication Research, 21,* 223–240.

Barley, S. (1983). Semiotics and the study of occupational and organizational culture. *Administrative Science Quarterly, 23,* 393–413.

Barnard, C. (1968). *The functions of the executive.* Cambridge, MA: Harvard University Press. (Original work published 1938)

Barnet, R., & Cavanagh, J. (1994). *Global dreams.* New York: Simon & Schuster.

Barnlund, D. (1994). *Communicative styles of Japanese and Americans.* Belmont, CA: Wadsworth.

Barrett, F. (1998). Creativity and improvisation in jazz and organizations: Implications for organizational learning. *Organizational Science, 9,* 605–622.

Barry, D., & Elmes, M. (1997). Strategy retold: Toward a narrative view of strategic discourse. *Academy of Management Review, 22,* 429–452.

Bartlett, C., & Ghoshal, S. (1994, November–December). Changing the role of top management: Beyond strategy to purpose. *Harvard Business Review,* 79–88.

Bastien, D., & Hostager, T. (1988). Jazz as a process of organizational innovation. *Communication Research, 15,* 582–602.

Bateson, G. (1972). *Steps to an ecology of mind.* New York: Ballantine.

Bauer, T., & Green, S. (1996). Development of leader member exchange: A longitudinal test. *Academy of Management Journal, 39,* 1538–1567.

Baxter, L. A., & DeGooyer, D. H., Jr. (2001). Perceived aesthetic characteristics of interpersonal conversations. *Southern Communication Journal, 67,* 1–18.

Baxter, L. A., & Montgomery, B. (1996). *Relating: Dialogues and dialectics.* New York: Guilford.

Bell, A. H., & Williams, G. G. (1999). *Intercultural business.* Hauppauge, NY: Barron's.

Bellah, R., Madsen, R., Sullivan, W., Swidler, A., & Tipton, S. (1985). *Habits of the heart.* Berkeley: University of California Press.

Bell-Detienne, K. (1992). *The control factor: An empirical investigation of employees' reaction to control in an organizational work environment.* Unpublished doctoral dissertation, University of Southern California, Los Angeles.

Bendix, R. (1956). *Work and authority in industry.* New York: Wiley.

Benne, K., & Sheats, P. (1948). Functional roles of group members. *Journal of Social Issues, 4,* 41–49.

Bennis, W., & Nanus, B. (1985). *Leaders: Strategies for taking charge.* New York: Harper & Row.

Berger, P., & Luckmann, T. (1967). *The social construction of reality.* Garden City, NY: Anchor.

Berlo, D. (1960). *The process of communication.* New York: Holt, Rinehart & Winston.

Bhabha, H. (1990). Dissemination: Time, narrative, and the modern nation. In H. Bhabha (Ed.), *Nation and narration* (pp. 291–322). London: Routledge.

Bingham, S. (1991). Communication strategies for managing sexual harassment in organizations: Understanding message options and their effects. *Journal of Applied Communication Research, 19,* 88–115.

Blair, C., Brown, J., & Baxter, L. (1995). Disciplining the feminine. *Quarterly Journal of Speech, 81,* 1–24.

Blake, R., & Mouton, J. (1964). *The managerial grid.* Houston: Gulf.

Block, P. (1993). *Stewardship.* San Francisco: Berrett-Koehler.

Blumer, H. (1969). *Symbolic interactionism: Perspective and method.* Englewood Cliffs, NJ: Prentice-Hall.

Bochner, A. (1982). The functions of human communication in interpersonal bonding. In C. Arnold & J. Waite-Bowser (Eds.), *Handbook of rhetorical and communication theory* (pp. 544–621). Boston: Allyn and Bacon.

Bohm, D. (1980). *Wholeness and the implicate order.* London: Ark.

Bohm, D. (1996). *On dialogue.* New York: Routledge.

Boje, D. (1991). The storytelling organization: A study of story performance in an office-supply firm. *Administrative Science Quarterly, 36,* 106–126.

Boje, D. (1995). Stories of the storytelling organization: A postmodern analysis of Disney in "Tamara-Land." *Academy of Management Journal, 38,* 997–1035.

Boland, R., & Hoffman, R. (1983). Humor in a machine shop. In L. Pondy, P. Frost, G. Morgan, & T. Dandridge (Eds.), *Organizational symbolism* (pp. 187–198). Greenwich, CT: JAI Press.

Brandenburger, A., & Nalebuff, B. (1996). *Co-opetition.* New York: Doubleday.

Brass, D. (1984). Being in the right place: A structural analysis of individual influence in an organization. *Administrative Science Quarterly, 29,* 518–539.

Braverman, H. (1974). *Labor and monopoly capital: The degradation of work in the twentieth century.* New York: Monthly Review Press.

Brett, J. M., & Okumura, T. (1998). Inter- and intracultural negotiation: U.S. and Japanese negotiators. *Academy of Management Journal, 41,* 495–510.

Browning, L. (1992a). Lists and stories as organizational communication. *Communication Theory, 2,* 281–302.

Browning, L. (1992b, May). *Reasons for success at Motorola.* Paper presented at the applied communication pre-conference of the International Communication Association, Miami.

Browning, L., & Shetler, J. (2000). *Sematech: Saving the U.S. semiconductor industry.* College Station: Texas A & M University Press.

Brzezinski, M. (2002, June 23). The re-engineering of the drug business. *New York Times Magazine,* pp. 24–29, 46, 54–55.

Buckley, W. (1967). *Sociology and modern systems theory.* Englewood Cliffs, NJ: Prentice-Hall.

Bullis, C. (1999). Forum on organizational socialization research. *Communication Monographs, 66,* 368–373.

Bullis, C., & Bach, B. (1989). Socialization turning points: An examination of change in organizational identification. *Western Journal of Speech Communication, 53,* 273–293.

Bullis, C., & Glaser, H. (1992). Bureaucratic discourse and the Goddess: Towards an ecofeminist critique and rearticulation. *Journal of Organizational Change Management, 5,* 50–60.

Bullis, C., & Stout, K. R. (2000). Organizational socialization: A feminist standpoint approach. In P. Buzzanell (Ed.), *Rethinking organizational & managerial communication from feminist perspectives* (pp. 47–75). Thousand Oaks, CA: Sage.

Bullis, C., & Tompkins, P. (1989). The forest ranger revisited: A study of control practices and identification. *Communication Monographs, 56,* 287–306.

Burke, K. (1966). *Language as symbolic action.* Berkeley: University of California Press.

Burke, K. (1969). *A rhetoric of motives.* Berkeley: University of California Press.

Burke, K. (1989). *On symbols and society.* Chicago: University of Chicago Press.

Burke, R., Weir, T., & Duwors, R., Jr. (1979). Type A behavior of administrators and wives' reports of marital satisfaction and well-being. *Journal of Applied Psychology, 64,* 57–65.

Burrell, G. (1988). Modernism, postmodernism, and organizational analysis 2: The contribution of Michel Foucault. *Organization Studies, 9,* 221–235.

Burrell, N. A., Buzzanell, P., & McMillan, J. (1992). Feminine tensions in conflict situations as revealed by metaphoric analyses. *Management Communication Quarterly, 6,* 115–149.

Buzzanell, P. (2000a). Dialoguing. . . . In P. Buzzanell (Ed.), *Rethinking organizational & managerial communication from feminist perspectives* (pp. 257–264). Thousand Oaks, CA: Sage.

Buzzanell, P. (2000b). The promise and practice of the new career and social contract: Illusions exposed and suggestions for reform. In P. Buzzanell (Ed.), *Rethinking organizational & managerial communication from feminist perspectives* (pp. 209–235). Thousand Oaks, CA: Sage.

Buzzanell, P. (2000c). *Rethinking organizational & managerial communication from feminist perspectives* (pp. 3–23). Thousand Oaks, CA: Sage.

Calas, M., & Smircich, L. (1996). From "the woman's" point of view: Feminist approaches to organization studies. In S. Clegg, C. Hardy, & W. Nord (Eds.), *Handbook of organization studies* (pp. 218–257). London: Sage.

Calder, B. (1977). An attribution theory of leadership. In B. Staw & G. Salancik (Eds.), *New directions in organizational behavior.* Chicago: St. Clair Press.

Calvert, L., & Ramsey, V. (1992). Bringing women's voices to research on women in management: A feminist perspective. *Journal of Management Inquiry, 1,* 79–88.

Campbell, J., & Campbell, R. (1988). *Productivity in organizations.* San Francisco: Jossey-Bass.

Carbaugh, D. (1995). *Are Americans really superficial? Notes on Finnish and American cultures in linguistic action.* Unpublished manuscript, University of Massachusetts, Amherst.

Carey, J. (1992). *Sexual harassment in the workplace.* New York: Practicing Law Institute.

Carlone, D., & Taylor, B. (1998). Organizational communication and cultural studies. *Communication Theory, 8,* 337–367.

Cartwright, D. (1977). Risk taking by individuals and groups: An assessment of research employing choice dilemmas. *Journal of Personality and Social Psychology, 85,* 361–378.

Cavallo, K., & Brienza, D. (2001). Emotional competence and leadership excellence at Johnson & Johnson. Message posted to <http://www.eiconsortium.org>.

Chandler, C., & Ingrassia, P. (1991, April 11). Shifting gears. *Wall Street Journal,* p. 1.

Cheney, G. (1983). The rhetoric of identification and the study of organizational communication. *Quarterly Journal of Speech, 69,* 143–158.

Cheney, G. (1995). Democracy in the workplace: Theory and practice from the perspective of communication. *Journal of Applied Communication Research, 23,* 167–200.

Chiles, A., & Zorn, T. (1995). Empowerment in organizations: Employees' perceptions of the influences on empowerment. *Journal of Applied Communication Research, 23,* 1–25.

Clair, R. (1993). The use of framing devices to sequester organizational narratives: Hegemony and harassment. *Communication Monographs, 60,* 113–136.

Clair, R. (1996). The political nature of the colloquialism "a real job": Implications for organizational socialization. *Communication Monographs, 63,* 249–267.

Clair, R. (1998). *Organizing silence: A world of possibilities.* Albany, NY: SUNY Press.

Clegg, S. (1989). *Frameworks of power.* Newbury Park, CA: Sage.

Clegg, S. (1990). *Modern organizations.* Newbury Park, CA: Sage.

Cleveland, J., & McNamara, K. (1996). Understanding sexual harassment. In M. Stockdale (Ed.), *Sexual harassment in the workplace* (pp. 217–240). Newbury Park, CA: Sage.

Clifford, J. (1992). Traveling cultures. In L. Grossberg, C. Nelson, & P. Treichler (Eds.), *Cultural studies* (pp. 96–116). New York: Routledge.

Clifford, J., & Marcus, G. (1985). *Writing culture: The poetics and politics of ethnography.* Berkeley: University of California Press.

Cohen, H. (1985). The development of research in speech communication: An historical perspective. In T. Benson (Ed.), *Speech communication in the 20th century* (pp. 282–298). Carbondale: Southern Illinois University Press.

Cohen, R. (2002, September 22). Discounting teens. *New York Times Magazine,* p. 26.

Collins, J., & Porras, J. (1994). *Built to last: Successful habits of visionary companies.* New York: HarperCollins.

Collins, J., & Porras, J. (1996). Building your company's vision. *Harvard Business Review, 74,* 65–78.

Conger, J., & Kanungo, R. (1988). The empowerment process: Integrating theory and practice. *Academy of Management Review, 13,* 471–482.

Conlin, M. (1999, September 20). 9 to 5 isn't working anymore. *Business Week, 94,* 98.

Conquergood, D. (1991). Rethinking ethnography: Towards a critical cultural politics. *Communication Monographs, 58,* 179–194.

Conquergood, D. (1992). Ethnography, rhetoric, and performance. *Quarterly Journal of Speech, 78,* 80–97.

Conrad, C. (1983). Organizational power: Faces and symbolic forms. In L. Putnam & M. Pacanowsky (Eds.), *Communication and organizations* (pp. 173–194). Beverly Hills, CA: Sage.

Conrad, C. (1988). Work songs, hegemony, and illusions of self. *Critical Studies in Mass Communication, 5*, 179–201.

Conrad, C. (1991). Communication in conflict: Style-strategy relationships. *Communication Monographs, 58*, 135–155.

Conrad, C., & Poole, M. S. (Eds.). (1997). Communication in the age of the disposable worker. *Communication Research, 24*.

Contractor, N. (1992). Self-organizing systems perspective in the study of organizational communication. In B. Kovacic (Ed.), *Organizational communication: New perspectives*. Albany, NY: SUNY Press.

Contractor, N., & Eisenberg, E. (1990). Communication networks and the new media in organizations. In J. Fulk & C. Steinfeld (Eds.), *Organizations and communication technology* (pp. 143–172). Newbury Park, CA: Sage.

Contractor, N., Eisenberg, E., & Monge, P. (1992). *Antecedents and outcomes of interpretive diversity in organizations*. Unpublished manuscript, University of Illinois, Urbana.

Contractor, N., & Seibold, D. (1992). *Theoretical frameworks for the study of structuring processes in group decision support systems*. Unpublished manuscript, University of Illinois, Urbana.

Cooper, C. J. (1984). Executive stress: A ten country comparison. *Human Resource Management, 23*, 395–407.

Cooper, R. K. (2002). *The other 90%: How to unlock your vast untapped potential for leadership and life*. New York: Three Rivers Press.

Covey, S. (1990). *The 7 habits of highly effective people*. New York: Simon & Schuster.

Craig, R. (1999). Communication theory as a field. *Communication Theory, 9*, 119–161.

Csikszentmihalyi, M. (1990). *Flow: The psychology of optimal experience*. New York: Harper & Row.

Daft, R., & Lengel, R. (1984). Information richness: A new approach to managerial information processing and organizational design. In B. Staw & L. Cummings (Eds.), *Research in organizational behaviors* (Vol. 6, pp. 191–233). Greenwich, CT: JAI Press.

Daniels, T., & Spiker, B. (1991). *Perspectives on organizational communication*. Dubuque, IA: Brown.

Dansereau, F., & Markham, S. (1987). Superior-subordinate communication: Multiple levels of analysis. In F. Jablin, L. Putnam, K. Roberts, & L. Porter (Eds.), *Handbook of organizational communication* (pp. 343–388). Beverly Hills, CA: Sage.

D'Aveni, R. (1995). Coping with hypercompetition: Utilizing the new 7-S model. *Academy of Management Executive, 9*(3), 45–57.

Davis, J., Schoorman, F., & Donaldson, L. (1997). Toward a stewardship theory of management. *Academy of Management Review, 22*, 20–47.

Davis, K. (1953). Management communication and the grapevine. *Harvard Business Review, 31*, 43–49.

Davis, K. (1972). *Human behavior at work.* New York: McGraw-Hill.

Davis, S., & Davidson, B. (1992). *2020 vision.* New York: Fireside Press.

Deal, T., & Kennedy, A. (1982). *Corporate cultures: The rites and rituals of corporate life.* Reading, MA: Addison-Wesley.

De Certeau, M. (1984). *The practice of everyday life.* Berkeley: University of California Press.

Deetz, S. (1991). *Democracy in an age of corporate colonization.* Albany, NY: SUNY Press.

Deetz, S. (1995). *Transforming communication, transforming business.* Albany, NY: SUNY Press.

Dentzer, S. (1995, May 22). The death of the middleman. *U.S. News & World Report,* p. 56.

Derrida, J. (1972). Structure, sign, and play in the discourse of the human sciences. In R. Macksay & E. Donato (Eds.), *The structuralist controversy: The language of criticism and the science of man.* Baltimore: Johns Hopkins University Press.

Dessler, G. (1982). *Organization and management.* Reston, VA: Reston.

Dillard, J., & Miller, K. (1988). Intimate relationships in task environments. In S. Duck (Ed.), *Handbook of personal relationships* (pp. 449–465). New York: Wiley.

Dillard, J., & Segrin, C. (1987). *Intimate relationships in organizations: Relational types, illicitness, and power.* Paper presented at the annual conference of the International Communication Association, Montreal, Canada.

Dixon, T. (1996). Mary Parker Follett and community. *Australian Journal of Communication, 23,* 68–83.

Donnellon, A., Gray, B., & Bougon, M. (1986). Communication, meaning, and organized action. *Administrative Science Quarterly, 31,* 43–55.

Drucker, P. (1957). *The landmarks of tomorrow.* New York: Harper & Row.

Drucker, P. (1974). *Management: Tasks, responsibilities, practices.* New York: Harper & Row.

Drucker, P. (1992a). *Managing for the future: The 1990s and beyond.* New York: Truman Talley Books/Dutton.

Drucker, P. (1992b, February 11). There's more than one kind of team. *Wall Street Journal,* p. 16.

Drucker, P. (1993). *Management.* New York: Harper & Row.

Drucker, P. (1996). Introduction. In *Mary Parker Follett: Prophet of management.* Cambridge, MA: Harvard Business School Press.

Ehrenreich, B. (2001). *Nickel and dimed: On (not) getting by in America.* New York: Holt.

Einstein, A. (1961). *Relativity: The special and general theory.* New York: Bonanza Books. (Original work published 1921)

Eisenberg, E. (1984). Ambiguity as strategy in organizational communication. *Communication Monographs, 51,* 227–242.

Eisenberg, E. (1986). Meaning and interpretation in organizations. *Quarterly Journal of Speech, 72,* 88–98.

Eisenberg, E. (1990). Jamming: Transcendence through organizing. *Communication Research, 17,* 139–164.

Eisenberg, E. (1995). A communication perspective on interorganizational cooperation and inner-city education. In L. Rigsby, M. Reynolds, & M. Wang (Eds.), *School-community connections* (pp. 101–120). San Francisco: Jossey-Bass.

Eisenberg, E. (1998). Flirting with meaning. *Journal of Language and Social Psychology, 17,* 97–108.

Eisenberg, E. (2001). Building a mystery: Toward a new theory of communication and identity. *Journal of Communication, 51,* 534–552.

Eisenberg, E., Farace, R., Monge, P., Bettinghaus, E., Kurchner-Hawkins, R., Miller, K., & Rothman, L. (1985). Communication linkages in interorganizational systems: Review and synthesis. In B. Dervin & M. Voight (Eds.), *Progress in communication sciences* (Vol. 6, pp. 231–258). Norwood, NJ: Ablex.

Eisenberg, E., Monge, P., & Farace, R. V. (1984). Co-orientation on communication rules in managerial dyads. *Human Communication Research, 11,* 261–271.

Eisenberg, E., Monge, P., & Miller, K. (1983). Involvement in communication networks as a predictor of organizational commitment. *Human Communication Research, 10,* 179–201.

Eisenberg, E., Murphy, A., & Andrews, L. (1998). Openness and decision-making in the search for a university provost. *Communication Monographs, 65,* 1–23.

Eisenberg, E., & Riley, P. (2001). A communication approach to organizational culture. In L. Putnam & F. Jablin (Eds.), *New handbook of organizational communication.* Newbury Park, CA: Sage.

Eisenberg, E., & Weller-Gregory, K. (2000). *Ethics of the urgent organization.* Unpublished manuscript, University of South Florida, Tampa.

Eisenberg, E., & Witten, M. (1987). Reconsidering openness in organizational communication. *Academy of Management Review, 12,* 418–426.

Eliot, T. S. (1949). *Notes toward the definition of culture.* New York: Harcourt, Brace.

Ellis, C. (2002). Shattered lives: Making sense of September 11 and its aftermath. *Journal of Contemporary Ethnography, 31,* 375–410.

Emerson, C. (1983). Bakhtin and Vygotsky on internalization of language. *Quarterly Newsletter of the Laboratory of Comparative Human Cognition, 5,* 9–13.

Emery, F., & Trist, E. (1965). The causal texture of organizational environments. *Human Relations, 18,* 21–32.

Erez, M., & Earley, P. (1993). *Culture, self-identity, and work.* New York: Oxford University Press.

Evered, R., & Tannenbaum, R. (1992). A dialog on dialog. *Journal of Management Inquiry, 1,* 43–55.

Fairhurst, G., & Chandler, T. (1989). Social structure in leader-member interaction. *Communication Monographs, 56,* 215–239.

Fairhurst, G., Green, S., & Snavely, B. (1984). Face support in controlling poor performance. *Human Communications Research, 11,* 272–295.

Fairhurst, G., & Sarr, R. (1996). *The art of framing: Managing the language of leadership.* San Francisco: Jossey-Bass.

Farace, R. V., Monge, P., & Russell, H. (1977). *Communicating and organizing.* Reading, MA: Addison-Wesley.

Fayol, H. (1949). *General and industrial management.* London: Pitman.

Feldman, M., & March, J. (1981). Information in organizations as signal and symbol. *Administrative Science Quarterly, 26,* 171–186.

Feldman, S. (1991). The meaning of ambiguity: Learning from stories and metaphors. In P. Frost, L. Moore, M. Louis, C. Lundberg, & J. Martin (Eds.), *Reframing organizational culture* (pp. 145–156). Newbury Park, CA: Sage.

Ferguson, K. (1984). *The feminist case against bureaucracy.* Philadelphia: Temple University Press.

Fiedler, F. (1967). *A theory of leadership effectiveness.* New York: McGraw-Hill.

Fine, M., & Buzzanell, P. (2000). Walking the high wire: Leadership theorizing, daily acts, and tensions. In P. Buzzanell (Ed.), *Rethinking organizational & managerial communication from feminist perspectives* (pp. 128–156). Thousand Oaks, CA: Sage.

Fisher, A. (1980). *Small group decision making* (2nd ed.). New York: McGraw-Hill.

Fisher, R., & Ury, W. (1981). *Getting to yes.* New York: Penguin.

Ford, R., & Fottler, M. (1995). Empowerment: A matter of degree. *Academy of Management Executive, 9,* 21–31.

Foucault, M. (1972). *The archaeology of knowledge.* London: Tavistock.

Foucault, M. (1979). *The birth of the prison.* Hammondsworth, England: Penguin.

Fox, M. (1994). *The reinvention of work.* San Francisco: HarperCollins.

Franklin, B. (1970). *The complete Poor Richard almanacs published by Benjamin Franklin.* Barre, MA: Imprint Society.

Franz, C., & Jin, K. (1995). The structure of group conflict in a collaborative work group during information systems development. *Journal of Applied Communication Research, 23,* 108–122.

Freeman, S. (1990). *Managing lives: Corporate women and social change.* Amherst: University of Massachusetts Press.

Freire, P. (1968). *Pedagogy of the oppressed.* Berkeley: University of California Press.

French, R., & Raven, B. (1968). The bases of social power. In D. Cartwright & A. Zander (Eds.), *Group dynamics* (pp. 601–623). New York: Harper & Row.

Friedman, M. (1992). *Dialogue and the human image.* Newbury Park, CA: Sage.

Friedman, T. (2002, August 13). India's leaders think twice about war with Pakistan thanks to GE. *St. Petersburg Times,* p. 8A.

Frost, P., Moore, L., Louis, M., Lundberg, C., & Martin, J. (1991). *Reframing organizational culture.* Newbury Park, CA: Sage.

Fulk, J., & DeSanctis, G. (1995). Electronic communication and changing organizational forms. *Organization Science, 6*(4), 337–349.

Fulk, J., & Mani, S. (1986). Distortion of communication in hierarchical relationships. *Communication yearbook* (Vol. 9, pp. 483–510). Newbury Park, CA: Sage.

Fulk, J., Schmitz, J., & Steinfeld, C. (1990). A social influence model of technology use. In J. Fulk & C. Steinfeld (Eds.), *Organizational and communication technology* (pp. 143–172). Newbury Park, CA: Sage.

Gabarro, J., & Kotter, J. (1993). Managing your boss. *Harvard Business Review, 58,* 92–100.

Galbraith, J. (1973). *Designing complex organizations.* Reading, MA: Addison-Wesley.

Gardner, H. (1996). *Leading minds: An anatomy of leadership.* New York: Basic Books.

Garfield, C. (1992). *Business in the ecological age* (Audiotape). San Francisco: Berrett-Koehler.

Garfield, C. (1999, September/October). Peak performances and organizational transformation: An interview with Charles Garfield. *Educom Review, 34.*

Gates, B. (1999). *Business at the speed of thought.* New York: Time Warner.

Geertz, C. (1973). *The interpretation of cultures.* New York: Basic Books.

Geist, P. (1995). Negotiating whose order? Communicating to negotiate identities and revise organizational structures. In A. M. Nicotera (Ed.), *Conflict and organizations: Communicative processes* (pp. 45–64). Albany, NY: SUNY Press.

Geist, P., & Dreyer, J. (1993). The demise of dialogue: A critique of medical encounter ideology. *Western Journal of Communication, 57, 233–246.*

Gendron, G. (1999). Seizing opportunities for meaning. *Inc., 21,* 87.

Gergen, K. (1991). *The saturated self.* New York: Basic Books.

Gersick, C. (1991). Revolutionary change theories: A multi-level explanation of the punctuated equilibrium paradigm. *Academy of Management Review, 16,* 10–36.

Gibson, D., & Rogers, E. (in press). *Synergy on trial: Texas high tech and the MCC.* Newbury Park, CA: Sage.

Gibson, J., & Hodgetts, R. (1986). *Organizational communication: A managerial perspective.* New York: Academic Press.

Giddens, A. (1979). *Central problems in social theory.* London: Hutchinson.

Giddens, A. (1984). *The constitution of society: Outline of the theory of structuration.* Berkeley: University of California Press.

Gitlin, T. (1987). *The sixties: Years of hope, days of rage.* New York: Bantam.

Glaser, H., & Bullis, C. (1992, November). *Ecofeminism and organizational communication.* Paper presented at the annual meeting of the Speech Communication Association, Chicago.

Gleick, J. (2000). *Faster: The acceleration of just about everything.* New York: Vintage Books.

Gluesing, J. (1998). Building connections and balancing power in global teams: Toward a reconceptualization of culture as composite. *Anthropology of Work Review XVIII*(2/3), 18–30.

Goes, J., & Park, S. (1997). Interorganizational links and innovation: The case of hospital services. *Academy of Management Journal, 40*, 673–696.

Goleman, D. (1995). *Emotional intelligence*. New York: Bantam.

Goodall, H. L. (1984). The status of communication studies in organizational contexts: One rhetorician's lament after a year-long odyssey. *Communication Quarterly, 32*, 133–147.

Goodall, H. L. (1989). *Casing a promised land*. Carbondale: Southern Illinois University Press.

Goodall, H. L. (1990). Interpretive contexts for decision-making: Toward an understanding of the physical, economic, dramatic, and hierarchical interplays of language in groups. In G. M. Phillips (Ed.), *Teaching how to work in groups* (pp. 197–224). Norwood, NJ: Ablex.

Goodall, H. L. (1991a). *Living in the rock 'n' roll mystery*. Carbondale: Southern Illinois University Press.

Goodall, H. L. (1991b). *Unchained melodies: Toward a poetics of organizing*. Blair Hart lecture on communication, University of Arkansas, Fayetteville.

Goodall, H. L. (1994). *Casing a promised land: The autobiography of an organizational detective as cultural ethnographer* (Rev. ed.). Carbondale: Southern Illinois University Press.

Goodall, H. L., Jr. (1995). Work-hate narratives. In R. Whillock & D. Slayden (Eds.), *Hate speech*. Thousand Oaks, CA: Sage.

Goodall, H. L., Jr. (1996). *Divine signs: Connecting spirit to community*. Carbondale: Southern Illinois University Press.

Goodall, H. L., Jr. (2000). *Writing the new ethnography*. Newbury Park, CA: Alta Mira Press.

Goodall, H. L., Jr. (2002). Fieldnotes from our war zone: Living in America during the aftermath of September 11. *Qualitative Inquiry, 8*, 203–218.

Goodall, H. L., Jr., & Goodall, S. (2002). *Communicating in professional contexts: Skills, ethics, and technologies*. Belmont, CA: Wadsworth/Thomson Learning.

Goodall, H. L., & Kellett, P. M. (2003). Dialectical tensions and dialogic moments as pathways to peak experiences. In R. Anderson, L. A. Baxter, and K. N. Cissna (Eds.), *Dialogic approaches to communication*. Thousand Oaks, CA: Sage.

Graen, G. (1976). Role making processes within complex organizations. In M. Dunnette (Ed.), *Handbook of industrial and organizational psychology* (pp. 1201–1245). Chicago: Rand McNally.

Graen, G., Liden, R., & Hoel, W. (1982). Role of leadership in the employee withdrawal process. *Journal of Applied Psychology, 67*, 868–872.

Graham, P. (1997). *Mary Parker Follett — Prophet of management*. Cambridge, MA: Harvard Business School Press.

Gramsci, A. (1971). *Selections from the prison notebooks*. London: Lawrence & Wishart.

Granovetter, M. (1973). The strength of weak ties. *American Journal of Sociology, 78*, 1360–1380.

Grant, L. (1992, May 3). Breaking the mold: Companies struggle to reinvent themselves. *Los Angeles Times*, pp. D1, D16.

Grantham, C. (1999). *The future of work: The promise of the new digital work society*. New York: McGraw-Hill.

Greenblatt, S. (1990). Culture. In F. Lentricchia & T. McLaughlin (Eds.), *Critical terms for literary study* (pp. 225–232). Chicago: University of Chicago Press.

Greenleaf, R. (1998). *The power of servant leadership*. San Francisco: Berrett-Koehler.

Grossberg, L. (1991). Review of theories of human communication. *Communication Theory, 1*, 171–176.

Grossberg, L. (2002). Postscript. *Communication Theory, 12*, 367–370.

Grossman, H., & Chester, N. (1990). *The experience and meaning of work in women's lives*. Hillsdale, NJ: Erlbaum.

Haas, T., & Deetz, S. (2000). Between the generalized and the concrete Other: Approaching organizational ethics from feminist perspectives. In P. Buzzanell (Ed.), *Rethinking organizational & managerial communication from feminist perspectives* (pp. 24–46). Thousand Oaks, CA: Sage.

Habermas, J. (1972). *Knowledge and human interests*. London: Heinemann Educational Books.

Hackman, R., & Oldham, G. (1975). Development of the Job Diagnostic Survey. *Journal of Applied Psychology, 60*, 159–170.

Hackman, R., & Oldham, G. (1980). *Work redesign*. Reading, MA: Addison-Wesley.

Hackman, R., & Suttle, J. (1977). *Improving life at work: Behavioral science approaches to organizational change*. Santa Monica, CA: Goodyear.

Hall, D. (1986). *Career development in organizations*. San Francisco: Jossey-Bass.

Hall, D. (1996). Protean careers of the 21st century. *Academy of Management Executive, 10*, 8–16.

Hall, E. T. (1973). *The silent language*. New York: Anchor.

Hall, K., & Savery, L. (1987). Stress management. *Management Decision, 25*, 29–35.

Handy, C. (1994). *The age of paradox*. Cambridge, MA: Harvard University Press.

Haraway, D. (1991). *Simians, cyborgs, and women*. New York: Routledge.

Hardin, G. (1968, December 13). The tragedy of the commons. *Science*.

Harrigan, B. (1977). *Games mother never taught you: Corporate gamesmanship for women*. New York: Warner.

Harrison, T. (1985). Communication and participative decision-making: An exploratory study. *Personnel Psychology, 38*, 93–116.

Harrison, T. (1994). Communication and interdependence in democratic organizations. In S. Deetz (Ed.), *Communication yearbook* (Vol. 17, pp. 247–274). Newbury Park, CA: Sage.

Harshman, E., & Harshman, C. (1999). Communicating with employees: Building on an ethical foundation. *Journal of Business Ethics, 19,* 3–11.

Hart, R., & Burks, D. (1972). Rhetorical sensitivity and social interaction. *Speech Monographs, 39,* 75–91.

Hatch, M. (1993). The dynamics of organizational culture. *Academy of Management Review, 18,* 657–693.

Hatch, M. (1999). Exploring the empty spaces of organizing: How improvisational jazz helps redescribe organizational structure. *Organization Studies, 20,* 75–100.

Hawken, P. (1994). *The ecology of commerce.* New York: HarperBusiness.

Hawking, S. (1988). *A brief history of time.* New York: Bantam.

Heald, M., Contractor, N., Koehlt, L., & Wasserman, S. (1998). Formal and emergent predictors of coworkers' perceptual congruence on an organization's social structure. *Human Communication Research, 24,* 536–563.

Helgeson, S. (1990). *The female advantage: Women's ways of leadership.* New York: Doubleday.

Hellweg, S. (1987). Organizational grapevines: A state of the art review. In B. Dervin & M. Voight (Eds.), *Progress in the communication sciences* (Vol. 8). Norwood, NJ: Ablex.

Herzberg, F. (1966). *Work and the nature of man.* New York: Collins.

Hirokawa, R., & Rost, K. (1992). Effective group decision making in organizations. *Management Communication Quarterly, 5,* 267–388.

Hirschman, A. (1970). *Exit, voice, and loyalty.* Cambridge, MA: Harvard University Press.

Hochschild, A. (1979). Emotion work, feeling rules and social structure. *American Journal of Sociology, 85,* 551–575.

Hochschild, A. (1983). *The managed heart: Commercialization of human feeling.* Berkeley: University of California Press.

Hochschild, A. (1993). Preface. In S. Fineman (Ed.), *Emotion in organizations.* Newbury Park, CA: Sage.

Hochschild, A. (1997). *The time bind.* New York: Holt.

Hofstede, G. (1983). National cultures in four dimensions. *International Studies of Management and Organization, 13,* 46–74.

Hofstede, G. (1995). *Culture and organizations: Software of the mind.* New York: McGraw-Hill.

Hollander, E., & Offerman, L. (1990). Power and leadership in organizations. *American Psychologist, 45,* 179–189.

Homans, G. (1961). *Social behavior: Its elementary forms.* New York: Harcourt, Brace & World.

Human, S., & Provan, K. (1997). An emergent theory of structure and outcomes in small-firm strategic manufacturing networks. *Academy of Management Journal, 40*, 368–403.

Hunger, R., & Stern, L. (1976). Assessment of the functionality of subordinate goals in reducing conflict. *Academy of Management Journal, 16*, 591–605.

Hurst, D. (1992). Thoroughly modern — Mary Parker Follett. *Business Quarterly, 56*, 55–59.

Huselid, M. (1995). The impact of human resource management practices on turnover, productivity, and corporate financial performance. *Academy of Management Journal, 38*, 635–673.

Hyde, R. B. (1994). Listening authentically: A Heideggerian perspective on interpersonal communication. In K. Carter and M. Presnell (Eds.), *Interpretive approaches to interpersonal communication* (pp. 179–195). Albany: SUNY Press.

Ilgin, D., & Knowlton, W., Jr. (1980). Performance attributional effects on feedback from supervisors. *Organizational Behavior and Human Performance, 25*, 441–456.

Infante, D., Trebing, J., Sheperd, P., & Seeds, D. (1984). The relationship of argumentativeness to verbal aggression. *Southern Speech Communication Journal, 50*, 67–77.

Isaacs, W. (1994, Fall). Taking flight: Dialogue, collaborative thinking, and organizational learning. *Organizational Dynamics.*

Isaacs, W. (1999). *Dialogue.* New York: Currency Doubleday.

Israel, D., et al. (1989). The relation of personal resources, participation, influence, interpersonal relationships and coping strategies to occupational stress, job stress, and health: A multivariate analysis. *Work and Stress, 3*, 163–194.

Ivancevich, J., & Matteson, M. (1980). *Stress and work: A managerial perspective.* Glenview, IL: Scott Foresman.

Jablin, F. (1979). Superior-subordinate communication: The state of the art. *Psychological Bulletin, 86*, 1201–1222.

Jablin, F. (1985). Task/work relationships: A life-span perspective. In M. Knapp & G. Miller (Eds.), *Handbook of interpersonal communication* (pp. 615–654). Newbury Park, CA: Sage.

Jablin, F. (1987). Organizational entry, assimilation, and exit. In F. Jablin, L. Putnam, K. Roberts, & L. Porter (Eds.), *Handbook of organizational communication* (pp. 679–740). Newbury Park, CA: Sage.

Jablin, F., & Putnam, L. (2001). *The new handbook of organizational communication.* Thousand Oaks, CA: Sage.

Jackson, M. (1989). *Paths toward a clearing.* Bloomington: Indiana University Press.

Jackson, S. (1983). Participation in decision-making as a strategy for reducing job-related strain. *Journal of Applied Psychology, 68,* 3–19.

Jacobson, R. (1992). Colleges face new pressure to increase faculty productivity. *Chronicle of Higher Education, 38*(32), 1, 16.

Janis, I. (1971). *Victims of groupthink* (2nd ed.). Boston: Houghton Mifflin.

Jantsch, E. (1980). *The self organizing universe.* Oxford: Pergamon Press.

Jassawalla, A., & Sashittal, H. (1999). Building collaborative cross-functional new product teams. *Academy of Management Executive, 13,* 50–63.

Jencks, C. (1977). *The language of postmodern architecture.* New York: Pantheon.

Jhally, S. (1998). *Representation in media* [Film]. (Available from Media Education Foundation, Amherst, MA)

Johnson, B. (1977). *Communication: The process of organizing.* Boston: Allyn and Bacon.

Johnson, D. (1993). *Circles of learning.* Edina, MN: Interaction Books.

Jones, B. (1972, June). Sex in the office. *National Times, 12.*

Jones, E., Jr. (1973, July–August). What it's like to be a black manager. *Harvard Business Review.*

Jorgenson, J. (2002). Engineering selves: Negotiating gender and identity in technical work. *Management Communication Quarterly, 15*(3), 350–380.

Jovanovic, S. (in press). Difficult conversations as moral imperative: Negotiating ethnic identities during war. *Communication Quarterly.*

Kanter, R. M. (1977). *Men and women of the corporation.* New York: Basic Books.

Kanter, R. M. (1989, November–December). The new managerial work. *Harvard Business Review, 67,* 85–92.

Karasek, R. (1979). Job demands, job decisions, latitude and mental strain: Implications for job redesign. *Administrative Science Quarterly, 24,* 285–308.

Katz, D., & Kahn, R. (1966). *The social psychology of organizations.* New York: Wiley.

Kellett, P. M. (1999). Dialogue and dialectics in organizational change: The case of a mission-based transformation. *Southern Communication Journal, 64,* 211–231.

Kellett, P. M., & Dalton, D. G. (2000). *Managing conflict in a negotiated world: A narrative approach to achieving dialogue and change.* Thousand Oaks, CA: Sage.

Kelly, J. (1992). *Scientific management, job redesign, and work performance.* London: Academic Press.

Kerr, S. (2001). Boundaryless. In W. Bennis, G. Spreitzer, & T. Cummings (Eds.), *The future of leadership* (pp. 59–66). San Francisco: Jossey-Bass.

Keys, B., & Case, T. (1990). How to become an influential manager. *Academy of Management Executive, 4,* 38–50.

Kiechel, W. (1994, April 4). A manager's career in the new economy. *Fortune,* 68–72.

Kiesler, C. (1971). *The psychology of commitment.* New York: Academic Press.

Kilmann, R., & Thomas, K. (1975). Interpersonal conflict handling behavior as a reflection of Jungian personality dimensions. *Psychological Reports, 37,* 971–980.

Kimberly, J., & Miles, R. (1980). *The organizational life cycle.* San Francisco: Jossey-Bass.

King, P., & Sawyer, C. (1998). Mindfulness, mindlessness, and communication instruction. *Communication Education, 47,* 326–338.

Kipnis, D., & Schmidt, S. (1982). *Profile of organizational influence strategies.* San Diego: University Associates.

Kipnis, D., Schmidt, S., & Braxton-Brown, G. (1990). The hidden costs of persistence. In M. Cody & M. McLaughlin (Eds.), *The psychology of tactical communication.* Philadelphia: Multilingual Matters.

Kipnis, D., Schmidt, S., & Wilkinson, I. (1980). Intraorganizational influence tactics: Explorations in getting one's way. *Journal of Applied Psychology, 65,* 440–452.

Kobasa, S., Maddi, S., & Kahn, S. (1982). Hardiness and health: A prospective study. *Journal of Personality and Social Psychology, 42,* 168–177.

Kotter, J. (1995). *The new rules.* New York: Free Press.

Kotter, J., & Heskett, J. (1992). *Corporate culture and performance.* New York: Free Press.

Kraatz, M. (1998). Learning by association? Interorganizational networks and adaptation to environmental change. *Academy of Management Journal, 41,* 621–643.

Kramer, M., & Miller, V. (1999). In response to criticisms of organizational socialization research. *Communication Monographs, 66,* 358–367.

Kreps, G. (1991). *Organizational communication: Theory and practice* (2nd ed.). New York: Longman.

Krippendorff, K. (1985, June). *On the ethics of constructing communication.* Presidential address of the International Communication Association, Honolulu, HI.

Krivonos, P. (1982). Distortion of subordinate to superior communication in organizational settings. *Central States Speech Journal, 33,* 345–352.

Kunda, G. (1993). *Engineering culture: Control and commitment in a high-tech corporation.* Philadelphia: Temple University Press.

Laine-Timmerman, L. (1999). *The emotional experience of floor nursing.* Unpublished doctoral dissertation, University of South Florida, Tampa.

Laing, R. D. (1965). *The divided self.* Harmondsworth, England: Penguin.

Langer, E. (1998). *The power of mindful learning.* New York: Perseus Publishing.

Langewiesche, W. (2002). *American ground: Unbuilding the World Trade Center.* Boston: North Point Press.

Larkey, P. (1984). The management of attention. In P. Larkey & L. Sproull (Eds.), *Advances in information processing in organizations* (Vol. I). Greenwich, CT: JAI Press.

Larson, J., Jr. (1989). The dynamic interplay between employees: Feedback-seeking strategies and supervisors' delivery of performance feedback. *Academy of Management Review, 14,* 408–422.

Lawler, E., III. (1986). *High involvement management.* San Francisco: Jossey-Bass.

Lawler, E., III, & Finegold, D. (2000). Individualizing the organization: Past, present, and future. *Organizational Dynamics, 29,* 1–15.

Lawrence, P., & Lorsch, J. (1967). *Organization and environment: Mapping differentiation and integration.* Boston: Graduate School of Business Administration, Harvard University.

Leavitt, H. (1951). Some effects of certain communication patterns on group performance. *Journal of Abnormal and Social Psychology, 46,* 38–50.

Leidner, R. (1993). *Fast food, fast talk: Service work and the routinization of everyday life.* Berkeley: University of California Press.

Lennie, I. (1999). *Beyond management.* London: Sage.

LeVine, S. (1984). *The flight from ambiguity.* Chicago: University of Chicago Press.

Lewin, R. (1997, November 29). Ecosystems as a metaphor for business. *New Scientist.*

Lewis, M. (2000, March). The artist in the gray flannel pajamas. *New York Times Magazine,* 45.

Liden, R., & Graen, G. (1980). Generalizability of the vertical dyad linkage model of leadership. *Academy of Management Journal, 23,* 451–465.

Likert, R. (1961). *New patterns of management.* New York: McGraw-Hill.

Locke, E., & Latham, G. (1984). *Goal setting: A motivational technique that really works!* Englewood Cliffs, NJ: Prentice-Hall.

Loher, B., Noe, R., Moeller, N., & Fitzgerald, M. (1985). A meta-analysis of the relation of job characteristics to job satisfaction. *Journal of Applied Psychology, 70,* 280–289.

Longworth, R. C. (1998). *Global squeeze: The coming crisis for first world nations.* New York: McGraw-Hill.

Louis, M. (1980). Surprise and sense-making: What newcomers experience in entering unfamiliar organizational settings. *Administrative Science Quarterly, 23,* 225–251.

Luhmann, A. D., & Albrecht, T. L. (1990). *The impact of supportive communication and personal control on job stress and performance.* Paper presented at the International Communication Association, Chicago.

Lukes, S. (1986). *Power.* New York: New York University Press.

Lunneborg, D. (1990). *Women changing work.* New York: Greenwood Press.

Lyotard, J. F. (1984). *The postmodern condition: A report on knowledge* (G. Bennington & B. Massumi, Trans.). Minneapolis: University of Minnesota Press.

March, J., & Olsen, J. (1976). *Ambiguity and choice in organizations.* Bergen, Norway: Universitetsforlaget.

March, J., & Simon, H. (1958). *Organizations*. New York: Wiley.

Marcus, G., & Fischer, M. (1986). *Anthropology as cultural critique*. Chicago: University of Chicago Press.

Markham, A. (1998). *Life online*. Newbury Park, CA: Alta Mira Press.

Marshall, A., & Stohl, C. (1993). Participating as participation: A network approach. *Communication Monographs, 60*, 137–157.

Marshall, J. (1984). *Women managers: Travelers in a male world*. New York: Wiley.

Marshall, K. (1993). Viewing organizational communication from a feminist perspective: A critique and some offerings. In S. Deetz (Ed.), *Communication yearbook* (Vol. 16, pp. 122–141). Newbury Park, CA: Sage.

Martin, J. (1992). *Cultures in organizations: Three perspectives*. New York: Oxford University Press.

Maruyama, M. (1994). *Mindscapes in management: Use of individual differences in multicultural management*. Dartmouth Publishing.

Maslach, C. (1982). *Burnout: The cost of caring*. Englewood Cliffs, NJ: Prentice-Hall.

Maslow, A. (1965). *Eupsychian management*. Homewood, IL: Irwin.

Maslow, A. (1994). *Religions, values, and peak experiences*. New York: Viking Press.

Mattson, M., Clair, R. P., Sanger, P. A. C., & Kunkel, A. D. (2000). A feminist reframing of stress: Rose's story. In P. Buzzanell (Ed.), *Rethinking organizational & managerial communication from feminist perspectives* (pp. 157–176). Thousand Oaks, CA: Sage.

May, S. (1988). *The modernist monologue in organizational communication research: The text, the subject, and the audience*. Paper presented at the annual convention of the International Communication Association, San Francisco.

May, S. (2000). *Silencing the feminine in managerial discourse*. Unpublished manuscript, University of North Carolina at Chapel Hill.

Mayo, E. (1945). *The social problems of industrial civilization*. Cambridge, MA: Graduate School of Business Administration, Harvard University.

McDonald, P. (1988). The Los Angeles Olympic Organizing Committee: Developing organizational culture in the short run. *Public Administration Quarterly, 10*, 189–205.

McGregor, D. (1960). *The human side of enterprise*. New York: McGraw-Hill.

McLarney, C., & Rhyno, S. (1999). Mary Parker Follett: Visionary leadership and strategic management. *Women in Management Review, 14*, 292–302.

McLuhan, M. (1964). *Understanding media: The extensions of man*. New York: McGraw-Hill.

McPhee, R. (1985). Formal structures and organizational communication. In R. McPhee & P. Tompkins (Eds.), *Organizational communication: Traditional themes and new directions* (pp. 149–177). Beverly Hills, CA: Sage.

McPhee, R., & Corman, S. (1995). An activity based theory of communication networks in organizations, applied to the case of a local church. *Communication Monographs, 62*, 132–151.

McPhee, R. D., & Poole, M. S. (2001). Organizational structures and configurations. In F. M. Jablin & L. L. Putnam (Eds.), *The new handbook of organizational communication: Advances in theory, research, and methods* (pp. 503–543). Thousand Oaks, CA: Sage.

Mead, G. (1991, May 30). The new old capitalism: Long hours, low wages. *Rolling Stone, 27*(3).

Mead, G. H. (1934). *Mind, self, and society.* Chicago: University of Chicago Press.

Meyer, G. J. (1995). *Executive blues.* San Francisco: Franklin Square Press.

Meyer, J., & Rowan, B. (1977). Institutionalized organizations: Formal structure as myth and ceremony. *American Journal of Sociology, 83,* 340–363.

Miller, D., & Form, W. (1951). *Industrial sociology: An introduction to the sociology of work relations.* New York: Harper.

Miller, J. G. (1978). *Living systems.* New York: McGraw-Hill.

Miller, K. (1995). *Organizational communication: Approaches and processes.* Belmont, CA: Wadsworth.

Miller, K. (2003). *Organizational communication: Approaches and processes* (3rd ed.). Belmont, CA: Wadsworth.

Miller, K., Ellis, B., Zook, E., & Lyles, J. (1990). An integrated model of communication, stress, and burnout in the workplace. *Communication Research, 17,* 300–326.

Miller, K., & Monge, P. (1986). Participation, satisfaction, and productivity: A meta-analytic review. *Academy of Management Journal, 29,* 727–753.

Miller, K., Stiff, J., & Ellis, B. (1988). Communication and empathy as precursors to burnout among human service workers. *Communication Monographs, 55,* 250–265.

Miller, V., & Jablin, F. (1991). Information seeking during organizational entry: Influences, tactics, and a model of the process. *Academy of Management Review, 16,* 92–120.

Minh-Ha, T. (1991). *When the moon waxes red: Representation, gender, and cultural politics.* New York: Routledge.

Mitchell, T., & Scott, W. (1990). America's problems and needed reforms: Confronting the ethic of personal advantage. *The Executive, 4,* 23–35.

Mitroff, I., & Kilmann, R. (1975). Stories managers tell: A new tool for organizational problem-solving. *Management Review, 64,* 18–28.

Mohan, M. (1993). *Organizational communication and cultural vision.* Albany, NY: SUNY Press.

Monge, P., Bachman, S., Dillard, J., & Eisenberg, E. (1982). Communicator competence in the workplace: Model testing and scale development. *Communication yearbook* (Vol. 5, pp. 505–528). New Brunswick, NJ: Transaction.

Monge, P. R., & Contractor, N. (2001). Emergence of communication networks. In F. Jablin & L. Putnam (Eds.), *The new handbook of organizational communication* (pp. 440–502). Thousand Oaks, CA: Sage.

Monge, P., Cozzens, M., & Contractor, N. (1992). Communication and motivational predictors of the dynamics of organizational innovations. *Organization Science, 3*, 250–274.

Monge, P., & Eisenberg, E. (1987). Emergent communication networks. In F. Jablin, L. Putnam, K. Roberts, & L. Porter (Eds.), *Handbook of organizational communication* (pp. 204–342). Beverly Hills, CA: Sage.

Monge, P. R., & Fulk, J. (1995). *Global network organizations*. Paper presented at the annual meeting of the International Communication Association, Albuquerque, NM.

Morgan, G. (1986). *Images of organization*. Newbury Park, CA: Sage.

Morrison, E., & Bies, R. (1991). Impression management in the feedback-seeking process: A literature review and research agenda. *Academy of Management Review, 16*, 522–541.

Moskowitz, M., & Townsend, C. (1991, October). The 85 best companies for working mothers. *Working Mother,* 29–64.

Motley, M. (1992). Mindfulness in solving communicators' dilemmas. *Communication Monographs, 59*, 306–317.

Moxley, R. (1994, September). *Foundations of leadership*. Paper presented at the Center for Creative Leadership, Greensboro, NC.

Moyers, B. (1989). *A world of ideas*. New York: Doubleday.

Mumby, D. (1987). The political function of narratives in organizations. *Communication Monographs, 54*, 113–127.

Mumby, D. (1988). *Communication and power in the organization: Discourse, ideology, and domination*. Norwood, NJ: Ablex.

Mumby, D. (1993). *Narrative and social control*. Newbury Park, CA: Sage.

Mumby, D. (2000). Communication, organization, and the public sphere: A feminist perspective. In P. Buzzanell (Ed.), *Rethinking organizational & managerial communication from feminist perspectives* (pp. 3–23). Thousand Oaks, CA: Sage.

Mumby, D., & Putnam, L. (1993). The politics of emotion: A feminist reading of bounded rationality. *Academy of Management Review, 17*, 465–486.

Mumby, D., and Stohl, C. (1996). Disciplining organizational communication studies. *Management Communication Quarterly, 10*, 465–486.

Murphy, A. (1998). Hidden transcripts of flight attendant resistance. *Management Communication Quarterly, 11*, 499–535.

Murphy, A. (1999). Managing "nowhere": The changing organizational performance of air travel. *Dissertation Abstracts, 59*(11-A), 4012.

Murphy, A. (2002). Struggling for organizational voice. *Management Communication Quarterly, 15*(4), 626–631.

Murphy, D. (1999, May 30). A new attitude. *San Francisco Examiner,* pp. J1–J2.

Myerson, D. (2003). *Tempered radicals: How people use difference to inspire change at work*. Cambridge, MA: Harvard Business School Press.

National Communication Association. (1999, September). Credo. *Spectra,* p. 4.

Neale, M. A., & Bazerman, M. H. (1985). The effects of framing and negotiator overconfidence on bargaining behaviors and outcomes. *Academy of Management Journal, 28,* 34–49.

Nicotera, A., Clinkscales, M., & Walker, F. (in press). *Understanding organizations through culture and structure: Relational and other lessons from the African-American organization.* New York: Erlbaum.

Noer, D. (1995). *Healing the wounds: Overcoming the trauma of layoffs and revitalizing downsized organizations.* San Francisco: Jossey-Bass.

Ochs, E., Smith, R., & Taylor, C. (1989). Detective stories at dinnertime: Problem solving through co-narration. *Cultural Dynamics, 2,* 238–257.

Ogden, C., & Richards, I. A. (1936). *The meaning of meaning.* New York: Harcourt Brace & Co.

Oldham, G., & Rotchford, N. (1983). Relationships between office characteristics and employee reactions: A study of the physical environment. *Administrative Science Quarterly, 28,* 542–556.

Orbe, M. P. (1998). *Constructing co-cultural theory: An explication of culture, power, and communication.* Thousand Oaks, CA: Sage.

Ortner, S. (1980). Theory in anthropology since the sixties. *Journal for the Comparative Study of Society and History,* 126–166.

Osborn, J., Moran, L., Musselwhite, E., & Zenger, J. (1990). *Self-directed work teams.* Homewood, IL: Business One Irwin.

Ouchi, W. (1981). *Theory Z.* Reading, MA: Addison-Wesley.

Ouchi, W., & Wilkins, A. (1985). Organizational culture. *Annual Review of Sociology, 11,* 457–483.

Pacanowsky, M. (1988). Communication in the empowering organization. In J. Anderson (Ed.), *Communication yearbook* (Vol. 11, pp. 356–379). Newbury Park, CA: Sage.

Pacanowsky, M., & O'Donnell-Trujillo, N. (1983). Organizational communication as cultural performance. *Communication Monographs, 50,* 126–147.

Papa, M. (1989). Communicator competence and employee performance with new technology: A case study. *The Southern Communication Journal, 55,* 87–101.

Papa, M. (1990). Communication network patterns and employee performance with new technology. *Communication Research, 17,* 344–368.

Papa, M., Auwal, M., & Singhal, A. (1997). Organizing for social change within concertive control systems. *Communication Monographs, 64,* 219–249.

Parks, M. (1982). Ideology in interpersonal communication: Off the couch and into the world. In M. Burgoon (Ed.), *Communication yearbook* (Vol. 5, pp. 79–108). New Brunswick, NJ: Transaction.

Parsons, C., Herold, D., & Leatherwood, M. (1985). Turnover during initial employment: A longitudinal study of the role of causal attributions. *Journal of Applied Psychology, 70,* 337–341.

Parsons, T. (1951). *The social system.* New York: Free Press of Glencoe.

Peppers, D., & Rogers, M. (1996). *The one to one future*. New York: Currency Doubleday.

Perrow, C. (1986). *Complex organizations: A critical essay* (3rd ed.). New York: Random House.

Peters, T. (1987). *Thriving on chaos*. New York: Knopf.

Peters, T., & Waterman, R. (1982). *In search of excellence*. New York: Harper & Row.

Peterson, L. (1995). *The influence of sharing a semantic link on social support in work relationships at a hospital*. Paper presented at the annual meeting of the Speech Communication Association, San Antonio, TX.

Pfeffer, J., & Sutton, R. (1999, May–June). The smart talk trap. *Harvard Business Review, 77*, 134–142.

Pfeffer, J., & Veiga, J. (1999). Putting people first for organizational success. *Academy of Management Executive, 13*, 37–48.

Phillips, G. (1991). *Communication incompetencies: A theory of training oral performance behavior*. Carbondale: Southern Illinois University Press.

Pinchot, G., & Pinchot, E. (1993). *The end of bureaucracy and the rise of the intelligent organization*. San Francisco: Berrett-Koehler.

Pine, B. J., Gilmore, J., & Pine, B. J., II. (1999). *The experience economy*. Cambridge, MA: Harvard Business School Press.

Poole, M. S. (1983). Decision development in small groups II: A study of multiple sequences in decision making. *Communication Monographs, 50*, 321–341.

Poole, M. S. (1996, February). A turn of the wheel: The case for a renewal of systems inquiry in organizational communication research. Conference on Organizational Communication and Change, Austin, TX.

Poole, M. S. (in press). Organizational challenges for the new forms. In G. DeSanctis & J. Fulk (Eds.), *Shaping organizational form: Communication, connection, and community*. Thousand Oaks, CA: Sage.

Poole, M. S., & DeSanctis, G. (1990). Understanding the use of group decision support systems: The theory of adaptive structuration. In J. Fulk & C. Steinfeld (Eds.), *Organizations and communication technology* (pp. 173–193). Newbury Park, CA: Sage.

Poole, M. S., & Roth, J. (1989). Decision development in small groups V: Test of a contingency model. *Human Communication Research, 15*, 549–589.

Porter, L. (2003). *Organizational influence processes*. New York: M. E. Sharpe.

Prigogine, I. (1980). *From being to becoming*. San Francisco: Freeman.

Pritchard, R., Jones, S., Roth, P., & Steubing, K. (1988). Effects of group feedback, goal setting, and incentives on organizational productivity. *Journal of Applied Psychology, 73*, 337–358.

Putnam, L. (1982). Paradigms for organizational communication research: An overview and synthesis. *Western Journal of Speech Communication, 46*, 192–206.

Putnam, L. (1985). Contradictions and paradoxes in organizations. In L. Thayer (Ed.), *Organization and communication: Emerging perspectives* (pp. 151–167). Norwood, NJ: Ablex.

Putnam, L. (1995). Formal negotiations: The productive side of organizational conflict. In A. M. Nicotera (Ed.), *Conflict and organizations: Communication processes* (pp. 183–200). Albany: SUNY Press.

Putnam, L., & Fairhurst, G. (2001). Discourse analysis in organizations: Issues and concerns. In F. Jablin & G. Fairhurst (Eds.), *The new handbook of organizational communication* (pp. 78–136). Thousand Oaks, CA: Sage.

Putnam, L., & Kolb, D. M. (2000). Rethinking negotiation: Feminist views of communication and exchange. In P. Buzzanell (Ed.), *Rethinking organizational & managerial communication from feminist perspectives* (pp. 76–106). Thousand Oaks, CA: Sage.

Putnam, L., & Pacanowsky, M. (1983). *Communication and organizations: An interpretive approach*. Beverly Hills, CA: Sage.

Putnam, L., & Poole, M. S. (1987). Conflict and negotiation. In F. Jablin, L. Putnam, K. Roberts, & L. Porter (Eds.), *Handbook of organizational communication* (pp. 549–599). Newbury Park, CA: Sage.

Pynchon, T. (1973). *Gravity's rainbow*. New York: Viking.

Quick, J., & Quick, J. (1984). *Organizational stress and preventative management*. New York: McGraw-Hill.

Quinn, R. (1977). Coping with Cupid: The formation, impact, and management of romantic relationships in organizations. *Administrative Science Quarterly, 22*, 30–45.

Raban, J. (1991). *Hunting mister heartbreak: A discovery of America*. San Francisco: HarperCollins.

Rabinow, P., & Sullivan, W. (1986). *Interpretive social science — a second look*. Berkeley: University of California Press.

Rafaeli, A., & Sutton, R. (1987). The expression of emotion as part of the work role. *Academy of Management Review, 12*, 23–37.

Rawlins, W. K. (1994). Being there and growing apart: Sustaining friendships during adulthood. In D. J. Canary & L. Stafford (Eds.), *Communication and relational maintenance* (pp. 275–296). San Diego, CA: Academic Press.

Ray, E. (1987). Supportive relationships and occupational stress in the workplace. In T. Albrecht & M. Adelman (Eds.), *Communicating social support* (pp. 172–191). Newbury Park, CA: Sage.

Redding, W. C. (1972). *Communication within the organization*. New York: Industrial Communications Council.

Redding, W. C. (1985). Rocking boats, blowing whistles, teaching speech communication. *Communication Education, 34*, 245–258.

Redding, W. C. (1991). *Unethical messages in the organizational context*. Paper presented at the Annual Convention of the International Communication Association, Chicago.

Reuther, C., & Fairhurst, G. T. (2000). Chaos theory and the glass ceiling. In P. Buzzanell (Ed.), *Rethinking organizational & managerial communication from feminist perspectives* (pp. 236–256). Thousand Oaks, CA: Sage.

Rice, R. E., & Aydin, C. (1990). Social worlds, information systems and intraorganizational boundaries. In D. Henderson (Ed.), *Proceedings of the American Society for Information Science* (Vol. 27, pp. 256–260.) Medford, NJ: Learned Information.

Richards, I. (1936). *The philosophy of rhetoric.* New York and London: Oxford University Press.

Richmond, V., Davis, L., Saylor, K., & McCroskey, J. (1984). Power strategies in organizations: Communication techniques and messages. *Human Communication Research, 11,* 85–108.

Richmond, V., & McCroskey, J. (1979). Management communication style, tolerance for disagreement, and innovativeness as predictors of employee satisfaction: A comparison of single-factor, two-factor, and multiple-factor approaches. In D. Nimmo (Ed.), *Communication yearbook* (Vol. 3, pp. 359–374). New Brunswick, NJ: Transaction.

Rider, A. (1992, September 15). Wishful thinking. *Los Angeles Times Magazine,* p. 10.

Rifkin, J. (1995). *The end of work.* New York: Tarcher/Putnam.

Rifkin, J. (1999). *The biotech century.* New York: Tarcher.

Riley, P., & Eisenberg, E. (1992). *The ACE model of management.* Unpublished working paper, University of Southern California, Los Angeles.

Robert, M. (1993). *Strategy: Pure and simple.* New York: McGraw-Hill.

Roberts, K., & O'Reilly, C. (1974). Failures in upward communication: Three possible culprits. *Academy of Management Journal, 17,* 205–215.

Robertson, J. (1985). *Future work: Jobs, self-employment, and leisure after the industrial age.* New York: Universe Books.

Robin & Associates. (2002). *A better workplace: Dealing with difficult people.* Retrieved from <http://www.AbetterWorkplace.com>.

Rogers, E., & Kincaid, D. (1981). *Communication networks: Toward a new paradigm for research.* New York: Free Press.

Rose, D. (1989). *Patterns of American culture.* Philadelphia: University of Pennsylvania Press.

Rose, H. (1983). Hand, brain, and heart: A feminist epistemology for the natural sciences. *Signs, 9,* 81.

Rosen, M. (1985). Breakfast at Spiro's: Dramaturgy and dominance. *Journal of Management, 11,* 31–48.

Rosenberg, T. (2002, August 18). The free-trade fix. *New York Times Magazine,* pp. 28–33, 50, 74–75.

Rounds, J. (1984). Information and ambiguity in organizational change. *Advances in information processing in organizations, 1,* 111–141.

Roy, D. (1960). Banana time: Job satisfaction and informal interaction. *Human Organization, 18,* 156–180.

Rummler, G., & Brache, A. (1991). *Managing the white space in your organizational chart.* New York: Free Press.

Rushing, J. (1993). Power, Other, and Spirit in cultural texts. *Western Journal of Communication, 57,* 159–168.

Sackmann, S. (1991). *Cultural knowledge in organizations.* Newbury Park, CA: Sage.

Sahlins, M. (1976). *Culture and practical reason.* Chicago: University of Chicago Press.

Said, E. (1978). *Orientalism.* New York: Pantheon.

Said, E. (1984). *The world, the text, and the critic.* Cambridge, MA: Harvard University Press.

Sailer, H., Schlachter, J., & Edwards, M. (1982, July–August). Stress: Causes, consequences, and coping strategies. *Personnel, 59,* 35–48.

Samovar, L., Jain, N., & Porter, R. (1998). *Understanding intercultural communication.* New York: Wadsworth.

Sample, S. (2001). *A contrarian's guide to leadership.* San Francisco: Jossey-Bass.

Sashkin, M. (1991). *Total quality management.* Brentwood, MD: International Graphics.

Scandura, T., Graen, G., & Novak, M. (1986). When managers decide not to decide autocratically. *Journal of Applied Psychology, 71,* 1–6.

Schaef, A. W., & Fassel, D. (1988). *The addictive organization.* San Francisco: Harper & Row.

Schaubroeck, J., & Merritt, D. (1997). Divergent effects of job control on coping with work stressors: The key role of self-efficacy. *Academy of Management Journal, 40,* 738–754.

Schein, E. (1969). *Process consultation: Its role in organizational development.* Reading, MA: Addison-Wesley.

Schein, E. (1988). *Organizational culture and leadership: A dynamic view.* San Francisco: Jossey-Bass.

Schein, E. (1991). The role of the founder in the creation of organizational culture. In P. Frost, L. Moore, & M. Louis (Eds.), *Reframing organizational culture* (pp. 14–25). Newbury Park, CA: Sage.

Schuler, R., & Jackson, S. (1986). Managing stress through PHRM practices: An uncertainty interpretation. *Research in Personnel and Human Resource Management, 4,* 183–224.

Schwartzman, H. (1993). *Ethnography in organizations.* Newbury Park, CA: Sage.

Scott, C., Corman, S., & Cheney, G. (1998). Development of a structurational model of identification in an organization. *Communication Theory, 8,* 298–336.

Scott, J. (1990). *Domination and the arts of resistance: Hidden transcripts.* New Haven, CT: Yale University Press.

Scott, W. R. (1981). *Organizations: Rational, natural, and open systems.* Englewood Cliffs, NJ: Prentice-Hall.

Selznick, P. (1948). Foundations of the theory of organizations. *American Sociological Review, 13*, 25–35.

Selznick, P. (1957). *Leadership in administration.* New York: Harper & Row.

Senge, P. (1991). *The fifth discipline: The art and practice of the learning organization.* New York: Doubleday/Currency.

Senge, P., Roberts, C., Ross, R., Smith, B., & Kleiner, A. (1994). *The fifth discipline fieldbook.* New York: Doubleday/Currency.

Shockley-Zalabak, P. (1991). *Fundamentals of organizational communication.* New York: Longman.

Shockley-Zalabak, P. (2002). Protean places: Teams across time and space. *Journal of Applied Communication Research, 30*(3), 231–250.

Shockley-Zalabak, P., & Morley, D. (1994). Creating a culture. *Human Communication Research, 20*, 334–355.

Shome, R., & Hegde, R. S. (2002). Postcolonial approaches to communication: Charting the terrain, engaging the intersections. *Communication Theory, 12*, 249–270.

Shorris, E. (1984). *Scenes from corporate life: The politics of middle management.* New York: Penguin Books.

Shorris, E. (1997). *New American blues.* New York: Norton.

Shuter, R., & Turner, L. H. (1997). African American and European American women in the workplace: Perceptions of conflict communication. *Management Communication Quarterly, 11*, 74–96.

Sias, P., & Jablin, F. (1995). Differential superior-subordinate relations, perceptions of fairness, and coworker communication. *Human Communication Research, 22*, 5–38.

Silverstein, S. (1992, January 1). Sabbaticals are costly for women. *Los Angeles Times*, p. D1.

Simon, H. (1957). *Administrative behavior* (3rd ed.). New York: Free Press.

Sivard, R. (1983). *World military and social expenditures 1983.* Washington, DC: World Priorities.

Sloan, A. (2002, January 21). Who killed Enron? *Newsweek*, pp. 18–24.

Small, A. (1905). *General sociology.* Chicago: University of Chicago Press.

Smircich, L., & Calas, M. (1987). Organizational culture: A critical assessment. In F. Jablin, L. Putnam, K. Roberts, & L. Porter (Eds.), *Handbook of organizational communication* (pp. 228–263). Newbury Park, CA: Sage.

Smith, A. (1898). *Wealth of nations.* London: G. Routledge.

Smith, D. (1972). Communication research and the idea of process. *Speech Monographs, 39*, 174–182.

Smith, H. (1982). *Beyond the postmodern mind.* New York: Crossroad.

Smith, H. (1995, May). *The three faces of capitalism.* Public Broadcasting System.

Smith, M., Cohen, B., Stammerjohn, V., & Happ, A. (1981). An investigation of health complaints and job stress in video display operations. *Human Factors, 23*, 387–400.

Smith, R., & Eisenberg, E. (1987). Conflict at Disneyland: A root metaphor analysis. *Communication Monographs, 54*, 367–380.

Somervell, D., & Toynbee, A. (1947). *A study of history*. New York: Oxford University Press.

Sparrowe, R., & Liden, E. (1997). Process and structure in leader member exchange. *Academy of Management Review, 22*, 522–552.

Speech Communication Association. (1991). *Pathways to careers in communication*. Annandale, VA: Author.

Spretnak, C. (1991). *States of grace*. San Francisco: HarperCollins.

Staimer, M. (1992). U.S. workers get little vacation. *USA Today*.

Stalk, G. (1998). Time: The next source of competitive advantage. In R. Gupta (Ed.), *Managerial excellence* (pp. 171–192). Cambridge, MA: Harvard Business School Press.

Stallybrass, P., & White, A. (1986). *The politics and poetics of transgression*. Ithaca, NY: Cornell University Press.

Steelman, J., & Klitzman, S. (1985). *The VDT: Hazardous to your health*. Ithaca, NY: Cornell University Press.

Steers, R. (1977). Antecedents and outcomes of organizational commitment. *Administrative Science Quarterly, 22*, 46–56.

Steers, R. (1981). *Introduction to organizational behavior*. Santa Monica, CA: Goodyear.

Steier, F. (1989). Toward a radical and ecological constructivist approach to family communication. *Journal of Applied Communication Research, 17*, 1–26.

Steier, F., & Smith, K. (1992). The cybernetics of cybernetics and the organization of organization. In L. Thayer (Ed.), *Organization-communication: Emerging perspectives*. Norwood, NJ: Ablex.

Stewart, J. (2000, April). *The practice of dialogue*. Grazier Lecture, Department of Communication, University of South Florida, Tampa.

Stewart, T. (1991, August 12). GE keeps those ideas coming. *Fortune, 40*(8).

Stewart, T. (1998, September 7). The cunning plots of leadership. *Fortune*, 165.

Stiglitz, J. E. (2002). *Globalization and its discontents*. New York: Norton.

Stoller, P. (1989). *The taste of ethnographic things*. Philadelphia: University of Pennsylvania Press.

Strine, M. (1991). Critical theory and "organic" intellectuals: Reframing the work of cultural critique. *Communication Monographs, 58*, 195–201.

Sullivan, J. (1988). Three roles of language in motivation theory. *Academy of Management Review, 13*, 104–115.

Sunwolf, & Seibold, D. R. (1998). Jurors' intuitive rules for deliberation: A structurational approach to the study of communication in jury decision making. *Communication Monographs, 65*, 282–307.

Talbott, M. (2002, October 13). When men taunt men, is it sexual harassment? *New York Times Magazine*, pp. 52–57, 82, 84, 95.

Tamaki, J. (1991, October 10). Sexual harassment in the workplace. *Los Angeles Times*, p. D2.

Taylor, B. C. (1990). Reminiscences of Los Alamos: Narrative, critical theory and the organizational subject. *Western Journal of Speech Communication, 54,* 395–419

Taylor, F. (1913). *The principles of scientific management.* New York: Harper.

Taylor, F. (1947). *Scientific management.* New York: Harper & Brothers.

Thomas, L. (1975). *The lives of a cell.* New York: Penguin.

Thompson, J. (1967). *Organizations in action.* New York: McGraw-Hill.

Tichy, N., Pritchett, P., & Cohen, E. (1998). *The leadership engine.* New York: Pritchett.

Tjosvold, D. (1984). Effects of leader warmth and directiveness on subordinate performance on a subsequent task. *Journal of Applied Psychology, 69,* 422–427.

Tjosvold, D., & Tjosvold, M. (1991). *Leading the team organization.* New York: Lexington.

Tompkins, P. (1984). Functions of communication in organizations. In C. Arnold & J. Bowers (Eds.), *Handbook of rhetorical and communication theory.* Boston: Allyn and Bacon.

Tompkins, P. (1987). Translating organizational theory: Symbolism over substance. In F. Jablin, L. Putnam, K. Roberts, & L. Porter (Eds.), *Handbook of organizational communication* (pp. 70–96). Newbury Park, CA: Sage.

Tompkins, P., & Cheney, G. (1985). Communication and unobtrusive control in contemporary organizations. In R. McPhee & P. Tompkins (Eds.), *Organizational communication: Traditional themes and new directions* (pp. 179–210). Beverly Hills, CA: Sage.

Tompkins, P., & Wanca-Thibault, M. (2001). Organizational communication: Prelude and prospects. In F. Jablin & L. Putnam (Eds.), *The new handbook of organizational communication* (pp. xvii–xxxi). Thousand Oaks, CA: Sage.

Torbert, W. (1991). *The power of balance.* Newbury Park, CA: Sage.

Tracy, K., & Eisenberg, E. (1991). Giving criticism: A multiple goals case study. *Research on Language and Social Interaction, 24,* 37–70.

Tracy, S., & Tracy, K. (1998). Emotion labor at 911. *Journal of Applied Communication Research, 26,* 390–411.

Tretheway, A. (1997). Resistance, identity, and empowerment. *Communication Monographs, 64,* 281–301.

Tretheway, A. (2000). Revisioning control: A feminist critique of disciplined bodies. In P. Buzzanell (Ed.), *Rethinking organizational & managerial communication from feminist perspectives* (pp. 107–127). Thousand Oaks, CA: Sage.

Trist, E. (1981). *The evolution of socio-technical systems.* (Occasional Paper No. 2). Toronto: Quality of Work Life Centre.

Turnage, J. (1990). The challenge of new workplace technology for psychology. *American Psychologist, 45,* 171–178.

Turner, V. (1982). *From ritual to theatre: The human seriousness of play.* New York: Performing Arts Journal Publications.

Tyson, L. (1991, November 10). U.S. needs new spending priorities. *Los Angeles Times*, p. D2.

UNCG Undergraduate Bulletin (2002–2003). Greensboro, NC: UNCG.

U.S. Bureau of Labor Statistics Web site, located at <http://stats.bls.gov/>.

Van Maanen, J. (1979). *Qualitative methodology*. Beverly Hills, CA: Sage.

Van Maanen, J. (1988). *Tales of the field: On writing ethnography*. Chicago: University of Chicago Press.

Van Maanen, J. (1991). The smile factory: Work at Disneyland. In P. Frost, L. Moore, & M. Louis (Eds.), *Reframing organizational culture* (pp. 58–76). Newbury Park, CA: Sage.

Varner, I., & Beamer, L. (1995). *Intercultural communication in the global workplace*. Chicago: Irwin.

Victor, D. A. (1994). *International business communication*. New York: Harper-Collins.

von Bertalanffy, L. (1968). *General systems theory*. New York: George Braziller.

Vroom, V. (1964). *Work and motivation*. New York: Wiley.

Waldera, L. (1988). *The effects of influence strategy, influence objective, and leader-member exchange on upward influence*. Unpublished doctoral dissertation, George Washington University, Washington, DC.

Waldron, V. (1991). Achieving communication goals in superior-subordinate relationships: The multi-functionality of upward maintenance tactics. *Communication Monographs, 58*, 289–306.

Watzlawick, P., Beavin, J., & Jackson, D. (1967). *The pragmatics of human communication: A study of interactional patterns, pathologies, and paradoxes*. New York: Norton.

Wayne, S., Shore, L., & Liden, R. (1997). Perceived organizational support and leader member exchange. *Academy of Management Journal, 40*, 82–111.

Weick, K. (1976). Educational organizations as loosely coupled systems. *Administrative Science Quarterly, 21*, 1–19.

Weick, K. (1979). *The social psychology of organizing* (2nd ed.). Reading, MA: Addison-Wesley.

Weick, K. (1980). The management of eloquence. *Executive, 6*, 18–21.

Weick, K. (1990). The collapse of sensemaking in organizations: The Mann Gulch disaster. *Administrative Science Quarterly, 38*, 628–652.

Weick, K. (1995). *Sensemaking in organizations*. Newbury Park, CA: Sage.

Wellins, R., Byham, W., & Wilson, J. (1991). *Empowered teams*. San Francisco: Jossey-Bass.

Wenberg, J., & Wilmot, W. (1973). *The personal communication process*. New York: Wiley.

Wentworth, W. (1980). *Context and understanding*. New York: Elsevier.

Wheatley, M. (1992). *Leadership and the new science*. San Francisco: Berrett-Koehler.

"White workplace frustrates many Blacks." *Tampa Tribune* (1995, October 30), p. 122.

Whyte, D. (1996). *The heart aroused*. New York: Bantam Doubleday.

Whyte, W. F. (1948). *Human relations in the restaurant industry*. New York: McGraw-Hill.

Whyte, W. (1969). *Organizational behavior: Theory and application*. Homewood, IL: Irwin.

Wilkins, A. (1984). The creation of company cultures: The role of stories and human resource systems. *Human Resource Management, 23*, 41–60.

Wilkinson, L. (1995, May). How to build scenarios. *Wired*, 4–81.

Williams, M. (1977). *The new executive woman: A guide to business success*. New York: New American Library.

Wilson, G., & Goodall, H. L. (1991). *Interviewing in context*. New York: McGraw-Hill.

Wood, J. (1992). Telling our stories: Narratives as a basis for theorizing sexual harassment. *Journal of Applied Communication Research, 20*, 349–362.

Yankelovich, D. (1999). *The magic of dialogue*. New York: Simon & Schuster.

Zedeck, S., & Mosier, K. (1990). Work in the family and employing organization. *American Psychologist, 45*, 240–251.

Zeithaml, V., Parasuraman, A., & Berry, L. (1990). *Delivering quality service: Balancing customer perceptions and expectations*. New York: Free Press.

Acknowledgments

Pages 40–43: R. Evered and R. Tannenbaum, excerpts from "A Dialog on Dialog" in *Journal of Management Inquiry 1*, 1992. Copyright © 1992 Sage Publications. Reprinted by permission of Sage Publications.

Figure 3.1: Gareth Morgan, "Organization Chart Illustrating the Principles of Classical Management Theory and Bureaucratic Organization" from *Images of Organization*. Copyright © 1986 by Sage Publications. Reprinted by permission of Sage Publications.

Pages 68–69: Mary Truscott, excerpt from *Brats: Children of the American Military Speak Out*. Copyright © 1989 by Mary Truscott. Used by permission of Dutton, a division of Penguin Group (USA), Inc.

Table 3.1: Charles Perrow, "Summary of Historical and Cultural Influences on the Classical Management and Human Relations Approaches to Organizations and Communication" from *Complex Organizations: A Critical Essay 3e*. Copyright © 1986 by Charles Perrow. Reprinted by permission of The McGraw-Hill Companies.

Figure 3.4: Abraham Maslow, "Maslow's Hierarchy of Needs" from *Motivation and Personality 3e*. Copyright © 1954 by Abraham Maslow. Reprinted by permission of Pearson Education, Inc., Upper Saddle River, NJ.

Pages 81–82: Douglas McGregor, excerpts from *The Human Side of Enterprise*. Copyright © 1960 by Douglas McGregor. Reproduced with permission of The McGraw-Hill Companies.

Pages 83–84: Earl Shorris, "The Politics of Middle Management" from *The Oppressed Middle: Politics of Middle Management: Scenes from a Corporate Life*. Copyright © 1981 by Earl Shorris. Reprinted by permission of Roberta Pryor, Inc.

Table 4.1: Ludwig von Bertalanffy, "The Hierarchy of General Systems Theory" from *General Systems Theory: Foundations, Development, Applications*. Copyright © 1968 by Ludwig von Bertalanffy. Reprinted by permission of George Braziller, Inc.

Figure 4.1: Karl Weick, "Weick's Model of Organizing" from *The Social Psychology of Organizing*. Copyright © 1979 by Karl Weick. Reprinted by permission of The McGraw-Hill Companies.

Pages 107–110: Karl Weick, "Seven Properties of Sensemaking" from *Sensemaking in Organizations*. Copyright © 1996 by Sage Publications. Reprinted by permission of Sage Publications.

Table 5.1: Kenneth Burke, "Burke's Definition of Man" from *Language as Symbolic Action: Essays on Life, Literature, and Method*. Copyright © 1966 The Regents of the University of California. Reprinted by permission of the University of California Press.

Pages 127–128: Tom Peters and Robert H. Waterman Jr., "Eight Characteristics of Successful Companies" from *In Search of Excellence: Lessons from America's Best Run Companies*. Copyright © 1982 by Tom Peters and Robert H. Waterman Jr. Reprinted by permission of HarperCollins Publishers, Inc.

Page 147: Michael Lewis, "The Artists in the Gray Flannel Pajamas" from *The New York Times Magazine*, March 5, 2000. Copyright © 2000 by Michael Lewis. Reprinted by permission of the author.

Pages 162–165: Judi Marshall, excerpts from "Viewing Organizational Communication from a Feminist Perspective" from *Communication Yearbook 16*, edited by Stanley Deetz. Copyright © 1993 by Sage Publications. Reprinted by permission of Sage Publications.

Pages 166–167: G. J. Meyer, excerpts from *Executive Blues: Down and Out in Corporate America*. Copyright © 1995 by G. J. Meyer. Reprinted by permission of International Creative Management, Inc.

Page 171: Randy Cohen, excerpt from "The Ethicist" from *The New York Times Magazine*, September 22, 2002. Copyright © 2002 by Randy Cohen. Distributed by the New York Times Special Features/Syndication Sales. Reprinted with the permission of the New York Times Syndicate.

Figure 6.1: Stanley Deetz, "Multiple Stakeholder Model of the Corporation in Society" from *Transforming Communication, Transforming Business*. Copyright © 1995 by Stanley Deetz. Reprinted with the permission of Hampton Press.

Pages 173–174: Stanley Deetz, "Four Steps toward Workplace Democracy" from *Transforming Communication, Transforming Business*. Copyright © 1995 by Stanley Deetz. Reprinted with the permission of Hampton Press.

Table 8.1: Vernon Miller and Fred Jablin, "Newcomer's Information-Seeking Tactics" from "Information Seeking during Organizational Entry: Influences, Tactics, and a Model of the Process" from *Academy of Management Review 16* (1991). Copyright © 1991 by the Academy of Management. Reprinted with the permission of the Academy of Management.

Figure 8.1: E. Eisenberg and P. Riley, "A Dialogic Model of Communication and Productivity" from "A Closed-Loop Model of Communication, Empowerment, Urgency, and Performance," unpublished paper, University of Southern California, 1991. Reprinted with the permission of the authors.

Figure 8.2: Richard Hackman and J. Lloyd Suttle, "The Job Characteristics Model of Work Motivation" adapted from *Improving Life at Work: Behavioral Science Approaches to Organizational Change*, published by Goodyear Publishing Company. Copyright © 1977 by Richard Hackman and J. Lloyd Suttle. Reprinted by permission of the authors.

Table 8.2: H. Sailer, J. Schlachter, and M. Edwards, "Strategies for Coping with Stress" excerpted from "Stress: Causes, Consequences, and Coping Strategies" from *Personnel 59*, July–August 1982. Copyright © 1982 by the American Management Association. Reprinted by permission of the American Management Association.

Page 233: Charles Garfield, excerpt from "Peak Performance and Organizational Transformation" from *Educom Review*, September/October 1999. Reprinted with the permission of the author.

Page 249: Linda Grant, excerpt from "Breaking the Mold: Companies Struggle to Reinvent Themselves" from the *Los Angeles Times*, May 3, 1992. Copyright © 1992 by the Los Angeles Times Syndicate. Reprinted by permission of the Los Angeles Times.

Figure 9.1: Jay Conger and Rabindra Kanungo, "The Five Stages of the Empowerment Process" adapted from "The Empowerment Process: Integrating Theory and Practice" from *Academy of Management Review 13* (1988). Reprinted by permission of the Academy of Management.

Table 9.1: Jack C. Hawley, "The Management/Spiritual Leadership Model" from *Reawakening the Spirit in Work: The Power of Dharmic Management*. Copyright © 1994 by Jack C. Hawley, Berrett-Koehler Publishers, Inc., San Francisco, CA. All rights reserved. Reprinted with permission of the publisher. <www.bkconnection.com>

Figure 10.1: Richard Wellins, William Byham, and Jeanne Wilson, "The Empowerment Continuum of Work Teams" from *Empowered Teams: Creating Self-Directed Work Groups That Improve Quality, Productivity, and Participation*. Copyright © 1991 by Jossey-Bass, Inc., Publishers. Reprinted by permission of John Wiley & Sons, Inc.

Figures 10.2, 10.3, and 10.4: Peter M. Senge, three figures from *The Fifth Discipline*. Copyright © 1990 by Peter M. Senge. Used by permission of Doubleday, a division of Random House, Inc.

Page 297: W. R. Scott, excerpts from *Organizations: Rational, Network, and Open Systems*. Copyright © 1981 by W. Richard Scott. Reprinted with the permission of Prentice-Hall, Inc.

Figure 10.5: W. R. Scott, "Small-Group Communication Networks" adapted from *Organizations: Rational, Network, and Open Systems*. Copyright © 1981 by W. Richard Scott. Reprinted with the permission of Prentice-Hall, Inc.

Figure 11.1: R. D'Aveni, "The Original 7-S Model of Strategic Alignment" from *Coping with Hypercompetition: Utilizing the New 7-S Model*. Originally published in *Academy of Management Executive 9* (1995). Reprinted with the permission of the Academy of Management.

Table 11.2: Jan Mouritsen and Niels Bjorn-Anderson, "Six Concerns in the Analysis of Communication Technology" excerpted from "Understanding Third-Wave Information Systems" from *Computerization and Controversy: Value Conflicts and Social Choices*, edited by C. Dunlop and R. Kling. Copyright © 1991 Academic Press. Reprinted with the permission of Academic Press.

Pages 355–356: NCA 1999 Communication Ethics Credo Conference, "NCA Credo for Ethical Communication" as published in *Spectra*, Volume 35, Number 9, September 1999. Reprinted by permission of the National Communication Organization.

Author Index

Adams, J., 14
Adelman, M., 213
Adorno, T., 148
Ahrne, G., 37
Albrecht, K., 235
Albrecht, T., 213, 220, 300, 303
Allen, B., 159, 161
Altman, S., 212–213, 218, 220, 250
Alvesson, M., 18, 132, 135
Anderson, R., 268
Andrews, L., 138
Argyris, C., 73, 103–104, 325
Arnett, R., 268
Arquilla, J., 182
Ashcraft, K., 160, 163
Ashford, K., 250
Ashforth, B., 205
Atkouf, O., 135
Atwood, M., 200
Auwal, M., 155
Axley, S., 23, 25
Aydin, C., 330

Baba, M., 282
Bach, B., 202
Bachman, S., 223
Baker, B., 203
Bakhtin, M., 31, 35
Bales, K., 61
Banta, M., 148, 152
Bantz, C., 135, 289, 290
Barabasi, A., 276
Barker, J., 205
Barley, S., 137
Barnard, C., 29, 71, 72, 77, 299
Barnet, R., 9, 166
Barnlund, D., 261
Barrett, F., 187
Barry, D., 313
Bastien, D., 187
Bateson, G., 35, 93, 163

Bauer, T., 246
Baxter, L., 160
Baxter, L. A., 267
Bazerman, M. H., 169
Beamer, L., 153, 258–259, 290
Beavin, J., 25
Bell, A., 357
Bellah, R., 16
Bell-Detienne, K., 330
Bemis, W., 222
Bendix, R., 64
Benne, K., 283
Bennis, W., 254
Berger, P., 29, 30
Berlo, D., 24
Berry, L., 236
Bertalanffy, L. von, 95, 97, 114
Bhabha, H., 121
Bies, R., 250
Bingham, S., 264, 266
Bjorn-Andersen, N., 333
Blair, C., 160
Blake, R., 168
Block, P., 172, 226, 254
Blumer, H., 31, 35, 70
Bochner, A., 245
Bohm, D., 41, 107, 348, 357, 358
Boje, D., 134, 138, 184
Boland, R., 241
Bougon, M., 27
Brache, A., 243
Brandenburger, A., 99
Brass, D., 301
Braverman, H., 330
Braxton-Brown, G., 240
Brett, J. M., 169
Brienza, D., 257
Brown, J., 160
Browning, L., 99, 202, 284
Brzezinski, M., 150
Buber, M., 42
Buckley, W., 93, 99

Bullis, C., 160, 201, 202, 204, 269
Burke, K., 54, 63, 67, 119–120, 198, 347
Burke, R., 221
Burks, D., 26
Burrell, G., 152
Buzzanell, P., 156, 159, 161, 164
Byham, W., 224, 278, 279

Calas, M., 132, 135, 161
Calder, B., 254
Calvert, L., 161
Campbell, J., 207
Campbell, R., 207
Carbaugh, D., 215
Carey, J., 176
Carlone, D., 154
Cartwright, D., 285
Case, T., 235, 240, 251
Cavallo, K., 257
Cavanagh, J., 9, 166
Chandler, C., 295
Chandler, T., 246
Cheney, G., 106, 198, 204, 268
Chester, N., 161
Chiles, A., 252
Churchman, 278
Cissna, K., 268
Clair, R., 156, 165, 265
Clair, R. P., 159
Clegg, S., 95, 104, 151, 175
Cleveland, J., 265
Clifford, J., 121, 123, 131
Clinkscales, M., 215
Cohen, B., 330
Cohen, E., 257, 313
Cohen, H., 330
Collins, J., 317
Commission on Achieving Necessary Skills, U.S. Labor Secretary, 326

409

Subject Index